October 2, 1999

Sometime after two, Tracey was ready. She'd loaded her shotgun and dressed in black. In her year-old maroon Pathfinder, she drove to the Toro Canyon house. When she reached the back entrance, the gate was open. She turned off the headlights and pulled forward.

Picking her way through the trees in the darkness, she walked along the back of the house to the patio. The house was dark, and the windows looked like blank eyes staring back at her in the night. She paused, thinking about what she was there to do, and felt ill again. *I can't do this,* she thought. For minutes she stood statue-still, thinking of some other way to save Celeste.

No, she thought. *This is the only answer. He'll never let her go. I have to do it. I promised. Just do it.*

Holding the shotgun in shaking hands, she felt her way around the house, saw the pool glistening in the moonlight, then the door. She opened it and, as Celeste had promised, it was unlocked. No alarm sounded.

To save Celeste's life, she thought, and walked through the door . . .

Books by Kathryn Casey

SHE WANTED IT ALL
A WARRANT TO KILL
THE RAPIST'S WIFE

SHE WANTED IT ALL

A True Story of Sex, Murder, and a Texas Millionaire

KATHRYN CASEY

AVON BOOKS

An Imprint of HarperCollinsPublishers

She Wanted It All is a journalistic account of the actual murder investigation of Celeste Beard and Tracey Tarlton for the 2000 killing of Steven Beard in Austin, Texas. The events recounted in this book are true; however, the following names are pseudonyms for people involved in the events: Gene and Sue Bauman, Lisahn Golden, Gail Sharkey, Alice, Samantha, Bruce Reynolds, Joey Fina, Bubba, and Jeannie Jenkins. For these people, I have also changed certain identifying characteristics. The personalities, events, actions, and conversations portrayed in this book have been constructed using court documents, including trial transcripts, extensive interviews, letters, personal papers, research, and press accounts. Quoted testimony has been taken verbatim from trial and pre-trial transcripts and other sworn statements.

AVON BOOKS
An Imprint of HarperCollins*Publishers*
10 East 53rd Street
New York, New York 10022-5299

Copyright © 2005 by Kathryn Casey
Front cover house photo by Greg Hursley; back cover mug shots courtesy of the Texas Department of Criminal Justice
ISBN: 0-06-056764-3
www.avonbooks.com

First Avon Books paperback printing: April 2005

Avon Trademark Reg. U.S. Pat. Off. and in Other Countries, Marca Registrada, Hecho en U.S.A.
HarperCollins® is a registered trademark of HarperCollins Publishers Inc.

Printed in the U.S.A.

10 9 8 7 6 5 4 3 2 1

*For Ann Rule and Carlton Stowers,
my favorite true crime writers,
with gratitude for their inspiration, guidance,
and friendship*

Acknowledgments

As always with a project of this scope there are many to thank. First: my readers—Claire Cassidy, Christie Bourgeois, Andrea Ball, Barbara Tavernini, and Pam O'Brien, who helped me weed my way through mountains of research on a complicated and twisted tale; for her astute suggestions, to Sandy Sheehy, who not only wrote the book on women's friendships but lives it; to Connie Choate for always being there; to Sarah Durand, my able editor at Avon Books, and Philip Spitzer, my agent.

Thank you to my legal heroes: David Weiser at Kator, Parks & Weiser in Austin, and Mark Pryor at Vinson & Elkins in Dallas. To Roger Wade at the Travis County Sheriff's Department and Michelle Lyons, Warden Rebecca Adams, and Warden Audrey Lynn at the Texas Department of Criminal Justice for their assistance in arranging interviews.

Thank you to Associate Psychology Professor Julia Babcock at the University of Houston and Nancy Parchois, MSW, for their insights into borderline personality disorder;

to Leslie Spry, M.D., with the National Kidney Association, for explaining the effects of high doses of alcohol on the body.

A very big thank-you to my favorite investigator, the man who so ably helped pull together documents and track down sources, Jim Loosen of JAL Data Services in Seattle, Washington. Jim, you're the best. Also to Eric Smits at ABC Legal Services in Seattle, Judy Owens of Owens Legal Service in Phoenix, Arizona, and Eleanor Richardson of Eleanor's Legal Support in Los Angeles for tracking down legal records, some decades old. A special thank-you to my able transcribers: Katie Guillory, Rebecca Anderson, and Barbara Benson, for their long hours of work.

Finally, thank you to my family for putting up with me when I'm preoccupied with work and to the Friday night bunch: Sue and Jack, Sherry and Jerry, Evan and Yvonne, Sharlene and Larry, and Juanita and Lynn, for helping me retain my sanity throughout the arduous year it took to pull this book together.

SHE WANTED IT ALL

Prologue

West of Austin, Texas, the earth surges upward from the coastal plain to form steep hills, and Glen Rose limestone tears jagged edges through a lush, deep green landscape. One hundred million years ago, during the Cretaceous Period when dinosaurs roamed, this part of Texas lay at the banks of a great shallow sea. When it retreated, a fierce wave wrenched the plains from the hills, birthing the Balcones, a fault line that remains hidden deep within the earth.

The Tonkawa Indians once claimed this land as their hunting grounds, harvesting the abundant deer. Gold Rushers were among the first white settlers, Carolina mountain folk whose broken wagons convinced them to abandon dreams of California fortunes. The land too rough to farm, they raised livestock, sheep and goats, intermarried and fostered bloody feuds. Later bootleggers hid stills in the thick woods atop remote hills.

Settlement proceeded slowly in the hills, the inhospitable terrain convincing many to root instead in the valleys below.

Eventually roads and electricity came. Then, in 1953, the town incorporated. Residents paid a mere $4.50 an acre in Westlake Hills. By the 1990s, when panoramic views convinced the well-off to spend up to millions to build hillside estates, the history of the land retained little use other than cocktail-party prattle.

By then some called Westlake "Lexusland." Others dubbed it "Austin's Hollywood Hills." The name fit; the landscape resembled the stony cliffs over Hollywood and housed celebrities, including movie stars Sandra Bullock and Matthew McConaughey.

Even in such imposing company, the house at 3900 Toro Canyon Road held its own. At the request of its owner, Steven Beard Jr., a founder of what became Austin's CBS affiliate, the architect sought inspiration from the Frank Lloyd Wright masterpiece Fallingwater.

A gentle creek ran beneath the house, and plump koi swam about a man-made pond. Three flights of stairs trimmed in black-granite diamonds led to heavy leaded-glass front doors that opened to a vast living room, replete with costly antiques and the best furnishings money could buy. From there, the house fanned back toward two bedroom wings, to the left the master and to the right the children's rooms. From nearly every room, windows overlooked a pool that glistened like black satin in the moonlight.

Just before three on the morning of October 2, 1999, all was quiet on Toro Canyon. Deer circulated peacefully through the surrounding woods, chewing on ragged tree bark and feasting on tall grasses. The only disturbances were the static buzz of insects, the rustling of squirrels, and the sporadic churning of scattered air conditioners, on a still warm fall night. In another month the leaves would turn gold and brown, but on this night lush green foliage muffled the crack of a single gunshot.

Inside her bedroom, at the back of the children's wing, eighteen-year-old Kristina Beard woke, without knowing why. A sound sleeper, she rarely stirred before morning, and as her eyes adjusted, an uneasy feeling engulfed her. All was not well. Lights flickered across the walls, white and blue. As her vision cleared, Kristina brushed her dark blond hair from her eyes and made out the form of a woman standing inside her bedroom door, staring out into the shadowy hallway.

"Mom," said Kristina, her voice hoarse with sleep. "What's wrong?"

First only silence, then Celeste Beard finally said, "I think it's the police."

Rising, Kristina joined her mother's vigil at the door. Peering out at the silent house, the teenager saw nothing out of the ordinary, only the unrelenting lights that whipped through the darkness. Kristina's twin sister, Jennifer, had stayed at the family lake house with friends. The only other person in the house was their adopted father, Steve Beard. An involuntary shudder ran through the teenager as she wondered who waited outside their front door and why.

"Are you sure it's the police?" she asked.

"I think so," Celeste said, but before Kristina realized it was happening, her mother pushed her into the hallway. "Find out what they want," she ordered.

The frightened teenager panicked. What if the intruders weren't police? What if someone had broken in? She darted into Jennifer's empty bedroom and dialed 911.

"It's EMS," the operator said. "Your father has a medical emergency."

"Mom, something's wrong with Dad," Kristina shouted, her heart racing as she ran toward the front door to unlock it for the ambulance crew, wanting them to reach her father as quickly as possible. Once there, she realized help was already inside, as a deputy emerged from the master-bedroom wing.

"Your father's in rough shape," he said. "We've called STAR Flight to transport him to the hospital."

"What's wrong?" Kristina asked. Steve had been her father for four years, and he'd given her and Jennifer much. More important than wealth, he offered love and stability.

"Has he had surgery recently?" the deputy asked. "His stomach is torn wide open."

"No," Kristina said as her mother ran into the room.

Moments earlier, Celeste had been dead calm. Now she shrieked, "What's wrong with my husband? What's wrong?"

The deputy did a double take. Kristina was used to his reaction. At seventy-four, Steve was nearly old enough to be her mother's grandfather. Strangers often looked twice at the couple. "We're helicoptering him to Brackenridge Hospital," he said. "You'll be taken there, too, in a squad car."

Not waiting for the conversation to ebb, Kristina hurried to the master bedroom to see her father. Hours earlier, when she'd looked in on him before bed, he slept peacefully. Now the sight of him made her feel ill, as EMS workers struggled to bind gaping wounds in his corpulent abdomen. His intestines spilled out onto the blood-splattered sheets. Kristina couldn't get close but she shouted, "Dad, they're going to take you to the hospital. You're going to be all right. We all love you. I love you."

Pale and weak, her father nodded.

"Is your mother all right?" he asked.

"Yes, she's fine," Kristina said, holding back tears. "Don't worry. Just get better."

In great pain, he smiled and nodded again, obviously relieved.

The longer the medics worked on her father, the more

Kristina worried. Even after the helicopter hovered over the house and drifted down to the road, they feared moving him. The wait felt like hours as she circulated between her sobbing mother and her critically injured father. On her third trip out of the master bedroom, she heard something that stunned her and she spun back into the room.

"I've found a shotgun shell," a deputy had said. "He's been shot."

"What?" Kristina shouted.

Later the EMS workers and deputies would talk about Kristina, how she, of the two women, remained calm, comforting both her parents as the horror of what had happened became apparent. In the darkness, someone had entered their home, raised a shotgun, aimed and fired directly into her father's ample belly. Then the intruder fled, leaving him for dead. Only sheer will kept him alive long enough to call for help.

The medical emergency now a potential murder investigation, Kristina and Celeste were surrounded as squads of police cars arrived. Throughout the chaos, the daughter comforted the mother, caring for her as if she were the parent. After the helicopter with Steve inside finally ascended into the darkness, an officer put the two women in the back of a squad car and sped down the hillside and onto the highway that led into the brightly lit streets of Austin.

By the time they arrived at the emergency room, Steve Beard had been wheeled on a gurney into surgery. His prospects weren't good. "We don't think he'll survive the night," a doctor told them.

Celeste sobbed as Kristina held her tight.

Minutes later in the hospital's austere family waiting room, Kristina realized that for the first time since she'd awoken to flashing lights and a deep sense of foreboding, she was alone with her mother. Suddenly, Celeste stopped crying. Her blue eyes narrowed as she focused intently on her young daughter.

"Kristina, the police are going to ask who could have done this," she said, her voice grave. "No matter what, don't mention Tracey's name."

Chapter
1

Only months later would Kristina allow herself to consider why Celeste ordered her not to mention the name of Tracey Tarlton to the police, even though many times throughout that strange summer she wondered about the odd relationship between her mother and the bright, funny woman who managed a large Austin bookstore. From experience, the teenager knew not to question her mother. To do so would be judged by Celeste as a betrayal, and the consequences could be bone-chilling. Throughout her life, she'd feared yet loved her mother as only a child can love a parent, with utter devotion. Only long after Steve Beard's cold body lay entombed in a rose-granite crypt did Kristina allow herself to wonder how much she truly knew about the woman she called "Mother."

Even if Kristina could see into the past, Celeste might have remained a mystery. For like the woman Celeste became, the household she grew up in was filled with contradiction. On the outside, Edwin and Nancy Johnson's brood appeared a typical 1960s middle-class family. Only decades later would a very different picture emerge.

Edwin and Nancy were an odd couple. They met after he'd left the Air Force, in the mid-fifties. Their first encounter took place in Ohio, where she worked as a telephone operator. They struck up a conversation, and Edwin told her he'd just returned to the United States after being stationed in Japan. "He talked about how he'd met a missionary who changed his life," says Nancy, a stern woman with horn-rimmed glasses and a bouffant hairdo. "Edwin talked a lot about God. He talked about morals and ethics."

A powerfully built man who'd been a mechanic in the service, Edwin bore the scars of a traumatic beginning; reared in Connecticut, he'd lost a brother to drowning. For a year and a half, Edwin's father blamed himself for leaving his son's stroller unattended. Finally, when Edwin was seven, his father shot himself. "When we'd go out east, he'd take us to the river where it happened," says Cole, the oldest of the Johnson siblings. "He had a morbid fascination about it."

The Johnsons followed the sunshine and settled in Camarillo, California, a small town straddling the 101 freeway in a valley between Santa Barbara and Los Angeles. In the sixties, Camarillo offered a peaceful life, the epitome of middle-class America. At the time, the population hovered just under 20,000. If children walking home from school were caught in the rain, local police offered rides. In the summer, families drove to the nearby beaches. School sports filled the weekends, and at the local beauty parlor and post office, gossip swirled like up-dos on prom night.

Using his Air Force nickname, Edwin opened Johnny Johnson's Vehicles of Wolfsburg, a Volkswagen repair shop, at a time when VW Beetles and buses swarmed the hip West Coast. He became a prominent businessman and joined the local Chamber of Commerce, while he and Nancy made plans to begin a family.

Six years into their marriage, after three miscarriages, however, the Johnsons were childless. "We decided it wasn't going to happen, so I put out the word that we were interested in adopting," says Nancy. In an era before legalized abortion and the pill, women needed homes for infants they couldn't keep. "I could have had as many children as I wanted," she says. The Johnsons adopted four babies in less than four years. The oldest, Cole, was a year when Celeste was born on February 13, 1963. Two days later, Edwin and Nancy claimed her. Nine months later, Caresse followed, then Eddy.

In years to come when her children asked about their biological mothers, Nancy offered few clues. Celeste once asked for her adoption papers, but Nancy refused. "They were mine, not hers," she says. To Cole, Nancy said he was the offspring of a wife beater and a prostitute she'd given five dollars not to have an abortion. "Mom could be brutal," says Cole. "She told me, 'You're with us because your real mother didn't love you.' I don't know why she adopted us. She'd say, 'I don't love you, either.' "

Nancy and Edwin would later disagree about where the discord in the family originated. He described her as unstable, while she pointed an accusing finger at him. "In those years, Ed was clean-cut, every hair in place," she says. "The shop was immaculate. But he kept me in the dark, at work, at home. He had secrets."

Just what life was like inside the small ranch house on a cul-de-sac where the Johnson brood lived would also remain a source of dispute. Nancy would later paint a picture of suburban tranquility. "We baked cookies, went rock hunting. I took the children to Disneyland, twice," she says. "We sang and danced."

Yet, her children recounted few of those carefree days.

"Dad was strange and Mom was always troubled," says Celeste's younger sister, Caresse. "She had psychological problems. It wasn't a happy place. Not ever."

One of Cole's earliest memories was terrifying. At five or six, he was in the bathtub with his brother and sisters when his mother held them underwater. "It was scary. It was like she was rinsing our hair, but she held us down too long," he says.

Afterward, Nancy briefly went to a psychiatric hospital. "I'd suffered a breakdown," she says. "I'd been taking diet pills, and I was under a lot of stress and had insomnia. At the time, I was thinking of a Bible passage, 'To wash away sins.' But I never hurt my children. I would never do that."

After treatment, Nancy returned home to care for her brood. Edwin was gone much of the day at the shop. "We had four kids. It was a full-time commitment to keep beans on the table," he says. When he talks of Celeste, it's in glowing terms; she was "Daddy's baby" and "a sweet child."

Following their parents' religious bent, the children attended West Valley Christian Academy. From the beginning, Celeste was a precocious child and in the program for the gifted. One year she drew greeting cards and sent them to patients in a nearby hospital. At the state fair, she and Cole entered their baked goods, cakes and cookies, and came home with ribbons. She had a wholesome, apple-cheeked look and bright, intelligent blue eyes. Everything—from her clothing to the room she shared with Caresse—was her favorite color, pink, making her the stereotypic, perfect, sweet little girl.

Cute and playful, Celeste charmed her parents. Even as a child she understood the power of a well-placed compliment. The year she turned twelve, Celeste told Edwin that a friend of hers had pointed at him and wanted to know who "that handsome guy is."

"I told her, 'He's my dad,'" Celeste said. Decades later, Edwin's voice grew emotional and proud at the memory.

In 1976, in honor of the country's bicentennial, Edwin helped her write a speech, and Nancy made her a red, white, and blue shirt. During her performance, Eddy marveled at the way Celeste controlled the audience of parents, students, and teachers. "Celeste gave the most persuasive speeches," he says. "She could convince people of absolutely anything."

Yet, little Celeste Johnson had another side, one her brothers describe as frightening and calculating. "One minute she would do everything for you, bend over backward," says Eddy. "Then she'd turn horrible, mean, positively psycho."

When they were four small children competing for their busy parents' attention, Cole describes Celeste as the family instigator, manipulating the others into acts that landed them in trouble. When Nancy fumed, Celeste ran to get the board used for spankings. Later, Nancy dismissed the tumult with a single sentence: "The whole family was dysfunctional."

As the years passed, signs that the Johnsons' second child was troubled mounted. Nancy would later describe taking Celeste to UCLA dental school for braces at the age of nine, only to have doctors remove them because she violently clenched her teeth. From an early age, she had horrific nightmares. When Nancy tried to awaken her, Celeste thrashed at her. "It was terrible," says Nancy. "I didn't know what was wrong."

At first the Johnsons were able to hide the turmoil within their home; that ended in the early seventies, when a financial setback sent the family reeling. When Celeste was eleven, Edwin's business failed. Rather than work, he went to college on the GI bill, attending Moorpark College then Pepperdine University, where he majored in speech. "Things changed," says Eddy. "Mom went to work as a cake decorator, and Dad put on airs, used big words, tried to impress people. Everything seemed strange."

With Edwin not working, the problem of finances escalated. The Johnson siblings later recalled violent arguments and their father's actions turning increasingly odd. At times he chased Cole, threatening to beat him. A neighbor saw Edwin, boiling over with anger, push a lawn mower into the front steps and scream, "There, take that."

"Edwin just got bizarre," says a neighbor, "while Nancy worked harder and harder to support the kids. Nobody could understand what was going on in that house."

Without money for tuition, the children were enrolled in public schools. At home, Celeste acted out. "She was hell on wheels when she turned thirteen," says Nancy. "I didn't know why. I was struggling just to keep food on the table. I left early in the morning and came home late at night."

Perhaps making the situation even more painful for Celeste than the changes in her father and the absence of both her parents was the contrast between her family and that of Nancy's wealthy friend Louise, who went to the same church as the Johnsons. Celeste and Louise's daughter were friends, and Louise's parents bought Celeste expensive presents and took her on trips. "Celeste liked the money," says Cole. "She saw what it could buy."

The tension at the Johnson house escalated. Edwin was a different man than the one Nancy married, scruffy, unshaven, and he called himself by a biblical name, Jedediah.

On Christmas Eve 1977, Nancy ordered him from the house.

For the next three years they waged a divorce that had such venom no one escaped its poison. They fought over money, Edwin's shop tools, and the children. "Dad was crazy," says Cole. "But Mom was vindictive. She brainwashed the girls to hate our dad."

* * *

"Celeste changed in junior high school," says Caresse. "She got in trouble, and she was angry all the time. She was a different person after my mom kicked my dad out."

By the time Celeste turned fourteen, everyone within the Johnson household agreed that she was out of control. She had fights with siblings that her youngest brother, Eddy, compares in violence to a Mike Tyson match. "We couldn't be together. She'd beat me up, and someone in the neighborhood would call the police," he says. "The cops were always there, making her stop."

One day, Cole arrived home to find Celeste pounding on their mother's back, screaming at her. "She had so much anger," he says. "It was awful."

Another day, Nancy woke her for school and a screaming match ensued that ended with Celeste putting her fist through a front-door window. Someone called the police, and the house was surrounded. "They took Celeste in, and the judge ordered her to do community service and go to counseling," says Nancy. "But by then I was already taking her to psychiatrists. They couldn't figure out what was wrong with her."

Once, when Nancy asked Celeste why she was so angry, the teenager simply said, "I'm just trying to get your attention."

At Camarillo High School, where the teams are known as the Scorpions, Celeste lettered freshman year on the varsity swim team and was a member of the debate team. She appeared a studious girl—always carrying a satchel of books—tall, with long legs, thick blond hair, and deep blue eyes. She had high cheekbones in a slightly elongated face, a carefree manner, and the body of a swimmer, lean and athletic, the very picture of the California girl the Beach Boys celebrated in song. She hung with other kids like herself, those from broken homes. Some remembered her big smile and a laugh that verged on a girlish giggle. She also had a way about her that friends later struggled to explain. "It was like Celeste could see inside of you," says one. "She sized people up, knew how to get what she wanted. She did it with teachers, even the rest of us kids."

In many ways, Celeste was an odd mix. She never dressed overtly sexually, instead preferring modest clothes. One friend teased her, saying that she looked like she'd raided her mother's closet. But she seemed to know without question what men were looking for. "She flirted, in a taunting way," says a classmate. "Then she'd come across as sweet and innocent. It was an amazing combination. It drove the guys in town crazy."

Along with her beauty, Celeste had an untamed, wild streak that some found fascinating. When she got her driver's license, she screamed down the streets in the family's VW Beetle. At night she teased the neighborhood boys, parading down the street in her nightgown, often with nothing underneath. Cole chased away the clique of boys who catcalled at her. "Celeste laughed, having a good old time with it," says Eddy.

One incident resonated for Cole; in high school, he had his first sexual experience. The girl then said something that shocked him: "I've already done it with Celeste."

"I always thought Celeste hated men and leaned toward being a lesbian," he says.

Still, men were attracted to Celeste and, from all appearances, she to them.

Decades later, Craig Bratcher told his family he met Celeste in a bar, when she nuzzled against him, then kissed him. Before long they were making out. Craig, then seventeen, was two years older than Celeste. With his parents divorced the house Craig lived in with his father and brothers was a magnet for the teenagers in the neighborhood, including Celeste. "There was something about Craig that I respected," says a friend of Celeste's. "He took things seriously."

Many would say there was something special about Craig. He was muscular, with a slight paunch. Long brown hair combed to the side fell over his forehead and brushed the tops of thick eyebrows, over sad, dark eyes. He came from a family of four brothers and worked with his father for a big produce company that harvested the bounty of the neighboring valleys.

Perhaps Craig was already troubled when he met Celeste. More than one friend describes him as extraordinarily shy. "Craig had his ups and downs," says his mom, Cherie Falke. "But he was young, just learning to get on in life, when he met Celeste. From the beginning, their relationship was a mistake."

In Camarillo, Craig, his father, and brothers lived just blocks from the Johnsons' home. Celeste skipped school and spent the days there with a batch of close friends, smoking pot and drinking. "We liked being with the older kids," says one friend. "It made us feel cool." By then Celeste's dark blond hair was shoulder length and chopped into a layered Farah Fawcett hairdo. She was fun, with a quick wit and an easy laugh. Craig fell in love. Celeste seemed as taken, and spent every available moment with him. By sophomore year she rarely went to school. "All she wanted was Craig," says Nancy.

From the onset their relationship was as troubled as Celeste's family life. "She brought out the worst in him. She'd get him so riled up that he'd go crazy," according to Craig's younger brother, Jeff. "Craig believed the things she told him, and that was a mistake."

After Celeste complained that her boss at a pizza restaurant sexually harassed her, Craig, Jeff, and their friends confronted the man. "The guy hit Craig with a hammer and we all got in trouble," says Jeff. "Later, Craig figured she wasn't even telling the truth." Another night, at a party, Celeste kissed Jeff, then screamed for Craig claiming Jeff had come on to her. "From that point on, I knew she was just no good," says Jeff.

The tricks she played often came back to haunt Celeste. By high school some teens didn't want her around. Gail Sharkey, one of her best friends, found Celeste full of life and exhilarating. She was perplexed by how others responded to her. On weekends when they circulated from house party to house party, they were often told to leave by teenagers who didn't like Celeste. Gail grew angry, but Celeste laughed and shouted curses at those who'd kicked her out.

"Why doesn't anyone like you?" Gail asked one evening, stating what she thought was the obvious. Celeste looked crestfallen. "Before, she never acted like she cared, but she looked as if she didn't realize it, and that I'd hurt her feelings."

Years later Gail would also remember her friend's recklessness. One afternoon they drove in Craig's Toyota truck, listening to Fleetwood Mac on the radio, when Craig and some friends came after them in a car. Laughing, Celeste gunned the engine and took off just as the passenger door flew open. Gail fell out. Her pant leg caught on the door and she was dragged for three hundred feet before Celeste pulled into a driveway. "I had a heavy jacket on, or I would have been hurt," says Gail. "My whole body was shaking."

Weeks later that same truck was a pile of scrap. Celeste chuckled telling Gail how she and Craig argued. She said she pulled on the steering wheel and drove it off the road, where the truck rolled. Uninsured, it was a total loss. For weeks after, Celeste wore a thick cervical collar and claimed her neck was broken.

* * *

Meanwhile, in the courts, the Johnson divorce ground painfully on, the proceedings progressively more bitter. On the stand, during testimony, Edwin was startled by one question in particular. Nancy's attorney asked: "Mr. Johnson, did you ever stab Celeste?" Edwin insisted he hadn't.

Later, testifying for her mother, Celeste insisted that her father had stabbed her. Edwin suggested his attorney ask where. Celeste pointed under her eye.

"Here," she said. "But the scar disappeared."

Not long after, Gail asked Celeste why she hadn't been at school. "I had to go to testify against my father," she said. "He tried to kill me."

Gail wondered why her friend never mentioned the attack before. They were together nearly every day, and she had never seen bandages on Celeste, except the cervical collar. All that was forgotten just weeks later when Celeste had yet another crisis: She discovered she was pregnant and dropped out of school. As usual, when she told Gail, the story was far from ordinary. It wasn't just a case of teenage pregnancy, it was a miracle. "I was told I could never get pregnant," Celeste said.

"I couldn't imagine why any doctor would say that to a healthy seventeen-year-old," says Gail. "The whole thing just seemed really, really odd."

On December 6, 1980, Celeste Johnson married Craig Bratcher. The seventeen-year-old bride was heavily pregnant with what by then doctors predicted would be twins. She wore a sleeveless red gingham maternity dress with a tuck-pointed front trimmed in white cotton lace that hung loosely across her rounded abdomen. The groom, by then nineteen, wore a blue and white shirt and jeans. It was a small affair, just family and close friends, and the cake had two tiers, with wedding bells and a brave little pouf of white netting at the top.

After the wedding, the young couple moved into a rented

flat in nearby Oxnard. Gail visited during the day when Craig was at work. On February 6, 1981, she drove up to find Celeste, who'd been ordered by her doctor to stay in bed until the births, walking down the street on her way home from a liquor store, where she'd bought junk food and candy. Gail parked the car and they went inside.

"I don't do bed rest," Celeste said. "But I've been feeling bad all day."

That evening at 7:27 P.M., two months early, Celeste gave birth to identical twins. Jennifer Lynn Bratcher was born first, followed by Kristina Ann Bratcher. The infants were tiny, weighting only two pounds seven ounces and two pounds eleven ounces. Doctors had hoped that on bed rest Celeste could have carried them longer, and now they feared the infants weren't breathing well. An ambulance rushed them to a larger medical center, where they were put on respirators, but the girls were strong and recovered quickly.

Months later the twins sat for a family portrait, the kind taken at department stores in front of a marbled blue background. In it, they wore matching yellow terry-cloth sleepers, their identical little faces flushed and red, eyes wide and intense, hands reaching toward the camera.

That day, Craig looked young and happy. Next to him, Celeste, dressed all in black, smiled shyly. Her dark blond hair framing her pretty face, she appeared the prototype for a content young mother. Barely more than children themselves, they were embarking on what should have been an exciting adventure: building a family with two perfect baby girls. A hint of what lay ahead, however, was also in that photo. While Craig wrapped a protective hand tightly around Jennifer, Celeste's grasp on Kristina looked reluctant. In the photo, Kristina frowns, her face red and her brow heavily furrowed. Perhaps she already sensed she would never be secure in her mother's arms.

* * *

Less than a year after the wedding the marriage was troubled. Young, with no money and two small babies, they lived like nomads, moving seven times in six months, from Craig's father's house, to sharing apartments with friends, to a guest house next to Craig's grandfather in Washington State, and back to California. When they were happy, friends say Celeste was all Craig could have asked for, vibrant and exciting, full of plans and launching schemes, sprinting through life. She had great dreams to go to college, to get a good job and buy a house. Yet as quickly, she became distracted, usually by another man, the next door neighbor or somebody she met while waitressing. At times she ran off, leaving the twins behind, with only Craig to care for them.

When she wanted him to take her back, Celeste explained away her behavior by saying she had demons in her childhood, dark secrets that haunted her. "From the beginning when she did something awful, she blamed it on what happened to her as a kid," says Craig's mother, Cherie. "Celeste told us her father sexually abused her and that was why she acted like she did."

Craig felt sorry for her and, despite everything, took her back.

Years later the Johnson family had conflicting theories on what happened between Edwin and Celeste and whether the abuse ever occurred. Edwin categorically denied ever sexually abusing either of his daughters. "It didn't happen," he says. Cole and Eddy agreed, insisting they saw no indication of anything improper. "It was a small house, and I saw nothing that even vaguely suggested it," says Cole. "As nosy as our mom was, she would have known. If Dad did anything wrong, he catered to my sisters too much. Did my father molest Celeste? No."

Nancy was less sure.

Recounting how she'd tried to get psychiatric help for Celeste, never understanding what was wrong with her, she would say, "I can't confirm the abuse, but I don't discount it." She remembered once walking in to find Edwin in bed with Celeste, yet both were clothed and he was on top of the blanket and sheet with Celeste underneath. Her most troubling memory, perhaps, was waking to find Edwin watching television—in the early hours of the morning—with their youngest daughter, Caresse, on his lap. "He said he couldn't sleep and got her up to keep him company," says Nancy.

"It started when I was five or six and went on for a long time," says Caresse. "Right up until he was thrown out of the house. He'd wake Celeste and me up and want us to watch television with him. Then he sent me to bed, and I heard Celeste crying. I don't remember it happening to me. Celeste says I don't want to. Maybe she's right."

If Celeste came to motherhood reluctantly, Craig's world revolved around the twins, giving them baths, feeding them, becoming both mother and father. Years later, when he and Celeste fought over the girls in court, he'd write an account of his life with her for the judge. "If I knew then what I know now, I would have written her off and raised the girls by myself," he wrote. "But I was young and ignorant, and I thought I was in love."

In Celeste's version, Craig was an abusive man who stalked and even raped her. There was no doubt that he had a temper. He would later admit that, saying, "I did a lot of things that I regret." When she took off with a new man, he fought to get her back. Once, he broke into a house where she and a boyfriend were staying. Another time he stood outside a window, pointing a gun at Celeste and a lover in bed. There were police reports, restraining orders, and Craig spent a four-month stint in jail for brandishing a firearm.

That time, he'd later claim, Celeste took his money and left with one of his fellow inmates, a man he introduced her to in the jail visiting room. When the affairs ended, Craig took her back. "I don't know if I was lonely or naive," he later wrote, "but I moved right back in with her . . . She stayed out all night. We had violent confrontations . . . She called the cops with wild stories and, because of my record, they believed her."

At one point she claimed that Craig put cat feces in her mouth as she slept. Another time she charged that he broke her arm. Did it happen? Later, many would be skeptical. "She was always bragging about how she had a high pain tolerance," says Kristina. "When I was little, I remember seeing her slam her arm in a car door on purpose, until it broke. I don't know if that's the time she said my dad did it. But I never saw him hit her."

One thing stood out: Craig felt powerless with Celeste, sucked into her world of chaos. To explain why she didn't enjoy sex with him, she talked of the sexual abuse she claimed she suffered at her father's hand. At their apartment, Gail once saw a hole punched in the wall. Inside, Craig had scrawled: *No Sex!* Yet, at the same time she rebuffed her husband, Celeste seemed driven by lust, jumping in bed with man after man. The message for Craig must have been that she was interested in sex, just not with him.

His mother, Cherie, spent enough time with Celeste to understand what kind of woman her son had married. One day a friend called to say she saw Celeste in the registrar's office of a business college she was attending, demanding a tuition refund past the cutoff date. When the clerk refused, Celeste cried and said she had a good reason for not attending classes. "One of my twin daughters died," she said.

The friend was distraught, calling Cherie with condolences over the death of her grandchild. Cherie knew it wasn't true. "I wasn't surprised," she says. "Money meant more to Celeste than anything, even her own children."

Eighteen months after they married, on May 18, 1982, Craig and Celeste divorced. Celeste was granted custody of the year-old twins, with Craig having a share of holidays, vacations, and weekends. He was ordered to pay $300 a month in child support, and Celeste was given their 1962 VW, a share of the furniture, her personal items and clothing. A $1,400 tax refund and money from the sale of Craig's 1974 Honda motorcycle were to be used to pay off bills, including $28 for a diaper service and three doctor bills. Both parties were ordered to restrain from harassing the other.

But rather than an ending, the divorce represented little more than an intermission.

"I hooked up with Celeste again after she left Craig," says Gail. "She was living with a woman with a bunch of kids on welfare. Celeste was on welfare, too, and working as a waitress at a pizza place. She asked if I wanted to live with her, and we got an apartment together. At first, it was fun. Then things got crazy. When I left, I fled for my life."

Years later Gail would remember Celeste being ill-equipped for motherhood. When Gail returned home from waitressing, Celeste was dressed and ready for work, leaving the babies with Gail, crying and dirty. Making their lives more chaotic, Craig often arrived at the apartment uninvited. To Gail, it seemed Celeste enjoyed manipulating him. Once, she found a love letter Celeste wrote him, which she'd signed with another woman's name. "One minute they'd be fine," says Gail. "The next, pots were flying. But I never saw Craig get physical. She'd throw things, but he'd just turn and leave."

Since the apartment had only two bedrooms, the girls' cribs took up one room, and Gail shared a bed with Celeste in the second bedroom. "There was nothing going on. It just worked better that way," says Gail.

Yet one morning she awoke to see Craig glaring down at them. "You're a lesbian," he said to Celeste. "That's why you never want sex with me."

Gail was horrified, but Celeste just laughed.

Soon Gail worried their friendship had taken an odd turn. Gradually, Celeste had become possessive, insisting Gail tell her where she went every moment of every day. "She got really strange. She treated me like a daughter or a boyfriend," she says. "I felt smothered." Seven months after she moved in with her, Gail wanted out. Hoping to avoid a confrontation, she packed her things in her car while Celeste worked. When Celeste arrived, Gail said she was going out. Celeste badgered her, insisting she say where. Gail refused. In a rage, Celeste cursed. As Gail walked to the door, something whizzed past her. When she looked, she saw a butcher knife embedded in the wall. Terrified, Gail ran.

At a friend's house the following morning, Gail hoped the worst was over, but a friend phoned and told her Celeste had called, claiming police were looking for her. "Celeste had pressed charges, claiming I stole her purse with her welfare checks and food stamps," says Gail.

Not knowing what to do, she called the Ventura County District Attorney's Office. "Are you looking for me? Do I need to come in?" she asked.

"No," the prosecutor said, explaining Celeste's purse had been found along the side of a road. "She won't bother you anymore. We'll take care of it."

"I don't know why he said that, except they knew she was lying," says Gail, who was so frightened of Celeste that she left the county and hid.

Later, Gail heard that after she moved out, Celeste abandoned the twins in a foster home. Over the years there would be a string of such periods, times when Celeste turned the girls over to others to raise. She'd later claim she couldn't afford to support them; others would charge she was distracted by her latest man. "My first memories are of her leaving us with strangers," says her daughter Jennifer. "We never knew if or when she'd come back."

Later, Celeste moved back in with Craig and regained custody of the twins. Living in an apartment, they must have looked to the outside world like the perfect young family, a handsome dad, beautiful mom, and two identical little toddlers. It was then that Celeste's father, Edwin, came to live with them. As she had with Gail, Celeste became demanding, insisting he report where he was and with whom. A few months after Edwin moved in, he spent a night with friends. He and Celeste argued, but he didn't realize how angry she was until he was picked up by police the next day. In the past, Celeste had claimed to others that she'd been sexually abused, but she'd never confronted him. Now, she made the accusation to the police. "I told them that it never happened," Edwin says. "I didn't abuse my daughter. I would never do that."

The deciding bit of information for Celeste's oldest brother Cole came from a detective. The day in 1985 when Edwin was taken in for questioning, one of the officers told Cole that Edwin had been given a lie detector test. In it he denied Celeste's charges. "The detective said Dad passed with flying colors. The police never pressed charges," says Cole. "Celeste was lying. Celeste was always lying. She was mad at our dad, and she was out to get him."

Months later, Celeste and Craig split once again and she dated a guy she'd known since high school, Pete Timm. An electrician, he came from a well-respected Camarillo family.

"Celeste was one of those people you wanted to be around," says Pete. "She wasn't drop-dead gorgeous, but she was pretty, and she loved to laugh . . . She kind of drew you in."

Attentive, Celeste said all the right things, including that she loved him. "Later, I wondered how I ended up with her, but I was only listening to my heart," Timm says.

When Craig warned him to beware of Celeste, saying she'd "raked him over the coals," Timm didn't believe him. With the twins in foster care, Celeste worked in a deli and cleaned houses in Leisure Village, a wall to do retirement community. She also went to school, first to be a hair stylist, then to Oxnard College, where she took a class in accounting. As she had with Craig, Celeste told sad stories about being abused by her father and having the twins so young she couldn't afford them. Pete opened up his life to her. She became a part of his family, even living with his parents. In love, he even took her to the bank when he made deposits. That turned out to be a mistake, when he discovered $7,000 had disappeared from his account.

"Your wife withdrew all the money," the teller told Pete. "She went through the drive-through taking out one to two thousand dollars at a time for a week."

When he confronted her, Celeste cried and said she needed the money for an attorney to reclaim the twins. After she pledged her love, Pete forgave her. Yet, things gnawed at him. One was that she never enjoyed sex. "It was a chore for her," he says. "She was really good at it, but it always felt like she wanted something in return. Celeste flipped the switch and acted upbeat, but there was never any real joy. She was beautiful and sad."

Even with the girls, he saw little happiness and rarely motherly love. "She did all the right things, acting like she cared, but never showed real affection," he says. On weekend visitations, a county caseworker dropped off the girls, then came to pick them up. The girls pleaded with her not to take them away from their mother. "It didn't faze Celeste," says Timm, who wondered how someone as caring as Celeste could be so cold.

Still, he loved her, and they made plans to marry. Once they did, Celeste told him caseworkers would release the girls to her and they'd be a family. As the wedding approached, his excitement grew. Celeste even told Pete's religious parents that she'd found God. Then, just months before the wedding, Celeste found an apartment she wanted. She asked Timm to lend her the money for the deposit. Remembering how she'd cleaned him out, he was apprehensive. But then Celeste surprised him by saying she'd get the money from her mother. While he listened, she phoned someone she called "Mom." When she hung up, she bubbled with excitement, saying Nancy had agreed. There was one catch: She wouldn't get the money for three days. "Pete, could you loan it to me?" Celeste pleaded. "I'll pay you back when Mom sends the check."

Pete agreed, and when she asked him to, he signed the apartment lease.

The next day Pete's money and Celeste were both gone. Compounding the blow, Celeste had turned in the lease, leaving him responsible for a full year's rent. Spinning from the betrayal, he searched but couldn't find her. In the end he didn't care about the money, only that the woman he loved had left him. "Maybe it was never love," he says. "But she broke my heart, and for three years I thought about her every day and wondered what I did to make her leave. In her own way, Celeste was intoxicating."

Craig hadn't been able to rid himself of his desire for Celeste, either, despite leaving California to flee her. It happened a few days after he was discovered sitting in a Camarillo hotel stairwell. He was drunk, morose, and had a shotgun poised under his chin. "I love her and she just does shit to me," Craig said to Jeff, who'd been called by the police. "Why does Celeste do these things? Why does she hurt me?"

Jeff took away the gun, and Craig was taken in for observation. Three days later he gave Craig his car keys and convinced him to move to Phoenix. "There was nothing good about Craig's relationship with Celeste except the twins," says Jeff. "I hoped Craig would never see her again. That didn't happen. He wasn't there for more than a few days when she called, begging him to take her back."

Chapter
2

Soon after Craig moved Celeste and the twins to Arizona, she was pregnant again. "I thought maybe it would calm her down and we could try to make it work," he'd later write. In November 1986, Celeste gave birth to a third baby girl and decided to put it up for adoption. The twins, then six, never saw their baby sister. "I remember Celeste being pregnant, then she wasn't," says Jennifer. "She never talked about it."

It was the way she handled the adoption, what Celeste got in return for the child, that rankled Craig. "She told the adoptive parent we had to pay the hospital bills, when my insurance did," he wrote. "She got ten thousand dollars cash for that baby."

Soon after, Celeste had yet another man in her life. Devastated, Craig stood helplessly by as she took the twins, their income tax refund, the $10,000 from the adoption, and left. Weeks later he tried to cut his wrists. When he was well enough, Jeff put him on an airplane for Washington State to live near their mother.

That fall, Celeste left the six-year-olds home alone at night and someone reported her to authorities. They were taken away to yet another foster home. Looking back, the twins had mixed feelings about the families that took them in. With a mother whose attention was spotty at best, it was a foster couple that took them for their first school vaccinations and to their first dental appointment. Yet, many of the homes were frightening and heartless. When they arrived, they were stripped and inspected for bruises. At one, the parents ridiculed Jennifer for wetting the bed, then pushed her into the swimming pool. "I couldn't understand why our mom did this to us," she says. "Kristina and I schemed about running away. We dug holes in the yard, trying to dig our way to China. When our mom came, we begged to go home. She walked away. She didn't even look sad."

That fall, Harald Wolf, an Air Force, jet-engine mechanic who worked on F-15 fighter planes at Luke Air Force Base, was the new man in Celeste's life. Six-foot-three, muscular, of German descent with prematurely gray hair, Wolf had eleven years in the service when they met. He'd grown up in a military family, traveled the world, and married once. Despite a divorce, he never considered that marriage a mistake. He'd feel vastly different about his connection to Celeste Johnson Bratcher.

"I felt drawn to her, but from the beginning, I never trusted her," says Wolf. "Call it spidey-sense, that feeling that makes the hair on the back of your neck stand on end." After they dated for a few months, Harald tried to break up. Celeste announced she was pregnant. When he resisted marriage, she suggested they go for counseling. At the sessions, the counselor pegged his distrust as irrational.

"If she hasn't given you reason not to, you should trust her," the counselor argued.

Maybe she's right, Harald thought.

In December 1988 they married. Not long after, Celeste called him at the base and said she'd lost the baby. "From that point on our lives went up and down like a drug addiction," he says.

The twins were released back to Celeste's custody, and they rented an apartment in Glendale, a bedroom community northwest of Phoenix near the base. Celeste was obsessed with keeping it clean, so much so that she and Harald argued about the pressure it put on the girls. "She insisted they pick up their rooms," he says. "They were little kids. I told her, just shut the door. She couldn't. She never left anything alone."

Sex was intense, but as with Craig and Timm, Celeste pulled back. "She was so good, it felt like paying a hooker," Harald says. "But she never seemed really interested."

When he wanted to know why, she cried. Only after he pushed did she whisper her claim that she'd been molested by her father. "Don't you feel sorry for me?" she asked.

"I did," says Harald.

After that, when they fought she reminded him of her past and sobbed. Harald felt his anger fade. "I'm not so bad, am I?" she asked, nuzzling against him.

In Phoenix in 1987, Celeste was hired on at Crystal Ice, an ice wholesaler. Claiming to have a junior college degree, she was made head of accounts payable; Lue Thompson was in charge of accounts receivable. Years later, Lue—twenty-two years older than Celeste and married with grown sons—believed she understood how Celeste insinuated herself into her life. "She saw something in me even I didn't understand," she says. "Celeste knew I'd spent my life wishing for a daughter."

First at work then during their off hours, the women became inseparable. "I wish I had a mom like you," Celeste said that Mother's Day, when she gave Lue a brightly wrapped box with a dress inside. She remarked on Lue's acceptance of her gay son, Jimmy, complaining that her own mother would never accept such news. Lue grew sad thinking about all Celeste had been through. Soon she was buying her presents and doing the things a mother does for a daughter, even brushing her long, curly blond hair.

"Mom, I wish you could adopt me. I wish I could really be your daughter," Celeste told her, and Lue dreamed it, too, that Celeste would truly be hers.

When Celeste and Harald fought, she ran to the Thompsons'. One night she cried in Lue's arms while Lue's husband, Gary, listened to Harald's complaints then ordered him to go home. By morning both their tempers had cooled. Harald, however, still felt ill at ease. Just too much about Celeste seemed suspicious. At times she arrived home hours late. She said she was having her hair done, but it looked the same as when she'd left for work. "Can't you see it's different?" she'd say.

On the other hand, Lue believed everything Celeste told her. She worried about her new "daughter," whose life was constantly in turmoil. Celeste complained often of being ill, once telling Lue she had a virus that went to her heart and could have killed her. She cried about Harald, claiming he abused her. When she said Harald didn't want the girls, Lue and Gary, who'd often helped children in trouble, offered to take them weekdays.

From the first, the Thompsons fell in love with Jen and Kris. At six, they were miniature versions of their mother, with dark blond hair and large blue eyes. Lue signed up the girls, natural athletes, for baseball, and she and Gary went to the games. Evenings, they gabbed as she cooked dinner. After the years with Celeste, it was a welcome break for the girls. Off and on, for nearly two years, the girls lived with the Thompsons, who grew to think of them as their own.

Financially, Celeste was better off with Harald than she'd been with Craig. They lived in a good neighborhood, and he bought her a car, a yellow Ford Taurus. But from the beginning she hated the car, so much so that she ordered a vanity plate that read: Lemon. One morning she left for work and ran back in the house, shouting that someone had attacked the car. When Harald got outside, the fenders were scratched and the seats slashed. "It was weird," he says. "The cuts were perfect lines at the seams."

When police arrived, the officer, too, thought the damage suspicious. "It's funny they didn't slash the tires," he said, mentioning that Celeste could still drive it to work.

"Deep down, I knew Celeste did it," Harald says. "I couldn't admit it, even to myself."

Something else happened that year, something the twins would remember vividly. Sobbing, Celeste told them that their grandmother, Nancy, had died. At the California funeral, the twins stretched on tiptoe to see into the coffin. They hadn't seen their maternal grandmother since infancy and didn't recognize the white-haired woman inside.

Along with the stability they found at the Thompsons,' summers in Washington with their father brought solidity to the twins' lives, playing sports and spending time with Craig's mom, Cherie, and their circle of relatives. Coaching the teams, Craig never looked happier. Weekends they camped in mountain parks, where the trees towered. On Sundays, Cherie brought doughnuts for Craig and her eight-year-old granddaughters and found them fishing in a stream, their baseball hats turned backward.

Those were happy times, and Jennifer cried at the thought of leaving her father to return to the chaos of her mother. In contrast, for Kristina every minute apart from Celeste filled her with pain. She was their mother's favorite. Celeste whispered in her ear that she was special, that she was the daughter she truly loved. She called her in Washington State, urging her to hurry home. "Kristina was a little girl who wanted a mother," says Lue. "Jennifer began pulling away, but Kristina couldn't. When Celeste screamed, Jennifer was angry, but Kristina was devastated."

At home, Kristina panicked every time Celeste seemed blue. She didn't complain when Celeste kept them out of school, hauling them on shopping trips or running errands. "I knew she hated being alone," says Kristina. "She just couldn't stand it."

From an early age, Kristina understood her mother had a sadness about her that never totally went away. As manic and happy as Celeste acted, it seemed a hollow ruse, as she quickly flipped back to depression and anger. She had children, a home, and a husband, but it wasn't enough. Celeste filled every minute, planning weeks in advance: doctor appointments, movies, going out with friends. She shopped without regard, filling her closet with clothes she never wore.

The longer she and Harald lived together, the more erratic her behavior became. One weekend he arrived home to find a note saying she was visiting a friend. That night, two men from his unit came to the apartment to drink beer. An hour later Celeste burst in, angry that he wasn't missing her. Harald and his friends sprinted for the door as beer bottles flew. "I stayed away for the night," he says. "I knew the marriage was a mistake, but every time I tried to leave, Celeste went crazy."

One time, she took a handful of pills; another, she stood

next to a full bathtub with a hair dryer, threatening to step in and drop the hair dryer in the water. Their eyes wide with terror, the twins pleaded with her not to, and Harald agreed to stay if they saw a counselor. From that point on, while other little girls pondered friends and homework, Kristina worried about keeping her mother alive.

The sessions began as couples counseling, but within a few visits the therapist zeroed in on Celeste, suggesting her suicide threats needed intense treatment and checking her into the base hospital's psychiatric unit. "I thought she was trying to get better," says Harald. "At times, she could be loving, wonderful."

By then Celeste had become a regular in the Phoenix court system. When Jennifer fell off of a swing set at school and broke her arm, she sued. She tried to sue again after she quit her job at Crystal Ice, saying one of the men in charge sexually harassed her. "The attorney refused the case," says Lue. "The man she complained about seemed like a nice guy. But I believed Celeste."

Lue always believed Celeste, even when her niece told her she shouldn't; that she'd seen Celeste being manipulative and mean and that she wasn't the woman Lue believed. Craig, too, warned Lue that Celeste could be dangerous, but Lue scoffed, "You don't know the real Celeste."

"I do, and someday you'll meet her, too," Craig countered. "Please, be careful."

In 1989 the Air Force notified Harald he was being transferred to Kadena Air Force Base in Okinawa, Japan. Word came down that due to her hospitalization in the psychiatric unit, Celeste wouldn't be allowed to go. Furious, she mounted a campaign, calling his superiors and arguing that they were being treated unfairly. She complained so vociferously that the transfer was eventually cancelled. "Tell your wife to stop calling," Harald's sergeant told him.

At home, their arguments escalated. One night, in bed, Celeste screamed at him. He turned his back, and she kicked him. Harald hit her with a pillow and then went outside to cool off. As he stood in the darkness, the police drove up. Celeste had called in a domestic violence report. When the officers questioned her, Celeste pulled up her shirt to display an angry red bruise on her back and claimed Harald had punched her. He suspected she'd done it to herself, by ramming into a door knob. "I never saw a pillow leave a mark," he says. That night, Harald had time in jail to think. The next day she bailed him out, but he refused to go home and moved in with a friend.

Looking back, it would seem Celeste was incapable of letting go of anyone. As soon as they pulled away, she became frantic to win them back. One night she showed up at a bar where Harald played pool. When he refused to take her back, she dug her long nails into his arm until it bled. Later, he stood on the outside balcony at the apartment. When he looked down, Celeste glowered up at him. Smiling, she popped the lid on a can and poured a Coke over his Camaro. When he turned to go inside the apartment, the door wouldn't open. "She'd gotten inside and bolted it," he says.

A little over a year into their marriage, his career in the Air Force was in shambles. Before he'd married Celeste, his reviews had been high. After two years with her, he was barely satisfactory. Why he'd take her back was something he could never explain, even to himself. But he did, weeks later, at the pool at the apartment complex. His roommate said, "She's here," and he looked up and saw Celeste.

When he approached her, she held out a box. Inside was a ring she'd bought for him. "I love you," she said. "I want us to be together."

They argued, she pleaded, and Harald relented. "I got so deep in a rut with her I couldn't see above the rut to find a way out," he says. "I was like a beaten dog. I didn't want to be confrontational anymore. Looking back, the orders to Iceland saved my life."

He'd been told to report to Keflavik Air Force Base for a one-year tour of duty a few weeks after they reconciled. On the plane, he felt the sting of separation. "I missed her," he says. "Even after everything, I still missed her."

In Phoenix, Celeste moved in with Lue, Gary, and the twins. She quickly had an affair with a bartender and became pregnant. After she lost the baby, she had a hysterectomy. The reason was not clear. Years later she claimed she had ovarian cancer, an insidious disease with few symptoms that is often deadly. Lue Thompson remembers it differently: "Celeste told me she had the hysterectomy because she never wanted to worry about getting pregnant. I never remember her having any type of cancer."

Two months later Celeste left the girls with Lue and moved into an apartment with Jimmy, Lue's son, and his male partner. At the time, Celeste was dating a middle-age lawyer she met hanging out at a Phoenix bar frequented by the big-money crowd. He gifted her with something she'd often talked of wanting: breast implants.

When not out with her wealthy beau, Celeste partied with Jimmy and his crowd at gay bars. Because of her giggle, they nicknamed her Silly. "Celeste can be sweet, but she can turn backstabbing," he says. "There's something about her that you go back to her."

Still, their friendship soured. Jimmy complained to Lue that Celeste had come between him and his partner, pitting one against the other. As she had when anyone criticized Celeste, Lue defended her, this time instead of believing her own son.

From Jimmy's apartment, Celeste, who had a string of jobs from office work to waitressing, moved into an apartment with the girls. By then they'd become her shadows. Jennifer ached to play ball or spend time with friends, but that was out of the question. Celeste wouldn't permit it. Often they weren't even allowed to attend school, not when Celeste preferred to have them with her, to follow behind her as she shopped or ran errands. Through it all, Kristina kept silent, rarely complaining. She watched their mother with anxious eyes, afraid anything could send her over the suicidal edge.

Lue, too, was frightened, but for a different reason. Celeste drove at breakneck speeds and had one wreck after another. The nine-year-olds were terrified as their mother careened around corners. When a check-engine light came on in the yellow Taurus, Celeste screamed, "The car's going to explode."

The twins panicked as she shouted to hold onto the doors. "Be ready to jump," Celeste ordered, but nothing ever happened. Years later Jennifer remembered holding so tight her knuckles turned white, terrified they would all die. "I think she did it so we'd be quiet," she says. "We were so scared, and she laughed like it was all a joke."

At night Celeste left the girls alone in the apartment and partied. Hour after hour they waited for her return. "From when I was little on, what I remember most about being with her was that I was always hungry," says Jennifer. "She spent money on herself and never had any for food."

Despite all she'd learned about Celeste, Lue still thought of her as a daughter, and there were things she could never imagine she was capable of. That winter, the girls seemed afraid of their mother, and after much prodding, they told Lue why. Celeste, they said, ground something up and put it in their food, something that made them sleep. The girls begged Lue not to tell their mother. She agreed. While Lue found the conversation disturbing, she suspected it was nothing more than overactive childish imaginations.

Years later Kristina would have other memories of her mother: days an angry Celeste hit them with wooden spoons so hard they broke. And when Kristina suffered unexplained seizures, Celeste rarely visited her in the hospital. In the evenings, Kris called the apartment, but it was her sister, Jen, home alone, who answered. Those nights, Kris fell asleep watching the *Cosby Show* and wishing for a mother like Claire Huxtable, one who loved her children.

In 1990, Celeste reported the yellow Taurus stolen. When the insurance money came in, she purchased a brand new Thunderbird.

That summer, Celeste's landlord called Lue complaining about unsanitary conditions in the apartment. More and more, Kristina and Jennifer were alone and burdened with cleaning and cooking. Kristina even ironed the white tuxedo shirts from Celeste's waitress uniforms. In the mornings, waking Celeste was an unhappy task. She cursed and shouted. "I never woke her up when she didn't make me feel bad," says Kristina.

That fall, someone reported Celeste to Maricopa County's Children's Protective Services, and the girls were taken away. Despite the abysmal conditions they lived in, Kristina and Jennifer cried. "That was the last time I let myself care about her," says Jennifer. "From then on I couldn't love her, because she didn't love Kristina and me."

Not long after, police found the charred remnants of the Taurus in the desert outside Phoenix. Excited, Celeste asked Lue to bring her video camera and drive to the site with her. Once there, she filmed the car's blackened skeleton and giggled.

"What's so funny?" Lue asked.

"I burned it," Celeste answered with a wide grin. "I did it for the insurance."

"You're going to get caught, honey," Lue said. "You can't do things like that."

"People do it all the time," Celeste scoffed. "It was a piece of crap."

Perhaps Lue should have thought of that day when, weeks later, on October 14, Celeste called, crying. The Thompsons were in California, where they'd just returned to Gary's mother's house after a funeral. "Someone robbed your house!" Celeste screamed into the telephone. "They took a bunch of your stuff and my things."

When they arrived the next day, Lue realized how much was gone. They'd lost the television and VCR, as well as family heirlooms, including silver candlesticks and Lue's late mother's jewelry, Gary's class ring, even silver dollars commemorating their children's births. The point of entry was a single, small, neat cut in the back door screen.

"This was done by someone you know," an officer who stopped by told them. "They didn't mess up the place to look for things, and they knew what to take."

Days later Lue and Celeste filled out insurance forms. By then the Thompsons had more bad news: They weren't insured for replacement value and would collect nowhere near enough to restore all they'd lost.

"Why don't you add some things to your list?" Celeste urged.

"It's wrong, and I'll get caught," Lue told her.

"My attorney says everyone does it," she said. "That's what he told me to do."

Lue thought it over, and then, despite knowing that she was doing something wrong, padded the list of stolen valuables.

As always, Celeste's world changed quickly and without warning. At the end of 1990 she called Craig and announced that she wanted to join the army. She was willing to sign papers giving him custody of the twins. The girls, finally out of the foster home, left for Washington. But an odd thing happened that year while they lived with their father—they received a postcard in the mail, signed "Grandma."

"Who is this?" Jennifer asked her father. "This isn't from your mom."

"Your mother's mother, your grandmother," Craig explained. "She lives in California."

Jennifer and Kristina never asked their mother about the postcard or whose body they'd looked at in a coffin years earlier. They heard from Celeste rarely that year. When she did call, it was never good news. "She screamed at Craig, threatening to take the girls back," says his sister-in-law, Denise. "She never left him alone."

That spring, 1991, Celeste had her first serious brush with the law. Like all of her plots, her plan to join the army quickly dissipated. Instead she'd decided to stay in Phoenix. It was there, on May 6, that she became furious with the Thompsons. Celeste demanded they return a dog she'd given their youngest son. They refused, and she called the police. When Celeste claimed to the officer who responded that the Thompsons had staged the previous fall's robbery, Detective R. T. Phillips was put on the case.

In his nearly two decades on the force, Phillips, a lean man with a well-groomed mustache, specialized in uncovering insurance fraud. He was so good at it that he'd been written up in an insurance industry publication. "I felt like they [insurance frauds] were ripping me off," he says. "I had to pay my insurance, and they were driving up the rates."

When Phillips questioned her, Celeste told him she'd seen many of the items the Thompsons reported stolen in their house months after the robbery. She said she believed they'd staged the robbery, then inflated their losses. Based on her information, Phillips went to the Thompsons' house.

"Celeste loves me. She'd never hurt me," Lue told Phillips that day.

Yet, Phillips assured her, Celeste had made serious allegations against her and Gary. Quickly, the Thompsons admitted their guilt; they had inflated their insurance claim by $13,000. But they insisted they hadn't staged the robbery. In fact, Lue gave Phillips one more bit of information, recounting the story of the incinerated Taurus.

Phillips's gut told him the Thompsons were telling the truth, and he brought Celeste in for questioning. Each time he pointed out inconsistencies with the evidence, her story changed. When he found the stolen items in her two rented storage units, he felt certain she was the one behind the robbery. When he asked about the incinerated Taurus, Celeste just laughed. "Sure, I took it out in the desert and torched it," she said. "The damn thing didn't work half the time."

"She was cool the whole time," says Phillips, who wrote in his report: "Based on the inconsistencies in what Celeste Wolf has told me and her insurance company, it appears no burglary ever occurred at the Thompsons' . . . in fact, Celeste Wolf took property belonging to the Thompsons to make it look like a burglary occurred, then made false reports to her insurance company."

Despite all the evidence Phillips had, when he called Craig in Washington State to ask about Celeste's past for her pretrial report, Celeste's first husband laughed at the notion that she'd be punished. "Celeste gets away with everything," he said. "I'll bet my hard-earned money—every penny I've got—that she'll talk that judge into letting her go."

In 1991, while the insurance fraud case ground on, a new man, Jimmy Martinez, entered Celeste's life. It was he who would bring her to Texas and into Steve Beard's world.

Swarthy and handsome, Martinez was thirty—nearly three years older than Celeste—had a stable job planning and managing security systems, and had never been married. Like Celeste, he exuded a palpable sexual tension and a flirtatious manner. Someone who knew them both would later say, "I don't think it was ever love between them. To me, it always looked more like lust."

They met at Mr. Lucky's, a legendary Phoenix country bar, famous for its mechanical bulls. With a mischievous grin and a cowboy's swagger, Jimmy had just left a country western concert when he saw Celeste with a woman he'd once dated. They were quickly attracted. "I'm a leg man," he says. "And Celeste looked great in a miniskirt."

On August 24, 1991, Celeste was twenty-eight and marrying for the third time. At least one matter remained unresolved the day she promised to love Jimmy Martinez until death they did part: She was still legally married to Harald Wolf. In her busy life, she'd never gotten around to filing for divorce.

In Washington State, Jennifer and Kristina learned about the marriage on a postcard. The girls must have been on Celeste's mind often that fall. She didn't like having anyone out of her reach, and just months after voluntarily giving them up, she called Craig, demanding he send them to her. He refused. Many who knew him gave the credit for his ability to stand up to Celeste to the new woman in his life, Kathryn Morton, a bright, determined woman who worked at the Snohomish County Attorney's Office. They met at a park, while he was camping with Jennifer and Kristina, and it was his dedication to them that attracted Kathryn, who had two young children of her own. "Craig described Celeste as a Coyote Bitch," says Morton. "He was exhausted from battling her."

The battle became a war as Celeste began a court fight to reclaim the twins.

That summer, Jen and Kristina were ten and about to enter fourth grade; they lost a year when they had to repeat second grade, after Coleste kept them out of school so often that they couldn't keep up. A thousand miles away, Celeste called often and pulled the strings that attached Kristina to her. The youngster sobbed as Celeste put the weight of the world on her thin, young shoulders, telling her she couldn't live without her, at times threatening suicide. "It was awful. She was my mother. I loved her," says Kristina.

Her identical twin couldn't have been more different in her reaction to their mother. Even the thought of seeing Celeste gave Jen terrible nightmares. "She'd be killing us," says Jennifer. At times she saw herself firing a gun at her mother. The bullet ricocheted, then struck her instead, as if embodying an unspoken fear that anything she did to hurt Celeste would come back to injure her.

In Arizona, Celeste moved to Tucson with Jimmy, but soon this marriage, too, was troubled. When they argued, she raged, then explained away her erratic behavior by saying she forgot to take the hormone supplements given to her after her hysterectomy. "That's why the girls are so important," she said. "I can never have other children."

As far as Jimmy was concerned, Celeste had so much else to offer that he overlooked her tantrums. He loved watching her at a party, proud of the way she talked to anyone, not relying on him for support. "She made people laugh," he says. Where Celeste held back with others, their sex life couldn't have been better. In the end he would wonder if he was swept up in the passion and the lure of finding someone who needed him. "I was there to protect Celeste," he says.

Meanwhile, in May 1992, Celeste arrived at Craig's, demanding to see Kristina. When they dropped her twin off, Jennifer didn't even look at her mother's car. With tears in her eyes, she watched Kristina walk away, wondering if she'd return. She came home later that night, but Jennifer instinctively knew Celeste wasn't finished with them.

All the next day, Jen watched Kristina at school, assessing her face to see what she was thinking. Kris seemed quiet, with faraway thoughts. In final period, Jen lost track of her sister, and when she arrived at the bus stop, Kristina wasn't there. At home, Craig called the police. When they found Kristina with her mother, Celeste had cards she said Kris had written her. In them, Kris described Craig as abusive, saying he'd hit her. The following day, Jen was pulled out of school and questioned. Police even asked the girls' friends if they'd seen signs of abuse. The investigation came up empty. After seventy-two hours Kristina was released to Craig. On the way home she cried and told him that she was sorry. Later, she'd deny that her father ever hit her or Jen. "Kris was just doing what our mom told her to," says Jen.

In Phoenix, on May 28, 1992, Gary and Lue Thompson stood before a judge and were sentenced to probation—Lue to three years and Gary to five—and they were ordered to pay $8,000 in restitution to their insurance company. For Lue, the sentence paled in comparison to who was there to witness it: a group of schoolchildren on a class trip. "I thought of all the troubled kids we'd taken in and all the good we'd tried to do," she says. "I couldn't look at those kids. It just tore me to pieces."

Adding insult to injury, the Phoenix P.D. refused to prosecute Celeste for burglarizing their house. "We had no rights, because we lied on the insurance form," says Lue.

Later that summer, Harald returned from Iceland. By then Celeste and his possessions had disappeared. When he tried to rent an apartment, his credit report came back with six pages of bad debts he didn't know they had. Celeste's legacy was $60,000 in unpaid bills. "My credit was toast," he says. "She'd taken everything. My clothes, my books, my furniture, my photographs, even the stamp collection I started when I was a kid."

In his truck—the one thing she'd left behind—he drove to the East Coast, eager to forget her. There, he filed for divorce, and on December 14, 1992, it became final. The process servers never found Celeste to serve the papers, and, as far as Harald knew, Celeste never learned of the divorce. Years later, married and happy, Harald saw a woman resembling Celeste at a mall. "My wife said my face was so full of hatred it scared her," he says.

The following summer Jen was furious at her father and refused to even look at him when he took her and Kristina to the airport to fly to Arizona to spend two weeks with Celeste. In Tucson, Celeste put both the girls to work. The security company had transferred Jimmy to Austin, and he was already there. The furniture had been moved, but the apartment needed to be packed. Celeste didn't plan to do it herself, not with the girls available. Besides, she was busy. She didn't let being married infringe on her social life. The night before they were supposed to move, she had a date with a cop. "Finish packing," she said. "I want it all done when I get home."

After she left, the eleven-years-olds looked about them,

not knowing how one went about packing an apartment. They started to put clothes in boxes while they watched television, but the food ads made them hungry. As usual, Celeste had left them nothing to eat. Not knowing what else to do, Jennifer searched and found change. Then the frightened little girls, holding hands walked through the dark streets to a convenience store where they bought TV dinners. Back at the apartment, they ate and fell asleep.

The following morning Celeste was livid to find the packing not completed. "You never do anything for me," she screamed as she gathered their belongings. Months earlier the girls had watched a movie on TV based on the autobiography of screen siren Joan Crawford's daughter. In it, Faye Dunaway, playing Crawford, shrieked at her children. That day, as on many others, Celeste lived up to the nickname the twins had given her, the title of the movie: *Mommie Dearest*.

On the nine hundred mile trip to Austin, Celeste was exuberant. She always seemed excited about change, and this was no exception. They stopped at one convenience store after another, where she loaded up on junk food and Cokes. Munching away, Celeste coached the girls on what they were and weren't supposed to tell Jimmy. "Remember when I was in Phoenix, and I had cancer and all my hair fell out?" she said.

The twins had no such memories but nodded in agreement.

That afternoon, with her mother in a good mood, they talked. "How did you take care of us and go to high school?" Kristina asked.

"I graduated two years early, so I was out of high school," Celeste lied, then, continuing her tale, told them, "After you were born, I went to college."

When Jennifer asked why she'd married Jimmy Martinez, Celeste laughed smugly.

"Because of his BMW," she answered.

"He has a Pontiac and a truck," Jen said.

Celeste giggled. "No, his big Mexican wiener."

Driving into Austin on Interstate 35, as Celeste and the twins did that day, one can look toward the east, to valleys that dwindle off to a flat coastal plain. Looking west from I-35, the landscape beckons to the rugged Texas Hill Country. Some say Austin's main attribute is its quirkiness. At dusk on summer nights the city's prime attraction is the exodus of more than one million Mexican free tailed bats, the largest urban colony in the world, from under the Congress Avenue Bridge. For decades before the advent of skyscrapers, the city's skyline was dominated by the Texas State Capitol's dome and the University of Texas clock tower. It was there on August 1, 1966, that Charles Whitman climbed the stairway to the twenty-eighth floor and opened fire. The siege left sixteen dead and thirty injured. It was a rude entry into the chaos of the sixties for a gentle city that had always welcomed a healthy dose of wildness.

Austin is a city where tie-dye never went out of fashion, and local merchants ran a campaign to "Keep Austin Weird." One year the roster of mayoral candidates boasted a thong-wearing cross-dresser and a former hit man. The mideighties brought an influx of high-tech companies led by Dell Computer, and the city grew and prospered, making the new Austin not only part cowgirl and part flower child, but part Silicon Valley yuppie.

From the beginning, the free-spirited city matched Celeste well. Jimmy rented a town house on a street full of such double houses. Of the three bedrooms, when they visited, Kris and Jen shared one, Celeste and Jimmy another, leaving the last to serve as Celeste's closet. After years of frenetic shopping, she had 160 pairs of shoes and enough clothes to fill the room. Many remained unworn and price-tagged, making it resemble a small, private boutique.

Throughout the two weeks Jennifer and Kristina spent in Texas, Jimmy and Celeste fought often. One day, Celeste covered a wall writing "I hate Jimmy Martinez" with a felt-tip pen. During another argument, Celeste stabbed herself in the wrist with a scissors, shouting that she would kill herself, while Kristina sobbed.

One afternoon as the family drove on a freeway, Celeste threatened to jump from the car. The girls screamed as their mother threw open the front passenger door. Jimmy grabbed her arm and yanked her back in. Later, just as she had with Craig and Harald, Celeste called police and claimed Jimmy had hit her. As proof, she showed officers a bruised hand-print on her left arm, not explaining that it came from her husband pulling her back into the car as she attempted to throw herself onto a busy highway. Jimmy was locked up overnight. When he threatened to end the marriage, Celeste went to a psychiatrist and was put on medication for depression. "She was better for a while," he says. "She was trying."

Meanwhile, Celeste begged the twins not to return to Washington. She pleaded with them to stay with her. Unswayed, Jennifer boarded a flight home; but Kristina couldn't part from her mother. Craig pushed Celeste to live up to the custody agreement and return her. She refused. "My whole life I felt bad for my mom. I felt like one of us needed to love her," says Kristina. "She always said that she loved me and needed me. Two seconds later she was screaming that I wasn't good enough or didn't love her enough. Then she'd be sorry. I'd say it was okay. What else could I do?"

For the first time in their young lives, the girls were separated, and they missed each other dearly. Still, Celeste wasn't satisfied. While Craig fought for Kristina, she wanted Jennifer. "The phone rang at the house, and it would be her," says Jen. "She'd laugh and say she was going to take me away from my dad, that she'd get even with us for what we did to her. Once she told me that she had cancer and tried to make me feel sorry for her."

After she had Kristina, Celeste changed her phone number. For months Craig was unable to call. When he finally got through, Kristina told him she loved him and missed him, but then he heard Celeste in the background, ordering Kristina to tell him she didn't love him. At first Kristina said nothing; then she mumbled something into the telephone.

"You don't ever want to live with your dad again, do you?" Craig heard Celeste prod.

Eventually he stopped calling.

Six months after the Thompsons' sentencing, on November 27, 1992, Celeste returned to Phoenix on the insurance fraud charges. In the courtroom, Kristina sat beside her mother as the Thompsons watched from the gallery. "I didn't know what was going on, but I knew Celeste had done something to cause them trouble," says Kristina. "I couldn't talk to them with Celeste there. So I didn't even look at them."

In his report to the court, Detective Phillips painted a damning picture of a woman who cared for no one but herself. He'd discovered Celeste had devastated lives wherever she'd gone and had a record of twelve insurance claims, each for an escalating amount. Nothing—not even her children, it appeared—mattered to Celeste as much as money.

As always, Celeste told a very different story that day to the judge, one in which she was a victim, not a predator. After her sad account of abuse at the hands of her parents and Craig, Celeste deflected responsibility for the offense by blaming a nameless attorney she said had advised her to inflate her report. Finally, she argued that she had a young daughter to support and—the key issue—she'd left Arizona.

"She basically said, 'I won't bother you anymore. I'm Texas's problem now,'" says Phillips. "And the judge bought it."

As Craig predicted, Celeste received no jail time. Instead, the judge gave her two hundred hours of community service, four years' probation, and ordered her to pay $20,000 to the insurance companies, then set her free to "proceed to the state of Texas."

That day in the courtroom, Phillips shook his head in disgust. "I knew that woman wasn't any good and that she'd only get worse," he says. "I never kept files on old cases. I made an exception with Celeste. I kept those files until I retired, because I had no doubt I'd hear her name again, and the next time it would be for something truly bad."

A month later Jimmy took Celeste and Kristina to spend the holidays with his family in El Paso. Kristina enjoyed the warmth of his large extended family. One night as they watched the news, a reporter warned the public to beware of con artists, people who weren't what they seemed. *That's what my mom is,* Kristina thought. *She hurts everyone.*

In Austin, Celeste first waitressed at the Springhill Restaurant, north of the city in a suburb called Pflugerville. A red clapboard structure with a saloon-shaped facade, it had a menu featuring chicken-fried steak, fried catfish, and burgers. Then, in early 1993, she applied at the exclusive Austin Country Club, where the city's wealthy played tennis, golfed, dined, and mingled. Her first day working the main dining room opened up a new world for Celeste, one of money and prestige, a world she'd soon make her own.

Founded in 1899, the club was the first of its kind in the state, and over the decades the membership list read like a Who's Who of Texas. Tucked next to Westlake Hills, where the city's new money migrated to homes perched atop craggy bluffs, the club had sweeping fairways surrounded by gnarled live oaks, boat slips along Lake Austin, and a clubhouse with expansive windows framing breathtaking scenery.

There, Celeste became one of a staff of waitresses, bartenders, and busboys. She reported to Fernando von Hapsburg, the maitre d'. He'd remember her as a good waitress, popular with the members. At first Celeste was well-liked. She told more than one member about troubles at home, claiming she was hiding out from an abusive ex-husband, like Julia Roberts had in the 1991 movie *Sleeping with the Enemy*. Few knew she was actually living with Jimmy. "She always seemed to be dating some new guy," says a waitress. "I felt sorry for her that she didn't have anything positive in her life."

After work, the staff traveled downtown to Sixth Street, where run-down storefronts housed Austin's music and bar scene, mingling taverns with vintage clothing stores and tattoo parlors. There they listened to music and drank. Celeste was often the center of attention. When she imitated von Hapsburg or a snooty member, she was dead-on, and the others roared. One night, while they circulated from bar to bar, Celeste flirted with a chauffeur, then took the others with her for a limo ride. "This is the only way to live," she said, throwing back her head and laughing.

On such nights, Jimmy wondered about her absence, but the next morning she always had a good excuse. Often, she would tell him she'd been home all along, arriving after he'd fallen asleep. Instead of waking him, she claimed she'd slept with Kristina. Perhaps he didn't investigate, or maybe he was beyond caring, for the marriage was already cooling. By the summer of 1993—not quite two years after their wedding—the bills were streaming in. Jimmy, who'd always been fastidious about his credit, discovered that Celeste had run up tens of thousands of dollars in debt. He called the credit card companies saying they were Celeste's cards, not his, and asking to have his name taken off the accounts.

"Your wife opened these accounts, and you're responsible," he was told.

"When I tried to talk to Celeste about it, she'd take Kristina and leave," he says.

As usual when all didn't go well, Celeste told those around her that she was sick. That year, she had herself tested for throat cancer. At the club, some members felt sorry for the pretty young waitress with the sad stories; others had a different impression. "She was husband-shopping," says one woman. "She flirted with every man with a bankroll."

In June 1993, when the twins were twelve, the custody battle escalated. Craig and Kathryn, who had by then married, went to Austin for a hearing. In the courtroom, Kristina looked tired and bowed, as if she'd gone through a horrific ordeal. "The brief glances we received from her were full of fear, trepidation, and sadness," Craig wrote in his letter to the judge. "She is obviously going through a great deal of emotional turmoil."

"Why didn't you bring Kristina home?" Jen asked Craig when he returned.

"She told the judge she didn't want to come," he answered.

"Mom told her to say that," she replied.

In July, Craig and Kathryn wrote their letters to the judge, detailing reasons Kristina would be better off with them: *"Celeste is a pathological liar . . . She often takes the facts of situations . . . and twists them . . . taking something she did to someone and twisting it around as if they did it to her. It almost seems as if she believes it herself after a while.*

"Celeste Martinez is a greedy, uncaring, cruel and evil in-

dividual . . . She is an accomplished con artist and is extremely dangerous."

A month later, on August 10, in Washington, Jennifer met with the lawyer the court appointed to represent her interests. She was nervous, fidgeting in the chair as they talked. But when he asked, she was resolute: She never wanted to visit or live with Celeste again.

"Why?" she was asked.

"Mom makes me tell people lies, and I don't like that," she said.

At the country club, many members grew fond of Celeste. Among them were Anita Inglis and her husband Jerry. "She was charming. And she talked a lot about trying to regain custody of her daughters," says Anita, an attorney and former prosecutor. "Some members slipped her hundred dollar bills to help pay for an attorney."

One week, Celeste called Anita and said she had nasal cancer and needed surgery. She said she had nowhere to leave Kristina. Although she hardly knew Celeste, Anita told her she'd care for her daughter.

Forty-five minutes later Celeste and Kristina rang the bell. When Anita opened the door, she saw Celeste with a slight, quiet young girl with her mother's athletic build, dark blond hair, and large blue eyes. "She was a little mouse, just scared to death," says Anita, whose heart went out to the girl.

That week, Anita, a kind woman with thick, dark hair and a motherly manner, took Kristina to school and helped with her homework. At night she and Jerry tucked her in. "The whole time, Kris worried about Celeste. She kept asking when she'd be coming back," she says. "She was this very sad but very sweet little girl."

A week later Celeste returned and reclaimed Kristina. Not long after, she called again, this time asking for legal help with the custody battle. Craig had won, and the Washington court had ordered her to send Kristina to him in Washington. Anita met with her and with Kristina. Without Celeste in the room, Anita asked Kris, "Honey, what do you want? Do you want to live with your mom or with your dad?"

"I want to live with my mom," Kristina answered.

Anita wrote petitions and tried to help, but the decisions went against Celeste. Days later Celeste put Kristina on an airplane in Austin, but Kristina never arrived in Seattle. During a Dallas layover, she refused to reboard. Although Celeste had repeatedly abandoned her, Kristina loved her mother so much she refused to leave her.

In Washington, Craig told Jennifer, "We have to let it be."

That fall, many at the Austin Country Club noticed Steve Beard, a wealthy television executive, sitting alone at a table, eating dinner and staring out the window as darkness fell over the golf course. The death of his beloved wife had left the once gregarious man an empty shell. He asked around, looking for someone to hire as his house manager. Days later Celeste had the job.

In late 1994, Steve had no way of understanding who Celeste really was. Instead, he must have seen an attractive young mother who needed help and protection. As she had with so many others, Celeste told him her twisted version of her life, in which she was a victim, not someone who had destroyed lives across three states. "Steve was the kind of guy who figured he was a good judge of character. He went with his gut about people," says a friend. "And Celeste was beautiful and persuasive."

Chapter

3

"**S**teve Beard was an old-fashioned Texas busi-nessman," says a friend. "He was the kind of guy who'd take a little bit to get to know you, maybe even give you a little shit about something at first, but if he liked you, he was your friend for the rest of your life."

Born on November 27, 1924, Steven F. Beard Jr. grew up in a modest Dallas neighborhood and came of age in an era when men earned a living while women stayed home and raised families. He was a member of the old school, a successful businessman who worked hard and made his own way in the world, relying on his wits and talents. He believed in keeping his private life private, and that it was his duty to take care of his wife and children. Later, his youngest son, Paul, would remember little about his father's father, except that Steve had a falling out with him and rarely talked of the man. But Steve loved his mother, a tall, proud woman with a well-carved profile.

In early pictures, Steve was a handsome boy, with a crop of dusty brown hair combed determinedly to the side. Even then he had a wide smile and a slight paunch around the middle. After high school he had a hard time finding himself. He migrated to three colleges: Texas Christian University, Southern Methodist University, and the University of Georgia, majoring in advertising and marketing. He earned a degree in chiropractic medicine, although he never practiced. In World War II, with the nation in turmoil, Steve joined the navy and trained as a pilot and an engineer at the U.S. Maritime Academy in Kings Point, New York. He worked as a supply officer on a ship, and after the war, joined the Coast Guard for a stint.

Out of the service, with thousands of GIs returning home, jobs were scarce, and Steve felt lucky to land a fifteen-dollar-a-week shoe salesman's job at Neiman Marcus in Dallas. There he met a young model from Arkansas, Elise Adams. A pretty girl with a petite figure, she'd attended the University of Texas at Austin and played clarinet in the band during the time Tom Landry, the legendary Dallas Cowboy's coach, played football for the school.

Steve and Elise had much in common. Both loved the outdoors. For all her grace on a runway, Elise was a tomboy at heart. They went camping and fishing, and quickly fell in love. "I don't know that it was love at first sight, but I think it must have been," says Paul. "My mom and dad had their ups and downs, but they loved each other dearly."

In their wedding photo, Elise is stunning in a flowing chiffon wedding gown and carrying a bouquet of roses. She looks so thrilled to be marrying Steve that looking at the photo, one might have assumed her groom was Neiman's chairman of the board, not a young shoe salesman. At twenty-three, Steve has a boyish face, dark eyes, and generous cheeks. He is wide in the girth, giving him an ample appearance in his white dinner jacket and slender, Errol Flynn–style bow tie.

The future media exec first got interested in TV and radio in college, when he worked as a student broadcaster at TCU. Knowing where his interests lay, as soon as he could he quit Neiman Marcus and joined Dallas's KRLD radio, doing whatever they asked, even sweeping floors. From KRLD he signed on at Tracy-Locke Advertising Agency. It was there Steve came into his own, finding his niche, selling ads. He produced TV commercials for the nation's top companies, including Haggar Slacks, Borden Dairies, and Imperial Sugar. In 1948, Locke transferred Steve to New York where he and Elise had their first child, Steven III, while living in the suburbs.

From Tracy-Locke, Steve signed on in 1950 with John Blair & Company, a nationwide firm that sold radio and television commercial time, and he returned to Dallas to open the firm's southwest regional sales operation. While they were there, their second child, Becky, was born. In 1953 their third and final child, Paul, made his entrance.

At just twenty-six years old, Steve was a superstar at Blair. He was committed, hardworking, and bright. And he had a way about him, a boisterous, effervescent personality that advertisers liked. When he entertained clients in New Orleans, he introduced himself to the proprietors of the city's best restaurants. They remembered him when he returned, and he got top-shelf service. Soon, Steve could walk into any of that city's top restaurants without reservations and get a center-stage table. "We called him the mayor of Bourbon Street," says a friend. "Everybody knew Steve. He was the kind of guy who made an impression. He was easy to do business with, ethical, never a question about him honoring a promise, and fun to be around. Just an all-around good guy."

Quickly, Steve was promoted and brought back to New York to work for Blair's television division, where he was responsible for sales development with many of the city's largest ad agencies. But he never truly settled in back East. He loved Texas and asked to be transferred home to Dallas. In 1954 he got his wish and returned as Blair's vice president and manager of the southwest regional operation. He and Elise bought a two-story, five-bedroom house in exclusive North Dallas. With a putting green and a swimming pool in the backyard, the Beard house became a destination on July Fourth, when Steve manned the grill and closed the festivities with fireworks. "On holidays, he always assumed we'd be together with family," says Paul. "Family was important to Dad and Mom both."

When Paul joined the YMCA swim team, Steve rushed home from the office early to be his coach. He timed his son's laps in the backyard pool, pushing him to be competitive. One day, Paul was hit by a car while bicycling. Steve, in his Jaguar, rushed to the scene so fast the police couldn't stop him on the freeway. When he finally pulled over, he informed them that they could follow him and write the ticket but that he was headed to the accident. "He was a good dad, always there for us," says Paul.

There was little that Steve liked better than giving gifts. At Christmas he presided over the celebration, grinning as the family opened their presents. One year he surprised Elise with a beautiful gold watch; another year, he parked a brand new 1962 Oldsmobile F85 station wagon out front, visible from the bay window. "Don't you notice anything?" he said, growing exasperated as he waited with excitement for Elise to see the car.

The truth was, Elise never liked station wagons. She preferred sportier cars, like another of Steve's presents, a 1969 Camaro with a black and orange houndstooth interior, just like that year's Indy pace car. "He knocked her socks off," says Paul.

As his success grew, Steve bought the family a three-hundred-acre weekend ranch with two creeks and a lake, near Gainesville, Texas, where they raised Beefmaster cattle, horses, and 150 head of sheep. Steve worked long hours, but in his time off, he took Paul and Steve fishing and hunting for dove, geese, and quail. Later, when beef prices plummeted and Steve's allergies worsened, he sold the ranch and bought a twenty-five-foot cabin cruiser they kept on Lake Dallas. Summer vacations were car trips to Padre Island, a Texas barrier island that forms a long string of beach fringed by high-rise hotels. In 1964 he took the entire family to the New York World's Fair.

A man with a big appetite, over the years Steve grew round at the waistline. He slicked his hair back and wore a small mustache. With a ruddy complexion, he resembled the rotund comic Jackie Gleason. His laugh as full of life as the star of the *Honeymooners*, friends described Steve as "hale and hearty," "a man's man," "boisterous," and "fun."

Known for never mincing words and telling friends exactly what she thought, Elise was his match. Never shy, she sang in a women's barbershop quartet wearing a fringed, 1920s flapper dress on her petite and athletic frame. After the early years of raising three children, she took up golf and became an exceptional player, one year winning the championship at Brookhaven Country Club, where they were members. She taught Paul and Steven III to golf and spent so much time on the links, three to four days a week, that at times Steve resented her dedication to the game. Yet, as active as she was, Elise was a chain smoker. Friends rarely saw her without a cigarette in her mouth. And, they both enjoyed their cocktails. "Dad liked his vodka," says Paul. "He wasn't an alcoholic, but he definitely liked to drink."

Yet, Steve was a careful man. He often told friends that while young he'd been pulled over for drinking and driving.

From that point on, he never drank more than he knew he could manage if he planned to get behind the wheel. "He called his drinks 'Whitey Loudmouths,' because he got happier when he was drinking, and louder," says a friend. "But he never drank before five and never that I saw to the stage that he was sloppy drunk."

As they aged, Elise and Steve remained very much a conservative and traditional married couple. She spoke her mind, but he ruled the family. As he grew successful, they became wealthy, but never threw around money. "Steve remembered the Great Depression," says one old friend. "He didn't much care for people who bought just to buy. He wasn't cheap, but he expected to get something for his dollar."

At work, Steve's employees called him Mr. Beard, but he didn't treat them as underlings. Instead, he had a deep interest in people and worked hard to bring along those who showed promise. When Blair purchased KOKH-TV in Oklahoma City, Steve was appointed to the board of directors and helped plan programming. He did well at Blair, but then, with the children grown and gone, he eyed a new challenge. In 1982, Steve heard that the FCC was offering a license for a new Austin television station. Steve called Darrold Cannan, a wealthy friend and a customer throughout his years at Blair, and asked him to be his partner in the deal.

Until the late seventies, the three networks—NBC, ABC, and CBS—ruled the marketplace, and independent stations weren't considered viable. The availability of sitcom reruns changed that, making independents suddenly attractive investments. Cannan readily agreed that the new Austin station appeared to be a good opportunity. With his own money and Cannan's to back him, Steve spearheaded a bid to win the FCC license. Out of five applications, three made it to the final stages: Steve's and two others. To win the license,

Steve negotiated an alliance, bringing one of the competing applicants in as a third partner. The strategy worked, and in 1982 he won his bid to found Austin's new, independent television station. When Steve left Blair and Dallas, his staff threw him a party. As a parting gift, they commissioned a caricature of him as a cowboy in chaps and spurs heading toward Austin.

The owner of fifteen percent of the stock in the new station, Steve moved quickly. He and Elise rented an Austin apartment, and he took on the formidable job of general manager. In a smart marketing move, he named Channel 42 KBVO after the University of Texas football team's beloved mascot, Bevo, a Texas longhorn steer. Running the operation on a shoestring, he opened a small office and hired a skeleton staff. At the opening party, Steve was an enthusiastic host, introducing KBVO to the city and potential advertisers.

"Steve was nearing sixty when he came to Austin, and he was older in body but had a young mind and a young heart," says Ray McEachern, KBVO-TV's financial officer, and later its station manager. "Lots of the television stations ran ads in the little towns in the viewing area. Steve hired the local high school bands and put on parades. People loved it. He drove his BMW in the parades and waved at people, with a big smile on his face."

Yet Steve wasn't all sunshine and smiles. If someone crossed him, he stood his ground. One afternoon McEachern came to him about a client who owed the station more than $100,000. Steve was furious. It was in the first months of the station, when ratings weren't commanding big ad dollars and drawing in ads wasn't easy. McEachern feared alienating the customer, a media buyer for a large soap company. Steve had no such qualms. He picked up the phone and called the man. "I have to pay when I buy at the store. You've got to pay here," he said. He then told the man that in the future he'd have to pay cash to advertise on KBVO.

McEachern thought that Steve had lost a big client, but the following day a check for the client's arrears arrived plus another $20,000 for future ads. When Ray showed him the check, Steve wasn't surprised. "Never, ever let anyone mess with you," he said.

Over the years, the one blind spot McEachern noticed in Steve involved women. "They seemed to be able to hoodwink him," he says, saying Steve made exceptions for women that he wouldn't for the men, such as not questioning when they needed time off. "Steve never thought badly of a woman. He respected them."

At KBVO, Steve's acumen quickly paid off, making the station a resounding success. "There was a real opening for a fourth station," says one observer. "Steve ran old movies and sitcom reruns, and the ads came in, and the revenues climbed."

In 1986 the Fox network mushroomed across the nation. Under Steve's guidance, KBVO became Austin's Fox affiliate, and more success followed. Throughout Austin, Steve became a familiar sight, driving his BMW with his KBVO license plates. He affixed magnetic FOX 42, KIDS' CLUB placards on the sides, advertising the station's children's show, where the main character dressed as Bevo, the steer. Children waved and called out to him, and Steve waved back, loving the attention.

Living the good life, Steve loved food and drank, and his weight climbed until he flirted with 300 pounds on his five-foot-ten-inch frame. Yet his weight never seemed to bother him. On the golf course he was too wide to bend down to tee his ball. His friends did it for him. When McEachern drove in his car with him, Steve snickered at joggers. "Look at that guy," he said playfully. "Hell, he's all red in the face, huffing and puffing. You can't tell me that damned exercise is good for people."

He told a friend: "Elise loves me the way I am, and I'm happy. That's all that matters. Life is good."

And Elise did love him. Throughout their years together, they were a team. "She adored him," says a friend. "When she looked at him, you could see she'd never stopped loving him."

Steve felt the same way about her. Each day at five-thirty he stopped what he was doing, straightened his desk, then called Elise and asked what he could pick up for her at the grocery store. "Do you need anything?" he'd ask, taking out his pen to write a list.

Of the three children, Becky visited the most often. By then she was teaching school in Dallas. Steve was settled in Chicago and Paul had joined the navy. "Dad convinced me," Paul says. "He said the navy would give me a chance to find myself and to see the world."

When it came time to buy, the Beards chose a house in West lake Hills, on a bluff overlooking the city. On Terrace Mountain Drive, it was one of the best examples of why Austin's moneyed crowd was migrating to the hills. The land had a rugged charm, a rough-and-tumble wildness that fit Texas, and incredible views of the city skyline.

The one-story house rambled across the crest of a hill. From the street it resembled giant blocks with Mediterranean arches. Beige stucco, it appeared to be formed out of the same pale earth as the hills on which it stood. Inside it boasted rough-hewn Spanish tile floors and a wall of windows. In the panorama visible from nearly every room lay downtown Austin, striking upward from a bed of trees. At night, Steve and Elise swam in the enclosed pool or gazed out at the city lights while drinking cocktails in their hot tub.

The former owners had built a hothouse on the property and raised orchids. Elise, who laughed about having a black thumb, took up the calling and won a garden club competition with an orchid her second year in the house.

The Beards added on, bringing the house to more than 4,700 square feet. It had a study, game room, formal living and dining room, and four and a half baths. Steve was so proud, he photographed the renovated house, and Elise put together a before and after album to show friends. In his study, Steve hung mementoes, including photos of himself with *Bonanza*'s Hoss, Dan Blocker, from a promotional trip when KBVO bought the rights to air the reruns, and White House Christmas cards signed by Ronald and Nancy Reagan.

While KBVO flourished, all Steve's money wasn't from the new station. He'd left Blair a wealthy man. McEachern estimated the Beards were already worth three million dollars when they arrived in Austin. "Steve did well, and he and Elise were both careful. They saved," says Ray. "He was the kind of man who knew how to build wealth."

At lunch, Steve had a rule: Although he could have easily afforded it, he rarely spent more than five dollars. Later, McEachern would chuckle remembering how one day in a Chinese restaurant Steve looked at the menu and asked for the owner. When the man walked up, he said, "Is this the dinner menu or lunch?"

"Lunch," the man, who spoke little English, replied.

"Hell, I can't afford your prices," Steve growled, handing it back to him. "Just bring me a bowl of egg drop soup and an egg roll."

At first the man didn't know how to take the big, brash customer. Then Steve's laugh echoed through the restaurant, and soon the man laughed along with him. From that day on, Steve was a regular, and the owner greeted him by name.

"Steve wasn't cheap. He just liked to know what he was getting for his money," says Ray. "He didn't give it away."

Once, in a rare moment of candor, Steve confided in McEachern about his past, saying that when he and Elise were newlyweds, he lost their savings in a bad investment. "I learned my lesson," he said. "I won't ever let myself be poor again."

By the late eighties Steve was well-known in his adopted city. He was active on the city's Red Cross, volunteering as director one year. At the Headliners, a private club for media types, including execs, editors, and reporters, he made many good friends. Among them were Austin's former mayor, Roy Butler, who owned the city's main beer distributorship, and Gene Bauman, who ran Butler's two popular country western radio stations. Steve advertised KBVO on Butler's stations, and every year he and Elise went on the radio stations' advertising trip. They were extravagant, all-expenses-paid outings, often to points in Europe. And in China, Steve and Elise purchased an intricate embroidered silk kimono they hung over the fireplace.

At the station, Steve's management style reflected his roots, in an era when successful men drew careful boundaries. Although he cared deeply about the people who worked for him, he kept a certain distance. Still, when he knew someone needed help, he often quietly did what he could. One year, when a custodian fell upon hard times, Steve brought the man clothing. When his secretary's car broke down, he talked a friend who ran a dealership into giving her a good deal on a new one.

With Elise's love of golf, one of the first places the Beards set up roots was the Austin Country Club, just minutes down the hill from the Terrace Mountain Drive house, paying the then-going rate for a membership of $50,000. One of the top women players, she teed off three to four times a week and was jubilant the day she made a hole-in-one. While Elise, whose voice grew gravelly from the cigarettes—and her skin leathery from years in the sun—never hesitated to offer an opinion, she did it with such gusto that the other women enjoyed the give and take. At night the Beards often drank and dined with friends. "They were always there," says a waitress. "Mr. Beard would tell me to cut him off after a few drinks, and I did. Sometimes he'd want more and grumble, but he'd say, 'Good girl.'"

Elise and Steve loved animals, and in the early nineties she bought him a dog, Meagan, a yellow lab–golden retriever mix, from a local shelter. Meagan quickly became Steve's shadow, following him through the house and sleeping at the foot of their bed. When strangers arrived, Meagan announced their presence with a formidable bark, then eyed them, looking for cues from Steve.

In 1992, Steve and his partner, Cannan, bought out KBVO-TV's third investor, and his share of the station jumped to thirty percent. He threw a party for the staff at the Headliners Club to mark the station's tenth anniversary. It was a grand event, with food and drink, and he presided proudly. It seemed his life just kept getting better. Then his success became bittersweet.

Elise fell ill.

"It started when Mom had this backache," says Paul. At first doctors speculated that Elise, whose words were slurred, had suffered a small stroke. But that wasn't it. "Mom had a brain tumor."

It happened in March 1993, and at first Steve told no one. Lisa Ottenbacher, his personal secretary, didn't understand why he seemed so preoccupied until the day he finally called her to his office. She knew he was carefully controlling his emotions as he explained that Elise was gravely ill. It was a family matter, and he didn't discuss it further, except to tell Lisa that she might have to cover for him, since he'd be absent more than usual. From that day on, he left often, first to take Elise to doctors, then to be with her while she underwent chemo and radiation. When Lisa saw Elise at the hospital, she was struck by her courage. Some friends affectionately called Elise "a tough old broad" for speaking her mind. That strength served her well as she waged a battle for her very life.

That spring and summer, Elise's doctors seemed hopeful. In July, Steve came into the office with good news. "She's cured," he told Lisa. "No signs of the tumor."

"Steve was on cloud nine," says Lisa. "He was sure they'd gotten it all. Her doctors told Elise she didn't even have to return for a checkup until December."

That summer, Steve and Elise took a trip, a Panama Canal cruise. They were thrilled at her progress, believing she'd escaped death and that they had more years together. They celebrated their forty-fifth wedding anniversary and made plans to take the annual radio station trip that fall to Italy. Then, in September, their world fell apart for a second time.

"The cancer was back," says Paul.

It returned with a vengeance. In the hospital, Elise suffered horrific headaches. One day, McEachern walked in and found Steve tenderly massaging her forehead. As the cancer spread, she grew weaker. Steve stayed beside her, holding her hand and running to get her cool compresses for her head.

As the end approached, Paul flew into Austin. Becky picked him up at the airport. At the hospital, Steve tried to control his mounting grief but couldn't. "Dad broke down and cried," says Paul. "He talked about how much he loved her."

When Paul saw his mother, the cancer had taken a terrible toll. She was pale and weak, and for the second time chemo and radiation had caused her hair to fall out. Still, she'd asked Becky to bring her wig and makeup to the hospital. "She wanted to look good for Dad," says Paul. "Here she is dying, married all those years, and she still wanted to look pretty for him."

Finally, on October 13, 1993, Elise Adams Beard died at the age of sixty-seven. Paul, by then back on his aircraft carrier, received a call from Steve.

"She's gone," he said.

After the funeral, Steve asked Becky to move to Austin, to live with him. She had a life and a teaching career in Dallas. "I couldn't just leave everything I'd built there," she says. "I wanted to help him, but I couldn't move."

For the first time in the nearly half a century since he'd met Elise, Steve was alone. That fall, Steve III and his wife took the radio station trip to Italy, and Steve stayed home. He was despondent, and complained to Ray, "I'm the type of person who needs to be married. I need someone to take care of. The saddest thing is a rich, lonely old man."

To Paul, Steve complained that he was uncomfortable with wealthy women of his age, widows who asked him to escort them to functions or approached him in the local grocery store to offer their condolences then invite him to dinner. "He complained he couldn't go anywhere without some woman hitting on him," says Paul.

Steve's friends worried about him, too, that fall and winter. He appeared lost without Elise, tired and broken. Most nights, he sat alone at the nineteenth-hole dining room at the Austin Country Club, drinking his two vodkas, eating his dinner, and staring out the window, not wanting to look at the couples spread throughout the dining room. Friends invited him to their homes, and he went, but eventually he had to leave, and when he did, it was to go home alone to a dark, empty house. Before long Steve began talking about hiring a house manager to keep the place up for him. One evening at the club he asked a bus girl if she might be interested in the job. She refused, but offered to pass the word around to others on the staff.

The first anyone knew that Steve had hired Celeste Martinez for the job was when she drove into Austin Country Club's parking lot in his brand new white and gold Explorer with its Channel 42—KBVO placards on the sides. Those who did notice weren't surprised. Celeste was a beautiful woman, just thirty years old, with a glow about her, tall, with a wispy voice and a playful manner. Still, not everyone at the club believed she was as wholesome or as harmless as she appeared. "She flirted endlessly with the men. Some of them just lapped it up," says one member. "There was a group of women who never had a doubt what Celeste Martinez was all about."

As Christmas approached, Steve called his secretary, Lisa, into his office. Spread across his desk, he had women's clothing catalogues. "I've got this housekeeper, and I need to buy her a Christmas gift," he said. "What would a nice young woman wear?"

Amused at her gruff boss stewing over buying the housekeeper a present, Lisa paged through the catalogues. They appeared to be from companies that catered to older women in the country club set, probably places where Elise bought her clothes.

"How old is this woman?" she asked.

"About thirty," he said.

Lisa flipped through the pages of shapeless dresses and found one that had a youthful flair. "How about this?" she asked.

"That might work," Steve said, smiling. "I think we'll give it a try."

Days before Christmas, Kristina left to spend the holiday with Craig and Jennifer in Washington, and Jimmy drove to see his family in El Paso. Celeste stayed home, saying she had to work at the country club. "When I got home, Celeste had already moved out. She told me she'd found someone else," says Jimmy. "She was moving in with Steve."

"It's for the best," she told him. "Steve can afford to support me and Kristina."

Friends would later say that they believed Celeste had broken Jimmy's heart. "He changed after Celeste," says one. "Jimmy was just a different, a little sadder, guy."

Reeling under all the debts she'd amassed during their short marriage, Jimmy didn't argue and soon after he filed for divorce. "You fall in love, get married, and think it's supposed to be forever," he says. "It didn't work that way."

On Christmas Eve, Gene Bauman and his wife, Sue, invited Steve to dinner.

"I'd like that, but is it okay if I bring my house manager?" Steve asked.

"I didn't know you had one," said Gene. "Who is she?"

"You know, Celeste, the blond waitress from the club."

"I can't picture her, but sure, bring her," Gene said.

"We'll be there," Steve said.

At dinner that night, the Baumans' Christmas tree glowed and they were in a festive mood. Gene, tall, gray-haired, and ruggedly handsome, looked carefully at his old friend. Steve was in high spirits, more buoyant than he had been since Elise relapsed. Understanding what Steve had gone through, he couldn't help but be happy for him. Celeste was attractive and young, and making it clear that she wasn't just on Steve's payroll.

"I needed someone to let in the repairmen and do some light cooking and laundry," Steve said.

"Except that I don't cook, and I send out the clothes," she said, giggling, with her arm through Steve's. "That's just not me."

Gene laughed, and decided he wouldn't take Steve's fling too seriously. "He was just having a bit of fun with a girl who was younger than his own kids. I never thought it would turn out to be anything serious," he says. "I figured, he'd have his fun, buy her some baubles, maybe give her some money—Steve had plenty—and then move on."

However, Gene's wife, Sue—pencil thin with short blond hair—was more concerned. From the beginning, something about Celeste Martinez bothered her. She seemed evasive about who she was and where she'd come from. Sue had nothing tangible to pin her fears on. Celeste acted charming, solicitous of Steve and devoted to him. But Sue wasn't buying it.

"To me, it all looked like an act," she says.

Chapter
4

From their first days together, Celeste moved gracefully into Steve's life, artfully filling the void left by Elise's death. Startled by his age, Kristina asked her mother why she was with him. Celeste didn't hesitate.

"Steve's rich," she answered.

While she was blunt with Kristina, to others Celeste professed her love of Steve. In January she quit her job at the Austin Country Club and brought Anita a crystal vase to thank her for her help during the custody battle. "Sorry I couldn't have done more," Anita said, mindful that they'd lost. The final decision came down early that month, granting Craig custody of both twins. Aware of the pressure on her, Craig agreed to allow Kristina to live with Celeste. When it came to Jennifer, the judge granted Celeste visitation, but at Jennifer's discretion, and she refused to see her mother.

But, Celeste wasn't interested in the twins that day. Instead she gushed to Anita about the new man in her life, Steve Beard, a country club member. "I want you to meet him," she said. "It's magic." She explained that she'd moved in as his housekeeper and they'd fallen in love.

While some might have been shocked in the difference in their ages—Steve was sixty-nine and Celeste just thirty-one—Anita wasn't fazed. Her husband, Jerry, was older than Anita, and they had a happy marriage. "I never thought age mattered," she says.

Steve's daughter had no such romantic notions about her father's new girlfriend.

Becky Beard learned about Celeste Martinez when her father said he had a new housekeeper. Becky was surprised to see the young blonde who appeared at her door in Dallas that same month, holding some of her mother's jewelry. Steve had wanted her to have a few of her mother's things, Celeste said. They sat and talked, Celeste telling Becky a web of lies, including that she'd graduated with an accounting degree from Pepperdine University. "I got tired of accounting," Celeste said. "It was boring."

From that first meeting, Becky never believed Celeste was who she claimed to be. Rather, she worried about what her father was getting into. Her apprehension grew in January, when Steve had tickets for the Super Bowl, the Cowboys against the Buffalo Bills in Atlanta. Becky called his hotel room and Celeste answered. "I didn't like what was happening, but I didn't know what to do," she says.

When Celeste invited Anita and her husband, Jerry, to the house for cocktails, the Inglises knew him only slightly from the club and had never spent any time with him. That night, Anita thought she understood why Celeste was attracted to Steve, as he joked and laughed, often poking fun at himself. Meanwhile, Celeste bragged about his accomplishments and the fun they had together.

"She appeared devoted to him," says Anita.

It was abundantly clear that Steve was crazy about Celeste. He beamed just looking at her. As so many other men before him had found, being with Celeste was invigorating. It wasn't just her physical beauty. She exuded a playful, highly sexual manner, an infectious enthusiasm. To Steve, who'd just endured the most painful year of his life, she must have represented the promise that his life hadn't ended with Elise's death. She offered a new beginning, the opportunity to be loved again, and the chance—with Kristina—to start a whole new family.

In the months that followed, Steve's secretary Lisa, grew accustomed to hearing Celeste's wispy voice when she answered his phone. At first Celeste called about household matters, like getting the rugs cleaned or problems with the hot tub. Then, gradually, the reasons changed. As she had throughout the years, Celeste quickly shifted the spotlight back to herself. In early 1994 the issue that consumed her was the fight to recover Jennifer.

That summer, when the girls were twelve, Celeste left Austin, telling Steve she was traveling to Washington and intended to return with Jennifer. She was gone a few days when the phone rang at KBVO. "Celeste called and said she was in jail in Washington, for trying to see Jennifer," says Lisa. Steve tried to calm Celeste, who sounded frantic. He hired an attorney and spent more than $20,000 on legal fees.

Later, Jennifer remembered nothing of her mother's supposed arrest. She would, however, never forget the phone calls Celeste made to her that year. "I'm going to take you away from your father," she said.

One night Steve answered the phone when Craig called to talk to Kristina. Craig's brother, Jeff, overheard the call. "Celeste isn't who you think she is," Craig told Steve. "Be careful. You think she's wonderful now, but she'll hurt you. You have no idea who you're dealing with. If you're not careful, you're a dead man."

Jeff couldn't hear Steve, but when Craig hung up he said, "He won't believe me. No one believes Celeste's as ruthless as she is until it's too late."

Death must have been on Steve's mind a lot that year. In February he'd been in for a checkup with Dr. George Handley, an avuncular man who'd been his personal physician and friend for many years. At five-ten and 312 pounds, Steve suffered from high blood pressure, asthma, and sleep apnea that forced him to use an oxygen machine while sleeping. Even worse, on a chest X ray, Dr. Handley discovered that Steve's heart was enlarged, a sign of heart disease. Rich foods, drinking, and a lack of exercise had taken their toll. As spry as he may have seemed, as young at heart as his friends found Steve, he was aging quickly and not well.

That spring, Celeste put Steve on a diet. He walked and paid attention to his health. In no time he'd dropped fifty pounds and looked better than he had in years. He went to see Dr. Handley and told him that he needed help with his sexual prowess, now that he was with a younger woman. Handley suggested monthly testosterone injections. Steve laughed and agreed, jokingly dubbing the shots his "Vitamin T."

At KBVO, Ray McEachern wondered if he'd been wrong about Celeste. From the first day they'd met, he hadn't liked her, sizing her up as an opportunist out to cash in on a lonely, rich old man. "But I couldn't deny that Steve looked happy," he says. "He told me older women had bankrolls of their own and didn't appreciate what he had to offer. But he could spoil Celeste, and she enjoyed what he could give her. He could bring stability to her life, and for the first time since Elise's death, he wasn't lonely."

Yet Craig had been right. There was much Steve didn't know about Celeste. As she had with Jimmy, she'd reinvented her past, spinning a web of lies. She failed to tell

Steve about her second marriage, to Harald Wolf, only admitting to having been married twice, to Craig and Jimmy. "It was hard to know what to say," says Kristina. "She told one person one thing and another something else. I just kept quiet."

Although she was technically the housekeeper, Celeste knew little about how to care for a home. At one point she went to the store to buy new sheets. She bought four-hundred-thread-count cotton sheets that came out of the dryer in a ball of wrinkles. Since Celeste didn't iron, the sheets went with all the clothes, even the underwear, to the dry cleaner.

Yet, Celeste knew what was important to Steve. He was a careful man, one who'd spent a lifetime keeping his world in order. He'd retained habits he learned in the navy, where he had little room aboard the ship, and kept his possessions neatly folded and stored. She didn't wash his shirts, but made sure they were organized, neatly stacked, and arranged by color in his closet. Celeste smoked, but only outside, often commenting that she was being careful of Steve's house, making sure the smoke from her Marlboro Light 100s didn't ruin the paint.

Yet her talents as a housekeeper undoubtedly meant little to Steve, who wanted a companion and lover, not someone to wash his floors. He wasn't accustomed to a woman he could rule. Elise had always spoken her mind, and Celeste did the same, giving him back everything he shot at her. Steve liked that. He'd never wanted an anemic woman who danced around issues. He told friends he liked Celeste's spunk.

From her first days there, Celeste slept in Steve's bedroom and moved Kristina into an extra bedroom, enrolling her in Hill Country Middle School, where the students came from affluent families. "Kristina wasn't like a lot of the kids," says another student. "She wasn't spoiled. She hadn't grown up with money."

Perhaps remembering her own girlhood when she was considered odd, Celeste appeared determined to see that her daughter fit in. To that end, she threw a slumber party, inviting thirty girls from the soccer team. Celeste made up the guest list and reigned over the party, laughing and gossiping with the girls. Instead of talking like a parent, she joked about sex and Steve, saying he was fat and old but that his money made him good-looking. Late that night, she took them to a neighbor's house, loaded down with shopping bags of toilet paper. Stifling giggles, Celeste and the girls threw roll after roll into the air, allowing the long strands to hang from the trees. Through it all, Celeste laughed like the teenagers. When they finished, it looked like the site of an aberrant snow storm, one that had befallen one house without touching the rest of the block.

"Celeste wasn't like the rest of our moms," says one girl. "She was young and pretty and liked to have fun. I thought she was just the coolest mom."

In the shadow of her mother, Kristina was Celeste's opposite. As mercurial and outgoing as Celeste was, Kristina was soft-spoken and shy. Yet there was a connection between the mother and daughter that seemed almost unnatural. Steve's secretary Lisa learned quickly that when Celeste was in turmoil, Kristina was the only one who could calm her. "Kris would talk to her, tell her that it would be all right," says Lisa. "No matter how upset Celeste was, she'd calm down with Kris."

After all he'd been through, Steve appeared both taken aback and overjoyed by the turmoil and excitement Celeste brought to his life. When he complained that he couldn't keep toilet paper in the house, blaming Celeste for using it to T.P. the neighborhood, he'd ask, "Is this what teenagers do?" When Celeste said it was, he laughed heartily.

As always, Celeste was on overdrive, hustling through her days with enough energy to take her well into the night. With Steve, her youth brought a special charm. He was a man who saw old age staring him in the eye. Being a dad again also held its allure. He talked about Kristina with friends, discussing the differences between teenagers in the nineties and when his own daughter had entered her teen years, thirty years earlier. In the mornings, Steve drove her to school while Celeste slept in. "Steve loved Kris from the start," says Anita. "We all did."

On Mountain Terrace Drive their lives took on a routine. As long as the house was well cared for, Celeste was free to do as she pleased, while Kristina was at school and Steve at work. Sometimes, Steve even found himself taking over the household tasks, as on the morning Becky called and discovered her father at home. Celeste, the alleged housekeeper, was out, and he was waiting for a maid to arrive to do the actual cleaning.

Each evening at five Steve poured himself and Celeste their first cocktails of the night and started cooking dinner. While he drank martinis made with Wolfschmidt, an inexpensive vodka, and two olives, Celeste only drank top brands, usually Stoli. He wouldn't buy it for himself, but he bought it for her. "Celeste kept up with him," says Gene Bauman. "She matched him drink for drink."

That summer, Steve purchased a lot in the Windermere Oaks subdivision in Spicewood, Texas, thirty-five miles west of Austin, in an unincorporated area of Burnet County, on the south shore of Lake Travis. The homes in the area started at $200,000, and his corner lot was covered with gnarled live oaks and across the street from homes that overlooked the lake. Down a winding road lay a row of covered boat slips and a pier. From dam to dam Lake Travis, a constricted stretch of the Colorado River, measured sixty-four miles, and on summers and weekends it buzzed with boats, skiers, and jet skis.

Once he had the lot, Steve hired a local home builder, Jim Madigan, to construct a one-story house. It was small, just three bedrooms and two baths, but well-appointed. Constructed of limestone, it had a solid look. Steve installed two heavy wood front doors bearing elaborate carvings of nymphs riding seahorses, and the flower beds were lined with white stone. "The idea was that it would someday be Celeste's," says Anita. "By then he cared about them and didn't want Celeste and Kristina to ever be without a home."

In August, Celeste's divorce from Jimmy Martinez became final, clearing the way for her to marry Steve, if he asked. His bankroll must have looked ever more attractive to her as that year drew to a close. In October, an offer to purchase KBVO came from Granite Broadcasting Corporation, a New York media giant that was buying up stations across the country. Steve grew excited as it appeared he'd be able to cash in on more than a decade of hard work. He negotiated hard. Granite offered $54 million, and since Steve owned thirty percent, his share came to $16.2 million. Later, Granite flipped networks, turning it into KEYE, the city's CBS affiliate. "Steve was proud of what he'd built," says Lisa. "He said he was ready for a new chapter."

As 1994 drew to a close the KBVO staff gathered to bid Steve good-bye. As a remembrance, they gave him a plaque bearing a branding iron that read: "You really made a mark on Austin." Steve packed up his office and walked out the door a very rich man.

In no time at all he was bored.

"It wasn't as sweet as Steve thought it would be," says McEachern. "His two great loves in life had been Elise and the station, and now they were both gone." Steve had always had an eye for art, and he tried painting, but that failed to catch his interest. One day in early 1995 he called McEachern. "I'm going to marry Celeste," he said. "Hell, we're already living together. We might as well."

In hindsight, Steve's friends wondered if they should have tried to talk him out of the marriage. Early on there were signs that Celeste had only contempt for him.

As the wedding drew near, Steve called Gene and asked a favor. "Celeste hasn't any friends in our group," he said. "Would Sue go to lunch with her?"

"Sure," Gene agreed. "I bet she'd be happy to."

Days later, Sue and Celeste met at a Mexican restaurant. What began as an ordinary lunch suddenly took an odd turn. Although Celeste knew that Sue and Gene were close to Steve, she confided in Sue as if they were old friends. Celeste called Steve a fat slob and bemoaned the way she said he ruled her life. "I have to turn my cell phone off to get away, otherwise he'd call me twenty times a day," she said. "I never have any peace."

By the time the check arrived, Sue couldn't wait to leave. That evening she told Gene, "They're not even married yet, and she's saying awful things. It makes me uncomfortable. If Steve asks, tell him I'm not going out with Celeste again."

When Steve's children heard about his upcoming wedding, they, too, worried. "Why would a woman of thirty-two marry a seventy-year-old man except for his money?" says Becky. She called Paul and Steven III, and they all talked. Afterward, Paul called Steve's ex-brother-in-law, Judge Harold Entz, who'd remained a close friend. A state district court judge in Dallas, Entz listened patiently, then said what Paul expected to hear: that their father was a bright man and had to be trusted to know what he was getting into. "The bottom line was we all agreed we had to abide by Dad's decision," says Paul.

Steve, too, must have remained at least somewhat unsure of the match. As the time for the ceremony neared, he asked David Kuperman, his attorney, who'd handled his personal and business matters for years, to write a prenuptial agreement, limiting his losses if his marriage to Celeste failed.

On the papers Kuperman drew up, Celeste estimated her net worth—mainly clothes and jewelry—at $20,000. She listed no liabilities, ignoring her credit card bills and the $20,000 she'd been ordered by the Arizona court to pay in restitution for the fraud case.

Meanwhile, Steve estimated his net worth—after paying taxes on the sale of KBVO—at $11 to $12 million. Under the agreement, Steve and Celeste each retained their personal property, including Steve's separate ownership of the house on Terrace Mountain Drive and the lake house. If they divorced before their third anniversary, Celeste agreed she would receive nothing. If the marriage lasted a minimum of three years, however, she was entitled to a onetime payment of $500,000. If married when he died, he doubled that bequest to $1 million.

Yet, that was only a fraction of his money. It was a conservative document engineered by a conservative man. Steve wanted to share his life with Celeste but didn't intend to act rashly. As in love with her as he appeared, he'd spent a lifetime building his fortune, and he didn't intend to lose it.

It must have seemed the ultimate triumph, as Celeste stood beside Steve under an arch in Harvey's, the main dining room at the Austin Country Club, on February 18, 1995, near windows that overlooked a garden. Little more than a year earlier she'd been a waitress in that same room. Now, surrounded by fifty or so guests, many from Austin's elite, she was becoming the bride of a very wealthy man.

The ceremony didn't escape the notice of the staff. "There

was a lot of talk," says the maitre d', Fernando von Haps-
burgh. "We'd never had a waitress marry a member before."

As her matron of honor, Celeste had Ana Presse, a petite
and pretty woman with frosted hair. She and her attorney
husband, Philip, had been acquaintances of Steve's and
Elise's, meeting in the early nineties on a radio station trip to
Hong Kong. Some would wonder why Celeste asked Ana,
whom she'd only recently met through Steve, when such
honors are often reserved for old, dear friends.

Meanwhile, Steve's best man was someone he'd known
since boyhood, his first cousin, C. W. Beard. A tall, dour-
looking Dallas banker with large ears and horn-rimmed
glasses, C. W. had handled Steve's financial affairs since the
eighties.

Paul was on a ship and couldn't attend the ceremony, but
Becky was in the audience, watching apprehensively as her
father recited his vows. In her heart she knew it was a terrible mistake. Celeste was a full fourteen years younger than
Steve III, and Becky was acutely aware that her father was
nearly old enough to be Celeste's grandfather. But that
wasn't what bothered her. There was something about Celeste she simply didn't trust. "She was fake," says Becky.
"We could see it. We just wished Dad could have seen it."

If he sensed his daughter's apprehension, Steve didn't acknowledge it. That day, he exuded happiness. He must have
believed he had good reason to be proud. Dressed in a cream
brocade suit cut to show off her trim waistline, with her
blond hair swept up in a sophisticated French twist, Celeste
looked truly lovely. She was dressed with exquisite care and
taste. Her jewelry was simple, a strand of pearls around her
neck with matching earrings, and on her left-hand ring finger a beautiful diamond solitaire. "It wasn't flashy big, but it
was stunning," says a friend.

After the ceremony, the group dispersed to tables adorned

with rose centerpieces for a four-course dinner as waiters circulated with trays of crystal flutes bubbling with champagne. As they mingled, Steve grinned so broadly one friend said that a young wife must be the road to happiness.

Still, many of his friends had a sense of impending trouble. In the men's rest room one asked another, "What the hell is Steve doing?"

"I've got no damn clue," the other answered.

At the wedding, Kristina was delighted for her mother. Celeste was exuberant, flushed with excitement, and Kris wondered if this, perhaps, would be it—the match that gave her mother everything she'd ever wanted, the marriage that would finally make her happy. Halfway through dinner, Kristina left for softball practice. At the door, as she walked out, she took one last look at the happy couple. "I hoped it worked," she says. "Steve seemed like such a nice man."

Jennifer learned the way she had always did about Celeste's wedding. "I got a postcard," she says. "I just threw it away. I figured, well, here's another new guy."

On March 3, 1995, after they returned from a New Orleans honeymoon, Celeste and Steve signed a postnuptial agreement confirming the terms of their prenup. It must have made Celeste pause, realizing she hovered so close to wealth and all it could buy, but it still wasn't hers. Even as Steve's wife, she had no claim to his money. Only if he died while they were married would she be entitled to any substantial portion of his fortune.

That same month, Kristina saw her mother do something odd. Steve, who fashioned himself a gourmet cook, made dinner, but she and Celeste set the table and served. That night, Celeste ground up pills in a bowl, then mixed the powder into Steve's food.

"What's that?" Kristina asked.

"Sleeping pills. I can't stand being here all night with that fat fuck," she said. "This way, he'll have a couple of drinks and pass out. Then I can go out."

When she put the food on the table, Celeste beamed at Steve, from every appearance the dedicated wife. Kristina would later say that she was so used to her mother doing odd things, she thought little of it, never thinking the pills could be dangerous.

About that same time, little more than a month after the wedding, Ray heard rumors around the television station. A friend had seen Celeste out on Sixth Street, partying at night. "I figured it was true," says Ray. "But it wasn't my business. I never told Steve."

Celeste had made it amply clear to Kristina that money was the reason she was with Steve, and she lived the part. As his wife, she had a wallet full of credit cards and spent with abandon. She had a beautiful home, and he bought her jewelry and presents. Yet, it must have troubled her that she had little she could truly call her own. That summer, Steve was furious when she overdrew the checking account, and an incident from her past loomed—Celeste still owed the $20,000 in Arizona.

In June, Steve went to his safe deposit box at the Bank of America, where he'd banked since the eighties. When he opened the box, he called out for an officer. In moments he was complaining to a teller and the branch manager that his valuables had been stolen. When they couldn't explain it, Steve called Chuck Fuqua, who'd handled his affairs with the bank since he arrived in Austin. "Someone's stolen Elise's jewelry out of my box," Steve told him. "It's all gone."

"We'll look into it," Fuqua told him. The bank ran a records check, and later that same day Fuqua, who'd been at the wedding, reluctantly called Steve. It was a duty he dreaded. "Celeste's been in your box," he said. "She's been in twice, once on May third and again on the twenty-second. She signed the register. No one else has been in there."

The phone was silent. Then Steve said only, "Thank you."

That day, he ordered Celeste to leave his house, and within a week he'd hired a divorce attorney. He brought the prenuptial agreement and the postnup that reaffirmed it to the first meeting. Celeste was frantic. If Steve divorced her then, she'd have nothing more than her personal possessions, no share of his fortune, no alimony. The message must have come through loud and clear when he brought in a locksmith and changed all the locks on the Austin house and the lake house.

When Anita encountered her at a shop, Celeste looked awful, tired, with large circles under her eyes, as if she'd been crying through sleepless nights.

"What's wrong?" Anita asked.

"Steve and I are getting a divorce."

"You've only just married," Anita said, shocked.

On June 18, Celeste wrote a letter to Steve saying: "*I don't know where to begin. 99% of our problems are my fault.*" She then bemoaned the horrors of her past, saying that even if she explained it, he couldn't envision all she'd endured. Perhaps by then Steve knew about Harald, for she wrote that his leaving had devastated her. Or perhaps it was something else she said in the letter, something that must have been true—that she'd told so many people so many different stories she couldn't keep them all straight. "*I don't remember how much I have told you,*" she wrote.

In the letter, Celeste said she'd fallen in with bad friends: *"What I didn't tell you is that I was fined $20,000 in order to remain in Texas so I could fight for the girls."* When it came to the overdrawn checking account, she wrote: *"When you told me I didn't believe you . . . I really didn't realize I had spent so much money. So I went to the safety deposit box and got a loan on the missing jewelry. I owe about $2,500 . . . I know by telling you all of this our marriage is over . . . no matter what, I need to be honest with you. I am so sorry."*

In the end, she professed her love, saying: *"I am hurting so much that I seem to screw everything up. I really do want to get help . . . Whatever you want to do to me, I'll accept it."* She closed by writing that she and Kristina would be staying at the Harvey Hotel, and signed the letter, *"I love you—Celeste."*

As she had when Harald and Jimmy threatened divorce, Celeste then held out the promise that she could change. Maintaining that she wanted to stop feeling and acting the way she had been, she checked herself into a psychiatric hospital. There, for perhaps the first time, she was diagnosed with borderline personality disorder,

One of the most controversial of diagnoses, BPD describes a cluster of personality traits often tied to early trauma. Some experts believe that from birth, borderlines have biological tendencies to overreact to stress. Their emotions are volatile and violent, plunging from despair to euphoria. Even small slights become gaping emotional wounds. Without filters to keep them from fulfilling every desire, borderlines binge on food, sex, gambling, or compulsive shopping. They self-mutilate or threaten suicide, often using such threats to control others. They fear being alone, even for short periods, and experience anxiety at any sign of being abandoned. Borderlines push people away, then panic when they leave.

Often bright and witty, fun to be around, borderlines are

the life of the party. Yet for those who love them, the road is a hard one. They breed chaos and judge people without context, based not on an entire relationship but solely the most recent interaction. Years of devotion can be ignored for the slight of one unkind look. All the while, borderline personalities search for a rescuer, someone to save them from the disarray they create.

Steve was a bright man, one who'd lived long enough to learn when to be skeptical, and, at least initially, he didn't accept Celeste's excuses. On June 25 she was discharged from the hospital. Four days later he filed for a divorce.

His marriage crumbling, Steve told few about the impending divorce. Lifelong lessons are hard to ignore, and he was a reflection of his time, when such matters were not discussed. Perhaps he was embarrassed, fearing his friends and family thought him an old fool for marrying Celeste. To him, a divorce would prove them right.

Finally, in August, like the husbands before him, Steve took Celeste back. What convinced him would remain a mystery, but he told one friend that everyone deserved a second chance and that, with the difficult life she'd lived, he understood that Celeste would make mistakes. By then he'd recovered Elise's precious things from a pawnshop. "Money is just money," he said.

Soon after, Kristina and Celeste moved back into the house on Terrace Mountain Drive, and Steve paid off her debts—including the $20,000 restitution for the insurance fraud. On August 29, 1995, he withdrew his petition for divorce.

"Maybe it was just that Steve knew what it was like before Celeste, when he was lonely," says a friend. "And by then he was in love not just with Celeste, but Kristina. Losing Celeste meant losing her as a daughter." That fall, Kristina moved a step closer to becoming Steve's child, when he agreed to have her name legally changed to Beard.

Later, it would seem Celeste learned from Steve's threats of divorce. She'd nearly lost everything: her beautiful home and access to his millions. After living a life of wealth, how could she be forced back to her old life? It must have seemed impossible. From that point on, divorce was Celeste's enemy. She'd forestalled losing Steve and his millions, but did she wonder how long she could hold him? Later, it would seem she had a motive: manipulating him into giving her a greater claim to his wealth.

"We need to get Steve to sell the house," Celeste told Kristina. "If he dies, the kids get it. If he builds or buys us a new one, it becomes community property."

Days after he dropped the divorce, Steve put the house up for sale. The plan was that they'd live at the lake house while he built a new home. To friends, he said Celeste saw the house as Elise's, not hers. He wanted her to have a home of her own.

In September, Richard Oppel relocated from D.C., where he'd been Washington bureau chief for Knight Ridder newspapers, to take the editor's job at the *Austin American States-man,* the city's daily. Oppel and his wife, Carol, drove by the house and jotted down the address. The following day they were waiting on the doorstep with their realtor when the door swung open and Celeste glared at them. After persuading Steve to sell, she didn't want to give the house up.

"Go away. We don't want to sell," she snapped.

The realtor argued, "It's listed on the market, and I made an appointment."

Then, Steve pulled Celeste out of the doorway from behind and ushered the Oppels and their realtor inside. For the rest of their house tour, Celeste remained out of sight. Oppel found Steve, in his Sansabelt slacks and golf shirt, an affable host. Enthralled with the view of the city, the Oppels made an offer, and negotiations produced an agreement. Before the closing, they stood in the study while Steve sat at his desk, ordering Celeste to retrieve items he needed. "He was clearly in charge," says Oppel. "Very much the elderly gentleman."

On another preclosing visit, Richard and Carol again found Steve, dressed in slacks and an open-collar plaid shirt, sitting at his desk in the library. This time he had a large checkbook in front of him. As they talked, Celeste shuffled in, wearing sandals, shorts, and a loose shirt. "Steve, Kristina and I are having so much fun on the jet ski up at the lake," she said. "While you're writing out checks, we really need another one."

"Honey, those cost a lot of money," Steve answered.

Celeste leaned over his shoulder, playfully wrapped her arms around his chest and said, "Oh, honey, you've got a lot of money."

Without further comment, Steve laughed and wrote her a check.

As well as he appeared to be adapting to the move, Steve had a deep sadness about leaving a home that held so many happy memories. One day, after the Oppels moved in, Steve stopped by. Inside the house, he stood before a window in the bar that overlooked the orchid house, where Elise had spent many happy hours. Pointing at an orchid etched on the glass, he said, "That was a gift to my first wife."

Years later, Oppel remembered the melancholy look on Steve's face that day. "He was clearly very much in love with Elise," he says. "He was still visibly sad at losing her."

As Mrs. Steven Beard Jr., Celeste segmented her life into two distinct slices: time in Austin and at the lake house. While his friends remained cordial to Celeste, they never welcomed her into the group. It was with women more like those she'd come of age with that Celeste bonded. At Tramps, an upscale salon frequented by many in Austin's old guard, she befriended her hairdresser, Denise Renfeldt. A small woman with the figure and the enthusiasm of a teenager, Denise immediately liked Celeste. "We were a lot alike," she says. "We both liked to have fun."

Over the years, Denise became Celeste's confidante. In a station in the center of the salon—a busy establishment that smelled of shampoo and nail polish—Celeste talked of her life. In her account, Steve met her at the club and fell head over heels in love with her. "He offered me two million dollars to marry him," Celeste told her. Calling Steve fat and old, she complained about having sex with him. Others overheard her, and the stories spread. "Austin is a big city, but it's like a small town. Talk travels," says Denise.

If Austin had a fast-paced edge, life at the lake took a more leisurely turn. Celeste spent much of the day in sandals, T-shirts, and shorts. The house was small for Celeste, Steve, Kristina, and the two dogs—Steve's Meagan and Celeste's constant companion, a black and white cocker spaniel named Nikki.

At the lake, Celeste made friends with Dawn, the wife of Jim Madigan, the builder Steve hired to put up the house. A petite woman with thick dark amber hair, she lived in a house her husband had built nearby. Another friend was an elderly, stocky woman named Marilou Gibbs, the mother of the realtor who'd sold Steve the lot. From the beginning, Kristina thought little of her mother's friends. "Celeste was always buying them things," she says.

One friend would later say that Celeste turned shopping into an Olympic sport, spending up to $50,000 in a single day. When the stores were closed and she couldn't sleep, she took Kristina to a Super Wal-Mart that was open twenty-four hours, where she bought albums and books. Celeste loved to read mysteries and true crime books, working through the plots and figuring out what the bad guys did that got them caught.

At night, Celeste continued to sprinkle Steve's food with ground-up sleeping pills, but it was while they were living at the lake house that Kristina noticed her mother do something else: pour half a bottle of Steve's Wolfschmidt vodka down the drain and refill it with Everclear—pure grain alcohol. "This will help him pass out early," Celeste said, laughing. "Then I can do what I want to do for the rest of the night."

From that day on, Steve would sip his ritual cocktails, never knowing that rather than 80 proof vodka he was drinking half 190 proof Everclear. While Celeste filled his glass with alcohol, Kristina noticed she filled her own with water. Yet the teenager said nothing, afraid of her mother's volcanic wrath. "I just never crossed her," she says.

Kristina maintained her silence even after she overheard Celeste laughing and bragging to a friend about the Everclear cocktails. "I've got a name for them," she said with a giggle. " 'The Graveyard.' "

Chapter
5

A year into their marriage, Steve's finances were becoming ever more enmeshed with Celeste, much of it by his own hand. In early 1996 he brought in Brian Rahlfs, a vice president and portfolio manager with Bank of America, Dallas, to meet with them about investing his fortune. Over lunch at the country club, where Celeste ordered her usual chicken-fried steak and Coke in a can, they discussed his plans for the eventual disbursement of his money, the Steven F. Beard Jr. Trust. Without counting the lake house, his IRAs, and personal property, Steve's fortune totaled more than $10 million. That same month, Steve had his lawyer, David Kuperman, draw up a new marital agreement. In the event of his death, Steve wanted to leave Celeste not only the $1 million, but half of both the lake house and a lot he purchased at 3900 Toro Canyon Road in Austin.

In the more than a decade since Steve and Elise moved into the house in Westlake Hills, Austin had grown westward. Million-dollar estates proliferated; so much so that by the time he married Celeste, the Terrace Mountain Drive house had been surpassed by neighborhoods of stately homes in Georgian, English Tudor, and modern design.

After selling the house in 1995, Steve purchased the prime undeveloped acre lot little more than a mile from Terrace Mountain Drive, in an exclusive, gated enclave called the Gardens of Westlake. The slice of land was just down the street from thick metal gates that guarded the mega-million-dollar estate of Michael Dell. In Austin, Dell was royalty. As the founder of the highly successful Dell Computer Corporation, he was the poster boy for the city's burgeoning high-tech industry.

One day the phone rang in the office of Gus Voelzel, who specialized in high-end residential and commercial construction. "I hear you're a great architect," Steve said.

"Some people say I am," Voelzel replied. "Who told you?"

"My builder. He tells me that I need to get you to design my new house."

Two days later Gus pulled up in front of the Toro Canyon lot and Steve was already there, standing outside his Cadillac with his dog, Mcagan. When Gus got out of his car, the lab growled and bared her teeth. "Now you stop that, girl," Steve said, walking forward. "She just needs to know we're friendly, and she'll be okay."

Steve took a good look at Voelzel, a tall man with shoulder length white hair and a beard. Around the waist, Voelzel was nearly as broad as Steve. "Looks like you're about my size," Steve said. "I think we might be able to do some business."

Voelzel laughed. "Sounds good to me," he agreed.

With that, the two men walked the property. Steve's lot was wooded with gnarled oaks and rough cedar that appeared as ancient and rugged as the rocky hills. Eventually, five houses would be built behind the Gardens of Westlake gate, but as yet, only one was under construction, a rustic, ranch-style house with a long front porch that recalled the Texas Hill Country. Although beautiful, it wasn't what Steve had in mind.

"I've always loved Fallingwater, and I'd like something with that kind of feel," Steve said, referring to Frank Lloyd Wright's cantilevered design in Bear Run, Pennsylvania. Perched over a rushing mountain spring, it epitomized Wright's concept of organic architecture, design so well integrated with its setting that it appeared unified with nature.

"This site won't work," Volezel said. "We need a creek."

"Hell, can't we build one?" Steve said with a twinkle in his eye.

Voelzel laughed. "I guess we could."

Steve told Voelzel how he envisioned the house. He wanted a sprawling one-story, with a separate master wing and a wing for Kristina and guests. "Does your wife have some ideas? Should we include her?" Voelzel asked.

"Nah, we made a deal. I build the house and she decorates it," he said with a grin. "You're going to be really surprised when you meet my wife." He then went on to say that his first wife had died just three years earlier and he'd married a "younger woman. I dated older women, but they didn't appreciate me for what I could provide: money."

Voelzel laughed again.

In the ensuing months, Gus worked closely with Steve, translating his ideas to paper. The two men formed a quick friendship, and the house, as it evolved, took on a contemporary look with expansive windows. The first time Voelzel met Celeste, as Steve had predicted, he was surprised. "I didn't expect her to be quite that young. She didn't say much," he says. "She kind of looked over the plans and nodded."

The one change Celeste did make was to her closet. The original plan called for cubbyholes to store three hundred pairs of shoes. "She said that would never be enough. She needed room for five hundred," says Voelzel.

As Gus designed it, visitors walked up three short flights of stairs to reach double stained-glass front doors set into a panel of glass. Squared columns held up a wide overhang, and, emanating from a backyard koi pond, a man-made stream bubbled out from beneath the house and ran along the front flower beds into two large ponds.

Inside, the house fanned out in a U from the entry to a full 5,800 square feet. Walking straight ahead, one entered a grand living room with a high coffered ceiling. Three steps up to the right brought visitors into an elaborate gourmet kitchen and dinette area that overlooked the koi pond. The fireplace, entrance, and walls leading into the dining room and kitchen were constructed of the same Golden Arkansas ledge stone as much of the exterior. The master wing, three steps up from the living room to the left, housed Steve's office, a large bedroom, and a bathroom with a room-size glass shower and closets. If one walked from the entry to the right instead, there were two additional bedrooms with separate baths, one for Kristina, the other a guest room.

On the blueprint, Steve had concerns. "He wanted the living room bar as a command post," says Gus. "He wanted to serve drinks and look out at a party. Steve was a people person, he liked seeing people happy, and he wanted to see them enjoying his house."

When Voelzel estimated a seven-figure price tag to build the house, Steve sucked in a whistle. "I'm going to need a really big credit card for this," he joked. A week later at lunch, Gus gifted him with the house floor plan shrunk down and laminated to look like a credit card. "He loved it, showed it to everyone," Gus says.

Planning quickly gave way to construction. After the

groundbreaking, Steve, with Meagan at his side, became a constant presence, sitting in a lawn chair under an umbrella with a cooler of water, watching as the house grew out of the lot. He was there the day the masons laid out the stone. When it came to the fireplace mantel, Gus had the stone beaten with chains and coated with buttermilk to age it. Once installed, the mantel was held up by carved lions, a symbol from the Beard family crest.

His soon-to-be next door neighbors, Bob and Bess Dennison, a retired orthopedic surgeon and his wife, in the throes of building their own home, stopped over often to see Steve. It was obvious that he was immensely proud of the house. On more than one occasion Steve told Bob it would have the perfect living room: one with a big screen television and a wet bar. "Steve wasn't overly impressed with his money. He had fun with it," says Dennison, who quickly decided he liked his new neighbor.

When it came to Celeste, Dr. Dennison wasn't as sure. Steve bragged about her, telling Dennison she had a degree from Pepperdine. "She's beautiful," Steve said, "and smart as a whip." The Dennisons weren't impressed. Around them, Celeste barely spoke. It was as if their money and genteel manners intimidated her.

That year, Steve brought Celeste and Kristina to Virginia to meet his youngest son, Paul, and his wife, Kim. A hospital corpsman, at the time of the wedding Paul had been aboard ship, unable to attend. When Paul entered the bar at the Williamsburg Country Club, it stung to see Celeste wearing his mother's gold watch. Still, dinner went well. Celeste was affectionate toward Steve, bragging about him to his son and daughter-in-law. When Paul and Kim left to smoke cigarettes, Celeste joined them, but not before she bent over and kissed Steve on the cheek. "She seemed all right," says Paul.

"I thought maybe things would be okay. Maybe she loved him and he'd be happy."

Yet his misgivings quickly returned. From that point on, whenever he attempted to visit his father, Celeste rebuffed them. "She'd say it was never the right time. They were always going somewhere, something was happening," he says. "She kept all of us kids away from our dad. There was always a reason we weren't welcome."

"Mom didn't want the older Beard kids around," says Kristina. "She didn't want them poking their noses into her business."

If Paul had been at the lake house that summer, he would have seen much to disturb him. Kristina did. She'd grown to care about Steve. In her young life, with the exception of her father, he was the first man who'd stayed long enough to become a presence. Yet, she loved her mother and felt responsible for her. She said nothing when she saw Celeste combing grocery store shelves for dented and bulging cans, then bringing them home and feeding the contents to Steve. She never connected it with a memory out of her own childhood. Years earlier, Kristina and Jen had faint recollections of being rushed to a hospital, where doctors pumped their stomachs. Steve never did get sick, convincing Kristina that Celeste wasn't *really* hurting him.

That year as the house construction continued and summer beckoned, Kristina's school counselor asked her what she'd like to be when she grew up. She answered, "A vet, because I like animals." She listed her hobbies as volleyball, basketball, and watching television, and her teacher commented that she was conscientious. Yet the counselor's note reflected something else, something about how Kristina had closed off her emotions in order to live with her mother: "Kristina's affect is flat. She seems distant from her feelings.

She was unable to generate three wishes when asked." Her teacher added, "Kristina is friendly, easygoing, likable, responsible, and willing to work." But she displayed "a significant amount of emotional distress as related to family issues."

In July 1996, Kristina left to see Jennifer at their paternal grandfather's ranch in California. The two-week vacation had been an annual event since the girls were very young, and she was eager to go, even more so that year because she'd missed Jennifer. In Washington State, however, Jennifer hesitated, unsure she should leave their father. She worried about Craig, whose life had taken a dangerous turn.

In April of that year, when the girls were fifteen, after just two years of marriage, Kathryn filed for divorce. Later, she'd say Craig was drinking and taking methamphetamines. He'd become sullen and angry. Hoping she'd come back to him, Craig joined AA, quit drinking, cut out the drugs, and went for counseling. With Jennifer, he moved into a small apartment. It was during that time that Celeste and Craig began talking. "I called Kristina a lot," says Jennifer. "That's how it got started." Before long they were on the telephone nightly. When she heard, Cherie was concerned. Whenever Celeste entered her son's life, something bad happened.

"They were even making plans to take the girls to Disney World that fall," says Jeff. "Celeste was married to Steve, but she wanted to see Craig. It was the typical old stuff."

Yet, Craig continued to be morose. At times he cried, telling Jennifer he missed Kathryn. To Jeff, he said he couldn't survive another divorce. "I told him it wouldn't be that way, that Kathryn wasn't Celeste," says Jeff. "But he didn't believe me."

Everyone around him knew Craig was deeply depressed in the summer of 1996. Cherie tried to talk to him, but to no avail. Jennifer panicked when her father missed one of her softball games. It was the first time Craig wasn't in the stands. When she got home, he admitted he was thinking about suicide.

With the trip to her grandfather's approaching, Jennifer refused to go, afraid of what might happen unless she was there to watch over her father. Craig insisted and promised he'd be all right. "I believed him," she says.

The day after she arrived, Jennifer called home, but Craig didn't answer. Cherie called, too, and got no response. For nearly two days Craig's phone rang without an answer. Finally, on July 19, 1996, Cherie pounded on his door. When he didn't open it, she went to the landlord and returned with a key. Her heart pounding, she walked in and saw blood splattered against a wall. "I didn't go any farther. I knew," she says.

Craig's dad tried to break the horrible news to his granddaughters gently, but there was no way to soften the blow. Immediately, Jennifer screamed, "No," over and over, while Kristina tried to comfort her. Later, Jennifer wouldn't remember anything about that afternoon, except Kristina whispering in her ear, "Jen, I'm so sorry."

On his death certificate, the cause was listed as a contact gunshot wound to the head; suicide. Craig had left behind letters to Cherie and Jennifer, saying he simply wasn't strong enough to keep fighting. "He said God didn't hear him, and he couldn't handle it anymore," says Jeff.

Cherie and Jeff, however, would never agree with the finding of suicide. "We always believed Celeste pushed him to do it," says Jeff. "That she was the last person he talked to, and that she told him she was married to a rich man who could take care of the girls better than he could. Celeste may not have pulled the trigger, but she loaded the gun."

Later, Celeste would tell her mother, Nancy, that she did talk to Craig the day he died, but insisted that "if she'd known, she would have stopped him."

The day after the body was discovered, Celeste rushed to California to claim the girls. Jennifer was in shock. "When I was with my dad, everything was all right," she says. Of her mother, she says, "She frightened me."

In the small town of Stanwood, where he'd lived, Craig's remains were cremated. The Bratchers so hated Celeste that Jeff went to the police and cautioned them to keep her away from the funeral. "I told them that if I saw her, I'd kill her," he says.

Perhaps they relayed the message, for Celeste dropped the girls at the funeral but didn't go inside. Something, however, did happen that day to rupture the family. After the funeral, Jennifer begged her grandmother to let her move in with her. Cherie refused. "I'd just lost my son, and I had to let go of my granddaughters," she says. "I wasn't strong enough to handle the interference that I knew Celeste would bring into my life."

As a result, the girls had only their mother to turn to, the same mother who had abandoned them to foster homes whenever they'd been inconvenient, the same mother who'd yelled and screamed at them, insisting they were never good enough. That point must have been driven home further when, as soon as they got off the plane in Austin, Celeste stopped at Jimmy's house to tell him what happened. After comforting Celeste and the girls, he told them, "You girls better take care of your mother, be there for her and do whatever she needs. Because now she's all you have left."

That was something Kristina understood—that she only had Celeste and that Celeste needed her. For Jennifer, it was very different. She grieved for her father. "For the first four days after we got to Austin, I stayed in the bedroom and cried," she says.

Now that he was gone, Celeste, too, became preoccupied with Craig. In the months that followed, she badgered

Cherie, demanding his ring, watch, and even her last letter from Craig. Cherie refused. When Celeste wanted photos of Craig, Cherie told her no. Not to be denied, Celeste bought a full-page ad in a Stanwood newspaper that read:

WANTED
ANY PHOTOGRAPHS
OF
J. CRAIG BRATCHER

His 15-year-old daughters are distraught.
We did not receive any physical memories of our father.
Just one photo would help ease the pain of his death.
PLEASE HELP US!
We Will Pay All Expenses
Jennifer and Kristina

The ad ended with a P.O. box and phone number. The twins knew nothing of the ad until she came to them giggling and said, "Look what I did." Spurred by the ad, a Seattle television station requested an interview with the girls, and Celeste happily agreed. During the news footage, the twins said they missed their father and that his family had refused to give them photos. "I was a zombie, still really missing our dad," says Jen. "Celeste told us to do it, and we didn't refuse. You didn't tell Celeste no. You just didn't."

In Stanwood, Cherie felt humiliated to have her family troubles so publicly aired. What remained of the relationship between her and her granddaughters dissolved the following year, when a Mother's Day card arrived. Amid tiny hearts and a cheery verse that thanked Cherie for being an inspiration, was a letter that began: "Grandma, we really mean this." It went on to voice an indictment of Cherie for turning her back on the girls and to gushingly praise Celeste.

Years later, Kristina would look at the letter and insist she didn't write it. "That's not my handwriting," she says. "It's Celeste's."

In Texas, Celeste must have seen the grief in Jennifer's eyes, as, for the most part, she left her alone. She did complain to Steve about the way her newly reclaimed daughter dressed: baggy pants and big T-shirts; Seattle grunge. While Celeste didn't appear to know what to do with Jennifer, Steve opened his arms wide to the sad teenager. Each day, he drove the girls to Westlake High School for their freshman year. On Sundays, while Celeste and Kristina slept in, he and Jennifer began a weekly ritual: breakfast at the country club. "We'd just go and talk," says Jen, smiling at the memory. "It was fun."

On weekends, Steve, Jennifer, and Kristina loaded into his Cadillac and, while Celeste had plans with friends, explored the small Texas Hill Country towns, stopping for lunch at hole-in-the-wall restaurants. Before long Jennifer became Steve's companion, driving to Home Depot with him to pick up things for the house, spending time together. For a girl whose heart ached for her lost father, he filled a painful void.

As time passed, Celeste's world was becoming Steve's as she methodically cut him off from his own children. Looking back, it would seem that he was trying to do for her and the twins what he'd done for Elise and his children: build a secure world, one based on solid footing. But Celeste undermined his best efforts. Although he showered her with gifts, it was never enough. No matter what she had, Celeste always wanted more.

That summer at the lake house, Kristina walked in and found her mother standing at a window, holding up a blank check over a cancelled one. With the light shining through illuminating the checks from behind, she traced Steve's signature onto the blank check. Again, Chuck Fuqua called, this time to tell Steve that his personal checking account was overdrawn. "I'm not sure how Steve figured it out, but what he came up with was that Celeste had gotten very, very good at forging his signature," says Fuqua.

After that, Steve had his financial papers, including his bank statements, sent to a P.O. box. For a short time he again pondered divorce, telling Kuperman that all wasn't well, but he never went forward with it. "I guess he just decided against it," Fuqua would say later. "He did love Celeste and the girls. He thought of them as his family."

Throughout that summer, Celeste was in a whirlwind. While Steve had controlled the design of the home itself, inside he gave her free reign. Little from the first house except personal mementoes would be moved. Instead, as the house neared completion, Steve took Celeste to Louis Shanks, Austin's top-end furniture store, where he introduced her to Michael Forwood. Decades earlier Steve had bought furniture from Forwood's grandfather, the original Louis Shanks, who founded the chain in 1945. With the house plans under his arm, he showed Forwood the vast rooms they'd need to furnish. "I don't mind paying what's fair, but I want a good price," Steve said.

"We'll take care of it," Forwood assured him.

From then on Celeste took over. The first time Greg Logsdon, a salesperson at the store, met Celeste, he saw an attractive blonde wandering the store in jeans and a T-shirt.

"Is anyone helping you?" he asked.

"No," she said, flippantly adding, "probably because of the way I'm dressed. I want to see your Henredon and Baker catalogues."

Fifteen minutes later Celeste had flipped through the Henredon catalogue and chosen $20,000 in occasional tables and benches. When she instructed Logsdon to put in the order, he asked for a deposit.

"You won't need that," she said. "Tell Mike Forwood that Celeste Beard was in."

Later that day Logsdon relayed the message. "Order anything she wants. Mr. Beard is good for it," Forwood instructed.

Over the next three years, Celeste was Logsdon's best customer. She never quibbled about price, and she chose only the very best. For a woman who'd had little money in the past, everyone at Louis Shanks had to admit that Celeste knew what to buy. Sometimes, her requests were exceptional, however, even for a store as upscale as Shanks. There was the time she bought a heavily carved bedroom suite from the Henredon line named Natchez, after the Mississippi city. The king-size, four-poster bed alone ran more than $4,000. Celeste had Logsdon custom-order a heavy damask bedspread and pillows. While such a purchase wasn't unusual, Celeste's next request was: She wanted a duplicate of the bed made including the bedding but on a small scale, for her cocker spaniel, Nikki.

They did, at a cost of $3,000.

"I think that's the first time we ever had a request like that from a customer," says Forwood. "We were all frankly amazed."

Steve, however, never questioned the expenditure. In fact, he rarely balked at any of her purchases. The one exception: the day Celeste spent $7,000 on throw pillows. When the bill arrived, Celeste called Logsdon.

"Steve got the bill," she said. "He called me every name in the book, except my own."

To mollify the situation, Logsdon gave Celeste an adjustment on the bill. But the next time she walked into Louis Shanks, Steve was beside her, watching over her shoulder as she made purchases. At times, he shook his head no. Celeste bristled.

"That's why I don't like to bring him shopping," she said

to Logsdon, loud enough for Steve to hear. Looking back, Logsdon would say it was as if Steve were a father with an errant child, paternal, wanting her to be happy, yet monitoring her actions.

"She was clearly unhappy he was there," he says.

Throughout the three years she bought from him, Celeste spent more than $100,000 each year, for a total of nearly $400,000. She was always polite, always easygoing, never questioning prices or asking for discounts. "She was a dream customer," he says.

Logsdon, then, found it difficult to understand why the women at Louis Shanks grated at having to deal with Celeste. While she was calm with him, with the women Celeste's mood turned churlish with little provocation.

"Do you know who I am?" she said, irritated when things weren't going her way.

The Bank of America teller who refused to cash Celeste's check that summer when she went through the drive-through without identification was a woman. Celeste caused a scene, screaming, "Do you fucking know who I am?" Steve's banker, Chuck Fuqua, was called. "She read me the riot act," he says. All the while she was yelling he was recalling the way she'd talked about Steve at the last party. "She said he was disgusting."

At the end of August, Brian Rahfls flew in from Dallas to discuss funding Steve's trust. That day at the country club, Steve stopped Rahfls frequently to ask Celeste questions, making sure she understood the trust with its $7 million in cash, stocks, and bonds, explaining what her situation was should they remain married when he died. In a grand gesture, he had made Celeste the main beneficiary. *If* she remained his wife at his death, she wouldn't have access to the principal but would receive all the earnings from the estate.

At a twelve percent return, Rahfls estimated the trust would produce $290,000 a year.

That October, Steve and Celeste went on the radio station trip, this time to Madrid. During their stay at the palatial Ritz Hotel, Celeste grew angry. That night, she took his American Express card and left. The next morning she was gone, flying home on a first-class, one-way ticket. At breakfast Steve looked sheepish, not wanting to tell the others what had happened. Instead, he said that Celeste had something at home she had to attend to. But he told the truth to Roy Butler and Gene Bauman. "He kind of grinned, like ain't this wild," says Butler. "I got the feeling Steve thought he had a wild pony by the tail."

Afterward, Butler and Bauman compared notes and figured Celeste's impulsive departure probably cost Steve in the neighborhood of $7,000. Four days later the travelers returned to Austin. When they got off the plane, Celeste waited for Steve, waving and calling his name, as if she couldn't wait to have him home.

That fall, Steve, Celeste, and the girls finally moved into the Toro Canyon house. Two months later they hosted an elaborate holiday open house. More than a hundred guests arrived to view the house and the treasures the Beards had amassed. Celeste had so many antique Staffordshire dogs, she couldn't display them all, keeping many in closets. Over the living room fireplace hung a painting Celeste had commissioned for Father's Day the previous year. It depicted Kristina, Jennifer, and Celeste in the forefront, with the koi pond fountain in the background. Buried in the fountain pedestal was a small medallion bearing Steve's face. "Mom wanted it that way for a reason," says Kristina. "She said it would be easy to paint over him when he died."

The following February, 1997, a full year before she would have been entitled to the money under the prenup,

Steve funded a $500,000 trust for Celeste. Perhaps he thought she'd be happier with money of her own. To counsel her on investing the sum, he brought in a specialist from Bank of America. Six months later every penny was gone. Celeste had spent it all. From that point on, his financial obligation to her in a divorce was satisfied. Even if they remained married for a decade, if they were to divorce, he owed her nothing, and she'd leave the marriage with only her half interests in the houses and her personal property.

From that point on Steve was worth considerably more to Celeste dead than alive and divorced.

Chapter
6

Throughout 1997 and into 1998, life at the Toro Canyon house resembled an advertisement for living the American dream. The whole family traveled to St. Thomas for Christmas. One summer, the girls studied biology in Hawaii for two weeks. At home, Celeste played on the country club bunco league—evenings she called "drunko bunco"—took golf lessons, and had her hair styled twice a week and nails manicured. And she doted on Steve, throwing him elaborate parties, once reserving an entire restaurant for his friends. He showered her with jewelry, and she gave him a bronze fountain of a young girl reading a book for the front yard. To those who didn't know what lurked beneath, Steve and Celeste, the twins, and their menagerie of pets—cats Priscilla and Ollie and dogs Meagan and Nikki—seemed picture perfect. And when Celeste wasn't wrestling with yet another crisis, Steve did appear happy. Ray called one day, and Steve answered the phone.

"What are you doing?" Ray asked.

"Playing Mr. Mom. I'm getting ready to take the girls to soccer practice."

"Boy, things have sure changed."

"Yeah," said Steve. "But not in a bad way."

"Steve was crazy about the girls," remembers Anita. "And when Celeste wasn't doing something awful, he was crazy about her, too."

Even when she was furious, yelling and screaming, Steve dismissed her tantrums. "She doesn't mean it," he told Kristina. "Your mother's a firecracker, and sometimes she blows up. Don't pay attention. She'll get over it."

"I don't know why he loved her, but he did," says Kristina.

To visitors walking in the front door, the Toro Canyon house, too, looked perfect. If the maid jarred a knickknack, Celeste rushed to reposition it. It was as if the house had to testify to her perfection, no blemish ignored. Yet, out of the sight of guests and Steve, it was very different. Like their marriage: faultless on the surface and troubled beneath.

Celeste barred Steve from the girls' wing—Kristina's bedroom and the guest room, now Jennifer's territory— telling him it was improper for a man to go into young girls' quarters, even his daughters.' There, in the attic crawl space and closets, Celeste hid what she didn't want him to see, including credit card bills that poured into her four P.O. boxes. She was so bent on keeping them secret that one afternoon when Steve was out and she fell and broke her arm climbing down from the attic, she staged a second fall in the living room in front of him, to explain the injury.

When sleeping, Steve wore an oxygen mask for his sleep apnea, one that hummed and thumped throughout the night. Sometimes Celeste slept with him. Other nights she complained that the machine kept her awake, and she bunked in a spare bed in Kristina's room. Until late in the night, Celeste sat at the computer, typing, searching the Internet. "It got so I had to be able to sleep with the light on and typing in the background," says Kristina. "Sometimes she stayed awake all night."

When she did sleep, Celeste had some odd habits. Not liking her toes to touch, she packed tissue between them. She felt the same way about her enhanced breasts, and wore a bra to bed to keep them from pressing against her chest. "No matter how late she was up, she put the tissue between her toes," says Kristina. "She was obsessive about it."

As perfect as she kept the front of the house and the master bedroom, she threw the twins' wing into chaos. Celeste kept extra clothes in their closets, often throwing them on the floor so she could change after Steve fell asleep and go to the bars or shopping. She had a voracious appetite for reading, especially crime books, finishing three or four a week. Her books were scattered everywhere.

Many things seemed to occupy her thoughts that year. As she had been since childhood, she was fascinated with finding her biological mother. She hired a private investigator, tracked the woman down, and Celeste and Steve left for California to meet the woman who'd given her birth. They stayed at a country club, and she hired a limo to take them to the meeting. Celeste arrived dripping in jewelry, but the woman, whom she described as married to a wealthy and powerful man, wasn't impressed. "She told me she was just an incubator," Celeste said later. "I felt like renting a billboard and putting her name up there, with a picture of me that read, 'I'm her illegitimate daughter.' "

The story of how she met her biological mother became fodder for the beauty salon circuit. At Tramps, Celeste confided in Denise Renfeldt about the injustice. She never lowered her voice to keep others from hearing, even when she grumbled about Steve. One day she laughed, saying, "He's so dumb he thinks my breasts are real." Another afternoon, when she was particularly animated, Celeste groaned about their sex life, although it wasn't true, complaining she had to give Steve shots in his penis for him to get an erection. "I threw the needles away, so now he just makes me give him oral sex," she whined. "Once a week, every Sunday, I go make some money. I call it the Sunday suck."

Word traveled back to Steve's friends, including the Baumans. As upset as they were, Gene decided not to tell Steve. "I told a friend once that his wife was unfaithful, and he wasn't grateful," he says. "I figured the worst that would happen was Steve's reputation would get tarnished. I never thought it could be more serious."

A businessman at heart, Steve kept to his old habits. He had a daily planner in which he carefully jotted down each day's schedule, and he asked Celeste and the girls to do the same. The appointment book was filled with social events, commitments with the girls and Celeste, doctor appointments and vacations. But it wasn't enough. Steve was used to running a television station, and he was bored. That spring he called Gus Voelzel, complaining, "Now that the house is finished, I don't feel like I have a job."

Voelzel told Steve about Eatsies, a trendy grocery store, gourmet carryout in Dallas and Houston. Robbie Mayfield, a contractor Voelzel knew, was developing an exclusive shopping center down the hill from the Beards' new house, on Capitol of Texas Highway, next to a dress shop where Susan Dell, Michael Dell's wife, sold the expensive little frocks she designed. "Why don't you open an Eatsies in it?" Voelzel asked.

Intrigued by the idea, Steve went to Dallas to see Eatsies and considered the possibility, ultimately deciding it would entail too much work. Instead, he bantered about the idea of a liquor store in the new shopping center. Voelzel made the introductions, and Steve came away from the meeting with Mayfield convinced he wanted to be involved not as a lessee, but as one of the lessors. So, instead of renting space in the center, Steve became the money man, supplying the funds to back the development.

That year, Jennifer played on the Westlake High School softball team, and Steve was a frequent spectator, clapping for her in the stands. Celeste never made it to one of the games. "Where's your mom?" the coach asked. When Jennifer replied that she wasn't coming, he made light of the situation. Years later Jennifer would remember the sting of knowing that of all the players' moms, only hers never came. When she'd finished her required physical education credits, Celeste wouldn't let her play. "I think she just wanted to make me miserable. Or maybe it reminded her of our dad," says Jen. At times Celeste yelled at her for the way she opened Coke cans, saying it reminded her of Craig. As many times as Celeste screamed at her, Jennifer did it anyway.

Before long many at Westlake High knew Celeste better than they cared to. She had arguments with teachers and counselors, and pulled the girls out at a moment's notice for capricious reasons. Once, a shouting match with the girls' biology teacher became so heated that a security guard was called. Another day, when Jen forgot a book, Celeste brought it to school. She fumed when the office staff told her to leave it with them and wouldn't let her take it into Jennifer's classroom. Furious, Celeste screamed that they'd better call Jennifer to the office. When Jen arrived, she told her they were leaving. Soon, the staff stopped questioning the girls' absences. "They knew it wasn't us. It was our mom," says Kristina. "Jen and I did as we were told."

At times Bess and Bob Dennison wondered about the girls, who migrated to the house next door off and on during the week. Bess thought the girls seemed lonely, "like they wanted a little love." They were charmed by the teenagers, especially their naiveté. When Bob talked to them about college, they seemed reluctant to attend a large university and terrified to leave Austin and live alone. "I'd be afraid to do that," Kristina told him. "I'm not sure I could take care of myself."

"She was really a timid young girl," says Bess. "The girls looked like their mother, but they were like a shy reflection of her."

What the Dennisons didn't understand was that since they were toddlers, the girls had grown up afraid of their own mother. So much so that when Jennifer walked in one day to find Celeste grinding up sleeping pills and mixing them into Steve's food, she never asked why. Another day, she saw her topping off his Wolfschmidt bottle with Everclear. "You'd better not say anything," Celeste told her. "Keep your mouth shut."

"I did because I didn't think Steve would believe me. If I told him and he believed her, not me, she'd make my life miserable," she says. "And I didn't think it would really hurt him. I never thought it would give him more than a bad hangover."

By 1998 the twins had a tight group of friends, including Justin Grimm, a tall, dark-haired, shy teenager, who met Kristina when they were yearbook photographers. Kristina and Justin were just friends, but Jennifer was dating a sandy-haired, jowly teenager with small blue eyes, Christopher Doose, whose family had oil money. The fifth member of their tight-knit group was Amy Cozart, a pudgy, wide-faced girl with vivid blond hair. "Amy, Justin, and Christopher were the first friends we brought home," says Jennifer. "They liked us enough to put up with Celeste."

As extensions of her daughters, Celeste treated all five

teens as her servants, sending them to retrieve her mail from her secret P.O. boxes and ordering them to run errands. "You're my little niglets," she said, laughing. "Now go off and do as you're told."

Celeste always seemed too busy shopping or partying to run her own errands or fulfill her promises, even when her friend Dawn needed help raising money for her son's Montessori school. For months Kristina sold tickets to a fund-raising dinner and convinced local merchants to donate items for the auction. "Then Celeste took the credit," says Anita. "She acted like she'd done the work, never mentioning Kristina."

When the teens weren't off chasing about Austin as she directed, Celeste presided over them, flirting with Justin, teasing Christopher, and confiding all manner of things, including details about her sex life with Steve. When they were at the Beard house on Sundays, she made a show of getting ready for sex with Steve. "Time to make some money," she'd say, ordering them to take the dogs out of the master wing, complaining, "It takes him too long if he gets distracted."

Often when she was angry with him, Celeste raged, "That fat old man, I never thought he'd live this long."

Afterward, in front of the others, Celeste bragged about her sexual prowess, giving the girls pointers on what she considered the essentials of life, including her insights into the finer points of oral sex. Embarrassed, the twins tried to deflect the conversation.

Still, Celeste could be great fun. Rarely did she allow a quiet moment, and for the teens her enthusiasm could be infectious. There were pizza raids, when Celeste placed phone orders for stacks of pizzas and had them delivered to an unsuspecting family, then sat in the car with the teens giggling when the delivery man walked dejectedly back to his car still carrying the full cardboard boxes. When a family bought a lot at the lake, Celeste held a lot party, supplying orange juice and vodka screwdrivers and a grocery store cake. Celeste, the Madigans, the twins and their friends, and Celeste's other lake friends partied, laughing and carrying on. At one point Celeste drove around the subdivision pilfering For Sale signs to litter the new buyers' lot.

If the others were amused by her mother, Jennifer never lost sight of the real Celeste. "I walked on eggshells around her," she says. "When she'd be in a good mood, laughing and fun, it never seemed real, because any minute she could change."

When she did, her favorite subject was Steve, complaining that he was controlling and mean. At first the twins' friends believed her. "I thought Steve was evil," says Justin.

Over time, however, their views changed. Slowly they grew to like the girls' cantankerous stepfather, who often bellowed at them, as if for fun, then laughed. They noticed it wasn't Celeste who made it a point to be there for the girls, but Steve. Although Celeste fawned over her friends, showering them with gifts, she was very different with the girls. "She treated them like nonpersons," says Justin.

One day, driving the thirty-five miles from the lake house back to Toro Canyon with Jennifer, Justin, and Kristina in her new Ford Expedition, Celeste was in one of her flamboyant moods, smoking and laughing, when she suddenly became serious. "I don't like the way Steve's will is written," she told them. "I deserve more of his money. I'm his wife. I'm going to have to do something about getting it changed."

Whatever she did, it worked. On July 30, 1998, Steve not only finalized his trust, naming her beneficiary, but he drew up a new will. If he died and they remained married, she'd receive both houses, free and clear, mortgages paid up by the estate. On top of that, she was entitled to his personal property, including his IRAs and club memberships, plus the $500,000 gift in the original will. When Steve died, Celeste could expect to become a very wealthy woman. As before, if they divorced, she'd get much less.

That November, Steve took Celeste on a $14,000, seventeen-day tour of China, including two days in Hong Kong, two in Beijing, and a cruise down the Yangtze River. They walked on the Great Wall and saw Tiananmen Square and the burial grounds of the Ming emperors. Despite bringing home suitcases full of souvenirs, Celeste returned groaning that she hated every minute of the trip. At Tramps, she ridiculed how he'd hired rickshaws to "pull his fat ass up and down the street."

That year, Davenport Village I, the first stage of the shopping center Steve bankrolled, opened. In stone and stucco, with tile roofs, it soon boasted a pharmacy, a travel agency, a small restaurant, professional offices, and a shipping store named PakMail. At Koslow's, a tony furrier, Celeste bought furs, having only *Celeste* with no last name embroidered inside. "That way I won't have to change it when he dies," she told the girls.

After Studio 29, a posh second-floor salon opened, Celeste often went there to Joseph Prete, a tall man with extravagant gestures. Throughout her appointments, they gossiped, providing entertainment for the rest of the clientele, many residents of the surrounding hills. One day a manicurist overheard Celeste and Joseph chortling about Steve. "I thought that old man would be dead by now," she said.

The month after the China trip, things moved quickly in Celeste's life. That fall, she and Dawn went to Katz's, a downtown eatery with a sprawling bar. About ten that night Celeste called Jimmy Martinez, her last husband, who rarely minded going out at the drop of an invitation, and asked him to join them. Celeste and Jimmy flirted, the fire between them reigniting. He took her to his house and they made love. From then on she disappeared more often from Toro Canyon. She laughed about the affair with the teens, telling them, when Kristina asked why her knees were raw with scratches, that "sex with Jimmy got wild last night."

The affair presented a conflict for the twins. They'd grown up knowing they needed to look the other way with their mother. They'd kept their mouths shut—as ordered—about the sleeping pills and Everclear. Now, Celeste was being openly unfaithful. Still, Kristina and Jennifer said nothing. "We'd talk with our friends about it, how screwed up life with Celeste was," says Jennifer. "But we'd grown up with her always having some other guy on the side. We knew not to tell Steve. We knew it would only make our lives worse."

Experience had taught Celeste that her daughters knew how to keep their mouths shut, and she flaunted the affair, not even attempting to hide it from them. Yet, they'd both grown to love Steve. "We'd grown up knowing not to let anyone into our hearts, because they always left," says Kristina. "But Steve passed every test. We knew he loved us."

The girls, it seemed, lived in two worlds—one with Steve and the other with Celeste's secret life, where nothing was out of bounds. One night she took Justin and Kristina to a concert given by Jerry Jeff Walker, an aging rocker from Austin's cosmic cowboy days. Celeste drank and became belligerent, screaming at the stage, attempting to get Walker's attention. Justin thought she seemed determined to hook up with the artist, who ignored her. Afterward, she drove to Jimmy's house. When he didn't answer the door, she said a car parked on the street meant he was occupied with another woman. In front of the teens, she raised her skirt and peed on his grass.

That same month, in California, Celeste's adoptive mother, Nancy, and her husband, Al, were talking about moving. "Al and I wanted to live somewhere less expensive," says Nancy. "Celeste said, 'Why not live in the lake house for the winter?'"

Before Thanksgiving, the twins drove to California with Celeste to pick up the grandmother they'd once been told was dead. Although she'd played no part in their lives, Nancy fawned over them, telling Jennifer, "You're my favorite grandchild."

"She was strange," says Kristina. "She kept talking about how she loved us."

The girls took turns driving Nancy in one car while Celeste, Al, and the other twin drove a second car and a rental truck heavy with Nancy and Al's possessions. The girls took advantage of the time alone with the woman who'd raised their mother to ask questions. Kristina wanted to know what Celeste was like as a girl, if she'd had problems growing up. Jennifer asked if Celeste had really graduated from high school early and gone to Pepperdine. Nancy snapped at them and said it was none of their business.

In Austin, Nancy and Al moved into the lake house while they looked for a home, and they spent the holidays with Celeste, Steve, and the twins at the Toro Canyon house. But Celeste quickly tired of them, complaining to friends that she wished Nancy had never come. At Tramps she told Denise, "I hate that she's here. I just want her to leave."

That Christmas, Celeste told Steve she wanted a new diamond solitaire, like a ring she'd seen on a woman at the country club, a flawless eight-carat stone. "Buy it for me," she cajoled. Under the tree Celeste had professionally decorated for $3,000, waited a small box with her name on it. But it held a gold necklace, not the diamond ring.

"That fat fuck is going to regret this," she told the twins.

While she fumed about the ring, Celeste seemed unconcerned about something else that happened late that year: Steve was diagnosed with Type II diabetes. His risk factors were climbing. His mother had died of heart disease at sixty-seven, his father at seventy-five, and he was following quickly in their footsteps. Dr. Handley questioned him about his drinking habits. Steve said that he drank only two or three cocktails a night. Of course, he had no way of knowing that the drinks Celeste served him contained pure grain alcohol. On his chart, Dr. Handley noted the troubling results of Steve's blood tests: His kidney function was decreasing, often a result of high alcohol consumption.

One evening late that year, Becky called from Dallas and Steve got on the telephone. "He didn't make sense, like he'd had too much to drink," she'd say later. "I never even considered the possibility that he was drugged."

After he passed out at night, Celeste threw off her bathrobe. Underneath she wore her clothes for the evening, either something to wear out with friends or to meet Jimmy. One day she talked with the girls' friend, Amy, raving about the sex. Suddenly she looked worried. "Steve and I have a prenup," she said. "If he divorces me, I won't get any money. If he asks if I'm having an affair, will you lie for me?"

Amy didn't hesitate. "No," she said. "I don't lie for anyone." Celeste became suddenly silent.

The possibility that Steve might ask didn't seem out of the realm of possibility. He'd begun acting suspicious about Celeste's whereabouts, asking her where she was off to, dressed up to go out. "To get my hair done," or "Just out with friends," she'd say, pausing to peck him on the cheek on her way out the door.

Despite Amy's insistence that she wouldn't lie for her, Celeste continued to confide in all the teens, and didn't appear worried that she'd lose control over them. Amy was there the day Celeste ordered Kristina to grind up sleeping pills and mix them into Steve's food. For one of the few times in her life, Kristina refused. Celeste then insisted Amy do it. "I wouldn't do it, either," she says. "So Celeste did it. The whole time, she was cackling, like she thought it was really amusing."

That same month, Celeste, the teens, and a group of her friends from Tramps—including Denise and Terry Meyer, Celeste's manicurist—drove to Houston on an antiquing trip. When they arrived at the Doubletree Hotel across from the city's Galleria shopping complex, Celeste plopped down her credit card and paid for the rooms. When the charge was rejected by the credit card company, she said, "Try this one," and rattled off another number. That credit card was accepted. On the way to the room, she laughed and told the teens, "That's Steve's. It always works."

At a large warehouse complex dedicated to antique dealers, the women shopped. Many collected antique pickle jars, and Celeste bought the most expensive one they found that day, made out of cranberry glass, for $950. That night, the twins went to the Galleria to eat at the food court, while Celeste, Denise, and the others had reservations at Café Annie, a rosewood-paneled restaurant that caters to Houstonians who make the society column. At dinner, Celeste rattled on about Jimmy.

"Are you having an affair with him?" Denise asked.

"No," Celeste lied. "Don't be ridiculous. We're divorced."

At the bar, Celeste struck up a conversation with two well-heeled men in business suits. The men followed them to a disco, where the women drank and Celeste danced with both. Before long she told Denise they were taking her back to the hotel, but that night she didn't return to the room the two women shared. In the morning, Celeste arrived at the room she'd booked for the twins and their friends. "It's too embarrassing to show up in the same clothes I had on last night," she said, laughing. "Tell Denise I slept here."

She never asked if they'd go along with the ruse, and they did as they were told.

Still, the twins struggled with lying, especially to Steve. Months earlier Celeste had told them that he wanted to adopt them but he wanted them to ask him to do it, to be certain it was what they wanted. That day, Jennifer and Kristina walked outside and sat down next to him. "We'd like you to adopt us," Jennifer said. "We love you."

Tears filled his eyes. "I love you both, too," he said.

Weeks later they officially became his daughters.

In February the twins celebrated their eighteenth birthday. That night the teens, Celeste, Steve, and Al and Nancy had dinner at the country club, then gathered at the Toro Canyon house to open presents. As Celeste handed them to the girls, she told Steve who'd sent them. More than once she lied, about gifts from Jimmy, saying they were from Dawn or another friend.

The following night she rented a private dining room at Dick Clark's American Bandstand, an upscale TGI Friday's type restaurant, and hired a disc jockey for a surprise party. Fifty of Celeste's friends, a few of the girls', and even some of Steve's attended. He wasn't there, but Jimmy was.

To the guests, Celeste bragged that just the flowers—fresh-cut centerpieces—cost her $5,000. Music filled the room, the bartender poured liberally, and male dancers in G-strings gave the embarrassed twins lap dances. Steve's former secretary, Lisa, was there that night. "Steve didn't want to come," Celeste told her. Nuzzling Jimmy, she added, "Isn't he cute? I don't know why I ever divorced him."

Later the teens would say Steve hadn't known about the

party and that they were ordered not to tell him. On that day in the family planner, the one Steve had access to, Celeste had written: "Girls spending night at Amy's." Weeks later, however, Celeste's double life came into focus. Even if he wanted to, Steve could no longer ignore it. First he discovered $10,000 in bills from the party. It must have stung when he realized his wife hadn't wanted him there. Then Chuck Fuqua called from Bank of America. Steve's account had a $50,000 overdraft. When he investigated, Steve discovered that in a matter of months Celeste had gone through $300,000. When he demanded an explanation, she had no answers.

"I don't care about the money. I won't be mad. Just tell me what you did with it. Show me that you got something for the money," he pleaded.

"I bought stuff," she said, laughing. "Just stuff."

Seething, Steve soon discovered something else. Somehow he learned about her affair with Jimmy. Hurt and angry, Steve called Kuperman and again discussed divorce. Friends say he was sick about the turn of his marriage, but determined that it was time for his life with Celeste to end. He said little to the girls about the conflict, except one day, when he and Jennifer took one of their car rides. "Your mother's upsetting me," he said.

Days later Kristina walked into the kitchen and found Celeste holding a pistol to her head. "I'm going to kill myself!" she screamed. "You don't love me, nobody loves me!"

"I love you," Kristina pleaded, crying. "Jen loves you, Steve loves you. We all do."

"No, none of you love me," Celeste insisted.

Terrified, Kristina called 911.

A squad car and an ambulance screeched through the gates at the Gardens of Westlake and pulled up in front of the beautiful house with the man-made stream. Two deputies ran inside followed by EMS workers. They talked calmly to Celeste, asking for the gun. Finally, she handed it to them.

Just then Steve pulled up the long tree-lined driveway and parked off to the side. He rushed toward the house in time to see Celeste put in a squad car and driven away.

Inside, he talked to a deputy who explained what had happened. He comforted Kristina as the deputy wrote down a case number.

"You'll need this to get your gun back," he said.

But as soon as the deputy left, Kristina begged him, "Please don't pick the gun up. Don't bring it back into the house."

As she cried and he held her, Steve agreed. Later, Kristina would regret convincing her father to get rid of the gun, which he kept next to his bed.

Meanwhile, Celeste traveled through Austin's downtown traffic on her way to St. David's Pavilion, a critical care psychiatric unit. There she'd meet Tracey Tarlton, a smart, intense, and deeply troubled woman. From the first, Tracey felt drawn to the tall blond woman with the deep blue eyes. Later, after it was too late, she'd rethink that day and believe Celeste was already luring her into what would become a deadly dance.

Chapter

7

"The first time I remember seeing Celeste, she was smiling at me," says Tracey, shaking her head sadly. "It was like instantly there was something between us."

They may have been drawn together by a similar history, painful childhoods that left scars so deep they could never heal. Or perhaps it was something else Celeste recognized in Tracey that day. Some said Celeste had a talent for understanding the intrinsic traits that defined a person, then using them to her advantage. In Tracey, she'd discovered a woman who was her polar opposite and, in a strange way, her perfect match.

As a child, Tracey had been horribly violated, and someone she should have been able to count on to protect her did nothing to save her. The experience shaped her, leaving her as jagged inside as shards of glass from a shattered mirror. Her pain defined how she saw the world: as a collage of predators and victims. In the parlance of psychiatry, Tracey became what she'd most needed but never had as a child—a caretaker. Celeste had spent her life looking for someone to take care of her. Tracey cared more about those she loved than about herself, and she would do anything, absolutely anything, to protect them.

"I grew up in a beautiful house, and, from the outside, it looked like a good life. My father was successful, and we lived well. I loved my father. He was a kind, gentle person. My mother . . . my mother was . . ." she says pausing. "My mother was the problem."

The road that led Tracey at the age of forty-one to St. David's Pavilion and Celeste was a long and tortuous one, beginning when she was growing up in what should have been a privileged world, as the only daughter of a successful attorney, who specialized in international tax law, and his sociable and seemingly carefree wife. When Tracey was born, in May 1957, Kenneth and Mickey Tarlton lived in Ridglea, a posh Fort Worth golf course/country club community, and already had two other children, both boys, eight and ten years old. "I was an afterthought," Tracey says. "A surprise."

Of her parents, Mickey was the more gregarious, playing cards with friends, often at the country club, where she dangled a Herbert Taryton cigarette from one hand and held a drink in the other. A stocky blonde with a poodle cut and a craggy face, she resembled Rosemarie on the old *Dick Van Dyke Show*. In some ways, Mickey was like Celeste, a mom who treated the neighborhood teens like friends. She wanted the teenagers to like her and often slipped them cigarettes, a drink, or the keys to her car.

At the country club, she told the bartender, "George, I want some sour mash. My doctor says I can have all the sour mash I want, but only sour mash."

"Mickey was an alcoholic," says Tracey. "And a mean drunk."

Later, Mickey would be diagnosed as manic depressive. Self-medicating with alcohol, she spiraled from euphoria to the deepest of depression. At times she couldn't lift her head from the pillow, at other times she was giddy with happiness, and in between there were horrific outbursts of anger that cowered not only her children but her husband. "She'd yell and scream, just shriek at us," says Tracey. "She verbally abused us, telling us we were nothing, that we would never be any good."

With her daughter, Mickey did something else: She sexually abused her.

"Sometimes, I think the verbal abuse was worse," says Tracey. "But the other is, just, well, something I still find it difficult to talk about."

Whether or not her father knew of the sexual abuse, he knew about the constant verbal battering Mickey administered to his children, and he did nothing to stop it. In fact, he, too, was one of Mickey's favorite targets. "Mickey would be drunk by the time Dad got home," says Tracey. "She would just lay into him, and instead of making her stop, doing something, he'd go into the den and read."

With an abusive mother and a vacant father, home became a place Tracey dreaded. She escaped in books, spending every moment she could reading in her room. Mickey cooked dinner early and then was too drunk to manage the stove. Tracey ate it cold and left the house by four-thirty to play with the boys in the neighborhood. When they played baseball, Mickey screamed at her, calling her names in front of her friends. As night fell, the other children went home. Tracey hid in the darkness until she judged she could stay out no longer. When she entered the house, it was always the same. Her father had secluded himself in the den, and her mother was on a rampage. At times she even pounded with her fists on her husband's chest. Passive, he endured it until she stopped.

Later, Tracey would be unable to find family photos of

herself in her mother's arms, as if even that were a comfort she'd been denied. Most of the time, her care was left to the maid or her father. But he stopped holding Tracey by the time she reached ten, when Mickey falsely accused him of incest. "Even then, he never stood up to her," says Tracey.

As an adult, she asked her father why he hadn't stopped Mickey. Her father grew angry and told her that it wasn't her place to question his actions. But she did. Perhaps it was harder because she truly loved him.

Her best times were spent with her brothers and father in the Texas wilderness, hunting and fishing. Her father taught her to shoot, and in the early 1970s he gifted her with a .20 gauge shotgun, a Franchi, lightweight and easy to shoot. For a few years she shot small animals, squirrels and rabbits. "But I didn't like killing," she says. "So I stopped and used it to shoot skeet."

From early on, Tracey's life revolved around animals. She had dogs and cats and adored them. They offered her the unconditional love she never received from her mother. "Tracey was dog crazy early on," says Pat Brooks, a friend whose father was also in the law firm. "She lived and breathed for her animals."

In many ways Tracey, despite the long brown hair she wore down to her waist, looked like her brothers, stocky and big boned. She idolized them. "They were there with me, I guess, in the trenches," she says. Once, when she was about ten, she talked to them about taking things into their own hands, by hiring someone to kill her mother. "It was never serious," she says. "Just one of those things you kick around when you're with someone else who understands how truly awful it is."

Tracey went to good schools, did well, and her summers were spent at Camp Longhorn on the Guadalupe River, a prestigious establishment whose campers have included the pampered scions of wealthy Texas families for generations. It was there that as children President George W. Bush and Senator Kay Bailey Hutchison swam, played tennis, golfed, and earned "attawaytogos"—kudos for jobs well done. "It's one of the top camps in the state," says one ex-camper. "Campers have to have a legacy—a mother or father who attended—to go there."

By adolescence, Tracey was an athletic tomboy, with shaggy brown hair. "From the beginning, she wasn't what you would describe as feminine," says Brooks. "She was always a burly girl." She became a popular camper, and was asked to be a counselor. "Tracey loved the outdoors, and she was just fun to be around, enthusiastic and good to talk to," says a former camper. "She loved books and animals, and treated people well. Tracey was the counselor you could count on to stand up for the kids who didn't fit in."

Looking back, Tracey would estimate that she took her first drink sometime before she turned fourteen. From that point on she drank nearly every day. It eased her feelings of being separate from the other girls. From early on she felt as if she didn't belong, not at home and not with the girls who raved about boys and clothes. Later, she'd think about that and believe the other girls saw a masculinity about her that she didn't yet realize. "I always felt out of place," she says. "Drinking was a crutch. It took the edge off."

In high school Tracey dated a football player. "It was what you were supposed to do," she says. "But my heart was never in it. I never did the boy crazy thing." That was the year she read *Going Down with Janis*, a book on Janis Joplin written by her woman lover. Tracey was fascinated with it, especially the love scenes. She read them over and over, until the pages were worn and dog-eared. Yet, she never thought about what that said about her or where her interests lay. "I didn't see myself in it," she says.

The "voice" first made its appearance in high school. When she drank, a man's soft voice belittled her, inside her head. She never thought it was real, always understanding that it was something inside of her that called to her, and from the very beginning it said the things she'd heard from her mother, that she was bad and worthless. "It told me that I should kill myself, that that was my destiny. I think I thought that was what my mother wanted," she says. Over the years, the voice left, then inexplicably returned.

After she left Fort Worth for Austin and the University of Texas, Tracey began to understand why she felt so distant from other young girls. As a freshman in the mid-seventies, she walked into a salon owned by Alice, a beautiful gay woman. Alice took one look at Tracey and recognized something Tracey hadn't yet realized about herself—a kinship and a mutual interest.

The next day, Alice sat with a group of friends outside a friend's rented house near the university. She'd invited Tracey to join them, and when Tracey walked up, it took her a few minutes to realize the attractive, bright women laughing and bantering between each other in lawn chairs were all lesbians. "It was like a light went on," says Tracey. "It was like suddenly I realized, hey, I'm like they are."

The other women recognized immediately that Tracey belonged. "She was like a young, handsome Kurt Russell," says a woman who was part of the clique. "Tracey wasn't trying to be a boy, it was just the way she was. She seemed to have an overload of testosterone. She had a husky voice, wore khaki pants, Ralph Lauren shirts, and Top-Siders. She carried herself and had the attitude of an adolescent boy, a splash of machismo." The women soon noticed that Tracey and her mother had a strained relationship. When she talked about her family, Tracey always referred to her mother as Mickey. "It was like she couldn't bring herself to say the word mother," says a friend.

Most of the women were UT students, and it was a time in Austin when gay men and women were coming out, acknowledging their sexuality and looking for others who shared their lifestyle. For a while Tracey lived a double life. Sororities ruled at UT, and Tracey belonged to Kappa Alpha Theta—the Thetas—which boasted girls from the wealthiest families in the state. "We called the gay sorority girls the Tah Tah's," says a woman who attended UT. "They were flighty and cute with lots of money."

One friend, Nancy Pierson, brought Tracey onto her team and taught her to be a goalie in the Austin Soccer League. She'd often tell Tracey that she was good because she was just crazy enough not to worry about getting hurt. "She was a star on the team, strong and athletic," says a friend.

Looking back, Tracey would say she never regretted coming out, but it did cost her dearly. She was drummed out of her sorority for "consorting with undesirables," which she translated to mean the clique of women she circulated the gay bars with at night. The day after she was kicked out, she saw a friend on the street, a woman she'd known since camp. Tracey said hello, but the woman walked by without acknowledging her. "That's the way it works," she says. "People pretend they don't know you."

In the rush of coming out, Tracey flitted from one relationship to another. While many of the women preferred to look androgynous, Tracey liked feminine lovers. "Tracey was a cute young thing, butch. She was into girlie girls," says a friend. "She liked them with curves, hips, and in dresses."

It was a fluid and lighthearted time in Austin's gay community, after centuries of living in the shadows and before the devastation of AIDS. "We weren't coming out making a statement. We didn't care," says Becky Odom, an artist and one of the original group. "People experimented, multiple partners, wild scenes. It was just the way it was."

Despite the new freedom, there was still an undercurrent of pain, of not fitting in, that many within the community didn't even like to acknowledge. "It's tough being gay. Most people wouldn't willingly put themselves outside the norm," says Odom. "We had a lot of abuse in the community, drugs and alcohol."

For Tracey, it was alcohol. And when she drank, like her mother, she became aggressive. "Alcohol made her cocky," says Odom. "We had similar personalities. We'd get loud and alienate people when we were drinking. We'd play pool at the gay bar and tell people to fuck off. Tracey and I were bad news drunks together."

There were bar fights, and Tracey had one car wreck after another. In the early years, she stayed with a lover briefly and then moved on. "She was like wow, so excited to be out there," says Odom. The women went skinny dipping at Canyon Rim, a favorite spot in Barton Creek, and rented a cabin where they sunbathed nude. All from prosperous families, they didn't flaunt or hide their sexuality. "Here were all these women out of the closet," Tracey remembers. "It was wild, and at the same time family."

The first of Tracey's true loves was a beautiful young blonde named Joan, wildly feminine and straight. "It was an unusual thing. Tracey would make friends with straight women and they'd become attracted to her," says Christie Bourgeois, a San Antonio professor and longtime friend. "They'd pursue her. They could make the leap with Tracey because she had a masculine quality."

While she never announced her sexuality to her parents, she brought her lovers home. Her father treated them well, going so far as to tell Tracey he particularly liked one woman. "You have good taste," he said. A few years later he died of leukemia. "He stayed with Mickey right until the end," she says. "He loved her."

When Mickey was sober, she was fun and lighthearted with Tracey's partners. When she was drunk, she became malicious. After Tracey and her lover went to bed, the phone rang in her bedroom. "I know what you're doing up there, and it's sick," her mother whispered in a raspy, drunk voice. "Lesbians," she hissed. "You're lesbians."

When her mother died, Tracey didn't mention it to anyone, as if nothing had happened. At a party, Odom asked her about Mickey.

"Still drinking?" she said.

"Mickey died," Tracey answered. "Finally kicked the bucket."

The official cause of death was pancreatic cancer, but the underlying root was alcoholism. By then Tracey had had an affair with another woman. When Joan found out, she left her. It was a pattern that would reemerge throughout Tracey's life. She'd fall in love, win the woman, then drink or have an affair, convincing her lover to leave.

If she hurt others, Tracey was never as hard on them as she was on herself. While she may have seemed brash and sure on the outside, she was plagued by doubts, magnified by the voice that came and went inside her.

The first time Tracey tried to kill herself was in Houston in 1981, when she was just twenty-four. After she'd attempted to overdose, a friend checked her into a ten-week treatment program. When she emerged sober, she felt as she had years earlier—as if she didn't fit in anywhere. Her friends were still drinking, and around them she bristled with self-doubt. AA gave her a home. Attending daily meetings for months, she kept her mind clear. "I was lonely, but I felt like I had my life back," she says. "I felt lucky to be alive."

Never having graduated at UT, she returned to college in the mid-eighties, this time to Texas A&M, where she completed a bachelor's degree in wildlife and fishery science. For three years she worked for the U.S. Fish and Wildlife service as a field biologist, first in Texas, then in Arizona. In November 1988 her old clique reunited, this time in Santa Fe for Thanksgiving. By then many had sobered up. It was a healthy weekend, full of hiking and horseback riding. One night, soaking in the hot tub, they talked about their favorite poems. When it was her turn, Tracey recited the first two lines from Langston Hughes's "Dream Deferred," a fierce warning about the danger of unrealized desire: "What happens to a dream deferred? Does it dry up like a raisin in the sun?" she asked.

"It was classic Tracey, intense and bright," says Odom. "Her friends loved her."

In 1989, Tracey returned to Austin, where she signed on as a biologist with BCI—Bat Conservation International—a nonprofit group that works to protect bat colonies and restore their natural habitats. It was a dream job for her, helping to protect a small, vulnerable little animal by working with government agencies and nonprofit groups. She ran educational trips to Africa and South America, where she brought groups into the bats' lairs. "It was an incredible place to work," she says, still visibly excited at the memory. "I got to be an advocate for an animal that's misunderstood and persecuted."

The small, furry, winged mammals became her cause. She worked for BCI for five years. Then, as she had with her lovers, Tracey made a mistake, and she was too stubborn to admit it and go on. "It was typical Tracey, adolescent boy in a woman's body," says someone she worked with.

Another woman remembers that Tracey interacted well with the women on the staff, but appeared uncomfortable with men. At the same time, she acted like "one of the boys." One day, Tracey walked up to two men in a hallway—one of whom was her boss. She grabbed one of them from behind and said, "How're they hanging?"

Neither man laughed.

In the days that followed, the entire BCI staff was ordered to attend a seminar on sexual harassment. Rather than apologize, Tracey became adamant about not having done anything wrong. She argued with her boss when he criticized her behavior, then circulated a memo he wrote her, detailing her transgressions, to the rest of the staff, asking them to join her in protest. "This was a minor thing, but she just blew it up," says a coworker. "It wasn't anything to lose a job over."

In April 1994, Tracey was fired, the official reason written in her employment record was "for displaying hostile conduct toward upper management."

It was a comedown for Tracey, who went to work as a receptionist in Alice's salon. But just a year later opportunity again presented itself. In 1995, BookPeople, Austin's largest independent bookseller, expanded to a new location, a three-floor store plus offices on Sixth and Lamar, next to another of the city's institutions, the trendy Whole Foods Market. Tracey hired on as manager of the third floor, which had sections on spirituality, health, philosophy, and men's and women's studies. She was dedicated, working long hours, and intensely interested. But not all was well. That year—after fourteen years of sobriety—she suddenly began drinking. She'd say later that it was a form of self-medication for the depression that had stalked her off and on since she'd been a child. Her friends called AA and asked the counselors to conduct an intervention. A petite straight woman, a hairdresser named Zan Ray, responded.

The intervention went off as planned, and Tracey was soon sober again, and determined to remain so. Her relationship with Zan Ray might have ended there, but in July of that year Ray arrived at the Austin airport after attending a trade show, and her husband wasn't there. Zan called Tracey, who picked her up and gave her a ride home. When the two women walked inside the house, they found his body. Days earlier, he'd overdosed. The coroner ruled it a suicide.

The discovery shook both Ray and Tracey. Months later Becky Odom saw Tracey at a party. "How terrible for Zan," said Tracey. "Suicide, it's just unfair to the people left behind."

At the time, Tracey was in a relationship with a bright, engaging woman. Yet that didn't stop her from having an affair with Ray. "I think the mutual experience brought us together," Tracey says. "We were there for each other, and it became more than that."

In the months that followed, Tracey and Ray lived together. But, again, she couldn't maintain the relationship. By late 1998 she was drinking again. As it had in the past, the alcohol opened the door where she kept her demons at bay. The voice returned.

"I would try to drown it out with alcohol," she says. "I just wanted it to stop."

On the evening of September 16, 1998, Tracey was anxious and lonely. She drove to a convenience store in a rough Austin neighborhood, where men milled around outside and cars drove by without stopping. There she met a dissheveled man named Reginald Breaux. For reasons she couldn't later explain, except that she wanted someone to drink with, Tracey invited Breaux into her truck. Together, they talked and drank a six-pack of beer while she drove around Austin. At one point he directed her to his brother's house, but then wouldn't take her inside. "I didn't want to bring some dyke into their house," he'd say later. "So we drove to another convenience store."

In the store parking lot, Tracey ordered Breaux out of her truck. What happened next they'd later explain in very different terms. Stumbling, he climbed down and started to walk away. Then he cursed at her and threw an open can of beer that hit her and splashed on her clothes. "I backed up and pulled forward, to leave," she says. "He lurched at me. I couldn't stop, and the truck hit him and he was down."

The police were called, and Tracey waited until an ambulance arrived to be sure Breaux was all right. Although he was only dazed, he claimed that she'd tried to run him over. Police noticed that she smelled of beer, so they booked her and took her in. Two days later all charges were dropped. Still, the incident haunted her, as if she were never completely clear in her own mind what she'd intended that night.

When Ray discovered that Tracey had been drinking, she told her she'd have to leave. With nowhere to go, Tracey bought one of Ray's rental properties, a run-down one-story corner house with a carport at 3601 Wilson Street, on the south side of Austin, near St. Edward's University. She called Pat Brooks, whose father had been her father's law partner, and asked for her help. Pat, a remodeling consultant, and her partner, Jane, a teacher, lived in a renovated home in one of Austin's better neighborhoods.

With the backdrop of their shared childhoods, Pat and Tracey renewed their friendship. Evenings, Pat helped with the renovations, while Jane grilled dinner on the back patio. It was easy to see what Tracey loved. All she cared about were her two cats and her dog, Wren, a Corgi and whippet mix, and her collection of first edition children's and animal books. "Tracey loved animals like they were her children.

She talked to them like they were people," Brooks says. "Jane and I are both animal lovers, and we understood that."

By 1998, Tracey's dedication and hard work at BookPeople had paid off with a string of quick promotions. Wearing her plaid shirts and khakis, her nails bitten to the quick, and carrying a backpack, she was a good fit for the bohemian feel of the store. If Austin's soccer moms and business execs bought their books at Barnes & Noble, its counterculture population, musicians, writers, and computer nerds frequented the aisles at BookPeople.

From floor manager and buyer, Tracey worked her way up to general manager. She had a staff of 150 employees to oversee and responsibility for the entire store. "It was an incredible responsibility, but I loved it," she says. In her fourth-floor office, Tracey had an open door policy for employees. Working long hours, she pushed hard to make sure schedules were met. As in the past, she sometimes became heavily invested in her decisions. Rick Klaw, a floor manager, at times saw things differently than Tracey and felt the sting of coming up against her. "We could both become confrontational, yelling and screaming," he'd say. "That was just Tracey. But we were still friends. We'd argue and then go out to dinner together."

On the surface, Tracey's life was on track and good, in every way except the alcohol.

Fueled by the run-in with Breaux, in early 1999 the voice grew louder. Soon, nothing drowned it out, not work or booze. Tracey fought to maintain control, but was barely holding on. At BookPeople, her staff noticed she was argumentative, issuing contradictory orders, as if she didn't remember one day to the next what she'd told them. Inside Tracey's head, the voice told her she was worthless and taunted her to end her life

At night she drank alone in the house on Wilson, then

called Pat and Jane, desperate for help. In those painful conversations she admitted secrets she'd hidden for decades, describing the horrors of her childhood, including what
Mickey had done to her behind closed doors. Jane tried to
help, but nothing seemed to lessen Tracey's pain.

At the end of February, Tracey called Jane again, crying.
She talked about the voice and said that she wanted to kill
herself to make it stop. "I've been playing Russian roulette,"
she said. "I've got one live bullet in the chamber."

It was a cry for help. Tracey didn't want to die.

"I'm not equipped to help you," Jane told her. "We're going to come for you."

Minutes later Jane and Pat pulled into Tracey's driveway.
When Tracey opened the door, her eyes were red and her
face anxious, reflecting the ache of the battle waging within
her. Jane put her arm around her and led her to the car. They
drove through Austin's darkened streets to St. David's Pavilion, a beacon of hope for Tracey, who wanted nothing more
than for the torment to stop.

Inside, they brought Tracey to Admissions, explained the
gravity of her situation, and asked for her to be checked into
the center's substance abuse program. They then watched as
she was led away to a ward. Tracey, shoulders slumped and
head down, looked as if she had no more energy with which
to fight. All her reserves drained, she resembled a small
child, helpless, vulnerable, and terrified.

Chapter

8

"Give one of those doughnuts to Tracey," Celeste told Kristina, motioning at a rumpled woman with shaggy hair who sat off in a corner in St. David's day room.

"Here," Kristina said, holding out the box to the woman. "Help yourself."

Appearing dazed, her eyes clouded with tears, Tracey glanced up at her, pulled out a frosted doughnut and placed it beside her. She said, "Thank you," but never took a bite. Something in the way Tracey looked, devastated by life, tugged at Kristina. "I felt sorry for her," she says. "She just hung her head and sobbed."

The black and white notebook Tracey used as her journal at St. David's reflected the pain that haunted her. On the first page she wrote:

In the name of Jesus, <u>shame & fear & doubt</u> must leave.
Jesus, give me peace in the storm. Calm my fears.

Perhaps what touched Kristina was Tracey's desperation. It was a stark contrast to Celeste's attitude since arriving at St. David's.

Despite the seriousness of her diagnosis—depression and suicidal ideation—Celeste acted more like a hotel guest than a patient since the first day she entered the hospital. She'd held a gun to her head, saying she was in so much pain only death could bring relief. But she treated the staff not like professionals she prayed would help her but as servants charged with doing her bidding. She even refused to eat the food, insisting that the teens and Steve bring her meals. At breakfast, Kristina stopped at IHOP for carryout waffles, pancakes, or eggs. That wasn't enough. In addition, Celeste wanted doughnuts for the other patients. Kristina did as she was told.

Steve brought lunch. If he couldn't, Justin, who took classes across the street from the hospital at Concordia College, filled in. In his heart, it wasn't for Celeste, but for Kristina. By then they'd grown to be more than friends. They were in love, and Justin wanted Kristina to do well, something Celeste rarely paid attention to. Due to their mother keeping the twins from school, both were behind and wouldn't graduate that May. Instead they hoped to attend summer school to graduate in August. The turmoil of the hospitalization and Celeste's demands threatened to make even that impossible. "She didn't seem to care about what was important for them," says Justin.

Evenings, Steve arrived with dinner. Tracey saw his round, robust figure lumbering through the hallways with a plastic carryout box or a dish from home. She wondered about the old man and his young wife. They seemed such an odd pairing.

At home, Jen was relieved to have their mother away. But the hospitalization devastated Kristina. She worried about her constantly. She barely ate and couldn't sleep. "Kristina was genuinely frightened," says Anita. "She had a hard time concentrating on anything else. She was devoted to Celeste, and having her sick threw her into a panic."

Meanwhile, Celeste displayed no such qualms about her own health. Within days of her arrival she acted as if she'd forgotten the suicide attempt that had brought her there. Instead, she spent much of her day avoiding therapy and complaining. Along with the quality of the food, she disdained the housekeeping service. "I ought to bring in my maid," she told a nurse. "The place is a fucking pigsty."

Tracey and the other patients laughed as Celeste ridiculed the staff. At times she imitated the way they walked or talked. "She just honed right in on people," says Tracey.

As always, Celeste flaunted Steve's money, bragging that instead of insurance, like the other patients, she was paying cash. Somehow, she convinced the nurses and orderlies to look the other way as she disregarded the rules. Visitors weren't allowed in patient rooms and treatment areas, but when Justin and the other teens arrived, they were waved through the electric security doors. "I heard one of the nurses say, 'Those are the special kids,'" says Justin. "Celeste said she'd made arrangements."

Suspicious of the way she was acting, one day Justin asked Celeste why she was there. She didn't mince words, replying, "I spent so much money, I don't know where it went, and I'm worried about Steve leaving me."

At St. David's, patients' days were devoted to therapy, working through the crises that brought them to the brink of suicide. An acute care facility, it emphasized stabilization. "They tried to maintain us until they could get us into another facility," says one patient. "It was emergency care, not long-term therapy."

In between sessions, patients who smoked congregated outside in a fenced yard near construction for a new medical office. It was there that Tracey and Celeste talked for the first time. Tracey noticed Celeste's little girl voice, with its soft lisp and the way she clipped off each word. Later, Tracey would say that even during that initial conversation, Celeste flirted openly with her. "She came on strong," she says. "We were both on heavy meds, but even then the attraction was there."

Curious, Tracey asked why Celeste was there, and Celeste told her about her suicide threat, then blamed her depression on Steve. She described him as overbearing and abusive. When Tracey asked why she stayed with him, Celeste said she was afraid to leave: He had power and money, and—despite the fact that he was the one threatening divorce—she insisted that he told her that he'd never let her go. "I never thought he'd live this long," Celeste complained. "I despise him."

Celeste went on to tell her that she had first married Steve after he helped her get custody of the twins. "I thought that was noble, that she'd given up her life for her daughters," says Tracey.

While Celeste was a distraction at St. David's, Tracey continued to wrestle with her own demons. A week after arriving she wrote in her journal: *"I'm being treated now with antipsychotic drugs and tranquilizers to try to quiet the voices in my head. They are very insistent about suicide . . . I am afraid what I would do if left to my own devices."*

While Tracey fought to reclaim her sanity, Pat talked with the owners at BookPeople, making sure they'd keep Tracey's job open for her. They agreed, and then Jane searched for a long-term facility for Tracey, one where she could finally unburden herself of her past. For her part, Tracey had heard of Hazelden, a Minnesota facility that specialized in treating patients with addictions. She was distraught when it turned her down, judging her too great a suicide risk. "*I am in the depths of sorrow and despair,*" she wrote.

In group sessions, Tracey talked of her childhood, including the sexual abuse, and listened sympathetically as Celeste recounted her past. "We seemed to have a lot of shared experience," says Tracey. "I never questioned those things had happened to her."

In St. David's, Celeste's allegations mushroomed. Now, not only did she contend that her father sexually abused her, but also that she'd been raped by one of her brothers and Craig. "It was a lie," her brother Cole would say later. "Just like the things she said about our dad. The most that ever happened was the normal show-and-tell stuff little kids do."

Photos from St. David's would later document the bond that developed between Celeste and Tracey. Reclining on a couch in one, Celeste had her legs stretched across Tracey's lap. In another, Tracey's arm draped over Celeste's shoulder. "When we'd visit, Celeste spent most of her time talking about Tracey," says Kristina. "She'd talk about how they were friends, how funny Tracey was. She said she was gay."

One day, Tracey would later say, the relationship took a turn. "Celeste followed me into my room," she says. "She kissed me on the lips."

Tracey kissed her back. From that point on there were stolen moments behind cabinets, in their rooms, wherever they had a moment of privacy. They kissed and touched, Tracey slipping her hands over Celeste's breasts. "Celeste didn't pull away," says Tracey. "She touched me back."

At other times they simply talked, telling each other about their lives, much of Celeste's conversation centering on Steve. "He's smothering me," she told Tracey. "He's the biggest issue in my life. I can't breathe with him watching everything I do. At times I think my only escape is suicide."

Growing to hate a man she'd only seen in passing, Tracey told her not to give up. "He's not worth it," she said. "And one day he'll be gone and you'll be free."

A week earlier, Tracey had entered St. David's a shell, so empty she hadn't wanted to live. Without realizing it was happening, Tracey was quickly filled by Celeste with expectations for the future. It was obvious to Pat and Jane that Tracey was entranced. When they called, she spent little time talking about therapy, just Celeste. "She's gorgeous," she told them. "Smart and funny. I want you to meet her."

Jane cautioned her, telling Tracey to consider where they'd met and that she needed to realize she and Celeste were both not well. "Concentrate on getting better, on your therapy," she said. "Not on this woman."

Her advice went unheeded. Days later, Tracey and Celeste had passes to leave St. David's for a dinner out. Pat and Jane pulled into the hospital parking lot to pick them up. When they saw a flashy woman in a fur coat and big jewelry smoking a cigarette near the door, Jane said, "I bet that's her."

Pat shook her head. "Can't be," she insisted.

Minutes later Tracey appeared and took the woman by the arm to bring her over to the car. "I want you to meet Celeste," she said.

Dinner was strained. Other patients from St. David's joined them in the small restaurant, and Pat felt ill at ease surrounded by people who appeared heavily medicated. She found Celeste amusing if odd. Much of the night she complained about Steve, calling him names and saying that he controlled her life.

Days later Celeste and Tracey made another public appearance, this time at BookPeople. On day passes, Tracey wanted to show her around the store, a place she loved. As soon as they entered, a small group of her floor managers gathered around. They hadn't told the staff that Tracey was in a psychiatric hospital, only that she was ill, and they didn't want them to see the drug-dazed look in her eyes. An argument ensued and Tracey's voice rose, until Celeste grabbed her by the arm. As the others watched, Celeste drew Tracey to the side and chastised her. Afterward, Tracey, looking embarrassed, apologized, and then both the women ꞏꞏꞏꞏꞏꞏꞏꞏ ꞏꞏꞏꞏ ꞏꞏ.

Soon, rumors spread through BookPeople and Austin's gay community that Tracey Tarlton had a new lover, a tall, beautiful, rich, married woman named Celeste Beard.

If Celeste initiated the relationship, Tracey latched on quickly. If nothing else, Celeste was a tantalizing distraction from the crisis that had brought her to St. David's. At times, Celeste entertained her with stories of the things she'd done to Steve. He was a despicable man, she said, one who deserved to be drugged and given Everclear. When she described how he'd once passed out in the closet, she imitated him so comically, splayed out and bloated, Tracey laughed as Celeste chortled wildly at the memory. "When I get frustrated, I cut myself. I've tried to slit my wrists," she said. "Steve's an old man and he's going to die soon, but not soon enough. If I can help him along, that's a good thing. When he dies, I get it all, all the money."

"I thought you didn't marry him for the money," Tracey replied.

"I didn't, but he'll never let me go until he's dead," she said. "If he dies, at least I'll be a rich woman. And if that doesn't happen, I'm just going to kill myself. At least if I kill myself, I'll be some trouble for him."

Pain was something Tracey understood. On Sunday, March 14, she wrote:

"I think that my left arm goes numb as a response to bad memories. I've noticed two times that were associated with some kind of Mickey behavior. Once when a girl on our unit wailed and another time when I noticed a cigarette burning in an ashtray, a long cigarette just left there to burn down. I wonder if she shook me by my arms—I seem to remember she did that often, or at least when I was little, but I can't bring it up clearly.

"MY SHAME AND MY SELF-BLAME BLOCK ME FROM MY GOOD SELF."

Despite the insights, Tracey's future remained uncertain. Jane told her about the Menninger Clinic, a renowned treatment center outside Topeka, Kansas. They accepted her, and two weeks after arriving at St. David's, on March 6, Tracey was released into Pat's care. Before she left, Celeste kissed her good-bye and promised to convince Steve to send her to Menninger as well. "The plan was that we would be roommates, free to explore the relationship," says Tracey.

On the plane to Kansas City she was heavily medicated and talked little. At one point she turned to Pat and asked, "Do you think this is the right thing for me?"

"Yes," Pat told her. "It is."

But when they drove up to the clinic, Pat grew worried. The facility reminded her of the haunted hotel in the old Jack Nicholson movie *The Shining*. In a rural setting, the hospital looked dreary and depressing. Inside, patients shuffled down the halls. "It felt foreboding," she says. "I hated leaving Tracey there."

By then Celeste had left St. David's and returned home to Steve and the girls. Her mood seemed little improved by her time away, and she and Steve argued bitterly. "She didn't want to be there," says Jennifer.

With the girls, she initiated the "Rule," an edict that banned them from being gone from the house at the same time. "We had to make sure one of us was home every evening and on weekends," says Kristina. "Celeste didn't want to be alone with Steve."

On March 8, two days after Tracey checked into Menninger, Celeste met with her psychiatrist, Dr. Michele Hauser, a prim and perfectly coiffed woman with dark brown, chin-length hair. A graduate of Tufts University Medical School, Hauser had served her residency at Atlanta's esteemed Emory University. After assessing Celeste, Hauser diagnosed her as narcissistic and histrionic and agreed with a former diagnosis that Celeste displayed a cluster of personality disorders.

Two days later Celeste returned to Hauser for another appointment. "I'm afraid Steve will commit me and divorce me," she told her doctor, crying. Unsaid was that if that happened, she would be left with nothing beyond her half share of the houses and personal property. There would be no big settlement and no alimony.

That night, Kristina found Celeste in a stupor. She hurriedly called 911, fearing her mother had downed a handful of pills. Again, for the second time in a month, an ambulance pulled in front of the Toro Canyon house. At midnight, after her stomach was pumped, Celeste was again checked into St. David's. Once there, she shrieked that she wanted the nurses to call Dr. Hauser. She screamed at Kristina, and then, at 1:30 A.M., announced, "I'm going to shower now. That's just the kind of bitch I am."

The next day in Menninger, Tracey wrote in her diary: *"Celeste is back at St. David's. She tried to kill herself."* Tracey would later say that she knew so quickly because Celeste called once or twice a day. But by then Tracey was battling her own wars. Compared to St. David's, Menninger seemed a bleak place that aggravated her depression. "It was just a bad match," she says. "I wanted out."

In Austin, Celeste was quickly released from St. David's. At her first meeting with Hauser after the suicide attempt, she told the physician she believed she needed inpatient therapy and asked about Menninger. She failed to mention that she had a relationship with a woman already there. By then Steve, too, had apparently come to the conclusion that the only hope for Celeste was an intensive program where she could work through her problems. Despite all she'd put him through, he hadn't given up on her.

That night on the phone, Tracey explained how much she hated Menninger. She described it as depressing, cold, and unfriendly. If not Menninger, they would need another alternative. Celeste brought up a posh Houston clinic, but Tracey had been there in the eighties, when she first quit drinking, and she didn't want to return. Then Celeste told her about Timberlawn, a clinic Steve had found outside Dallas. Tracey had heard of the facility and knew it had a good reputation.

"Celeste and I made a pact; I'd transfer to Timberlawn and she'd join me there," says Tracey. "If all went well, we'd be able to share a room."

Weeks earlier, Tracey and Celeste had been strangers, but by mid-March 1999 their lives were melding. On March 14, Celeste sent Tracey a card. The front bore a rising sun and the note: "*You're in my thoughts.*" Inside, in her fluid half printing, half writing style, Celeste scrawled a note: "*It's hard to think of something to write because I speak with you so often. My hopes are to see you soon and explore our friendship! You are in my thoughts and please take care of yourself. Love, Celeste.*"

In the days that followed, Tracey made arrangements to transfer to Timberlawn. Finally, on March 19, Celeste went to her Austin travel agent's office and purchased two e-tickets between Kansas City and Dallas for Tracey and an attendant from Menninger, charging them on her credit card. Considered a suicide risk, Tracey wasn't allowed to travel alone.

Arriving at Timberlawn buoyed Tracey's spirits. While Menninger felt oppressive, Timberlawn's parklike campus—a white Georgian colonial main building surrounded by satellite centers—gave her a sense of peace. Founded in 1917, the hospital began at a time when the chronically mentally ill were being released from prisons to long-term treatment centers. Eighty years earlier the stately white building had been a half day's buggy ride outside of downtown Dallas. By the time Tracey arrived, the city had grown up around it. Timberlawn had a national reputation for its post-traumatic stress disorder program. Begun after World War II to treat vets, it catered to patients suffering from all forms of PTSD, including the trauma of early childhood abuse.

"I've had issues since childhood that have manifested into substance abuse," Tracey told her admitting counselor on March 20, 1999. The diagnosis she brought with her from Menninger listed PTSD and bipolar disorder, in which moods swung rapidly from euphoria to depression. "Before St. David's, I was playing Russian roulette for five nights straight," she said. She then added that her problems had started in 1998, when she'd begun drinking again. Tracey described her clash with Reginald Breaux, the man she'd picked up at the convenience store. Instead of relating the incident as an accident, she said, "I tried to run him over with a car."

As she listened, the counselor assessed the exhausted, frightened patient before her. On the admission forms, she noted that Tracey was neatly dressed, a cooperative woman with above average intelligence. She wrote: "*Patient reports mother verbally assaulted her and her brothers and father . . . Patient says mother sexually molested her from the age of eight to sixteen. Verbal abuse continued until mother's death.*"

The counselor listed Tracey's goals as "*to understand her suicidality and lower her suicide ideology, to begin to like herself and process the shame she feels.*"

Judging her state of mind as dangerous, the counselor put Tracey on a suicide watch, and before she was brought to her unit, two women staffers searched her for contraband: razors, cigarette lighters, and drugs. Nothing was found. The night nurse gave her two Trazadone, and she quickly fell asleep.

The next day, Tracey made her first journal entry at Timberlawn, writing: "*Jane and Celeste love me & care about me & think that I am worthwhile.*" She drew a thick black box around her words, as if to give them the weight she wanted them to carry within her own soul. On the same page, she took notes during a group session: "*When perpetrator is bad, child sees it as child being bad to maintain attachment. Something happens and you feel little and helpless.*"

That afternoon, a nurse watched Tracey pace the halls, as if waiting for something or someone. She told her to calm down, but that was impossible; Tracey was waiting for Celeste. "I thought she'd be there that day," she says later. "That was our agreement."

That night on the telephone, Celeste explained that Steve was still making arrangements. Barely holding on to her resolve not to kill herself, Tracey felt the disappointment keenly. In her turmoil, she saw Celeste as a lifeline. Before she hung up, she asked for Celeste's birthdate and time of day. Tracey noted them in her journal: "2/13/63 and 7:15 A.M."

"That night on the phone was the first time Celeste said she loved me," Tracey says. "Before we hung up, I said I loved her, too."

Minutes later Tracey dialed another number. Lisahn Golden, an astrologer friend in Austin, answered. Years earlier, Tracey had been attracted to Golden, a straight woman with a husband. Golden had rebuffed her, but they remained friends. "I'd like you to do a couple's chart for me and a woman I'm seeing," Tracey said, giving Lisahn her own birthdate and time and Celeste's. "We'll come out and you can give us our readings."

Her life on full throttle once Celeste was involved, Tracey would never keep that appointment, but Golden would not forget the chart she drew, linking the two women's destinies. "They fit together like puzzle pieces," she says. "Celeste was Pisces in the twelfth house squared, self-centered, a woman totally without love, who cared about absolutely nothing more than money. Tracey desperately wanted to take care of someone. But it went beyond that. Apart they were troubled. Together, they were incredibly dangerous."

"I'm here for depression, and because I keep trying to kill myself," Celeste told the admitting counselor on March 24, 1999. She went on to elaborate the direness of her situation, saying she rarely slept and had lost twenty-five pounds in the last four months, sweated heavily, had a decrease in concentration, energy, and libido. She said she'd spent $250,000 in the past year, and that she was obsessive about cleanliness and organization. "I have panic attacks three times a day," she said.

Celeste's description of her alleged sexual abuse changed again. This time she claimed it had started at age four. She described herself as a college graduate. Celeste denied any imminent plans to kill herself, but said, "I just wish I was dead." The counselor judged her not a high risk of suicide—like Tracey—but a moderate risk, and wrote down her admitting diagnosis: Personality disorder, borderline and narcissistic.

"*She denies any homicidal ideation,*" the counselor noted.

Steve, sitting beside Celeste, answered questions as well, saying that he tended to give in to Celeste whenever she wanted things. Celeste described their relationship as "good" and "safe." Steve kissed her good-bye, then left, and Celeste was searched then escorted to her room, where Tracey waited for her.

"The minute the door closed, Celeste kissed me," says Tracey. "We were both euphoric. Everything had worked out just like we'd planned it. We were together."

In their journals that day, Celeste recorded notes from a class on how suicidal thoughts begin, drawing a diagram that led from stress to anxiety to suicidal ideation. Meanwhile, Tracey attended a class on relapsing addictions and the twelve-step problem so integral to AA. "*Relapse begins when you start thinking about it,*" she wrote.

Still, Tracey spent much of the day dreaming about being alone with Celeste. Her preoccupation caught the eye of a nurse who noted on her chart at nine that evening that Tracey paid an unusual amount of attention to her new roommate. "*Patient is having trouble maintaining her boundaries with her peer,*" the nurse wrote, adding that she'd cautioned Tracey against excessive touching.

Finally alone in their room that night, Celeste took off her shirt and lay on her stomach. On the bed, Tracey stroked and rubbed her bare back. "We'd been kissing," says Tracey. "It was foreplay."

When Tracey noted fine hair on her lower back, Celeste's face took on a pained expression. "That's from the chemo," she said, claiming she'd had ovarian cancer and had taken chemotherapy to treat it. Celeste's pain further endeared her to Tracey.

As they were becoming more intimate, a night nurse walked in and discovered them. She ordered them to stop and told Celeste to get dressed. She then explained that touching a peer was strictly forbidden. That night, the nurse's notes on Celeste's chart said: "*Patient was cautioned about appropriate touching and boundaries. Patient stated that she didn't know that 'massaging wasn't allowed,' and was very apologetic.*"

"We knew if we were caught again they might separate us," says Tracey. "From that point on we were more careful."

"Celeste didn't want to play by the rules," says Samantha, one of the patients. "From the beginning, she ordered people around, and she refused to attend sessions. She told us her husband was paying cash and she didn't have to do anything she didn't want."

For many, Timberlawn was a last resort. With its strong reputation, patients often waited for months to be accepted. Others, those without insurance, saved money to pay for care they hoped could turn their lives around. "It's a place, if you're serious about working, you're going to get the opportunity to take a good look at yourself and make changes," says Samantha. "It's a place where you can get real help."

In group sessions, Tracey peeled back the layers of her pain. At times she cried. "She spoke her mind," says Samantha. "She was out there, in the open."

Celeste, on the other hand, skipped groups whenever possible, and when she did attend, sat off by herself, acting as if she had no need to be there. On the rare occasion when the group leader cajoled her into the discussion, Samantha never saw what she believed to be a window into Celeste's soul. "I never saw any real emotion. It all seemed canned," she says. "I thought she hid behind a mask."

The PTSD program focused on cognitive behavioral therapy, a theory that function could be improved by reason. Desperate patients seeking help came from as far away as New York and California. A major tenet was that as adults such patients often fell into one or a combination of three groups: perpetrators, victims, or caretaker/rescuers. Within days of Celeste's arrival, Tracey's therapist, Susan Milholland, worried that her patient had become her roommate's rescuer.

It was as if Celeste had patched Tracey into the role Kristina filled at home—her entourage and staff. When Celeste wanted something, Tracey ran to the nurses' station to ask. The day a nurse reprimanded Celeste for wearing a tight sweater with a revealing neckline, Tracey sprang to her defense. During her sessions with Milholland, Tracey worried about Celeste, not concentrating on her own therapy. "*Patient defensive in response to encouragement that she focuses on her own issues not peer's, going on and on with repetition about what her roommate needs,*" Milholland wrote in her chart.

In her journal, Tracey pondered the way others perceived her relationship with Celeste. She knew that if the staff discovered they were lovers, they'd be separated. One thing particularly vexed her: A patient blurted out in the meeting room that when she and Celeste teased each other it sounded like "a lover's spat." It didn't help that later that day a nurse walked into the day room and found Celeste stretched out with her bare feet on Tracey's lap. "*Patient was reminded of her boundaries,*" the chart read.

In Celeste's journal, Tracey wrote a note of encouragement, trying to convince her to participate: *"You have a lot of anger you are not in touch with. You are afraid of your anger because you are afraid of the power you will have when you feel less vulnerable and you will have more personal power. Please participate; just TRY."*

That day, both women were given assignments—to write about their abuse.

Tracey wrote about her father. In four handwritten, highly emotional pages, she repeatedly asked why he hadn't stopped her abuse, why he'd turned his back on his own children and left them at the mercy of a madwoman. *"Why didn't he do something to protect me?"* she wrote. *"He probably didn't know about the sexual abuse, but when I would lock myself in my room he would allow her to beat on the door with a baseball bat."*

Celeste's letter was typed on a computer she'd had Steve send. It came to one and a half pages, a rambling and not always truthful account of her life. In it, she charged that Craig had raped her twice, that her marriage with Harald had ended not because of her wanton spending and temper but because she'd had two tubal pregnancies and ovarian cancer. She said she'd been unable to accept Jimmy's love. When it came to Steve, she accused herself of ruining the marriage: *"I freeze, withdraw, and manipulate any situation to avoid conflicts . . . I see my father on top of me. I feel him touching me. I feel him making me touch him. I can't take it anymore. I can't make it stop."*

When Tracey read Celeste's letter, she was deeply touched. Yet, she disagreed with her characterization of her relationship with Steve. If Steve was as Celeste described him, he was at fault. They argued, Tracey contending that around Steve, Celeste made herself powerless. "Well, screw you," Celeste said. "I don't need this at all." For days they didn't talk. When they did, Celeste told Tracey: "Let's just be friends."

Despondent, Tracey agreed. Then, days later, Celeste kissed her on the mouth. "I forgive you," she said.

On Fridays the twins drove the three and a half hours from Austin to Dallas. As soon as they arrived, Celeste put them to work. She ordered them to buy things, to smuggle banned goods onto the unit: razors, a cell phone, even cigarette lighters. More than once the items were later discovered, leading to arguments between the patients. "It was awful," says Jennifer. "Here we were smuggling in razors to a unit where people were suicidal."

One week the girls left Austin late, and Celeste was furious when they arrived. She ordered them to go to a convenience store. She had a cigarette order from the other patients and wanted a carton for each charged to her credit card. For Easter she sent them to Wal-Mart for baskets and candy eggs. They spent that night making fifteen baskets for Celeste to give the other patients. The next day they handed them out in the day room, and the patients with multiple personalities responded by acting like small children.

For all the complaining she did about the clinic, Celeste seemed to be having fun at Timberlawn. Often Kristina longed to be at a place like that, where she could rest. Between school and commuting to Dallas to do their mother's bidding, both the girls were exhausted. The one time Jennifer and Kristina told their mother that they didn't want to run her errands, that they'd spent hours driving to see her and didn't want to be shuttled off, Celeste cursed at them, saying they didn't understand all she'd been through, what it was like to have been abused as a child.

"You don't love me!" she screamed, sending shivers through them both.

After they left, Celeste changed her visitor list. They weren't allowed to return for nearly two weeks.

At home, Justin and Jennifer worried about Kristina, who'd lost twenty pounds and was down to a size two since her mother's hospitalization. "We'd be eating dinner with Steve and everyone would be laughing, then the phone would ring," says Justin. "Kristina would pick it up and it would be Celeste. When she hung up, Kristina was crying."

Kristina was struggling with a confluence of emotions. She worried about her mother, and yet since childhood, she'd had dreams of a life with a different family, one where she'd be happy and not burdened by her mother's constant demands.

Yet, as ever, Kristina was devoted to Celeste. When Steve made disparaging remarks about her, Kristina lashed out at him. They argued, and he blustered at her, perhaps taking out on the daughter all the frustration he felt toward his wife. "You don't know what you're talking about," Kristina said. She stormed out the door. When Kristina called, Celeste told her to stay at Jimmy's house until things cooled down.

For his part, Steve told few people where Celeste was; he said she was visiting friends. During the week, he often flew up for counseling sessions with Celeste and her psychologist, Bernard Gotway, a plump, gray-haired, bespectacled man; and her psychiatrist, Howard Miller, a short, quiet man with dark glasses and penchant for brightly colored suspenders. On weekends Steve arrived on Saturday, as the twins were driving home, and then left again on Sunday nights. Gotway and Miller noted on Celeste's chart that she did well during Steve's visits, as they discussed the problems with their marriage. But after he left, Celeste complained bitterly to Tracey. "She told me Steve smothered her.

Just seeing him made her feel like killing herself," says Tracey. "And there he was, showing up, involved in her therapy. How could she get better?"

When Steve visited, Tracey carefully watched the man whose very existence she'd grown to believe threatened her lover's life. He appeared as Celeste described him, big and boorish. Only once did they exchange words, and it unleashed a storm from Celeste. That day, Celeste argued with an attendant who wouldn't allow her and Steve to go to the lobby together. Steve turned to Tracey and said, "She has a hard time following rules."

Shocked that he'd said something to her, Tracey nodded, replying, "Yes, I'm afraid she does."

Later, Steve told Celeste what Tracey had said. Livid, Celeste tracked Tracey down on the smoking porch and screamed, "Why don't you mind your own fucking business!"

"Fine," Tracey replied, but inside she felt like something was waning. Later that day she wrote in her journal, "*I have lost my infatuation*" and "*MIND YOUR OWN FUCKING BUSINESS!!! Stay out of Celeste's shit.*" Then she scratched it out. The next day Celeste kissed her as if nothing had happened.

The days ground on, some better than others. Both the women were heavily medicated, everything from pills for depression, to anxiety, to ones to help them sleep. Over the weeks, Celeste threatened to sign herself out, and Tracey begged her to stay. Later, Tracey would say that their relationship progressed in surges: "We'd be close one day, and the next we were hardly talking."

While many noticed the unusually close relationship between the two women, it was Celeste's psychiatrist, Dr. Miller, who seemed troubled by it. More than once he brought it up to Tracey, asking her to explain their bond.

In Celeste's journal, during one group session, they wrote each other notes:

TRACEY: *"I told Dr. Miller that I have no sexual interest in you. So, I lied. But you should, too. He said as long as we follow the guidelines for touching (physical contact) & respect the room rules, there shouldn't be any problem. He had no problem with our being close as long as it doesn't interfere with our therapy. He says trauma abuse patients are prone to making impulsive life-altering decisions while in treatment."*

CELESTE: *"Did he bring it up—or did you?"*

TRACEY: *"Me—he asked if there were other issues & I told him I was really pissed off about the report from the night nurses* [about the backrub incident]. *By the way, I absolutely do have a sexual interest in you—He asked if we had a special relationship—he defined that as a relationship with more to it than other random patients—I said yes—He said that is not a problem. They don't discourage this unless it gets in the way therapeutically. We just need to go outpatient."*

Celeste ended by writing: *"Quick!"*

Timberlawn's outpatient program was waiting for them at the end of their inpatient stay, when they'd spend days at the clinic for therapy, then be free to do as they wished in the evenings. Tracey and Celeste already had plans. Steve had rented a room, number 103 at the Sumner Suites, across from the clinic, for $69 a night, for him and the twins to use while in Dallas and for Celeste to stay in when she graduated to the day program. There, Tracey and Celeste could explore their sexual relationship without fear of discovery. "Celeste told me she'd never been with a woman," says Tracey. "She said she didn't like sex with men and couldn't have orgasms. She wanted me to teach her."

At Timberlawn, Celeste and Tracey clutched together often, so much so that therapists noted it on their charts. Their journals were filled with affirmations: *"Believe in Ourselves! I am worthwhile! I am loved! I don't deserve all this self-hate. This self-blame. Helplessness becomes powerlessness. Be willing!"*

Tracey wrote: *"I want love . . . I want to be held . . . I want a safe attachment to someone."*

Yet, for weeks, Tracey made little progress, suicidal thoughts slipping in and out of her consciousness. Milholland pegged the stumbling block as her inability to place the blame for the abuse on her mother, not herself. It wasn't until a session in early April that the therapist felt she was making headway.

"Sometimes I think about going to hell to find my mother," Tracey told her that day. "When I find her, I hand over all the responsibility for what happened to her. I say, 'This was your fault, not mine. I was only a child. You were the adult.'"

"What do you worry about?" the therapist asked.

"I worry that I won't be able to leave, that I'll be stuck in hell forever with my mother," she answered, crying.

By early April, Tracey's insurance money was drying up, and she faced discharge to Timberlawn's day program. Her meds were still giving her problems. At times her speech was slurred and she appeared to be drunk. Yet, Milholland assessed the risk of her committing suicide as having decreased from a ten, on a ten-point scale, to a six. "I'm not free-falling to suicide anymore," she told the therapist. Tracey didn't say why, but much of her new peace centered on her relationship with Celeste, which, at the time, she says, was flourishing. She did, however, tell Milholland that they planned to room together again, off-campus, during the outpatient program.

"What's your relationship like?" the therapist asked.

"Just friends," Tracey answered.

Days later in Celeste's therapy, Dr. Miller questioned the wisdom of such a plan. *"Patient offended at being confronted on friendship with homosexual peer,"* he wrote in her chart. He advised Celeste that rooming with Tracey during outpatient sessions wasn't a good idea. As he saw it, Tracey was too possessive.

Tracey would later say that Celeste told her something very different that night—not that Dr. Miller questioned the wisdom of their plan, but that the clinic staff contacted Steve and made him aware of their friendship. "He doesn't want us to be roommates," she said. "He has money and power. You'll see. He'll get what he wants."

Frightened that she was losing the woman she'd made the linchpin of her recovery, Tracey panicked. The next days, she waited anxiously, hoping Celeste was wrong.

Two days later Miller brought up Celeste's discharge plans again and urged her to break off the friendship with Tracey. *"Counseled against rooming with peers when discharged. Discussed boundaries, caring but saying no,"* he wrote on her chart. It was decided Celeste would break off the entanglement with Tracey, but the clinic would help.

The following morning Tracey was called in for a meeting with Celeste and Melissa Caldwell, the art therapist. During the session, Celeste told her that she didn't want to room with her during outpatient treatment. Tracey was devastated.

That afternoon with Susan Milholland, Tracey bared her heart.

"Where did you see this relationship with Celeste going?" Milholland asked.

"My dream was only to have an affair with her," Tracey said. "Right now, I want to drink a bottle of beer, break the bottle, and kill myself with the glass."

As they talked, Tracey admitted she was reenacting an old pattern, falling in love with a straight married woman. Eventually, Tracey did something to end the relationships, drinking or acting out. "I force them to leave me," she told Milholland.

In her journal the next day, April 7, Tracey wrote:

"Celeste has decided to leave me. She had a meeting with her doctor and has already been moved to her new room. She will not room with me, and she will say only that I am too pushy. She wants to take the relationship one day at a time, but I can see she will not be interested in me. I believe that she is strongly attracted to me, and it has a whole tremendous lot of confusion for her."

In a session with Milholland, Tracey grumbled, "Her husband did this. He has money and influence and he wants me away from Celeste." The therapist disagreed, saying Steve wasn't behind Celeste's change of plans, but Tracey didn't believe her. Then Tracey said something that forced Milholland to take her very seriously: "My problems would all be solved if a certain person met an untimely death."

"Are you referring to Celeste's husband?" Milholland asked.

"I'm not homicidal now. I never have been," Tracey said.

Still, Milholland worried. Despite Tracey laughing it off as a joke, Milholland judged the statement a threat. She argued with Tracey, telling her Steve wasn't involved, but she couldn't shake her conviction. "I believed Celeste, and that's what she'd told me," says Tracey.

Frightened by Tracey's comment, Milholland called a meeting to inform the staff, including Dr. Miller. It was decided that the two women would be separated, and Tracey was immediately transferred out of the PTSD unit and into the adult program, for the chronically mentally ill. There, she felt as if she were back in Menninger, surrounded by shuffling, empty shells. By the next day Tracey had worked the transfer over in her mind, until she saw it as further proof of her lack of self-worth.

In between sessions, Tracey pulled Celeste to the side. "If you just want friendship without any sexual overtones, that's all right with me," she said.

"Sure," Celeste said.

But later Tracey wrote in her journal: "*Was Celeste just saying that because Celeste didn't want to say no?*"

The rest of the day, Tracey interpreted the actions of patients and staff at the clinic as if they were conspiring to keep Celeste from her. She watched Celeste through a glass door that separated the units and saw her with Steve. Tracey thought Celeste appeared sad, and she wondered if she missed her. "*I think it must be about losing me. But if it hurts that bad, why does she want to stay away?*" she wrote.

The next day, Tracey checked out of the inpatient program and into room 213 of the Red Roof Inn, across the street, to attend day sessions. Tormented by Celeste's absence and unable to stabilize her medications, on the pages of her journal she chastised herself for enmeshing herself with Celeste and squandering the time at Timberlawn. She vowed to use the final weeks to straighten out her life, and wrote in her journal: "*Dr. Montgomery wants me to realize that I am carved from the same stone as my mother . . . obviously my mother was very emotional & delusional. How am I delusional? I believe people will always leave me. I have known loneliness and sadness since I was a baby; I know how to live and thrive with these feelings. Turn my recognition into strength.*"

Yet, this time Tracey's expectation of abandonment

wasn't destined to come true. As Celeste had with Craig, Harald, and Jimmy, she had thrown Tracey away. What Tracey didn't know was that as Celeste had with the men in her life, she intended to reel her back in. Days after Tracey's discharge, Celeste, too, left Timberlawn for the day program.

"I was in my motel room when someone knocked," Tracey says. "I opened it, and Celeste was there. She walked inside and kissed me. She apologized and asked me to forgive her. Celeste closed the door, and we sat on the bed together. I asked her if she was sure, and she said she was. Then we consummated the relationship."

Chapter
9

As April passed, Tracey's time at Timberlawn drew to a close. Her insurance was running out and she had to return to Austin. Days before she was scheduled to leave Dallas, she found a new therapist, Barbara Grant, a middle-age, kindly faced woman with graying hair. Milholland seemed pleased with the progress she was making, but Tracey was apprehensive at the prospect of reclaiming her life. Not only was she worried about relapsing, but she feared the repercussions of leaving her new lover. The relationship, as she saw it, was as brittle and volatile as Celeste, whose moods surged and subsided as quickly as a changing breeze. Tracey thought the reason lay with Celeste's unfamiliarity with a gay relationship. "I thought she was conflicted," she says. "But I never felt like I was forcing her to have sex. With the separation looming, she was even more passionate, saying she didn't want me to go."

There was, however, a recurring issue with their sex life. "I could feel Celeste pull back before orgasm," says Tracey. "I worried about that. I wanted her to enjoy it. She said she felt guilty about enjoying any type of sex, because of her abuse." Understanding as only someone who has suffered such abuse as a child can, Tracey held Celeste as she sobbed, crying over what she described as the horrible violation of her childhood.

As sympathetic as she was, however, this was an issue on which Tracey wouldn't bend. "I wasn't interested in a platonic friendship," she says. "If we were lovers, I expected it to include sex." At times, when Celeste rebuffed her advances, Tracey grew angry, threatening to cut off the affair. When she did, Celeste apologized and pledged her love. Losing Tracey would send her into a spiral, Celeste said, since she counted on their relationship to keep her alive. "I loved Celeste," Tracey says. "I didn't want her to die."

As Tracey got ready to leave for Austin, Celeste checked back into the day program. She told her therapist, Bernard Gotway, that she hadn't been able to sleep. When he saw her, Gotway wrote in his notes: "*Patient presents rather superficial and avoidant, saying that the anxiety is manageable. She is irritable and focusing on extraneous issues.*"

"Structure your days at home," Milholland told Tracey that same day. After a phone conference with the owners at BookPeople, Tracey was near panic at the prospect of returning to work. She feared she'd be unable to maintain her tentative hold on calm in the outside world. The voice was quiet and her medications seemed to be working better than they had, but she still suffered tremors and fits of anxiety. Would her meds keep the voice still? Although she hadn't told her counselors, she was drinking again.

"Work, walk your dog," the therapist said. "Don't give yourself free time to panic."

The next day, armed with prescriptions for lithium, Wellbutrin, Neurotin, and other drugs, she said good-bye to Celeste. She was going home to Austin. "We didn't know how much we'd see each other," Tracey says. "We were both worried."

In Austin, Steve tried to keep the twins' home lives stable, watching over them, checking to make sure they did their homework. He looked into colleges, visiting one or two, and resurrected a tradition from the years he raised his first brood: Wednesday hamburger nights. One night a week they were allowed to bring friends home. He grilled burgers with all the fixings, and they spent evenings talking and catching up. It was easy to see he enjoyed the occasions. When his banker, Chuck Fuqua, stopped in for a burger, Steve was in good humor, laughing and telling stories about the years when he was just getting started in business. "He looked like a single dad with a houseful of kids," says Chuck.

In his black leather family date book, Steve faithfully recorded Celeste's arrivals and departures. For much of 1999, she'd been gone, living at St. David's, then Timberlawn, then the Sumner Suites and attending day sessions at Timberlawn. He'd married Celeste for companionship, but she was rarely with him. Instead, he had the twins and their friends filling the house. If the marriage ended, he didn't want to lose them all.

"If your mother and I divorce, will you live with me?" he asked one morning.

"I will," Jennifer said readily.

For Kristina the decision was more difficult. Since childhood, she yearned for a mother's love. So much so that she'd chosen Celeste over their father. Now, with Craig dead, that decision haunted her. Yet, she couldn't free herself from Celeste's grasp. "You're the one I love," her mother had told her. "Jennifer doesn't love me the way you do, Kristina. We're more than mother and daughter."

In her heart, Kristina believed that; in fact, she wanted it to be true. Yet such faith came at a terrible cost. Celeste forced her to lie and cover up for her, to not acknowledge the pain she caused. Kristina loved Steve, and now, as Celeste had with all her other husbands, she was being unfaithful. And Kristina said nothing.

When it came to money, Kristina understood only too well that Celeste was ruthless. Despite having access to all the money she could need, Celeste pocketed the little Kristina made working at her part-time job as a mail girl. "Lend me a little," she said. Kristina did, but her mother never repaid her. The only way Kristina kept any money was to open a bank account and have it automatically deposited. The teenager even went so far as to find a bank that put her picture on her ATM card so Celeste couldn't use it.

No one doubted the damage the conflict inside Kristina was doing to her. Jennifer and Justin worried about her, as she lost so much weight her collarbones protruded. With each visit to Timberlawn, Kristina came away more disillusioned. For a mother who said she loved her more than anyone else in the world, Celeste treated her like a servant.

Jennifer and Steve were both waiting for her to answer Steve. If he divorced Celeste, would Kristina stay with him or choose her mother, as she always had in the past?

It was then that Kristina realized Steve had given her the one thing she'd always wanted and never had: a stable home with a loving parent.

"I'll stay with you, too," Kristina told him, marshaling every particle of courage inside her. Then she and Jen hugged the man who'd truly become their father.

Life was less tranquil that week at Timberlawn. While they'd let her transgressions slide in the past, a nurse discovered Celeste had a cigarette lighter, and in a facility with suicidal patients, it couldn't be ignored. Instead of apologizing, Celeste cursed the nurse and fumed at being caught. She threatened to leave the program and go home to Austin, but returned to the day program. From then on she flitted back and forth between the resident and day programs. It seemed Celeste had no desire to return to Austin and Steve. The arrangement, in fact, suited her well.

During the day, she attended sessions at the clinic, taking voluminous notes like a high school student studying for a test: "*Beliefs create expectations. Feeling better does not equal getting better. Consciousness is the only game in town. If I can learn from my mistakes, it is more probable that the future can change.*" And at night she did as she pleased. She had her suite at the hotel, her freedom, and her credit cards. She even had the cream-colored Cadillac with gold trim Steve had bought her. It had every amenity, from leather seats to an OnStar navigation system. When it was dusty, she asked another of the day patients to take it to the car wash for her. When they returned, she handed them a tip, a crisp $100 bill.

Although Timberlawn's patients often remained only weeks in outpatient care, Celeste arranged to continue for months, rotating in and out of the hospital, with one crisis after another. With Steve paying the bills, there was no worry that insurance would be cut off. In her chart, a therapist noted that Celeste would be staying on for an unspecified period "to work on the hard issues."

Just days after she left Dallas, Tracey returned to BookPeople. At the store, she bought Celeste a note card with a jumping dog. "*You are so beautiful,*" she wrote. "*I think about your long, silky body and your incredible long legs and I just can't stand it. And then I think of your incredible face and I want to get in my car and drive to Dallas . . . please take care of yourself, do your work, and get better. I love you, T.*"

Despite Tracey's fears, it would turn out that their separations were short.

In the leather family date book, Steve wrote "Celeste Home" on Saturdays. He didn't know she actually left Dallas on Fridays. When Celeste flew into Austin, Tracey picked her up at the airport and brought her to her house for the night. The following morning, Kristina came for her, telling Steve she'd picked her up at the airport. One morning, when no one at Tracey's answered, Kristina used a key she'd been given to watch over the cats while Tracey was at Timberlawn. She'd often asked her mother where she slept at Tracey's—since only one bedroom had a bed—and Celeste always answered on the couch. But that day Kristina found the two women in bed and under the covers together; her mother, who always wore pink pajamas at home, had bare shoulders and her head on Tracey's shoulder.

After a lifetime of looking the other way, Kristina found it a hard habit to break. "I tried not to think about it," she says. Her mother had told her that Tracey was in love with her. "She's a bull dyke," Celeste said, laughing like it was the most hilarious of jokes.

Saturdays in Austin, Celeste ran between appointments, having her nails and hair done and shopping. Evenings, she had dinner and cocktails with Steve. After he passed out, she left, driving herself or having the teens drop her at Jimmy's or Tracey's.

On Sundays she flew back to Dallas for another week of sessions at Timberlawn.

In many ways Celeste's life was increasingly complicated. Where in the past she'd only had Steve and Jimmy to juggle, Tracey was now added to the mix. To keep track, Celeste kept a purse-size date book far from Steve's eyes. On the calendar pages, she scribbled her plans, the ones that didn't include him. She also recorded appointments she made for Tracey: *"Tracey haircut 4:00, Tracey dermatologist 1:15."*

At Tramps, Denise, Celeste's hairdresser, put highlights in Tracey's hair, and Terry Meyer, her manicurist, preened her nails. Tracey's staff noticed the change. Their bohemian leader started showing up with manicured nails, carrying a purse, and in freshly pressed Ralph Lauren shirts. More than one noted that they were pink, not knowing that since childhood that had been Celeste's signature color.

Her gay friends, too, started talking about the changes in Tracey when she and Celeste attended a beer garden fundraiser for Project Transitions, an AIDS hospice. Decked out in a Dale Evans cowgirl outfit with a flared skirt, Celeste had bought Tracey a matching cowboy shirt with pearl snaps, something Tracey would have ridiculed in the past. Throughout the evening, she fawned over Celeste, lighting her cigarettes and running to get her drinks. "It was like Tracey was putty and Celeste was rebuilding her," says Pat Brooks. "She didn't even look like Tracey anymore."

As usual, Celeste entertained the table. Wielding an imaginary spatula in one hand and a glass of vodka in the other, she blew out her cheeks to look fat and mimicked Steve flipping burgers. The entire time, she tittered with delight at her own cleverness.

On the weekends, however, when Celeste sat in Denise's chair, it wasn't Steve she ridiculed, but Tracey. "That dyke's in love with me," she told Denise, laughing. "I told her, I don't eat at the Y."

As summer descended on Austin, bringing with it blinding sunshine and intense heat, the twins and their friends wondered about Celeste's new relationship. Christopher, Amy, Justin, and Jennifer had all seen the signs, the way the two women looked at each other, the way they touched. "It didn't look platonic," says Amy.

The two boys, in particular, worried. They both had sinking feelings watching Celeste that summer. She seemed to be running too hot, as if she were headed toward a fall. "Save your money and I'll pay for things," Christopher told Jennifer. "You never know with Celeste when you'll need it." After all she'd been through with her mother, Jennifer didn't doubt that he was right. For months she'd worked part-time at Anita's investment firm. From that point on she deposited every dollar she made in a secret bank account.

Of them all, it was Kristina who couldn't bring herself to address Celeste's relationship with Tracey. In a sense, she told herself, it just didn't matter. From the beginning she'd liked Tracey more than Jimmy or many of the other men Celeste had paraded in and out of their lives. It seemed to her that Celeste's other friends only cared for her because she showered them with expensive gifts. Tracey, on the other hand, didn't appear to want anything material from Celeste. "She just seemed like a sad but a good person," says Kristina.

So, one night when Celeste called from Timberlawn saying Tracey had a gun and was threatening suicide, Kristina didn't hesitate to drive to Tracey's house in the family Expedition to stop her. When she arrived, Tracey sat at the kitchen table with two pistols beside her.

"I'm depressed," she told Kristina. "I'd really just like to end it and die."

They talked until Tracey went outside to smoke a cigarette. Judging that was her opportunity, Kristina picked up the guns. When Tracey returned, Kristina said good-bye, and quickly left. Before driving home, she found a squad car with two officers along the side of a road. Keeping her hands on the steering wheel, she said, "I have two guns on the floor that I took away from a woman who was threatening suicide."

They confiscated the guns, and Kristina went home to bed.

The first weekend in May was the girls' senior prom. That evening, Celeste and Steve stood together on the driveway in front of the house to wave as the girls left with their dates. To the world, they looked like proud parents watching their daughters depart on one of the most memorable events of their young lives. But as soon as Steve passed out, Celeste left, this time to Jimmy's. The next morning, when the girls picked her up, she bragged about the sex. "Jimmy had me up all night," she said. When Steve asked where she'd been, she told him she'd spent the night with the twins at the lake house.

The weeks were so busy she had little time for Steve. The following Friday she and Tracey met Pat and Jane at the City Grill to celebrate Tracey's birthday. Celeste brought a present, a beautiful stainless steel watch, and a card. The standard Hallmark variety, the greeting card bore a flowered heart and the words: "*A Birthday Message for the One I Love.*" The inside verse read: "*For bringing love to my world . . . And happiness to my heart . . . For making every day seem like a special dream come true . . . I hope your birthday and the year to come is filled with everything wonderful. Happy Birthday.*"

She signed it: "*Love, Celeste.*"

Celeste gave Pat, who was celebrating her own birthday, a hundred-dollar gift certificate to an upscale hardware store. That night, Celeste and Tracey were animated, talking about their plans to attend Tracey's niece's wedding in Atlanta.

"I told her she doesn't have to come," Tracey said. "These family things aren't fun."

"I want to be there," Celeste insisted.

That she spent so little time with Steve must have gnawed at him. The next night, he was in a foul mood. When he woke up about 10:00 P.M., the twins were out and, for once, Celeste was home asleep. Nearly every light in the house was on. It was a minor thing, but he was a careful man who had a routine, walking through the house at bedtime to turn off lights and arm the security system. To him, it must have seemed an insult.

Angry and hurt, he shouted at Celeste, challenging her to go back to Dallas. As he saw it, she didn't intend to spend any time with him. Enraged, Celeste left and drove back a day early. The following morning he called her at the Sumner Suites, saying that if she wanted a divorce she could have one. He was through with the marriage. That day, she wrote him a letter, blaming him for the incident. Although she spiked his cocktails, she wrote, "*I think your drinking is out of control.*" Then she begged him: "*Steve, I love you with all of my heart. If you truly want a divorce, then please tell me on Thursday when we meet with Dr. Gotway. I will have shown him a copy of this letter, so that he is apprised as to our current status. Please don't have me served while I am in the hospital. Tell me face to face on Thursday. I think I at least deserve that much. Love, Celeste.*"

It was a tactic that had worked well in the past. When Harald refused to marry her, she'd taken him to a counselor who had urged him to trust her. The following day, Steve called Gotway, maintaining he didn't really want a divorce but that Celeste avoided him. Gotway suggested Steve calm down and think about his actions, that perhaps it wasn't the time to make such a drastic decision.

In Austin, Celeste dominated Tracey's thoughts. Whether at work or at home with her dog, Wren, she couldn't get her out of her mind. Days after Steve talked with Gotway, Tracey mailed Celeste a card. On the front were two women and a dog. Inside she wrote: "I *woke up missing you with a fever better reserved for the dying. I woke up missing you and nothing I could do would shake it. Feeling like that, I would lie down and die just to smell your skin . . . I love you. T.*"

At BookPeople, Tracey combed the shelves and mailed Celeste books on sex, especially those that discussed putting past abuse behind to enjoy a healthy sex life. In a card, she expressed her discontent with the way Celeste pulled back before orgasm: "*I want to be part of your healing as we, together, explore ways to make you comfortable being intimate with me. I love you, T.*"

Steve, too, must have wondered about Celeste's sexuality, but for different reasons. One afternoon, on a weekend when she was home, he came right out and asked her something that must have been percolating within him for months, perhaps because he'd heard her talk so much of Tracey.

"Celeste, are you a lesbian?" he asked.

"I can't believe you asked me that," she shrieked. Then she got in the car and left, driving back to Timberlawn, where she didn't have to answer to him.

The following weekend, on Friday, May 21, Tracey flew into Atlanta and attended her niece's rehearsal dinner. Celeste joined her the next day. In the wedding photos, Celeste looked prim and proper in a light blue suit with matching buttons. Her blond hair was swept up, bangs brushed her forehead, and tendrils hung down her cheeks. She wore a blue sapphire pendant, and her diamond ring glistened on her hand.

Weeks before, Celeste had taken Tracey to the St. Thomas shop at Austin's posh Arboretum to choose the black suit she wore that day. An Armani, it cost $1,200, well above

Tracey's budget on her $55,000 salary. "It was an expense the old Tracey wouldn't even have considered," says Pat. "But with Celeste, there were no boundaries."

The wedding went well, and at the reception Tracey felt her family was accepting Celeste as her new girlfriend. But that night, when they went to the hotel bar, they hooked up with a group from the wedding and before long Celeste became the life of the party. She bragged about her rich husband, telling the women that her blue suit cost $2,200, then matched the men drink for drink, until she was visibly drunk. With the men in the bar egging her on, she opened her blouse and flashed her breasts. Embarrassed, Tracey urged Celeste to follow her upstairs to their hotel room. "Don't worry about these people," Tracey whispered to Celeste. "It doesn't matter."

At BookPeople, Tracey's staff had come to recognize Celeste, coming and going from the store. When she was in Austin on the weekends, she dropped by often, stopping on the fourth floor, where she'd walk into Tracey's office and close the door. Often, Celeste called. If someone were with her, Tracey waved them off and closed the door behind them. None doubted that the two women were lovers.

Twice a year Tracey threw a party for her managers. In the past it had always been at her house on Wilson, a casual affair consisting of deli trays and a keg of beer. The talk was about books and concerts, and the mood relaxed. In July, Tracey told Celeste she planned to throw a summer party, and Celeste had an idea.

"Let's do it at the lake house, and I'll do it for you," she said.

Tracey wasn't sure; a full thirty-five miles from Austin, without speeding, it took nearly an hour down winding roads

SHE WANTED IT ALL • 177

to get there, and after dark the turns were easy to miss. But Celeste insisted, and Tracey gave in.

Invitations went out announcing: *"Tracey's 'Fashion-Victim Party,' Come dressed in your fashion don't and spend the evening laughing and cavorting with your coworkers. Friday, July 9, 1999, at the Beard Retreat, 101 Bedford Drive, Spicewood, TX."* It was an odd fit for a group that cared more about literature than fashion, but Tracey didn't question Celeste's concept. Spending thousands, Celeste hired a caterer, a bartender, and even a photographer. Guests arrived early that evening, and the first found Celeste and Tracey dressing. Another walked in a bedroom and discovered the two women kissing. Without saying a word, she backed out of the room.

Music blared and the hot tub churned as the bartender served drinks and waiters passed trays of hors d'oeuvres. Earlier in the week Celeste had asked Tracey to arrange for one of the women to bring marijuana brownies, even giving her money to pay for the marijuana. When they arrived, she took the plate and placed it on the table with the other food. Fueled by the pot, Celeste was in a grandiose mood. That night, Cindy Light, the same photographer who'd shot pictures at Steve and Celeste's open house on Toro Canyon, snapped photos of Celeste on Tracey's lap, a vodka in one hand and a brownie in the other, along with pictures of the two women dancing, nuzzling, and kissing.

About eleven, Tracey and Celeste walked into the master bedroom and locked the door. As their guests partied outside, Celeste whispered, "After Steve's dead, we can live here together and wake up together each morning."

It was something Tracey dreamed of: to live freely with the woman she loved.

The crowd had already cleared out the following morning

when Kristina and Justin arrived to clean up, as Celeste had ordered. The tables were covered with half-full glasses and overflowing ashtrays. The bedroom door was locked and the house quiet. Wanting to wake Celeste, they opened and closed doors, but heard no one stir, so they left and drove to a convenience store to buy breakfast burritos they ate next to the lake. When they returned, the bedroom door was unlocked. Appearing to be naked under the covers, Tracey and Celeste lay together in bed, their heads touching. Silently, the teens left the room.

Minutes later Celeste and Tracey emerged, Celeste laughing about the party. "I can't believe I ate all those pot brownies," she said.

There'd been other indications that summer that the relationship between the two women wasn't platonic, but Kristina hadn't wanted to address them. Even the sight of them in bed which she'd seen before, was something she refused to consider. But the night they went to a movie together, she was once again confronted with it.

That evening, she and Justin went with Tracey and Celeste to see *The Love Letter*, directed by the actress Kate Capshaw. The plot centered on a found love letter. The teens grew bored and left. Later, Celeste and Tracey emerged laughing.

"How was the movie?" Kristina asked.

"The plot was, 'Oh relax, your mother's a lesbian,'" Celeste said, and laughed.

"Is that a hint?" Kristina asked Justin when they were alone. For months he'd been prodding her, but she hadn't wanted to confront what was obvious: that Celeste and Tracey were lovers.

"It could be," he said.

Not for the first time, Kristina was ambivient about it. She liked Tracey, after all. More than once when Celeste screamed for reasons that included not liking the way she and Jennifer looked at her, Tracey defended them. It cost dearly, as Celeste then turned her wrath on Tracey instead of the girls, but she never backed down. Tracey had grown to respect Kristina, too. She saw her as an old soul, a girl who was more woman than her mother. She also found the relationship between the mother and daughter intriguing. Wherever Celeste went, whether the beauty parlor or her appointments with her therapist, Kristina nearly always checked on her, just to make sure she was all right.

"It was like there was an unsevered umbilical cord," says Tracey.

In many ways, Tracey made Kristina's life easier. She was someone Celeste trusted and counted on, filling the space Kristina had always occupied—as her mother's keeper. With Celeste busy, for the first time the girls did the things normal teenagers take for granted. "Everyone goes to movies, but to us it was a big deal," says Jennifer. "Mom never gave us the time off to do that before."

Tracey was also someone who took the responsibility for Celeste's survival off Kristina. By that summer, although she'd kept her hotel room, Celeste was in Dallas infrequently. At times, when she was home, she'd languish in bed all day, saying she was depressed. When Kristina couldn't get her up and dressed, she called Tracey. Twice while Steve was away from the house, Tracey went to Toro Canyon to coax Celeste from bed. "I can't stand living with him. Death would be a relief," Celeste told her.

Whenever Celeste talked of suicide, Tracey's chest clamped up, like someone had a stranglehold on her heart.

As July drew to a close, Steve must have felt the end of his days as a single dad were finally in sight. After three months, Celeste was checking out of Timberlawn and coming home.

Through it all, she'd maintained that she loved him and wanted to be with him. On Father's Day she even gave him a beautiful sapphire ring. Maybe he believed she truly loved him, for that summer he told a friend, "All we need is time together to reconnect."

The Friday she took the twins and Amy to Dallas to help her move out of the Sumner Suites, however, she had no intention of leaving without one last fling. Telling Steve they were spending the weekend at Six Flags, an amusement park with acres of roller coasters and rides, she didn't mention that Justin and Christopher were going along, or that she'd invited Jimmy Martinez and his two nieces.

The ride there was a wild one; Celeste sped along the highway in the Expedition while Jimmy and his nieces followed. She was in one of her wild, talkative moods, entertaining the teens with stories, then rattling off her ex-husbands' social security numbers, like the answers to unasked Trivial Pursuit questions. She even dropped an enticing tidbit none of them had heard before: She said she'd had a secret husband—one she had never even told the twins about. "We were married just a couple of weeks and then had it annulled," Celeste said. The teens were intrigued, yet it was something else Celeste said that day that later resonated for Amy.

"You know, when Steve dies, I'll play the part. I'll cry and mourn," she said, laughing as if the thought of his death filled her with delight. "I'm such a good actress that no one will ever suspect that I never loved him."

Not long after they returned home to Austin, Celeste called Tracey and asked her to do something for her. "Buy some Everclear," she said. "Kristina's bringing Steve's vodka bottles over. Pour out half the vodka and fill them up."

At the time, Tracey thought little about it. After all, Celeste had been spiking Steve's drinks for years, and she wasn't the one handing him the cocktails. Later, that day would seem more significant. She'd recognize it as the first time Celeste enlisted her aid in her quest to hasten Steve to his grave.

Chapter
10

For nearly six months Steve had put his own life on hold to care for Celeste and the girls. Perhaps he thought the doctors at Timberlawn would make them a whole, healthy family. Now that she was home and on medication for her depression, he tried to return their lives to some version of normalcy. Perhaps, despite his five years with her, he didn't realize that with Celeste there was no such thing as "normal."

Through all the upheaval of the spring, the shopping center had thrived and the second phase, Davenport II, was under construction. The tenants included Tramex Travel, a small agency with branches across Austin. There, one afternoon, Steve approached Stacy Sadler, a young travel agent with strawberry blond hair, to plan a trip. Not just any trip, he said, but the best they had to offer. Stacy had booked two other trips for Steve that year—one to the Florida Keys and another to Cuba—both of which had to be cancelled because of Celeste's hospitalization. Although the relationship started out rocky, Steve pushing Stacy at every turn, she'd gradually realized he enjoyed teasing her, and she'd grown fond of him. "I found myself hoping that this time things worked out for him," she says. "He said this would be his trip of a lifetime."

From her files, Stacy retrieved a stack of brochures on the Rolls Royce of touring companies, Abercrombie and Kent. The possible destinations ranged from Antarctica to the Galapagos to Thailand. Steve didn't have anything so exotic in mind. He'd already decided the trip would be romantic and luxurious.

Days later, after poring over the possible destinations, Steve and Stacy designed a customized grand tour of Europe. He and Celeste would spend October traveling the Continent, to Berlin, Dresden, Munich, Lucerne, Bern, Dijon, Paris, London, York, Scotland, Stratford on Avon, and Dublin. They'd journey in private limousines with chauffeurs, eat at the best restaurants, and stay in only the finest hotels. Such extravagance carried a $53,000 price tag. To Steve, the trip may have had a special import. "It'll be an opportunity for us to get to know each other again," he told a friend. Left unsaid was that if they couldn't, he might finally admit the marriage was a mistake.

"You'll want the insurance, Mr. Beard," Stacy advised. "If you can't go, you won't want to be out so much money."

Steve thought about it for just a moment, then said, firmly, "No. I'm going. No matter what, I'm going. This time we won't be cancelling."

Celeste may have known what was riding on the trip. When he came home with the itinerary and brochures, instead of excitement she expressed dread. "I can't spend an entire month with him," she told the twins. "This will be torture."

From that point on, her aversion to Steve grew. She wanted him out of her life. But how could that happen and not cost her his fortune?

"If that old bastard died, he'd be out of the way," she told Tracey. "Then we could be together, forever."

Justin often arrived at the Toro Canyon house that summer to find Celeste giggling and watching *Serial Mom,* in which Kathleen Turner played a suburban housewife who kills a neighbor for not separating her recyclables. It happened so often, he bought her the DVD. At night, after Steve passed out, she told the teens to drop her at Tracey's, where the two women drank, talked, and made love. Yet, it was far from a carefree relationship. At times Celeste flared up, screaming at Tracey with little or no provocation. Stunned, Tracey fought memories of her mother's verbal barrages.

In bed on those nights, Celeste lay stiff and unresponsive. Unable to sleep, Tracey wondered why she wanted such an unsatisfying relationship with a married woman who had to sneak out to see her. Too often, with Celeste busy with Steve and the twins, she was alone and lonely. But there was that other side of Celeste, the charming and giving side. Celeste constantly surprised her, showing up at unexpected moments, bringing small gifts, and telling her that she loved her. Mornings after their arguments, she awoke to find Celeste curled against her, warm and loving.

When Tracey considered ending the affair, she worried that Celeste would have no one to talk her through the dangerous times. One day, for instance, Celeste drove down the road with the twins in the car, on their way home from the lake house. She screamed—why, they didn't know—and drove across lanes and onto the shoulder. Furious, she called Tracey. "Do you have a gun?" she shouted. "I'm coming over, and we're going to kill ourselves."

At the Toro Canyon house she told Steve, "I don't have to take shit from these girls. I'm going to kill myself." She left, and Steve paced the house, waiting for her to return.

At her house on Wilson, Tracey poured her lover a vodka from the bottle of Stoli she kept for her on a shelf and listened to her rave. When Celeste returned home the next morning, she acted as if nothing had happened.

Despite the turmoil she'd brought to her life, like Steve, Tracey thought Celeste was worth the effort, and she was willing to work to try to make the relationship better. When she told Celeste she wanted the two of them to go for counseling to work through their problems, Celeste agreed. Within days Tracey had a couple's session scheduled for July 21 with Barbara Grant, the therapist she'd gone to when she first left Timberlawn.

"I don't think I'm really a lesbian," Celeste told Grant that day. "I have to drink to have sex with Tracey."

In the therapist's office, Tracey listened. For months she'd been sexually involved with Celeste, and now her lover questioned whether she was attracted to her. Instead of anger, Tracey just smiled. She'd been in relationships with straight women before. "Was Celeste a lesbian? I don't know," she says. "What I knew was that she was sleeping with me."

Tracey explained that she worried about their relationship. "Neither of us have good track records. Both of us have been through lots of partners," she told the therapist. "We've got a lot invested emotionally. And I think we both want this to work."

Complicating matters, Celeste had plans to be gone much of the summer and fall, first on a driving trip to the Northwest with Steve, the twins and their boyfriends, then to Australia with the girls as a graduation trip, and in October, the month in Europe. "Celeste said when she got back, things would change," says Tracey. "Celeste was always promising things would get better, and I always believed her."

* * *

The trip to Washington State had a special purpose for Celeste: to comb through a storage shed in Stanwood that held Craig's possessions, where the girls hoped to retrieve mementoes from their father. Steve had outlined a route from Austin, through Salt Lake into California, up to Oregon and into Washington. Then, after completing their task, they'd loop up to British Colombia and backtrack through Phoenix to Texas and home. At first they planned to drive in two cars, the teens in the Expedition and Celeste and Steve in his Cadillac. That was something Celeste didn't want.

"I can't be alone with him," she told Kristina. "This isn't going to happen."

Somehow she convinced Steve to trade in the Expedition for a white Suburban equipped with a television and VCR. He had it parked in front of the house when his neighbor, Dr. Dennison, sauntered over to take a look. "It's got all the bells and whistles," Steve said proudly. "One hell of a machine."

They left early the morning after Celeste and Tracey's counseling session. Steve, Celeste, Jennifer, Christopher, Justin, and Kristina were in the brand new truck with their luggage in a rooftop carrier. On the road, Celeste moaned that Steve drove too slowly. "Speed it up," she said. "We'll never get there."

The trip turned into an arduous one for the teens, as Celeste, keyed up in the second row of seats, glared at Steve for driving the speed limit. As the road climbed into higher altitudes, Christopher drove and Steve sat beside him in a second captain's chair, his oxygen machine on to prevent altitude sickness. When he fell asleep, Celeste turned it off and lit a cigarette. When he asked for his medicine pack with his asthma medications, she threw them out the window and handed him sleeping pills instead.

"We didn't like it," says Justin. "But we didn't say anything. None of us did."

One morning in Ogden, Utah, Celeste ordered Kristina to smash up sleeping pills for her to slip into Steve's food. Kristina refused, but Celeste kept after her. "Just do it!" she screamed. Finally, Kristina did as she was told, sobbing as she ground them down to a powder. At the breakfast table, while Steve went to the rest room, Celeste poured some of the white powder into his orange juice.

When he sat down and took a sip, he grimaced. "This tastes funny," he said, looking for a waitress. "I'm going to send it back."

"Don't be wasteful. Drink it," Celeste cajoled him.

Steve looked at her and drank it down. "Happy now?" he asked.

"Yes, thank you," she said.

Minutes after they got in the car, he fell asleep. At lunch at a Red Lobster, she mixed more of the powder into his cottage cheese. This time Steve passed out at the table, and Justin and Christopher had to help him to the car. Barely coherent, he urinated on himself. When Celeste saw the yellow stain on his pants, she ridiculed him.

Later, they'd remember the trip in the snapshots Justin took, especially one of Steve taken along the side of a road, leaning against a railing. He'd just woken up from a drugged sleep. "We had dinner at a Sizzler, and Celeste gave him more pills," says Justin. "He passed out again."

By the time they reached Seattle, Steve was convinced there was something wrong. He called his personal physician, Dr. Handley, who blamed it on altitude sickness. "You have to get to a lower altitude," he said. "You're not getting enough oxygen."

At the airport, as Steve waited for a plane to Phoenix, he

handed Celeste a wad of cash and a Shell credit card for gas. She'd left Austin without her credit cards or driver's license. She tucked it in her purse, kissed him good-bye, and, when they walked out into the parking lot, shouted with exhilaration. "He's gone," she screamed. "The fat old fuck is gone. Now we can make some time."

Inside the Suburban, she tore the paper dealer's license plate off the back window and dropped it on the floor. "If we get stopped, tell the cops it fell off," she told the kids. Then she sat in the driver's seat, stepped on the gas, and they were off, speeding along the mountain roads, with the teens laughing nervously and looking over the edge to see the steep drop to the valleys below.

In Stanwood, north of Seattle, they drove to the storage shed. Although retrieving Craig's possessions was the reason for the trip, once there, Celeste was eager to leave. The girls had looked through their father's things for only minutes when she shouted, "Let's go." Each grabbed small mementoes, and then they were back on the road, headed toward the ferry to Victoria, Canada. On the way they stopped at Craig's old workshop at Twin City Foods. "Here, there's a bunch of junk in there, old tools," Celeste told one of his old friends, throwing him the keys. "You can have them."

Kristina and Jennifer wanted to shout at her, telling her that wasn't junk but all they had left of their father. Instead they said nothing.

On the way to Canada, Celeste pulled into an outlet mall. The wad of bills Steve gave her in Seattle waited to be spent, and she intended to do just that. In a Coach Leather shop, she bought shopping bags full of purses, spending nearly everything she had. Once they were hers, she threw them into the back of the Suburban, as if they meant nothing. At home she had hundreds more stacked in boxes, many with the tags still on. From that point on they ate only what they could charge on the Shell credit card, junk food, sodas, hot dogs, and doughnuts. Although Justin and Christopher had money with them, Celeste wouldn't allow them to spend it. Only one night, when they were all so hungry for real food that they were willing to argue with her, did she let them pay for a restaurant dinner. "It was just crazy," says Justin. "You couldn't talk to her. If you disagreed with her, she screamed, and Kristina would get so upset, it just wasn't worth it."

Three to four times a day they heard her talk to Tracey on her cell phone. Once she told the girls, "You're in trouble," then put Tracey on the telephone. Celeste had said they were disrespectful, and Tracey ordered them to "mind your mother." Another time she called her hairdresser friend, Denise, laughing about how she'd drugged Steve. "He was driving me crazy," she said. "He drove like an old man."

While Christopher drove, Celeste sat beside him, talking. "I don't expect Steve to live much longer, not with his age, weight, and health problems," she said. "Then the money will be mine. I can travel, buy whatever I want."

When they picked Steve up in Phoenix, Celeste was all smiles and asking how he was. He felt better, he said, and they loaded his suitcases into the Suburban and took off. Back in Austin, Celeste went to see Tracey at BookPeople. That night they slept together, and Tracey told Celeste about what had happened while she was gone. Drinking home alone, she'd grown depressed. She called her psychiatrist, who called in a suicide attempt on 911. By the time EMS arrived, her breathing was shallow. They released her the following day, after a night at the hospital. Tracey denied she'd tried to take her life, saying it was just a bad mix of her meds with alcohol. With her trip to Australia for the girls' graduation looming in just two days, the next day at her appointment with her therapist, Celeste was upset.

"I hope Tracey doesn't kill herself and interrupt my trip," she complained.

Earlier that summer Celeste had asked Tracey to order a book through BookPeople: *The Poisoner's Handbook*. It arrived while she was on the trip west, and when Tracey gave it to her, Celeste handed it back. Inside was a recipe for botulism, a dangerous nerve toxin produced by a bacterium found in soil, *Clostridium botulinum*. "I want you to make it for me while I'm gone," Celeste told her. "I'm going to feed it to Steve."

Tracey protested, refusing, but Celeste argued that she didn't expect her to feed it to him, just to grow the botulism while she was in Australia. "You're not going to even be there," she said. First Tracey had agreed to spike Steve's vodka; now it seemed a small step to grow a dangerous poison.

On August 4 the twins and Celeste left on their seventeen-day trip to Australia. Steve gave Celeste another wad of cash, and, just as she had on the trip west, she quickly spent it all, this time on a bagful of opals. From that point on she had no money for food or side trips, and the girls subsisted on the meals included in the tour package, sometimes only one a day. "It didn't matter to Celeste. She hardly left the room," says Jennifer. "She was talking to Tracey all the time on her cell phone."

What they were talking about, Tracey would later say, was the botulism. Tracey made it in an airtight jar, mixing corn, raw hamburger, and dirt. She then flooded the jar with water, sealed it, and left it in the Texas sun to bake. Just before Celeste returned home, Tracey put it to the test by feeding the putrid mix to three mice she bought at a pet store. That day Celeste called nearly nonstop.

"Are they dead yet?" she asked.

"No," Tracey answered. "It's not working."

When Celeste returned she took the jar home anyway, telling Tracey later that she fed the contents to Steve mixed into chili dogs. "The fat fuck didn't even notice. Didn't even upset his stomach," she said, laughing and looking miffed at the same time. Celeste brushed the botulism's failure off as a joke, yet Tracey understood Celeste's message when she said, "I can't go to Europe with him. I'd rather die."

Perhaps Steve wanted to meet the woman his wife spent so much time with, the one she'd called so incessantly from Australia that she'd racked up a $2,000 phone bill. The Wednesday after she returned, Celeste invited Tracey to the Toro Canyon house for hamburger night. Tracey didn't want to go. She remembered Timberlawn when she'd been transferred off Celeste's unit. At the time, Celeste told her it was because of Steve's interference, that he didn't want Tracey near her.

"Oh, that," Celeste said. "He's an old man. He won't remember that."

At the Toro Canyon house that night, Steve welcomed Tracey, shaking her hand warmly. When Celeste was out of the room, he said, "I want to thank you for being such a good friend to Celeste."

While the teens ate burgers in the kitchen, Steve, Celeste, and Tracey drank and talked outside. By ten that night none of the three had eaten and all showed the effects of the alcohol. When Steve went inside, Tracey and Celeste sat on the porch swing together, and, in front of Kristina, Tracey leaned over and kissed Celeste on the lips. Embarrassed, Kristina walked inside.

"I can't believe Tracey kissed mom," she told Steve.

With that, Steve walked outside. "I think it's time your guest went home," he told Celeste. "It's late."

When Tracey didn't move, he said it again, "You should leave now."

Jennifer and Christopher offered to drive her, judging she was in no condition to drive. As they stood at the door, they heard Steve ask once again, "Celeste, are you a lesbian?"

"Of course not," she shouted, then rushed out the door. While Christopher put Tracey in her car, Kristina and Jennifer got in the Cadillac to follow and drive him home.

"I want to ride in the trunk," Celeste said, motioning for them to open it. "I don't want Tracey to see me. She'll want me to come inside."

In her car, Tracey was in a talkative mood. "Celeste and I are in love," she told Christopher, who didn't know what to say.

At the house on Wilson, Christopher and Jennifer went inside, while Kristina opened the trunk to let Celeste out. She was choking and gasping.

"I couldn't breathe," she complained.

Inside the house, Tracey stumbled, appearing unaware anyone was with her. While the teens tried to steady her, she peeled off her clothes until she stood naked in the living room. Stifling giggles, they led her to the bedroom and helped her into bed. When they told Celeste what happened, she roared with laughter.

Later, Christopher told Jen what Tracey had said in the car, that she and Celeste were a couple. "Oh, my God. I had a feeling," she responded.

Despite the hamburger night clash, Steve wasn't angry at Tracey, at least not enough to keep him from extending a second invitation. The twins had worked hard to earn hours

in summer school, and the following Friday night was their
graduation. Steve had a celebration planned, including dinner at the Austin Country Club.

At the Tony Berger Center, the city's south side sports
complex, Kristina and Jennifer wore their blue Westlake
High School graduation robes. In the stands, Steve, Celeste,
Amy, Justin, Tracey, and Christopher sat together, cheering
as the girls walked across the stage. Another visitor sat separated from the family: Jimmy. He saw Steve seated next to
Celeste, happily unaware that he sat next to one of his wife's
lovers and across the auditorium from another.

Dinner at the club went well that night, without a replay
of the incident earlier that week. They had cocktails, talked,
and laughed. But Tracey watched Steve carefully, thinking
about what Celeste had told her. He was in an expansive
mood, happy and proud of the girls, yet under the magnifica-
tion of Celeste's words, she noticed small things she interpreted as confirming the worst about him. Steve ordered
Celeste's dinner without asking what she wanted, and her
drink before she seemed ready. In Tracey's mind she thought
he could easily be overbearing.

The following afternoon, Tracey met Celeste and the girls
at Tramps. They had a big night coming up. On the family
planner Celeste had written "girls and Celeste to As-
troWorld." In her own date book, however, she mentioned
nothing about an overnight at the Houston amusement park,
but instead had scratched in "Jimmy's for girls' graduation."
The party had been planned for weeks. At seven-thirty that
evening at Jimmy Martinez's house, the real celebration
would begin, one Steve wasn't invited to.

At Tramps, Celeste and the twins had their hair done.
Tracey, too, showed up. After Denise finished their hairdos,
Celeste asked, "Do you have time to do Tracey's?"

"Sure, sit down," she said. Denise went to work, fluffing and brushing. Then she looked at Tracey's lips. "You need some lipstick. I'll get some."

She came back with a tester tube she smoothed over Tracey's rough lips.

"You look dykey," Celeste said laughing, when she was finished. Denise laughed, too, but Tracey didn't seem to mind. Denise thought she seemed proud to get the attention.

That night, Jimmy served hamburgers and hot dogs to a group of forty that included a few of the twins' friends but mostly Celeste's buddies, everyone from Dawn and Jim Madigan, her friends from the lake, to both her hairdressers. On the buffet table Celeste placed trays of vegetables, cheeses, and fruit, a crockpot of chili con queso for chips, and cheese cake for dessert. Music blared, and many danced, including Jimmy and Celeste, so close that few who saw them wouldn't assume that they were lovers.

Among the crowd, Tracey watched Celeste's every move, wondering what was going on between her lover and her ex-husband. As the night wore on, Celeste announced another party, for Halloween. "Everyone will dress up as Jimmy," she said, visibly drunk. "You can all wear cowboy boots and jeans."

Soon after, she disappeared upstairs. Downstairs, the party continued, but Tracey, a short time later, followed her and found Celeste sleeping in Jimmy's bed. When Kristina walked in moments later, Tracey was draped over her mother, stroking her.

Upset, she found Jimmy. "Tell Tracey to get off mom," she said.

Jimmy ran upstairs and saw the two women in bed. "Get the hell off her," he ordered Tracey.

Tracey appeared not to hear, continuing to rub against Celeste.

"I said get out," he ordered, pulling her arm. Tracey stood, unsteady on her feet.

"Tell her I'm not a lesbian," Celeste mumbled.

Jimmy turned and followed Traccy downstairs, pushing her when she stopped and tried to go back upstairs. At the door, Kristina and Justin offered her a ride home.

"No," she shouted. "I'm fine."

She wove out the door, obviously drunk. At the street, she stopped and shouted, "You tell Celeste I want her at my house in one hour."

Jimmy slammed the door and locked it.

Inside, the party wound down. Amy had so much to drink she threw up and put her foot on the floor to keep the bed from spinning. Jennifer fell and scratched her face.

Half an hour later a guest who'd left called. "That gay woman got arrested," he told Jimmy. "We saw her on the side of the road with a squad car."

The phone rang and Travis County Jail came up on Jimmy's caller ID. He took the phone off the hook.

At the jail, Tracey tried Celeste's cell phone, then, in the early hours of the morning, the Toro Canyon house. When the operator told Steve he had a call from Tracey Tarlton at the Travis County Jail, he hung up, too. The next day he told Celeste what had happened and to bail Tracey out and stop seeing her. "I don't want you to spend any more time with that woman."

Celeste laughed that afternoon when she picked Tracey up at the jail. "Steve's really mad at you," she said. "He didn't even know about the party. He was so pissed."

In September, the month in Europe with Steve must have gaped before Celeste like approaching doom. She told Tracey to meet her at the lake house one afternoon, to brew a second batch of botulism. When Tracey got there, Celeste had all the ingredients, and they began stirring into the jar corn, a few tablespoons of chopped meat, and dirt from the yard. Then, just as Tracey had the first time, Celeste filled the jar with water and sealed it. *"Taken through the bloodstream, death is quick and relatively symptomless,"* the recipe read. *"Botulism is fun and easy to make."*

Once she'd screwed the cap on, Celeste placed it in a cabinet in the garage, where the Texas heat would bake it. It wasn't to be disturbed. But again the plan failed. Days later Justin noticed the jar with something that looked like liquid fertilizer brewing in it. He picked it up, unscrewed the top to look at it, and moved it, disturbing the growth of the botulism. When Celeste realized what had happened, she was despondent.

"Steve has to die," she told Tracey. "He just has to."

Within days she had another plan, asking Tracey to buy her ten tablets of ecstasy. "I'll take him to a bar and slip it in his drink. They'll think someone else did it," she said.

As before, Tracey did as Celeste asked, reasoning she was not the one who'd be putting it into his drink. Days later Celeste claimed to have used the drugs, again without success. "That fat old fuck. He's so big nothing can kill him," she said, laughing and crying at the same time. "It's like trying to kill an elephant."

"Mom won't get out of bed," Kristina told Tracey on the phone the next day.

Tracey rushed over. As before, Steve was gone and Kristina was frantic, worried about Celeste. Tracey urged Celeste out of bed and convinced her to dress. "Living with Steve is killing me," she said.

That day, Tracey told Kristina something she'd wanted to tell her for a long time. "Your mother and I are a couple," she said. "She's just not ready to tell you yet."

"Okay," Kristina said, not knowing what to think, except that in her heart she'd known it all along.

It seemed that Tracey was tired of hiding the relationship and was ready to tell the world. "I love Celeste," she told Terry Meyer, the manicurist, the next time she was at Tramps having her nails done.

"Everyone does. She's great," Terry said.

"No, I *really* love Celeste," Tracey emphasized. "And if that old man ever hurts her, I'll kill him." Terry was shocked, not knowing what to say. When Celeste came in, Terry told her what Tracey had said.

"Did she really say that?" Celeste said.

"She did."

At home, Celeste watched Court TV and homicide investigations on the A&E channel. One program on how murderers were caught seemed to fascinate her. On Celeste's desk Jennifer found a packet of grisly photos of dead bodies, mostly with gunshot wounds.

"Why's she have these?" she asked Kristina.

"I don't know," her sister replied.

Steve had been bored that August, while Celeste and the girls were in Australia. With Davenport II nearing completion, he had no pet projects in the works. Again he turned his attention to the house. Now that he had some time on his hands, he called Gus Voelzel and asked him to design maid's quarters and a guest house, one his grown kids could stay in when they visited. It had been years since any of Steve and Elise's children had come. Most kept a distance from Celeste, who'd called them more than once, raging, usually about nothing of importance. "I'll tell your father about this," she stormed, as if talking to small children.

* * *

By mid-September, Celeste was frantic. At Tracey's house three to four nights a week, she paced. Each time, they spent the evening drinking and talking about Steve. As Tracey saw it, Celeste was becoming increasingly unstable. "I'm giving him more sleeping pills and Everclear," she said. "Eventually, it's gotta kill him."

On September 10, Stacy, the travel agent, ran into Celeste and Steve at a restaurant, having lunch. Steve introduced her to Celeste and they talked about the trip. "I really think you ought to take the insurance," Stacy said again. "That's a lot of money to risk."

"I'm not going to cancel. Absolutely not," Steve said firmly. "We don't need insurance because we're going on that trip."

Many people noticed a change in Celeste that month. When she and Steve had dinner with Chuck Fuqua and his girlfriend, Celeste sat distracted at the table, not paying attention to the conversation, as if she had something else on her mind. Days later Anita and her husband ran into the Beards at a new posh, fusion restaurant in Davenport I. While Steve and the girls sat down for dinner, Celeste, her hair in a French twist and decked out in a designer dress and jewelry, paced outside. Through the windows they saw her smoking and talking on her cell phone.

"Should I go talk to her?" Anita asked.

Steve looked embarrassed and sad. "No," he said. "There's nothing you can do."

When Celeste finally came in, she sat with Steve and the girls, but it seemed to Anita that she wanted to be anywhere but in the restaurant with Steve.

The phone rang at Tracey's house on the night of September 12. "You need to come over right away!" Celeste screamed. "Steve's passed out. I need your help."

When Tracey arrived, Steve was in a kitchen chair, unconscious.

"I drugged him," Celeste said. "Help me get him out of the chair."

Tracey grabbed him under one arm and Celeste under the other, then they angled the chair beneath him, until he fell to the floor.

"Oh, God," Tracey said. "What do we do now?"

"Wait," Celeste said.

She left and moments later returned with a plastic kitchen garbage bag and a towel. She then wrapped the towel around his neck and pulled the garbage bag over his head, cinching it shut.

"I saw this on television," she said. "Now the bag won't leave marks."

On the floor, Steve moved slightly, and the bag went in and out with each breath.

Suddenly, Celeste handed the bag straps to Tracey.

"Hold these," she said.

Tracey did, and Steve's breathing continued. She thought: *I don't want to do this. I don't want to do this.* When Steve moved again, Tracey dropped the bag. "I can't do this," she said, horrified. "I just can't."

"I can't, either," Celeste said, pulling the bag from his head. "I'll call an ambulance."

After Celeste called 911, she dialed Kristina's cell phone. "Steve's had a seizure. I've called EMS," she said.

"Do you want me to come get you?"

"No, go to the hospital. Tracey's here. She'll take me."

But as soon as she hung up, Celeste changed her mind. "You should leave," she told Tracey. She dialed Kristina again. "Come get me," she said.

At North Austin Medical Center, Steve's blood alcohol level was high, .168, and his oxygen level was dangerously low. A social worker was called in to talk to him about his drinking, but he insisted he hadn't had more than two or three vodkas, not enough to cause such high blood levels. The social worker noted on his chart that Steve was not facing his drinking problem.

Two days later, at 2:00 P.M., a nurse called Celeste and said Steve was ready to be discharged. "I'm not going to be home today. I have plans," Celeste answered. "Why don't you keep him another day?"

"Your husband is fine. He doesn't need to be here," the nurse said. "He has to check out today, but you can wait until seven tonight, if you need to."

"Okay," Celeste said. "I'll be there at seven."

Steve took the news without complaint. For another five hours he stayed at the hospital, waiting for Celeste to arrive to take him home.

The morning after his release, it happened again. This time the maid screamed and Kristina came running. Steve was unconscious, facedown at the kitchen table with his eyes open. When Kristina shook him, he didn't respond.

Celeste and the girls lowered him onto the floor and called EMS for a second time in three days. At the hospital, Steve was prodded and examined, but the doctors found no reason for his fainting spells. They did, however, chronicle his declining health in his chart: bronchitis, high blood pressure, an enlarged heart, sleep apnea, and abnormal blood chemistry from the high doses of alcohol damaging his kidneys. Celeste was right. Eventually, the Everclear would kill him.

That week, Celeste brought in the final payment for the approaching trip to Europe, a check for $40,788, to Tramex Travel. Included was the money for the cancellation insurance. Stacy was surprised, wondering what had changed Steve's mind. He'd been so adamant about not wanting the policy, she'd given up hope that he would relent. Later, she'd wonder if he even knew, or if Celeste had been the one who bought the insurance, because she knew they'd never board the flight to Paris.

Despite all that happened to him, Steve worried more about his home life and Celeste than his health. When David Kuperman, his attorney, dropped in to see him at the hospital, he was morose, saying the marriage "wasn't working out."

"Do you want to call the divorce attorney?" Kuperman asked. "The one you used when you filed against Celeste in 1995?"

"I'll think about it," he told him.

Days after he was released from the hospital for the second time, he called Celeste's therapist, Dr. Michele Hauser, and complained about Celeste's behavior. She was tired all the time, seeing three to five doctors a week, everyone from an internist to a dermatologist. "She acts guilty, and she's spending money like crazy," he told Hauser. "When she's angry she screams."

There was more. Steve had found Celeste's stash of credit cards, four with aliases, including Celeste Martinez. "She doesn't include me in her plans," Steve said. "She does things with other people and doesn't tell me."

Still, Celeste had a hold on Steve he couldn't shake. Like the others before him, he found it impossible to leave her. When Steve finally talked to Kuperman again about a divorce, he told him he'd decided not to pursue anything, at least not yet.

Later, Tracey would say that it simply came up in conversation, and Celeste latched onto it as if fascinated. "I have my shotgun back," she told her.

For months one of Tracey's friends had kept the gun for her, because Tracey feared she might use it on herself during a weak moment. Finally, she felt stable enough to have it home. The shotgun was the .20 gauge Franchi her father gave her in the late sixties. A lightweight weapon, it had *Tracey Tarlton* etched on the stock.

Five days before Celeste and Steve were scheduled to leave for Europe, on Wednesday, September 29, Celeste brought the shotgun up again.

"I can't go with Steve," she said. "If I go, I won't come back. I don't know how to get away from him. He'll hunt me down. And if I stay, he'll see that I don't survive."

As Tracey listened, Celeste told her that Steve ridiculed her and pushed her to kill herself, telling her she was "too stupid to bail water."

"I want you to shoot him," she said, putting her arms around Tracey and kissing her.

"No," Tracey said, pulling away. "I can't do that."

Celeste covered her face and sobbed: "Then you might as well say good-bye to me. If I leave on that trip, I'll never come back. Go get your gun, and I'll use it on myself. I'll do it quickly, before I change my mind. Then, at least he won't ever touch me again."

Inside, Tracey fought a vicious battle. She didn't want to kill anyone, and it was Celeste's problem, not hers. Yet she felt she couldn't stand by and let Steve drive her lover to suicide. If she told her no, Celeste could do as she threatened, and kill herself that very night, driving off a freeway or finding a gun and pulling the trigger. She believed Celeste was powerless with Steve and desperate.

"I have no one else to turn to," Celeste pleaded.

"Fine," Tracey said. "I'll do it."

Smiling, Celeste took Tracey's face in her hands and kissed her hard on the lips.

Later, in a strange way, it would all make sense to Tracey. All her life she'd searched for the reason she'd been born. "I always felt unnecessary," she says. "I thought finally I'd found something I was necessary for. I had a purpose. I had to kill Steve to save Celeste's life."

Chapter
11

"Jennifer, why don't you, Christopher, and Amy stay at the lake house this Friday night?" Celeste said, during hamburgers. "That would be fun, wouldn't it?"

"Sure," Jen said, startled.

Celeste had first learned that the twins' boyfriends slept over earlier that year. At the time, she'd been furious—not because Jennifer was sexually active, but that Kristina was. She'd been so upset, she went to the teenager's next session with Peggy Farley, the therapist Kristina began seeing that spring. At the session, Farley attempted to calm Celeste, explaining that Kristina and Justin had been close for a very long time. "Don't you remember the first time you felt like that about a boy?" Farley asked.

"The first time I had sex, I was a little girl, and my father was raping me," Celeste screamed back. From that point on the session became less about Kristina than Farley calming Celeste's hysteria.

Soon, Celeste became comfortable with the fact that the girls had boyfriends and that both Christopher and Justin often stayed overnight in their rooms on the weekends. In fact, she'd goaded them, threatening to switch their birth-control pills for aspirins to trick them into getting pregnant. Celeste wanted a baby, she said, a new child now that they were grown. She didn't care who had it for her, Kristina and Justin, or Jennifer with Christopher; she even tried to convince Amy to have a child with Jimmy. At times she offered money, up to a million dollars. "We ignored her," says Justin. "We did that with a lot of things."

Still, Celeste rarely agreed to let the teens stay at the lake house alone, especially if Jennifer was the one who asked. All the teens knew that Celeste held a grudge over the years Jen had chosen Craig over her. "If I asked, she'd let us go," Christopher says. "But if Jen asked, the answer was almost always no."

Although it seemed odd, Jennifer didn't dwell on her mother's offer of the lake house. She was pleased. With Christopher attending college in San Angelo, Texas, four and a half hours away by car, they saw each other only on weekends.

"That'd be great," Jen said, meaning it.

That settled, Celeste turned her attention to Kristina, saying, "On Friday night I want you home by midnight. And Justin can't sleep over. I'll need your help."

"Why?" Kristina asked, less happy than her sister at her mother's plans.

"Because I said so."

Disappointed, Kristina didn't ask anything else. If Celeste needed her help, she assumed it was to pack for the trip. They'd all noticed that Steve was packed and ready to go, but Celeste had yet to start a single suitcase. Even Justin had offered to help her a couple of days earlier. Celeste had turned him down, saying there was plenty of time. What they didn't know was that while Steve had written "Leave for Europe" on the coming Sunday in the family planner, Celeste had made no such entry on her personal calendar.

"Okay," Kristina said. "We're going out to dinner with Justin's parents. Then I'll come home."

"Good," Celeste said. "Then it's all settled."

The following day, Thursday, Celeste called Tracey often, finalizing plans. "Steve will be gone tomorrow," she said. "You can come over and walk through the house. I've got it all figured out. Are you doing what we planned tonight?"

"Yeah," Tracey said.

Although they had plans to see Lily Tomlin perform, the tickets would never be used. Instead, Tracey's job was to make sure she and her shotgun were prepared.

As instructed, after work Tracey drove northeast of Austin, to a shooting range. She pulled her .20 gauge out of its beige case with brown trim and motioned for the attendant. Moments later skeet arched overhead. Tracey concentrated, pulling back the trigger and watching them shatter in midair. The entire time, as she worked her way through a full circuit, she thought about what she'd be doing. She'd stopped hunting years ago because she didn't like killing animals. Now, she was preparing to kill a human being.

"How's the shotgun working?" Celeste asked when she called that night.

"Fine," Tracey said. "No problem."

"I'll call tomorrow," she said. "I love you."

"I love you, too," Tracey said, but in her stomach she had a sinking feeling. She knew that no matter what happened, the next few days would change their lives, forever. Celeste said that after the murder they'd have to remain apart until the investigation was over. "Then we'll live together, at the lake house, you and me."

Tracey didn't believe it. She sensed that the fallout would be so great they'd never survive it. Still, she felt she had to do it. She'd agreed. And if she didn't follow through, she was convinced Celeste would take her own life. If it went bad, she'd asked Celeste for three things: that she'd find someone to care for her animals, pay for her attorney, and put fifty dollars a month in her prison account, to pay for extras. Celeste readily agreed.

"But you won't be caught. You won't even be a suspect," Celeste said. "I've read so many books on things like this, watched so many movies, I know what I'm doing. Wait and see."

So that night, Tracey sat alone, drinking beer, and trying not to think about what lay ahead of them both the following day.

Friday morning, October 1, two days before Steve and Celeste were scheduled to embark on their trip to Europe, Tracey left for work at BookPeople, just like every other morning. Kristina drove to her mail-room job and Jennifer to work at Anita's office. Throughout the morning, Celeste called Tracey at the store, often unable to reach her. She dialed and then redialed. Sometime in the early afternoon Tracey answered.

"He's leaving," Celeste whispered. "Come over now."

When Tracey drove up to the Toro Canyon house, she parked in the circular driveway in the front. Celeste was waiting for her.

"Okay, now tonight, you park right here," she said, pointing to a bend sheltered by trees. "Then walk around the house and come in through the bedroom."

Celeste led Tracey past the grand leaded-glass doors on the front of the house to a path that curved around the left side. She opened a gate and they entered a small patio. "He'll be in there," she said.

She slid back the door and brought Tracey into the bedroom. "Now wear all black, your black sweater, black jeans, tennis shoes, and a cap, so no one will see you. And don't drink. You don't want to make any mistakes."

As Celeste had it planned, Tracey would enter under cover of darkness, stand at the foot of the bed, point the gun at Steve, who would be sleeping, and pull the trigger.

"The shotgun will drop a shell," said Tracey.

"Look for it. If you don't find it, just leave. I'll pick it up," Celeste told her.

"What about the noise and the kids?"

"I've already taken care of that." Although she'd told Kristina to stay home, Celeste assured Tracey that she would be at Justin's house that night. Perhaps Celeste wanted Kristina as a witness to talk to the police when questioning began. After all, of the twins, Kristina not only slept soundly, but was the one Celeste could count on to do as she was told. She told Tracey that the other teens would be at the lake house, as they'd planned, and that she'd take the dogs, her cocker Nikki and Steve's Meagan, into Kristina's bedroom with her.

Celeste then gave Tracey vinyl gloves and a sheet of plastic to cover the seat of her car. After the shooting, Tracey was to drive to a convenience store on South First Street, to discard them in a Dumpster. "I've checked it out, and the Dumpster isn't visible from the store," she said. "You ought to be able to throw them away without the clerk seeing."

Tracey was then to return home, wash her clothing, clean her gun and put it away.

"By tomorrow morning, it'll all be over," Celeste said.

"If all goes well."

"It will," Celeste said. "Then we'll be together, you and me, without any worries."

"I hope so," Tracey said.

"I'll call you tonight to let you know for sure he's in bed, that he hasn't passed out in the closet," she said. "He does that sometimes."

Then Celeste had one more request. "When you shoot Steve, shoot him in the stomach," she said.

Tracey was alarmed. "If I shoot him in the stomach, he'll linger."

"I don't want blood all over the wall. I don't want to re-decorate." Anxiety churned inside Tracey as Celeste said, "I've read about this in books. He'll bleed to death."

Steve came home later that afternoon after picking up the fi-nalized itinerary for the trip and $1,000 in cash to leave with the twins for incidentals while they were gone. When Christopher arrived from San Angelo, they sat and talked. Steve was excited about the adventure of the month abroad, talking about all he and Celeste would do and see. Christo-pher enjoyed hearing details of the plans, including descrip-tions of the small villages with cobblestone streets they'd visit.

"So, what are you and Jennifer doing tonight?" Steve asked.

"We're going with Amy to the lake house," Christopher said. Steve didn't look pleased, and Christopher realized he probably shouldn't have answered as he did. Steve didn't know the boys slept over in the girls' rooms, and he wouldn't have approved. They came and went by a back entrance, without his seeing. Still, Steve didn't object.

By seven-thirty that evening Christopher, Amy, and Jen-nifer were on their way to the lake house at least a forty-five-minute drive, unless they went with Celeste, who drove so fast she could make it in half an hour. In Austin, Kristina and Justin were meeting his parents for dinner.

A few hours later, around ten, the phone rang at the lake house. "I'm going to bring Meagan over," Celeste said. "Steve's drunk and he's being mean, hitting her."

"Okay," Christopher said. When he hung up, he told Jennifer and Amy about the conversation.

"That's really strange. I've never seen Steve hit Meagan," Jennifer said. The others agreed. They'd never seen Steve abuse the dog in any way.

Just before eleven, Celeste arrived at the lake house with Nikki and Meagan.

"Steve's in a really bad mood. She's better off here with all of you," Celeste said. The teens all looked at each other. Celeste seemed even more manic than usual, walking hurriedly about the house, constantly looking at her watch. She talked just briefly, then called Kristina on the telephone.

"Will you be home by midnight?" Celeste asked.

"Yes," she said. "I'll be there."

"Good," Celeste said. "I'll see you at the house."

Quickly, Celeste turned and left, taking Nikki and leaving Meagan with the teens.

As soon as she was gone, Christopher said to the girls, "She's acting really strange."

"I'm surprised she took Meagan in the car," Amy said. "Meagan hates going in the car. Her legs just shake."

"Maybe it's just the whole thing about the trip," Jennifer said. "She's just dreading it."

After eleven, Justin and Kristina pulled into the driveway at Toro Canyon and went inside. It was dark. "Mom," Kristina called out. Celeste didn't answer.

Looking for her, Kristina walked into the master bedroom and saw Steve sleeping in bed, wearing his oxygen machine for his sleep apnea. He seemed peaceful, and she didn't notice that Meagan, who habitually slept at the foot of the bed, was missing.

"My mom's not here," Kristina told Justin. Then she

picked up the phone and called the lake house. Jennifer answered. "Where's our mom?"

"She should be home soon. She left here a while ago," Jennifer answered.

"Okay," Kristina said, and hung up.

Meanwhile, Celeste walked into Tracey's house on Wilson. Tracey hadn't been expecting her.

"Are you going to do it?" she asked.

"I'm ready," Tracey said.

Celeste was in an anxious mood as she paced around the house. "Kristina's home, but I'll have her in the bedroom with me," Celeste said. "And I dropped Meagan at the lake house. She's protective of Steve, and I don't want her there when you shoot him."

Tracey's mind was reeling. First, she didn't like Kristina being home, despite Celeste's assurances that she was a sound sleeper and wouldn't wake. But it was the comment about Meagan that Tracey found confusing. Celeste had told her repeatedly that Steve beat the dog. Why would a dog be protective of an owner that abused it? She asked, and for a moment Celeste faltered. Then she said, "Meagan's a barker. She barks at any noise. I just didn't want her to wake the neighbors."

That made more sense to Tracey. Especially when Celeste explained that she'd decided the neighbors could be a problem. In fact, she'd made some changes. The Dennisons directly next door investigated when they heard noises in the night. "If you drive up the front, they'll see you," Celeste said. Instead, Tracey was to back up to the workers' entrance to the house, off Westlake Drive, park near Kristina's room, and walk around the pool to enter the house through the patio door near the master bedroom.

"I'll be so close to her bedroom, Kristina will hear me," Tracey said.

"Don't worry about Kristina," Celeste said. "I'll take care of her."

"I don't know the house, and I've never come that way," Tracey argued. "This isn't a good idea."

"It is," Celeste said. Then she went on to say that she'd have the doors unlocked and the burglar alarm off. She'd also make sure the back gate was open.

Tracey wasn't sure.

"I've also set up a motive for the shooting," Celeste said, explaining that she'd staged a robbery by rifling through the master bath. She'd taken Steve's wallet, ring, and money clip. "I kept the cash out of his money clip but threw the rest in the lake."

Tracey felt physically ill.

"You're the only one I can count on," Celeste said. "If you don't kill him, I'll die."

Tracey nodded.

"Steve's passed out in the bed," she said, putting her arms around Tracey's shoulders and kissing her. "Just remember, you're saving my life."

At the Toro Canyon house, Kristina walked Justin to the front door. It was just after midnight, and Celeste wasn't home. When he arrived at his house, he called. It was twelve-fifteen and Celeste still wasn't there. Kristina had called her cell phone, but Celeste hadn't answered.

"I'm home," Justin said.

"Okay," Kristina answered. "I'm exhausted. I'm going to bed. Talk to you tomorrow."

"Good night."

Sometime after two, Tracey was ready. She'd loaded her shotgun and dressed in black. She took the sheet of plastic Celeste had given her, covered the car's front seat, then put on the rubber gloves. In her year-old, maroon Pathfinder, she drove toward the Toro Canyon house, trying not to think about why. When she reached the back entrance, the gate was open. She turned off the headlights, pulled forward, put her arm over the seat, and backed up. At first all went well as the car climbed the hill, but then she hit a loose patch of gravel and her wheels spun. She gunned it, praying the noise wouldn't wake Kristina. Finally, the wheels caught traction and the car pulled backward up the hill. At the top, she stopped, put the car in park and turned off the engine.

Picking her way through the trees in the darkness, she walked along the back of the house to the patio. The house was dark, and the windows looked like blank eyes staring back at her in the night. She paused, thinking about what she was there to do, and she felt ill again. For a moment she flattened her body against the wall and listened. Around her insects buzzed in the woods and a slight breeze ruffled the leaves. The house was quiet. *I can't do this,* she thought. For minutes she stood statue still, thinking, trying to find another way to save Celeste.

No, she thought. *This is the only answer. He'll never let her go. I have to do it. I promised. Stop thinking about it. Just do it.*

Holding the shotgun in shaking hands, she felt her way around the house, saw the pool shimmering in the moonlight, then the door. As Celeste had promised, it was unlocked and no alarm sounded.

To save Celeste's life, she thought as she let herself in.

Up three steps to her right and she was into the master bedroom wing. Her pulse quickened as she entered the bedroom itself. There, in the bed, she saw Steve's generous silhouette in the darkened room. She stopped where Celeste had instructed, five feet from the foot of the bed. Without pausing, without allowing herself to think, Tracey raised her shotgun and took aim. She squeezed the trigger, and a single shot echoed through the house. It reverberated through her so that she felt certain she'd awoken the neighborhood.

God, Kristina must have heard that, Tracey thought.

"Oomph," Steve said as the pellets struck his abdomen.

Quickly, Tracey glanced around the floor, looking for the shell, but then Steve moved. His arm wound around his body and held his abdomen, at the site of the gunshot wound. Startling Tracey, he sat up, searching the nightstand on his right, looking for something.

Maybe he has a gun, she thought.

Frantic, she ran for the patio door, following Celeste's route for her escape. Again, as promised, the door was unlocked. She slid it open, walked out onto the patio, closed the door and sprinted toward the car. Seconds later she was gone.

Chapter
12

The voice on the telephone was gruff yet polite, confused and frightened.

"Nature of the emergency?" a woman dispatcher asked.

"I need an ambulance, hurry," Steve told the 911 operator just before 3:00 A.M. on Saturday, October 2, 1999. "Thirty-nine hundred Toro Canyon Road."

"What's going on there?"

"My guts blew out of my stomach," he said.

"Are you alone?"

"My wife is somewhere in the house," Steve said, groaning.

"Okay. Help is on the way. How did this happen?"

"I just woke up and they blew out of my stomach," he said, fear clouding his voice. "I can't move. I'm holding them all."

"Sir, we're already on the way."

"Call my wife. She's in another part of the house," he said, repeating the phone number. The woman hung up.

Minutes after the 911 call, Travis County Deputy Alan Howard drove up Westlake Drive, turned right onto Toro

Canyon Road, and swung into the main entrance to the Gardens of Westlake enclave. A house was under construction inside, and the gate had been left open. By the time Howard pulled up in front of the house and parked his squad car with lights flashing on the circle drive, he'd been joined by Stephen Alexander, a captain with the Westlake Fire Department, and Sergeant Greg Truitt, also from the Travis County Sheriff's Department. Howard pounded on the Beards' heavy front doors, rang the doorbell, and shouted, trying to raise someone inside. He tried the door. It was locked. The house appeared completely dark. Howard called the dispatcher and asked them to call the number inside, to rouse someone to let them in.

Rather than wait, knowing someone was injured, Howard, Truitt, and Alexander followed the outline of the house, walking to the left. About that time he got a call from Dispatch, saying that no one answered the telephone inside the house. The answering machine had picked up the call. They continued on, by then joined by Deputy Russell Thompson. At the side of the house the officers walked through an opening in a chain-link fence and around a wall until they could turn back to the right, where they entered a small patio. Howard peered in through a window. Who was inside? Why had he called?

Seeing nothing out of the ordinary, Howard led the others past the wall, and found himself staring through French doors into a bedroom. In the semidarkness he saw a lamp shining on a nightstand and the figure of a large man in bed, his right hand holding a telephone receiver. Howard could see blood on the man's hands.

Grabbing the brass handles on the doors, Howard attempted to twist them. They didn't move. He pulled. They didn't budge. Inside, the man shouted something he couldn't hear. Howard knew from the look of the man's injuries that the situation was grave. He took his flashlight and cracked it hard against the glass. It didn't give. So he reared his hand back and swung again. This time the expensive tempered glass doors shattered into thousands of small pellets, like a car windshield in a traffic accident.

Howard stuck his hand through the opening and looked for a way to unlock the doors, but found nothing. He pulled on the doors again. Again they didn't budge.

"The door slides!" Steve shouted.

Howard pushed to the sides, and the doors opened. He rushed through, followed by the others, including two officers from the Austin Police Department who'd just arrived on the scene. Even with the noise of shattering glass, the house remained silent.

"What happened to you?" Howard asked.

"I don't know," Steve said. "I woke up this way."

At first glance Steve's abdomen looked as if someone had shredded it with a razor. Quickly, Alexander put in a call for STAR Flight, requesting an emergency helicopter.

"I heard a loud noise," Steve went on. "I woke up and my gut was like this, my insides spilling out."

Grasping for some explanation for the man's wounds, Howard asked, "Did you have surgery recently? Did your stitches open?"

"No," Steve said. "No, I didn't."

Alexander pulled bandages from his supplies and bound Steve's wide belly, hoping to keep him pieced together. Another EMS officer arrived, one who worked for the Texas Highway Patrol, and he pitched in dressing Steve's wounds. Minutes later Austin EMS arrived and pushed them both out of the way, hooking Steve up to an IV and putting him on a portable oxygen tank. Just then word came over Howard's radio that STAR Flight was on its way. To open the house for those he knew would be arriving, he told Truitt to unlock the front door. It was in the living room, as he approached the door, that Truitt encountered Celeste and Kristina making their way out from the opposite wing.

The lights woke Kristina. She was sound asleep when something flashed, then again, and again. She opened her eyes and realized they were white and blue, like the lights on a squad car. When her eyes focused, she saw her mother standing at her bedroom door dressed in a T-shirt and boxer shorts.

"What's going on?" Kristina asked.

"Someone's at the door," Celeste said.

Frightened by the prospect of strangers in the middle of the night, Kristina walked to the bedroom door. Before the teenager realized what was happening, her mother pushed her out into the hallway.

"Find out what they want," Celeste ordered.

Panicking, Kristina ducked into the guest room, where Jennifer normally slept, and dialed 911. When the operator answered, she recited her address, saying someone was at their front door. "It's the police and EMS," the dispatcher told her. "Your father called. He has an emergency."

"Mom, something's wrong with Dad," Kristina called out as she ran from the room.

"Who are you?" Celeste demanded of the uniformed officer when she emerged from the children's wing. "What's going on?"

"We've got a medical emergency," Truitt said as he came to the door. "Your husband called 911. Has he had recent surgery?"

"No. Is he okay?" Celeste asked.

When Howard told her that Steve appeared badly hurt, Celeste sobbed: "Don't let my husband die. Don't let him die."

Kristina moved forward, trying to comfort her mother.

As soon as Celeste quieted, the teenager rushed to the master bedroom. "Is he all right?" she asked one officer. "Is my father all right?"

"They're working on him," he said. "STAR Flight is on its way."

Kristina went to Steve's bedside but couldn't get near because of the crush of police and medics. "Dad, they're going to take you to the hospital," she said, looking directly into his eyes, not wanting to see the bloody bed. "We all love you. I love you."

Steve forced a fleeting smile then nodded. "Is your mother all right?" he asked.

"Yes, she's fine," she said, then urged, "Don't worry. Just get better."

Steve smiled weakly. With that Kristina left to check on Celeste in the living room. By the time she arrived, her mother was outside on the front steps, smoking a cigarette. She'd just said something that Truitt found surprising for a woman whose husband was critically injured: "This is perfect timing. We're supposed to leave for Europe tomorrow."

When she found her mother, Kristina noticed that Celeste had stopped crying. She stayed only moments, then returned to the bedroom to check on Steve.

In the bedroom, Deputy Thompson saw something yellow and round peeking out from under one of the medics' bags. While the others worked on Steve, he bent over and picked it up. It was a spent shotgun shell, .20 gauge.

"I've got a shotgun shell," he said. "He's been shot."

Another officer pointed toward the headboard and wall. Blood splatter and small bits of tissue fanned out in a pale, pinkish spray.

"This is a crime scene," Thompson announced. "From this point on."

At that moment Kristina was on her way out the door, after looking in on Steve a third time. She spun back into the room when she heard Thompson's announcement. "What?" she said. "How can that be?"

"Don't tell your mother. She's upset enough as it is," Thompson said. "Calm her down. We don't need her upsetting your dad and making things worse."

"Howard, we need to set up a perimeter and guard the crime scene," Sergeant Truitt ordered. "Take the front door."

While the medics worked on her husband inside, Celeste sat on the steps smoking. Later, the officers would disagree about her demeanor. Some said she appeared visibly upset and shaken, concerned about her husband's welfare, others that she was eerily calm. One would say that Celeste cried but shed no tears.

The Dennisons, who'd been awakened by the squad cars, rushed over when they saw the ambulance. Bob ran up to one officer. "I'm a doctor," he said. "Can I help?" The officer turned him away. Bess tried to comfort Celeste, holding her hand and talking to her. When Celeste saw her, she became hysterical again. Kristina put her arm around her mother and reassured her.

"He'll be okay, Mom," she said. "He'll be fine. I know it."

"It was like Kristina came of age that night," Bess would say later. "She was so protective of her mother. She took charge."

"Would you call Jennifer?" Kristina asked Bess. "She's at the lake house."

Bess Dennison agreed, just as the STAR Flight helicopter hovered overhead, its searchlight scanning for a place to land. Squad cars set up a barrier to hold back cars, giving it room to put down on the road. As Steve was carried on a stretcher past her, Celeste jumped up, but the EMS workers didn't stop.

Minutes later Celeste and Kristina were put into a squad car to follow the helicopter to the hospital. As they pulled onto Toro Canyon, Kristina saw Justin on the side of the road. She'd called him earlier, and he'd been arguing with officers, trying to get through the line of squad cars and to the house.

"We're on our way to Brackenridge Hospital," she shouted. "Meet us there."

In the squad car, the officer driving mentioned the shotgun shell.

"Steve was shot?" Celeste asked, and then she began wailing.

At that same time in the house on Toro Canyon, much attention was being paid to the shotgun shell. In the paramedic's rush, it had been pushed across the floor, where it lay, clear evidence that Steve's injuries weren't at all mysterious. No strange phenomenon had occurred. Instead it was a clear case of attempted murder.

Even before Steve had been whisked away, the officers began securing the crime scene and sweeping the house. There was much they didn't know, including if the assailant was still inside, hiding somewhere and ready to jump out at them or shoot at them from the shadows.

Deputy Howard guarded the front door, logging who went in and out. Inside, Thompson checked the other doors. He found two unlocked, one going out to the back patio and the pool, the other to a living room porch that had poor accessibility. From experience, Thompson knew that finding unlocked doors wasn't an unusual occurrence in a big house like the Beards'. It still seemed odd, however, that when they searched, they found no signs of forced entry. *How would the assailant know which door would be unlocked?* Howard wondered.

The more Deputy Thompson looked around, the more suspicious he became. Drawers in the cavernous master bedroom, closets, and vanities yawned open, the contents akimbo, but in a strangely orderly fashion. Rather than the chaos of a burglary scene, the Beard house looked, he'd say later, "like an amateur ransacking."

With the house a crime scene—and if Steve died, a murder scene—the criminal investigation unit was called in. The first to arrive was Sergeant Paul Knight, followed by Detective Rick Wines. Sergeant Truitt briefed Knight, a fortyish man with a boyish face framed by graying hair, and Wines, lanky and tall with shock white hair and a neatly trimmed goatee. Knight had a laid-back manner with a sardonic smile, while Wines's sharp features matched his hawklike demeanor and intent eyes that surveyed the room, seeming to absorb the scene. "One heck of a house," Wines said.

"Sure is," Knight agreed. "A shooting in this neighborhood is going to make headlines."

To that, Wines nodded. They both knew everything they did that night could one day be put under a microscope in a courtroom. "I'll handle things here," Wines told Knight. "Why don't you go to the hospital and talk to the family?"

Sergeant Knight agreed and left.

At the house, Wines, a Vietnam vet who'd worked as a cop for seventeen years, walked the scene. The house looked orderly, except for a living room lamp that lay on its side on the floor. It didn't appear to have been knocked over, but instead carefully laid down. In the master bathroom he found what the other officers had pondered before: clothing protruding from open dresser drawers. After seventeen years on the force, Wines had seen many burglary scenes. This didn't look like anything in his experience. It was too precisely done, not the chaos a thief causes looking for valuables.

Now that's odd, Wines thought. *Really odd.*

* * *

At Brackenridge at about five-thirty that morning, Knight learned that Steve was in critical condition and in surgery. His wounds were extensive. The bullet had shredded the lower right quadrant of his abdomen. He'd lost blood, suffered intestinal damage, and had been exposed to serious infection.

Unable to interview the victim, Knight found Celeste and Kristina in a family waiting room with the officer who had transported them there. He introduced himself and then explained that he was investigating the shooting. He'd brought a lab tech with him who had an absorption kit, swabs to use to detect gunpowder through the presence of nitrates and sulfides.

"You don't think I did it, do you?" Celeste asked.

"It's routine," he said.

"Am I a suspect?"

"We're just trying to rule people out," he said, thinking it odd that she'd be so concerned about being a suspect at such an early stage of the investigation. With that, Celeste and Kristina quickly agreed, holding out their hands for the lab tech to swab.

When that was done and the tests were negative, Knight asked questions.

"Any idea who would want to hurt your husband?" he asked.

"No," Celeste said.

"Anyone mad at him, have any reason to be angry with him?"

"No," she said again.

Celeste went on to detail that evening. She said Steve had gone to bed about nine or nine-thirty. She'd taken a ride to the lake house to see her daughter and her friends, returning before midnight and stopping at a Texaco station on Bee Caves Road for gas. It struck Knight as peculiar when Celeste offered, "You can check on it. They'd have a record of the transaction."

She then went on to tell Knight that Steve had cashed a check that afternoon for money for the girls to spend while she and Steve were in Europe. "He had a thousand dollars in his wallet," she said. Knight felt uneasy again when she then offered a motive for the shooting, "If it's not there, this must have been a robbery."

Later Knight would say that much of the way Celeste acted that night seemed peculiar. It was when he left to get an update from a nurse on Steve's condition that Celeste had her first moments alone with Kristina. Still stunned from all that had happened, and worried about her mother, Kristina listened intently as her mother whispered: "The police are going to ask who could have done this. No matter what, don't mention Tracey's name. She's not involved in this. Call Jennifer and the others and tell them, too."

Kristina thought her mother's request odd, but the obedient daughter, she did as she was told. As soon as she called Justin on his cell phone to tell him, he, too, wondered, *Why would Celeste say that?* When he arrived at the hospital, Kristina left Celeste in a waiting room and ran up to hug him.

"Is Steve all right? Where is he?" he asked.

"In surgery," Kristina answered, crying. "He's hurt bad. Really bad."

Justin and Kristina were still embracing when Knight returned and noticed Justin. As he had with Celeste and Kristina, he introduced himself and then asked if the lab tech could do a swab test. Justin agreed. Then Knight asked the same question he'd asked Celeste earlier. "Do you know anyone who might want to hurt Steve?"

Justin looked around to be sure Celeste wasn't listening. She was nowhere to be seen. He still worried. Celeste had a way of finding things out. But he had to say what was on his mind. "You won't tell Celeste if I tell you, right?"

"I won't tell Mrs. Beard," Knight agreed.

"You need to talk to Tracey Tarlton. My guess is that she did it."

Once Tracey's name had been mentioned, Kristina couldn't hold back. She'd been upset when her mother ordered her to remain silent, wanting to do all she could to find the person who'd hurt Steve. "Tracey's in love with my mom," she said. "And she has guns. One night, when she was threatening to kill herself, I went there and took two away and turned them in to the police."

Sergeant Knight made notes, listening carefully. "Where do I find this woman?" he asked.

"She has a house near St. Edward's, in south Austin," Kristina said.

About that time, Christopher and Jennifer walked in. The news had shaken Jennifer badly. She'd been hysterical when she got off the telephone, and Amy and Christopher had to calm her. She didn't stop crying until halfway to the hospital in the car. Now she threw her arms around her sister and the two twins cried in each other's arms.

After hugs and tears, they all sat in the waiting room, bunched together in a circle, seated on chairs while Kristina and Justin told them the little they knew about Steve's condition: He was critical and undergoing surgery. Wanting to make the session as relaxed as possible, Knight sat down with them. When he asked Christopher and Jen who might have shot Steve, Christopher immediately said, "You can't tell Celeste we said this, because she'd make our lives hell, but we think it was Tracey Tarlton."

Meanwhile, outside the hospital, Amy had stayed with Celeste, who leaned against the building smoking one of her

Marlboro Light 100s. With Steve precariously close to death, Amy watched her carefully, recalling what Celeste had once told her—that when Steve died she'd act so upset, no one would suspect she never loved him.

When Amy walked inside, she found the others with Sergeant Knight.

"So who do you think might have done this?" he asked her.

Amy, who thought of Steve Beard like a grandfather, didn't hesitate.

"Tracey Tarlton," she said.

Knight was intrigued. All five teens agreed Tracey had a motive, but Celeste hadn't brought up her name. What was she hiding? Before leaving to pursue the lead he'd just been handed, he gave Celeste another opportunity to help solve her husband's shooting.

"Does anyone have any reason to be angry with your husband?" he asked again when he found her in the waiting room.

"No," she said.

"Is there anyone who might want him out of the way because of feelings about you?"

"No."

Within a few hours of the shooting, word was out, and friends began arriving at Brackenridge. The first were Philip Presse, the attorney, and his wife, Ana, who'd been Celeste's matron of honor at her wedding to Steve. Celeste was crying, and Ana gave her a Xanax to help her relax. Soon, Gus and Linda Voelzel, and the Baumans and Ray McEachern, arrived.

"What happened?" Gus asked.

"Someone shot Steve," Celeste said. They asked questions, but Celeste's replies supplied few answers. Many of the things she said didn't make sense. At one point she turned to Linda and insisted, "There aren't any guns in our house."

Why is she telling me that? Linda wondered.

"Where was Meagan?" Linda asked. "Didn't she bark?"

"She was at the lake house with the kids," Celeste said.

The Voelzels exchanged bewildered glances; Steve's friends knew the old lab followed him like an obedient puppy. Then Celeste said something that left them all staring at her, searching her face for answers: Steve hadn't put the alarm on that night.

"Steve was neurotic about that alarm, made sure it was on every night," says McEachern. "There was no way he was the one who left it off."

A deputy stood nearby. While Celeste talked to the others, McEachern eased over to his side. "You watch that woman," he whispered, pointing to Celeste. "If she gets the chance, she'll pull the plug and finish him off."

"You're just upset," the deputy said. "We tested her for residue. She didn't fire a gun."

"I don't care what you tested. He's in danger with her here," Ray answered.

As McEachern spoke, Celeste praised Steve to the others and pledged her love for him. She said she didn't think she could live without him. And she cried.

With the exception of Kristina, the teens, too, were looking at Celeste suspiciously. As they discussed the events of that night, there were just too many oddities. Why did Celeste take Meagan to the lake? Why did she say the boys weren't allowed to sleep over and send Christopher, Amy, and Jennifer to the lake house? Of them all, Jennifer was the most certain that her mother had some involvement in the shooting. Celeste was ruthless; about that she had no doubt. In the hospital, Jennifer looked across at Kristina, who hovered protectively near their mother. She made a decision there, at that moment. She'd keep her distance from Celeste and watch. But she wouldn't tell Kristina her suspicions. "I love Kristina to death," she says. "But I didn't trust her not to tell our mother."

As Jennifer thought the situation through, she believed her mother was not only involved with the shooting but, under the right circumstances, capable of hurting not only Steve, but her and Kristina. She considered fleeing somewhere Celeste couldn't find her. But she couldn't. "Kristina wouldn't go, and I would never leave her behind."

Inside an operating room, doctors attempted to piece together Steve's abdomen. The birdshot had entered his body and fanned out, until it appeared on a portable X ray like a thin spray of white dots. His lungs already weak from asthma, he struggled to breathe on his own, so they inserted a ventilator. Using a tiny camera to guide him, Dr. Robert Coscia, a trauma surgeon, worked to repair the damage. In places, Steve's abdomen looked like ground meat. Parts of his skin were already decaying, poisoning his system. Coscia slowly and carefully resectioned his stomach and removed part of his colon and intestine, inserting an ileostomy. With so much to repair, he didn't have enough undamaged skin to close. Instead, he pieced Vicryl, six-by-six-inch panels of surgical mesh, over the wound. Eventually, if Steve lived, he'd require skin grafts, but for the time being Coscia wanted him out of surgery and stabilizing. With his enlarged heart and weak lungs, the longer he spent in the operating room, the more dangerous his situation became.

"At best, he has a fifty-fifty chance," Dr. Coscia told Celeste and the teens after the operation. "There's a good possibility that he won't make it through the night."

As Kristina held her, Celeste sobbed.

* * *

At the Toro Canyon house, Detective Wines made plans to have the place thoroughly searched and to bring in the forensic team. First, he wanted to make sure anything they found would later be admissible in court. He called Knight at the hospital. "Ask Mrs. Beard to sign a consent-to-search for us," he said. In case she refused, Wines then left and went to his office to write up a search warrant. That turned out to be unnecessary. Knight called just after he arrived and said Celeste had signed the forms. On the phone, Wines told Knight about all he'd noted at the house, including what looked to be a staged burglary. Knight told Wines about the teens' identification of Tracey Tarlton as a possible suspect.

"I'll come to the hospital," Wines said. "Let's see if we can talk to Mr. Beard."

At 9:30 A.M., Wines arrived at Brackenridge, and he and Knight went to the nurse in charge of the surgical ICU and flashed their badges. "We need to talk to Mr. Beard," he said. With no objection, she led them into his room.

In the bed, surrounded by machines pumping him with antibiotics, painkillers, and fluids, Steve had tubes protruding from his throat and nose. His abdomen was covered by layers of gauze. He'd been opened and pieced back together, but not all the birdshot had been removed. Some lay dangerously close to vital organs, including his heart.

"Mr. Beard," Wines said. "Would it be all right if we ask you some questions?"

In terrible pain, Steve nodded.

"Did you see who did this to you?" he asked.

Steve tried to shake his head no, but the tubes made it impossible. The nurse brought over paper and a pen, but he was too weak to write.

"Mr. Beard, try to communicate by blinking. One for yes, two for no," Knight said.

Steve blinked once for yes.

"Did you see who did this to you?"

Steve blinked twice for no.

The two officers went through a list of questions that morning, but came away with little. Steve didn't know who had shot him, but when Tracey's name came up, he blinked once. Yes, he knew her.

"Do you think this has anything to do with anyone in your family?" Wines asked.

Steve blinked once for yes.

When it appeared the questioning was taking a toll, Wines and Knight turned to leave. For the first time they noticed Celeste, glaring at them through the ICU window with what Wines would later describe as "pure hate."

Back at Toro Canyon the crime scene unit took over. They didn't find Steve's wallet or the thousand dollars Celeste had mentioned. When Sergeant Knight arrived, however, he found something he judged interesting. In the garage were three cars, two Cadillacs and a Ford Suburban. All had car phones, but Celeste's Cadillac also had a Nokia cell phone in the center counsel. Knight flipped through the recently called numbers and came up with two of special interest: "Tracey cell" and "Tracey home."

As the police searched, Kristina returned home. Steve's outlook wasn't good, and she'd come home to get his identification and insurance information. In the master bathroom, she searched for his wallet. It was gone. She couldn't find his Baume & Mercier watch, or his sapphire ring. While she rummaged around, Knight walked in.

"I've got a few questions," he told Kristina. "Can we talk?"

As exhausted as she was, Kristina agreed.

At the hospital, Celeste had warned Kristina to be wary of the police, that they could turn things around and make it appear that one of them was involved in the shooting. Now, in response to his questions, Kristina was nervous, trying to remember what her mother had coached her to say. When he asked, she told the lies that Celeste had told her to, that her mother had been home before midnight and that they talked briefly before going to sleep.

"How did your mother seem?" Knight asked.

"Normal," Kristina answered.

"Is it unusual for her to sleep in your room?"

"She does that sometimes," Kristina said.

Something had been mentioned to Knight on the scene—that when the police arrived, Celeste was wearing a bra under her nightclothes. "Is that unusual?" he asked.

"No," Kristina answered. "Mom always does that, because she was abused as a kid."

Little of interest was taken from the Toro Canyon house during the search that day, nothing beyond the shotgun shell that would yield any clues. From there Knight and Wines returned to their office, where they ran a computer check on Tracey Tarlton that produced a list of addresses. Using information Knight had gleaned from the teenagers, they narrowed the address down to one on Wilson Street, on Austin's near south side. They also checked Tracey's car registration and wrote down the license number on her maroon Nissan Pathfinder. Then they checked for weapons permits.

"Here we go!" Wines said when he discovered that Tracey was the owner of a .20 gauge shotgun, the same caliber as the casing found in Steve Beard's bedroom.

At three that afternoon Knight and Wines drove to the address on Wilson Street and parked in front of the address on Tracey's driver's license. The Pathfinder was in the driveway. They walked up to the front door of the unremarkable ranch-style house in the working class neighborhood and Knight knocked.

Tracey answered, as if she'd been waiting for them.

"We're here to ask a few questions," Knight said. "Do you know Steven Beard?"

"Sure," Tracey said. "Celeste's husband."

"He's been shot," Wines said. He didn't see surprise on Tracey's face, but dread.

"Can we come in?" Knight asked.

"Sure," Tracey said.

In the living room Wines asked, "Do you know why anyone would shoot Mr. Beard?"

"No. Do I need an attorney?" Tracey asked.

"Not unless you think you do," Knight answered.

Under questioning, Tracey said that she and Celeste had met at St. David's, in the psychiatric unit, after they'd both attempted suicide. "We had a brief affair," she told the officers. "It didn't mean anything to either of us. Now we're just friends."

"When did you last talk to Mrs. Beard?" Wines asked.

"I'm not sure. I guess it was Thursday or Friday."

As well as listening to Tracey, Wines watched her body language. While she appeared relaxed, her eyes flicked about the room, never resting on his face or Knight's.

"Do you have a gun?" Knight asked.

"I have a shotgun I use to shoot skeet," Tracey said. "A .20 gauge."

"We'd like to see it," Knight said. "Will you get it for me?"

Tracey hesitated.

"We can go get it, or I'll wait here while Detective Wines gets a search warrant and we'll find it ourselves," Knight said. "Take your pick."

With that, Tracey led them to a closet in a back bedroom she used as an office. From inside, she pulled the Franchi shotgun in its zippered case and handed it to Wines. The smell of cleaning fluid was so strong he didn't have to ask if it had been recently cleaned.

"When's the last time you fired this?" Knight asked.

"I shot skeet Thursday night," she said.

"Can we take this downtown to ballistics?"

"Sure," Tracey said.

She felt her chest tighten when he said, "We'd like you to come downtown to our office and make a statement."

Hours later Tracey had signed a statement at the Travis County Sheriff's Department headquarters. In it she described meeting Celeste at St. David's and then Timberlawn, and said again that they'd had a brief affair. Since returning to Austin, she said, they were just friends. "We talked on the telephone some and went shopping a couple of times." When it came to Steve, Tracey said Celeste told her that she didn't sleep with him and that they didn't have a good relationship. "There was no sex in the marriage, and I think that her depression was caused by her relationship with him," she said. When asked where she'd been at the time of the murder, Tracey said she'd had a few beers, ate pizza, and then went to bed. "I did not shoot Steve Beard, and I do not know who did," she said.

Wines brought Tracey back to the house on Wilson. As she turned to walk inside, he said, "You'll be hearing from us again."

Paul Beard was the first of the older children to hear of their father's shooting. He called the house Saturday to wish Steve a good trip to Europe. Christopher Doose answered and told him what had happened. Wines got on the telephone and explained what he knew about Steve's condition.

"Who shot him?" Paul demanded.

"We're investigating," Wines said.

"Make sure you take a good look at his wife," Paul said.

As soon as he hung up the telephone, Paul said to his wife, Kim, "Celeste is behind this. I'd be willing to bet my life on it."

That afternoon Paul left calls for his brother, Steve, and sister, Becky.

Meanwhile, at the hospital, Celeste was making phone calls of her own, one to Steve's Austin banker, Chuck Fuqua. "Steve's in the hospital and can't take care of the bills," she said. "I want to be put on his bank accounts."

Fuqua refused, but Celeste insisted. Then Fuqua reminded her that she had $10,000 in traveler's checks Steve had bought for the trip. "Use those," he said.

"What happens when those are gone?"

"We'll work it out," Fuqua said. "That should carry you over for now."

When Fuqua wouldn't release Steve's money to her, Celeste called C. W. Beard, Steve's cousin and his Dallas banker. The frantic message on his machine said, "Steve's been shot, and I need to be put on his bank accounts."

That afternoon, Celeste, Dawn Madigan, her friend from the lake, and Kristina and Jennifer returned to the house and picked up the Suburban. On the way back to the hospital, Celeste pulled over to a Dumpster. From under the seat she retrieved an empty Everclear bottle and a book entitled *The Poor Man's James Bond*. On the cover it touted recipes for poisons and explosives. Nearly unable to believe what she'd just seen, Jennifer looked at Kristina, hoping she'd recognize the importance of the book. Instead Kristina stared out the window, looking frightened and sad.

About then, Celeste's cell phone rang.

"I've been questioned," Tracey said. "The cops just left. And they took my shotgun."

"Steve's not doing very well," Celeste said. "I'll call you back."

Then the phone went dead.

At the hospital, Justin prodded Kristina. "Why would Tracey do this? Isn't it strange that Celeste took Meagan to the lake house?"

Kristina ignored his insinuations, not wanting to hear what he was saying.

When the teens were together, they made small talk. Christopher and Jennifer didn't know where Justin stood, if he'd tell Kristina that they believed Celeste was involved. "We couldn't trust her," says Jennifer. "We knew how loyal she was to our mom."

Her hands shaking and tears clouding her eyes, Tracey's next call was to Philip Presse, who'd been at the hospital much of the day with Celeste. Weeks earlier, Celeste had referred her to him to handle her DWI, and she'd hired him to represent her. Now she explained that the police had questioned her and taken her shotgun for ballistics. "I'm expecting it to match," she said. When she started to talk about Celeste, Presse stopped her. He was already representing Celeste, he said, and he couldn't talk to her. But he could refer her to another attorney, a man named Keith Hampton, who shared his office building. "He's good and he handles criminal cases," Presse said.

Tracey hung up and immediately dialed Hampton's number. When he got on the phone, she launched into her explanation again, but Hampton stopped her. "I think we need to talk at the office," he said. "When can you come in?"

Within an hour Tracey was seated in Hampton's office, detailing her relationship with Celeste and the circumstances surrounding the shooting, as the attorney's eyes grew wide. "Celeste had told me that you don't tell an attorney the truth. You tell him what you want him to represent," Tracey said later. "But I didn't believe that. I thought he should know everything, so he wouldn't be blindsided."

When she finished, Tracey told Hampton there was one thing she would never consider: turning on Celeste. "I pulled the trigger, and I'm taking the fall," she said. "I'm telling you the rest because I think you need to know. But I don't want you to use it."

Hampton explained what they could do, including fighting the admissibility of the weapon, since Knight and Wines hadn't had a search warrant. "And we could talk to the D.A. about a deal," he said. "If you're willing to tell the whole story . . ."

"Absolutely not," Tracey said. "Do what you can but if this thing goes bad, I don't want Celeste involved."

Afterward, Keith Hampton had a problem. He'd just been told that Celeste planned the shooting, that she wanted Steve dead. With Celeste at the hospital, Steve could still be in danger, and he had a duty to alert someone to keep her from finding a way to finish Steve off in the ICU. Hampton called Philip Presse. When Presse got off the telephone, he talked to Celeste, then put in a call for Charles Burton, Austin's premier criminal attorney, to represent her.

Early that evening Celeste and the twins were allowed into Steve's room. The girls were shocked by his condition. He was pale and barely responsive. When Jennifer touched his hand, it felt stone cold. He tried to talk, but the tubes running down his throat made it impossible. Instead they read his lips.

"Why am I here?" he asked.

"Someone shot you," Kristina explained. "You've had an operation."

Steve shook his head no and tears ran down his cheeks.

"Oh, Steve," Celeste said, standing at his bedside, the picture of the perfect wife. She held his hand. "You'll be all right. I love you."

Chapter
13

" I **f you'd been in the bedroom with Steve, Tracey**
could have killed you," Kristina told her mother.
Ever since the shooting, she'd worried about what might
have happened that night. To Kristina, Celeste was her
responsibility. She'd spent her young life caring for her
mother, watching over her, everything from waking her in
the morning to making sure she took her medicine. Now
her mother could be in danger, and she wanted to protect
her. "Promise me you won't talk to Tracey. Promise me that
you'll be careful."

Celeste agreed.

All of the teenagers were panicked. They didn't know if
or when Tracey would be back. They just knew that she'd
shot Steve and that she might come back for Celeste, maybe
even for them. They were too afraid to return to Toro
Canyon. The house still had yellow crime scene tape strung
across the front and fingerprint dust on the walls. Worried
about their safety, Christopher went to a Marriott just blocks

from the hospital and booked rooms. "Nobody is going to scare me out of my house," Celeste said.

The twins couldn't understand her reaction. They were terrified, but Celeste didn't seem afraid. Finally, she agreed to stay at the hotel, but only because they insisted.

At the hospital the following day, Sunday, Steve remained critical. A pulmonologist attempted to wean him off the ventilator. After twenty minutes of unassisted breathing, his oxygen levels dropped and the ventilator was reinstalled. As the doctors saw it, nothing about Steve's recovery would be easy. He was overweight, had an enlarged heart, compromised lungs, and a wound that was dangerous even for a healthy person.

In the waiting room, Celeste, the twins, and their boyfriends held a vigil, waiting for the ten minutes each hour they were allowed to see him. Steve's friends circulated in and out of the waiting room. To each, Celeste told the story, saying she'd awakened to find the police at the door. And to each she pledged her love for Steve, saying, "I just want him to come home, so we can take care of him."

No one really knew what Steve was thinking, not until early on Monday morning when a nurse called Brackenridge's social worker, Barbara Jefferson. When Jefferson responded, the nurse relayed a message. "Mr. Beard is afraid someone in his family might be involved in the shooting," she said. "He doesn't want them in his room, and he wants the police sent in as soon as possible to talk to him."

Jefferson went to Steve's room in the ICU, where the nurse waited.

"Do you want me to go through the names of your family members?" the nurse asked. "You can tell me who you don't want to see."

Steve, weak and pale, said nothing.

"Are you saying you don't want to see any of them?" she said.

Steve nodded yes.

With that, Jefferson left to contact the hospital's trauma social worker, while the nurse put in a call for Sergeant Knight at the Sheriff's Department.

When Knight arrived, he asked Steve, "Mr. Beard, I'm told you don't want your family in your room, your wife and daughters, is that true?"

Steve blinked once for yes.

Knight turned to the social worker. "That's it, then," he said. "Do as he says."

An order went out; the medical personnel and deputies standing guard were instructed not to admit anyone to his room, including his family.

Celeste arrived minutes later, with Kristina and Jennifer in tow.

"Mr. Beard doesn't want to see anyone," the nurse told her.

"I'm his wife," she said, indignant.

"He said no one, ma'am," she said. "I'm sorry."

"They can't do this," Celeste fumed. "He's my husband."

Furious, Celeste went back to the hotel. When she talked to Tracey that day, she was frantic. "They're trying to make Steve suspicious," she said. "And I can't talk to him."

"What are you going to do?" Tracey asked.

"I can handle Steve," Celeste said. "I just need some time to play the devoted wife."

Her defense attorney, Charles Burton, was due at the hotel later that afternoon to take statements. Before he arrived, Celeste sat the girls down. "She told us what she wanted us to say, that she and Steve were a loving couple," says Jennifer. "And she told us that he was representing all of us, Steve, Kristina and me, even Justin and Christopher."

When she spoke to them, Celeste concentrated on Kristina, telling her it was important she say they were both home by midnight and that they'd talked before going to bed. "They might try to say I'm involved in this," she told her. "The police could make anyone seem guilty, even you and Jennifer. We have to protect each other."

Then Celeste spent that morning as she had so many others, shopping. The telephone rang at Louis Shanks Furniture, and she asked for her regular salesman, Greg Logsdon.

"Greg, I need something," she said.

"How's your husband?" he asked. "I heard about what happened."

"In the hospital," she said. "Listen, I need a new mattress for the master bedroom, and a new rug for beside the bed. Would your men mind taking the old mattress with them? Would they mind moving a mattress with blood on it?"

That taken care of, Celeste drove to Foley's department store, where she purchased a replacement set of king-size Ralph Lauren sheets. The police had taken the bloodstained set that was on the bed when the bullet ripped through Steve as evidence.

Meanwhile, Jennifer followed orders and left a voice mail for Stacy Sadler, the travel agent. When Sadler played Jennifer's message back, she heard tears in the teenager's voice. There'd been an emergency, Jen said, and her parents' trip had to be cancelled. Later in the day Celeste called personally, demanding the money from the trip insurance she'd purchased, more than $50,000. Stacy explained it would take four to six weeks.

"I need the money now," Celeste insisted.

"I'm sorry Mrs. Beard," Stacy said. "There's nothing I can do."

* * *

Back at his office, Wines and an ID tech shipped Tracey's shotgun to ballistics at the Texas Department of Safety, DPS. A second shotgun was going as well. On a later search of the house, Jennifer had pointed out a shotgun she'd hidden in the attic, one she'd bought to give Christopher for their first anniversary as boyfriend and girlfriend. It, too, was a .20 gauge. This second shotgun was in the box. The tape sealing it appeared to be original and undisturbed, and Wines doubted it had anything to do with the shooting. But to be sure, he labeled and documented both guns to be tested.

That finished, Wines headed back to the hospital. If Steve could communicate, the detective wanted to have a preliminary interview to find out what he knew about the shooting and the days leading up to it. But when Wines arrived at Brackenridge's ICU, Celeste waited for him, and she was livid.

"You're not going in there," she said.

"Why not?" Wines asked. Victims and their families can act in odd ways, but in all his years on the force he'd never had any become as defensive as Celeste

"I'm his wife and I have a legal right to keep you out of his room. Our family has hired Charles Burton," she said. "If you need anything further from us, you'll have to go through him."

Wines had known Burton for years. His firm, Minton Burton Foster and Collins, was an Austin powerhouse, the most prestigious in the city. Wines looked at Celeste. This was another first. He'd never had a victim's family hire a criminal defense attorney before. *No doubt about it*, he thought. *That gun's going to be a match, and that woman's involved.*

Before the day was over, Celeste would also rescind her consent for further searches at the house on Toro Canyon and post a handwritten sign on the door to Steve's hospital room:

NO LAW ENFORCEMENT PERSONNEL ALLOWED TO INTER-
VIEW PATIENT EXCEPT IN THE PRESENCE OF HIS ATTORNEY.

That afternoon, Becky Beard arrived at Brackenridge to see
her father. The nurses turned her away, but Wines happened
to be there. The day before, he'd talked to all Steve's grown
children. He'd told them little except that the investigation
was under way. Individually, each had advised him to consider Celeste. They seemed sure she was behind the shooting. Wines assured them he was following every lead.

When Wines saw the nurse refuse to let Becky in, he went
up to the woman and talked to her, assuring her that Mr.
Beard would want to see his daughter. With that, the nurse
brought Becky into the room. Steve couldn't talk, but he
opened his eyes and saw that she was there. "Paul and
Steven send their love, dad," she told him. "I love you."

He smiled and held her hand.

Steve had another visitor that day, Harold Entz, a state district judge from Dallas and his old friend. This time Becky
intervened to get him in to see Steve, who held his hand,
squeezing hard, happy to see him. Days later, after the judge
returned home, Celeste called, screaming that he wasn't ever
allowed to visit Steve again. Entz hung up on her.

At BookPeople that Monday after the shooting, Tracey's
employees noticed she was distracted and jumpy. They were
all curious about the shooting at the Beard house, asking
what she knew and if she'd heard from Celeste. "I can't really talk to her now. She's busy," Tracey told one. "I don't
know anything about what happened."

Yet, the two women had been talking on the telephone
throughout the weekend, calling from pay phones, in case
their home phones were tapped.

"How's Steve?" Tracey asked.

"Not good," Celeste replied. "I can't believe he hasn't died."

Then Tracey asked something she'd wondered since the moment she learned that a shotgun shell had been found on the scene. "Why didn't you pick up the shell?"

"I fell asleep," Celeste answered. "I didn't wake up until the police broke into the house. By then it was too late."

By the time Charles Burton arrived at the Marriott, Celeste had made sure both the twins knew what she wanted them to say. As always, the girls did as they were told, saying Celeste was devoted to Steve.

After Burton left, Celeste pulled Kristina to the side, away from the other teens.

"He says Tracey is implicating me," she told her. "That's why I need an attorney, and why we have to be careful what we tell people."

Later at the hospital, Wines approached Kristina asking for the family's phone numbers. There were three lines coming into the Beard house; each of the Cadillacs had a car phone; plus all four of them, Celeste, Steve, Kristina, and Jennifer, had cell phones. It was a maze of phone numbers to weed through. But when Celeste saw Kristina talking to the detective, she shouted at her: "Kristina, come over here, now."

Quietly she whispered in her daughter's ear, "I don't want you talking to police or anyone from the D.A.'s Office. They're people we all need to be afraid of."

The next morning Wines drew up a request for a subpoena for all the Beard family phone records and Tracey Tarlton's cell and home phones. That done, he headed back to the hospital. When he got there, the sign was still on Steve's door and Celeste was standing guard. Rather than cause a scene, Wines decided to put off interviewing Steve, who nurses said was resting comfortably but was still in guarded condition.

Back at his office, he ran a more complete search on Tracey, coming up with not just her DWI, but the run-in she'd had with Reginald Breaux at the convenience store. Next, he expanded the search, looking for criminal records on Celeste. After a bit of searching, the database pulled up her insurance fraud conviction in Arizona. It was a minor charge, but to Wines it opened up another window into her true identity.

That done, he checked in at the District Attorney's Office and found out that Bill Mange had been assigned to the case. Wines had worked with Mange before and liked him. He was a good, resourceful prosecutor.

"Let me know what you find out from ballistics," Mange told him. From that point on there was little Wines could do but wait.

Finally, on the afternoon of Thursday, October 7, five days after the shooting, Wines stood outside Sergeant Knight's door and grinned.

"Ballistics got a match," he said. "We've got an arrest to make."

The report on the shell casing came back, and, as they'd both suspected, Jennifer's shotgun was easily ruled out. Tracey's Franchi, however, was an exact match. The rest of that day, Wines prepared the paperwork to arrest Tracey on charges of aggravated assault and injury to the elderly, with a possible sentence of life in prison. He also wrote up and had signed a search warrant for her house. Before he left the office, he named his file on the Beard case: "Victim (Beard, Steven); Defendant (Tarlton, Tracey), Case #9924038."

Early Friday morning, with a signed warrant in his hands, Wines called Tracey's attorney, Keith Hampton, and instructed him to bring Tracey in for booking.

"I'll take care of it," Hampton assured him.

Later that day, at the courthouse, Tracey was read her rights and booked for the shooting of Steve Beard. While she went through the system and made arrangements to put up a $25,000 bond, Wines went to her house with a search warrant.

Inside the house on Wilson, the crime scene unit combed through Tracey's possessions, looking for anything that tied her to the shooting. Many of the items they confiscated that day would yield no real clues. Tracey's computer and two zip drives and a stack of videos would all be deemed worthless to the investigation. The videos were nothing more than home movies, many with her cats and dogs. But on a backroom bookshelf Wines found framed photos of Tracey and Celeste. In a box he discovered even more, including photos from the lake house party, with Celeste sitting on Tracey's lap.

When Wines happened upon Tracey's journals from St. David's and Timberlawn, he put those in the box as well. Back at his office, he read through them. On page after page Tracey poured her heart out. It was obvious that her relationship with Celeste was much more than a brief affair. As Wines saw it, Tracey was obsessed with Celeste.

A birthday card completed the picture for him. With a flowered heart on the front it read: "*For the One I Love.*" Any doubts Wines had about whether Tracey's interest was reciprocated ended when he saw the signature: "*Love, Celeste.*"

Wines was cataloguing the evidence when Keith Hampton stopped in after walking Tracey through the process. They talked, and then Wines walked him to the door. "Thanks for taking care of this for us," he said. "Hope to see you again."

From the beginning, Celeste and Craig were a volatile mix. Here with twins Kristina and Jennifer in an early family photo.
Courtesy Cherie Falke

The twins had a name for their mother, Mommie Dearest, after the screaming portrayal of Joan Crawford in a book by her daughter. Both of them lived in fear of Celeste's mood swings, yet Kristina (*far right*) was devoted to her.
Courtesy Justin Grimm

After serving in World War II, the only job Steve Beard *(second from left)* could find was selling shoes at Neiman Marcus. That didn't matter to Elise Adams, a pretty young model he met there. Here on their wedding day.
Courtesy Paul Beard

The Beard family had always been close. "Someday everything we've built will be yours," Steve told his children. That was before Celeste.
Courtesy Paul Beard

Despite their more than four decades together, the love between Steve and Elise never tarnished. When she fell ill, he nursed her, and she still put on makeup and tried to look pretty for the man she loved.
Courtesy Paul Beard

The television station Steve Beard built, the former KBVO, now Austin's CBS affiliate, K-EYE. When it sold in 1994, it made Steve Beard a very wealthy man. *Photo by Kathryn Casey*

In February 1995, Steve married Celeste Martinez. His friends and family worried, but he looked like the happiest man in the world.

Celeste furnished the cavernous living room of their Toro Canyon house with Henredon and Baker furnishings. On the wall she hung a painting of herself with the twins, Steve's small face in the fountain. "That way we can paint over him when he dies," she told the girls. *Courtesy Greg Hursley*

By spring 1999, Justin (*far left*) pushed Kristina (*beside him*), wanting her to realize that her mother's actions toward her were abusive. Meanwhile, Christopher (*far right*) told Jennifer to save her money. "With Celeste as a mother, you may need it," he said. *Courtesy Justin Grimm*

The night of the twins' senior prom, Steve and Celeste posed outside the Toro Canyon house. After he passed out, she spent the night with Jimmy Martinez. *Courtesy Justin Grimm*

Celeste and Tracey Tarlton met in a psychiatric hospital in the spring of 1999. Here at the Fashion Victim party, Celeste sits on Tracey's lap, with a marijuana brownie in one hand and a drink in the other.

S eparated when Tracey returned to Austin, Celeste sent cards, among them a birthday card that read, "To the One I Love."
Photo by Kathryn Casey

A t the twins' graduation party, Celeste and Tracey danced. Later Celeste would claim that Tracey stalked her.

C eleste threw the twins' graduation party at Jimmy's house. Steve wasn't invited.

In February 1999, the girls turned eighteen, and Celeste threw a party. She bragged that the centerpieces alone had cost thousands. Male dancers embarrassed the twins, and Celeste told friends Steve didn't come because he wouldn't have approved.

One who knew them well said that what was between Jimmy and Celeste "wasn't love but lust." From the way they danced at the twins' birthday party, many suspected they were lovers.

I n New Orleans for Mardi Gras, Donna Goodson (in blonde wig) and Celeste drank and partied. Here clowning on a night on the town.

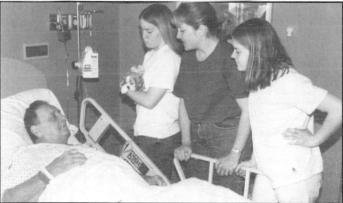

I n the hospital, Celeste catered to Steve. Here, on his seventy-fifth birthday, Kristina holds his present, a cocker spaniel puppy he named Kaci. Later, Celeste scoffed, "I can't believe he didn't die."
Courtesy Justin Grimm

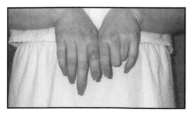

A fter Steve's death, Celeste's hands became infected. She asked Justin to take this photo, as evidence in case she sued the hospital.
Courtesy Justin Grimm

Tracey Tarlton's father gave her this .20 gauge when she was a teenager. At first she shot small animals, but then gave it up. "I didn't like killing," she said. "It just wasn't me." *Photo by Kathryn Casey*

A talented prosecutor, Allison Wetzel didn't want the Beard case but couldn't turn it down. Here she and Gary Cobb prepare for trial. *Photo by Kathryn Casey*

In the courtroom, Celeste, Catherine Baen, and Dick DeGuerin. Celeste looked more like a librarian than the femme fatale who had married five times. *Photo by Kathryn Casey*

Hampton shook his hand, then looked at Wines intently and said, "I'm sure you will."

As the defense attorney walked away, Wines thought, *He's telling me Tracey has something to barter with.*

While Keith Hampton insinuated the possibility of a deal, Celeste worried about evidence that she and the woman now charged with her husband's shooting were lovers. One afternoon in the car, she called Cindy Light, the photographer. Light had heard about the shooting and was surprised to hear from Celeste so soon.

"How's Steve? How are you?" she asked.

"He's in the hospital," Celeste said. "Do you have the photos from Tracey's party?"

Light thought for a minute, stunned. It seemed an odd request just days after an attempted murder. "No," she said. "I gave them to you, negatives and all."

"Okay," Celeste said, and hung up.

Afterward, Cindy realized that she'd been wrong. She'd given the photos to Tracey, not Celeste. What neither she nor Celeste yet knew was that they were already in evidence at the Sheriff's Department. *Celeste,* Light thought, *what have you done?*

The phone rang at Keith Hampton's office that week as well, and in weeks to come. Celeste wanted to talk with him about Tracey's case.

"I can't talk to you about that," he said. "Tracey's my client."

As many times as he refused, Celeste continued to call.

That afternoon at the hotel, Celeste pulled Kristina to the side. "Don't tell anybody, but I talked to Tracey," she said. "They've arrested her for Steve's shooting." She then repeated what Keith Hampton had advised Tracey in their meeting that day, that he would fight to keep the gun out of evidence by claiming the search was unconstitutional.

The knowledge that her mother had been talking to Tracey frightened Kristina. "You promised you wouldn't talk to Tracey," she said.

"Oh, don't worry," Celeste told her. "I won't do it again."

Days later Jennifer looked at the caller ID on Celeste's cell telephone and saw Tracey's name and phone number. Frightened, she confronted Celeste. "You're talking to Tracey, aren't you?"

"No," Celeste insisted. "She must be calling and hanging up."

Not long after, Celeste changed the password on her voice mail, so the girls could no longer pick up her calls.

With Tracey now charged, Wines had to inform Steve of her arrest. Ignoring the sign on the door, he went inside and found Steve still hooked up to a ventilator and appearing as if each breath might be his last. He took the news with little emotion and showed no surprise. After the detective left, Steve motioned for a pen and pad from the nurses. "*Let my family in to see me*," he wrote. Perhaps he reasoned that now he knew who the shooter was, and it wasn't Celeste.

Not knowing Celeste had already learned about the arrest from Tracey, Wines's last task that day was to tell her. He called Charles Burton and learned that she and the girls had changed hotels and were now staying at a La Quinta Inn near the hospital. When he arrived, the desk clerk called upstairs. "You have a visitor," he said.

"She doesn't want to see anyone," the man said when he hung up.

Wines pulled out his badge. "Tell Mrs. Beard that Detective Wines wants to talk to her."

Minutes later Celeste and the twins walked into the lobby. When Wines started talking, she pulled him outside, away from the ears of the clerk.

"Am I a suspect?" she asked.

"I'm here to tell you we arrested Tracey," Wines said.

"Is the investigation closed?"

"No," he said. She frowned when he added, "We're still investigating."

Although it had been nearly a week since the shooting, Steve's outlook remained dire. Much of the time he was heavily drugged and asleep. Over the coming weeks, Dr. Coscia would first try to stabilize Steve and then wean him from the ventilator. Repeatedly he'd have to be put back on as his oxygen levels plummeted. Since the gunshot tore through his intestines, it had polluted Steve's body with debris, raising the risk of serious infection. Signs at the door to his room asked visitors to don surgical gowns and wash their hands, to protect him from what in others might be a minor cold or flu, but to Steve could prove fatal.

Justin said nothing of his suspicions to Kristina, but he watched Celeste carefully. More than once he saw her walk into Steve's room without washing her hands. Once, when she had a sore throat, she went into his room in the ICU anyway. Inside, she took off her mask and kissed Steve full on the lips. Later, Justin reasoned that he was afraid to tell anyone what he was thinking. If he did, it would make it real.

At times Steve cried, depressed. At other moments, with the kids, he smiled, mouthing that the IV fluids and ice chips didn't match real food. Once, Jennifer put her ear to his lips, and he whispered, "I see hamburgers in my dreams."

Jen laughed, but when Steve chuckled, he stopped, holding his abdomen and squeezing the button on the drug dispenser for more pain killers. By then doctors had taken him in for more surgeries, including cutting a tracheotomy, a hole in his throat for the breathing tube. He was still being fed through tubes going directly into his stomach. Daily, nurses debreeded his wounds, cleaning out infection.

Long term, no one could predict how he'd mend, but the doctors agreed he'd be in a wheelchair for the foreseeable future. Although before the shooting he'd been a robust man, Steve was now in constant pain, bedridden and feeble, dependent on others to do the simplest tasks. The social workers talked to Celeste and Kristina about the future, a series of operations in which skin grafts would be transplanted over his gaping wounds. Once he healed, he'd be transferred to a rehab facility, where Celeste would be taught to care for him. Every conversation with his doctors began with, "If Mr. Beard survives . . ."

Even with Steve battling for his life, Celeste's attention seemed drawn not to him but to his accounts at the Bank of America, where his money remained out of her grasp. While Steve was incapacitated, C. W. Beard, the banker, and Steve's attorney, Kuperman, had agreed on a system to pay household expenses. With that go-ahead, Celeste spent lavishly. Some of the expenses claimed were for preparing the house for Steve's return home in a wheelchair, which included $26,000 for an ornamental stair railing.

Her handyman practically lived at the Toro Canyon house, building bookshelves and doing repairs. She had a gazebo built outside, telling the Dennisons it would be a place for Steve to sit in his wheelchair and look out at the trees. Dr. Dennison shook his head in wonder when she then had a pathway of loose river rocks laid to it, one on which it would have been nearly impossible to push a wheelchair.

Louis Shanks trucks pulled up weekly with new furniture

both at the Toro Canyon house and the lake house. The carpeting had been torn out and replaced, Celeste bought new wallpaper for the bathrooms, and, in what was still a brand new house, she hired painters to change the finish on the window ledges from satin to glossy.

Other expenditures, Celeste said, were for security. She paid $7,600 for chain-link fencing and razor wire, the spirals of thin steel blades often seen on the tops of fences and buildings in rough parts of large cities. For two weeks Jimmy Martinez worked daily at the Toro Canyon house, installing a cutting edge camera-equipped security system. From a central command center, Celeste could watch every door and every room.

It didn't help the girls' peace of mind that spectators drove by and stared at the house. Celeste posted a sign more often seen on dark country roads than in affluent neighborhoods: "No Trespassing. This property is under 24 hour video surveillance."

In mid-October she and the girls moved back to Toro Canyon. Jimmy left his German shepherd to guard them; and the teens, all on edge, slept together in Kristina's room, listening for Tracey's footsteps. "We were terrified she'd come back," says Kristina.

Jennifer was not only frightened of Tracey; she was afraid of Celeste, so much so that whenever she could, she stayed with friends. "I just knew she was involved, and I didn't know what she'd do to us," she says. "I wouldn't leave Kristina, but I shook every time I got in the car with Celeste. I was afraid she'd drive us off the side of a hill."

Meanwhile, the bills rolled into Kuperman's office. Along with all the house repairs, Celeste had purchased two Cadillac Cateras for the twins and a brand new $55,000 bronze mist Cadillac for herself. Combined, the three cars cost $105,000. With the bills climbing from the tens of thousands to the hundreds of thousands, Kuperman went to the hospital to see Steve. Celeste was with him, but Steve, still on a ventilator, was unable to talk. Kuperman stayed only briefly, getting no answers to any of his questions.

Ten days after Steve was shot, Becky returned to the hospital. This time she came armed with papers her father had signed years earlier that gave her his power of attorney for medical purposes. She took them to a social worker and had a notation made on his chart. When she went down to see him, Celeste tried to keep her from entering the room.

"He's been my father a lot longer than he's been your husband," Becky told her. "Get out of my way."

"He has a new family now. He doesn't love any of you!" Celeste screamed.

Becky stared at her. "I know my father loves me. I'm not going to take this up with him now, but when he's better, we'll have a talk." Then she went into his room.

After Becky left for Dallas, Celeste had Steve sign a new form, removing Becky and giving her his medical power of attorney. Once she had it noted on his chart, she began a code system; only people who knew the word of the day were given information about Steve's condition. From that point on, the older Beard children were rebuffed when they called the hospital and asked about their father. "Steven finally got someone at the hospital to help us," says Paul. "Celeste wouldn't even let us talk to our father."

Although she catered to him at the hospital, it gnawed at Celeste that Steve hadn't died. She hated going to the hospital, and complained to the twins that she had other things to do. The day the nurse put her hand over Steve's trach opening, so he could not just mouth words or write but talk, the kids were delighted. But his raspy voice struck a different chord with Celeste. Suddenly, all the weeks of pledging her love ended. "I can't believe she did that," she said. "Now I'll have to listen to that fat old fuck telling me what to do."

Many afternoons, Celeste and Tracey met at a picnic table in a small creekside park just north of downtown. Since her arrest, Tracey's friends at work stared at her. People treated her differently; many, including Pat and Jane, kept a distance. She felt alone. In mid-October she overdosed on prescription drugs and booze and spent another night in St. David's, barely pulling through. But when they were together, Celeste appeared unconcerned about Tracey. She was worried about her own future.

"I think the kids are suspicious of me," she said. "Not Kristina, but the others."

"Do they know anything?"

"I don't think so. They're just guessing," she said. Rambling on, she talked about Steve, saying that she'd never expected him to hold on for so long. She had to be at the hospital every minute, she told Tracey, watching to see who he was talking to. She didn't even want him talking alone to her attorney, Burton, afraid of what he might tell him. "And the will's not what I thought it was," she lamented. Celeste complained that she'd thought she'd have access to Steve's money, not be at the mercy of the bank. "I'm going to get him to change it," she said.

Perhaps Steve truly believed Celeste was innocent; still, there must have been a nagging doubt, a little voice that asked, "Why would Tracey do this?"

"Do you believe that crazy nut? She had the hots for Celeste and was jealous of a fat old guy like me," he said to one friend when he came to visit. The friend, who doubted Tracey had acted alone, only nodded. Around Steve, they all watched every word.

"His condition was up and down," says Jennifer. "We didn't want to upset him. We were afraid for him. And if we said anything, we were afraid he'd tell our mom."

Only Kristina, who had no doubts about her mother's innocence, asked Steve one day what he remembered from the night of the shooting. "Just waking up hurting like hell," he said. "Now don't you worry your pretty head about it."

Still, that doubt must have been there, perhaps fueled by a visit from Kuperman in early November, when he laid out Celeste's expenditures. In the month since the shooting, she'd spent nearly $300,000. Upset, Steve just shook his head. "I can't think about this now," he said. "When I get out of here, then I'll take care of it."

A month after the shooting, however, Steve was suddenly forced to confront his doubts. That afternoon, Celeste answered her cell phone in his hospital room. The girls listened as she talked, and they realized it was Tracey.

"Girls, wait outside. I want to talk to your mother," Steve ordered.

They did as they were told. Minutes later Celeste left Steve's room fuming. "Change all the phone numbers on the cell phones," Celeste told Kristina.

Later the twins would find out what went on in that room. Steve had looked at Celeste and asked her, "Did you put Tracey up to this?"

The following day, Celeste told Kristina to go to the hospital. She'd written a letter for Steve and wanted her to read it to him. Kristina didn't want to, but Celeste insisted.

In his room, Steve listened as Kristina read the rambling letter, in which Celeste maintained her innocence and pledged her love and devotion. "*I love you and I didn't do this,*" Celeste had written. "*Please believe me.*"

When Kristina finished, she looked up and realized

Steve was crying. Angry, he took a glass full of ice and threw it at her.

"Get out," he shouted.

Kristina ran crying from the room.

Later that day Celeste walked into Steve's hospital room and massaged away his doubts. Just like so many men before him, he couldn't extricate himself from her. Despite all he'd been through, all the reasons he had to doubt her, she reeled him back in

Chapter
14

Steve wasn't the only one asking if Celeste was behind the shooting. By November, rumors swirled through the city's social and media circles. At the Austin Country Club members whispered about the bizarre love triangle, a former waitress with her multimillionaire husband and the gay woman charged with shooting him. At Tramps and Studio 29, patrons and hairdressers swapped gossip. When Celeste entered, they held back, watching her every move. She presided as always, chattering and laughing loudly. The minute she left, the salons filled with nervous nattering. But the theories were just theories until an *Austin American Statesman* reporter, Laylan Copelin, called Celeste and asked very pointed questions.

Celeste refused to comment, but days later Copelin received an anonymous letter. The writer described herself as a friend and called Celeste *"one of the most giving people in the world . . . she helps out everyone and treats everyone as her equal, even though she is a very wealthy woman."* She said Celeste adored Steve and was the valiant survivor of a horrific past that included childhood sexual abuse, domestic violence, and ovarian cancer:

"The Beards were to leave for a month long trip to Europe the day after Steven was shot. Celeste was hoping that if Tracey did not see or talk with her for that length of time she would be able to be rid of Tracey for good. I am telling you all of this off the record . . . [Celeste] is tired, baffled and hurt by all of this. Making her a public humiliation serves no purpose. She trusted someone who is crazy. She feels tremendous guilt over the entire situation even though Steven has told her not to give it another thought. I know you want a story, but please do not further hurt a family that is already suffering."

Years later that same letter would be found on Celeste's home computer.

Despite the anonymous tribute, Copelin wrote his piece on the shooting, under the headline: A SHOT IN THE NIGHT; WIFE'S FRIEND CHARGED IN ATTACK ON TV EXECUTIVE.

"The 20-gauge shotgun blast ripped open Steve Beard Jr.'s belly while his wife and stepdaughter slept in another wing of his house on one of the highest points in Westlake Hills. The former television executive, 74, managed to dial 911.

"One month and three surgeries after the shooting . . . Beard remains in intensive care and his wife, Celeste, who is 36, spends most of her days at his bedside."

The article went on to detail Tracey's arrest and quoted Wines as saying the women met in a psychiatric hospital and that Tracey was "infatuated" with Celeste. There'd been no signs of forced entry into the house, and many questions remained to be answered. Copelin reported that Celeste had hired a defense attorney and wasn't cooperating with police.

That morning, Celeste's life moved from the beauty shop

rumor mill to fodder for Austin's morning, drive-time radio shows. Callers speculated on air about what type of relationship she'd had with Tracey and about the motives of a woman who married a man nearly old enough to be her grandfather. "Gold digger," some callers said. "Craziest thing I've ever heard of," another said.

"Sure, someone just leaves the door unlocked and the alarm off and this crazy woman just wanders in?" laughed one caller. "Give me a break."

Furious, Celeste went on the offensive. The day after the article ran, she phoned in to the *Sam & Bob* show, a drive-time staple for commuting Austinites, voicing what she described as her frustration. "I want you to know that the newspaper made it sound like the *National Enquirer*."

"Celeste, do you have any feelings about who did this?" one DJ asked.

"That part of the story may be right," she admitted, yet she denied a relationship with Tracey and labeled the coverage, "Sensationalism."

Days later Rich Oppel's phone rang at the *Statesman*. Four years earlier Oppel, the newspaper's editor-in-chief, had bought Steve's Terrace Mountain Drive house. Since then he'd run into him off and on at the Headliners Club, which catered to the city's media crowd. Oppel liked Steve. He judged him a good sort, a genuinely nice guy.

After a pleasant enough hello, Celeste said she wanted to bring her attorney to talk to Oppel about the news coverage. Oppel agreed.

Celeste may have assumed the meeting would be only the three of them. Instead, when she arrived with one of Burton's associates, they were escorted into a conference room, where Oppel waited with two of his editors and Copelin, the reporter who'd written the article. That morning, Celeste was dressed for business in a suit and big jewelry, looking like a woman of wealth. She got right to the point, complaining that the article raised questions about her relationship with Tracey and exposed her to public scrutiny. While she may have come hoping for sympathy and a retraction, Oppel didn't budge. Instead he shot questions at her, asking her to describe her relationship with Tracey and asking point blank, "Were you involved in the shooting?"

Celeste hesitated. Oppel thought she might answer, but the attorney interceded.

"We need to go," he said.

When she spun on her high heels and walked to the door, the room was cool with her anger.

With the eyes of Austin on her, Celeste paced restlessly about the picnic table when she next met with Tracey at the park. The twins had noticed Tracey's name on the caller ID on her cell phone and on the home phones, she said. They questioned how Tracey had the numbers, when they'd all been changed and were unlisted. "Buy me a cell phone," Celeste told Tracey. "I'll pay for it, but they won't know. We'll be able to talk."

Tracey agreed. She was willing to do whatever she could to stay close to Celeste. At her psychiatrist appointments, she talked of nothing but the toll the separation took on her. Not only was she charged with a felony that carried a possible life sentence, but the woman she loved was rarely in her life. They no longer even had stolen nights together, just the brief encounters in the park where they were careful not to touch. At times Tracey felt desperate to talk to Celeste, just to hear her voice.

"It'll be over, and then we'll be together," Celeste told her. "You'll see. If that old man would just go ahead and die."

Tracey tried not to listen to the doubt inside her, the certainty that it would never be over and that things would never be as they were.

Having Steve confined to the hospital appeared to fit Celeste's purposes well. She flitted in and out of his room during the day, on her way to have her hair or nails done or to shop. With the go-ahead from the bank to cover household and living expenses, money was no object. The work at the house continued, with new projects starting weekly. But as the costs continued to climb, Kuperman and the bankers asked questions.

In response, Celeste wrote a letter for Steve and brought it to the hospital for him to sign. In it, Steve agreed with all her expenditures, saying that she was making the house improvements to accommodate his needs and that he had planned to purchase the three Cadillacs. *"I'm coherent and Celeste read this entire letter to me before I signed it,"* it said. *"Everything she's doing is for my comfort and security."* The nurse who witnessed his signature noted that Steve blinked once to acknowledge the letter before signing it. When Kuperman received it, Steve's signature was jagged and barely resembled his old one. Kuperman went to the hospital, but Steve was so heavily medicated he was barely awake. When Kuperman returned two days later, Steve didn't remember that he'd been there.

When she was at the hospital, Celeste catered to Steve, running to get him water, holding his hand and kissing him. "We're going to get you home and take good care of you," she said.

Meanwhile, with Tracey, she raved about how she couldn't stand him and that she never wanted him to come home. In his weakened condition, she said, if he came home it would be easy to ensure that he never fully recovered. She'd been told the importance of keeping his wound clean. "I'll just spit on my hands and touch him. Eventually he'll get an infection and die," she said.

"If he dies, I'll face a murder charge," Tracey said, pleading. "Please, Celeste, don't."

"He's not out yet. Let's just not worry about it," she said, flipping the subject to something else.

Although the skin grafts Coscia applied healed reluctantly, Steve's condition slowly improved. In November he was moved from acute care into a regular room. From the window, he looked out on Austin's sports complex, and one day Justin joked that they could slip him out of the hospital for a basketball game.

Steve laughed. "I'm on this really excellent diet," he said. "I'm so skinny I bet I could fit through the chimney."

Just getting back on solid food, Steve had lost nearly a third of his weight, 100 pounds. Despite the weight loss, he looked far less healthy than before, his complexion pale from the sunless hospital rooms. Justin's heart ached for him when Steve said, "You know, I'd just like to be able to take a ride in a car."

As he became more aware of what was going on around him, Steve tried to reclaim bits and pieces of his life. He asked for small things, like his ring and his watch. Celeste gave Jennifer her credit card and sent her to the jewelry store to replace his sapphire ring and watch. Although no one had seen the items since the night of the shooting, Celeste never reported them stolen. In Texas, a murder in conjunction with another crime, like a burglary, can bring a capital murder charge and the death penalty. "I don't think we want to risk that," she told Tracey.

* * *

Meanwhile, Steve's older children worried about their father. They called Detective Wines at the Sheriff's Department often, asking how the investigation was coming. Wines assured them that he was working the case, but in reality he was doing little. When Judge Entz flew into Austin for another visit with Steve in November, he saw the sign barring police on the door, and he was furious.

"Are you honoring that?" he demanded when he called Wines.

"Yes," Wines said. "We are."

"Why?" the judge asked, but Wines didn't have an answer.

Days later Celeste called Entz, screaming, "You're not allowed to visit Steve ever again." He hung up. When she called back, he refused to take her calls.

Detective Wines would say later that he didn't know why he didn't ignore the sign and walk in. As a police officer, he had a legal right to interview the victim, whether or not his wife agreed. Was it Celeste's money, the big house and the expensive jewelry she wore, that made him wary to cross her? Perhaps he feared her high-profile attorney, Charles Burton? Later, all he'd be able to say was that he checked on Steve's condition and knew he was improving. "I thought I'd wait until he was out of the hospital," he says. "Then I could interview him without worrying about his health."

With the animosity they felt toward Celeste, Steve's grown children had kept a distance throughout the months since the shooting, only talking to their father on the telephone, but they made plans to come to Austin in November to celebrate his seventy-fifth birthday. Becky was driving down from Dallas, and Paul and his wife Kim flying in from Virginia. As the date approached, Steven, who'd thought at first that he couldn't make it, made plans to bring his family from Chicago.

"We wanted to throw him as much of a party as he was up to," says Paul.

Celeste was furious. She called all three, screaming, ordering them not to come. They said they had a right to see their father. Then she demanded to know where they were staying and who they'd be seeing. "Your father's not strong enough for you to come, and I'm too busy taking care of him to entertain you," she told Paul. When he still insisted he was coming, she said, "Stay by the telephone. You'll be getting a call from your father."

A short time later Paul's phone rang. Steve's voice sounded tired and sad when he said, "Paul, it's not a good time to come. Steven can't make it anyway."

"Yes, he's coming, Dad. He'll be there," Paul said. "All of us will be there."

Steve was silent. Then, in a voice filled with resolution, he said, "It's not a good time. You can't come."

In the end Steve's birthday was a quiet affair. In his hospital room, the girls, Justin, and Celeste gathered. Kristina smuggled in his present, a blond cocker spaniel puppy.

"What do I need another dog for?" Steve said gruffly, but minutes later the dog was licking his cheek and Steve was laughing. He named the puppy Kaci.

In December, Steve put in a call for Chuck Fuqua at the bank, asking about checks he'd expected but hadn't seen, including health insurance reimbursements. Chuck called back and told him that they'd already been cashed, the money put into an old joint account he had with Celeste, one that had been inactive, then pulled out and transferred into her personal account.

Steve thanked Chuck and hung up.

David Kuperman brought Steve more bad news in a briefcase full of bank statements and bills, including a spread sheet that showed Celeste's wild spending while he'd been in the hospital. It must have been a bad day for Steve, looking at the stacks of charges Celeste had incurred. In the months since he'd been hospitalized, Celeste had spent more than $550,000, money that would have to be raised by selling stocks out of his trust.

Kuperman pointed out that many of the expenses were onetime costs, like the security system at the house and the cars. "Hopefully, they won't be recurring," he said. "I've talked with Celeste and she says the expenses will be going down."

"This is out of line, but I can't do anything about this now. Not while I'm in here. All I care about is getting better," Steve said.

Yet Kuperman knew his old friend was fuming. "Do you want a divorce?" he asked.

"No," Steve said, shaking his head. "I'll talk to Celeste and put the brakes on."

That day, Kuperman also brought an addendum to the trust. Davenport II was nearing completion. In a phone call, he and Steve had discussed what to do with the property and the income it would generate. As with Davenport I, it was decided that Steve's interest in the property would go into the trust. Despite his anger, Steve signed the papers. It wasn't what Celeste told Tracey she wanted—control of the money without interference from the bank—but it increased the monthly stipend she could expect to get if he died.

"Steve changed the will," Celeste crowed when she met with Tracey. "It's all mine."

She arrived at the park that day in an expensive suit and sat smoking on the picnic table, looking out at the creek and the sun filtering through the bare tree limbs. Ahead of her waited all the wealth she'd dreamed of. All that stood in her way was Steve. That she didn't understand the trust, and that the changes hadn't given her access to his wealth, eluded her. As Celeste explained it to Tracey, the addendum meant she was the sole beneficiary to the estate and all of Steve's millions.

"Steve's such a sweetheart. I can't stand to watch him in so much pain," she said.

Celeste's words stung Tracey. "I thought you hated him," she said. "I thought you couldn't stand to have him touch you. Now, because he changed his will, he's a great guy."

"I just hate to see him in so much pain," she said.

It would turn out that her change of heart was short-lived. Early the following week, Celeste showed up at the park in her old humor, complaining bitterly about her husband. "I wish he'd just die," she said, "just fucking die and leave me the hell alone."

That winter, Celeste seemed intent on purging the house and her two storage areas of old papers and documents. Perhaps she worried about the secrets they held. Yet, she wasn't interested in doing the work herself. She had her little "niglets" for that.

"Just get rid of everything," she said. "I want it all gone."

They did as they were told, but they did something she hadn't counted on; they looked through what they were throwing out. As they pawed through boxes of papers, Jennifer and Christopher discovered four cards from Tracey to Celeste, and the three journals Celeste had kept at Timberlawn. In the cards, Tracey yearned for Celeste, talking about her beautiful body and how she wanted to run her hands over it. Black and white composition books, the journals were filled with page after page of Celeste's writing, notes from classes and accusatory letters to her mother and father, assignments from the psychiatrists at St. David's and Timberlawn. Also, scattered throughout, were notes from Tracey.

"Look at that," Jennifer said, pointing to one note after another.

"You have a lot of anger that you are not in touch with . . . TRY.

"I told Dr. Miller that I have no sexual interest in you, so I lied, but you should too . . . We need to go outpatient . . . QUICK.

"Celeste I believe you, Tracey."

From the beginning, the first night of the shooting, Jennifer and Christopher had both believed Celeste was involved. Now they held in their hands writings that tied her romantically to Tracey. They didn't know what to do, but sensed they could one day be important. That afternoon, Christopher slipped the journals and cards under his car seat and carted them off to his apartment for safe keeping.

"Should we tell Kristina?" he asked.

Jen shook her head no. Anything Celeste asked, Kristina would do. Jennifer believed Celeste was more than capable of murder, that she'd already tried to murder Steve. What stopped Celeste from coming after them? "If we tell her, it could put all of us in danger."

Justin and Kristina made a similar discovery in the attic and out in the garage storage area, where Celeste put them to work. They found the family planner from the house, Celeste's secret calendar, and photos of Tracey and Celeste together at St. David's, with Tracey's arm draped over Celeste's shoulders.

"What do you think these mean?" Justin asked.

"It means Tracey was telling the truth. That they were lovers," Kristina answered.

"Nothing more?"

Kristina believed in Celeste so much, she'd protected her for so long, she just couldn't let herself think any more than that Tracey loved Celeste and had shot Steve out of jealousy. So she didn't answer. As he'd done with his own suspicions since the night of the shooting, Justin tucked the calendars and the photos away where he would be prepared to share them with Kristina if and when she was finally ready.

The holidays approached, and Kristina thought little of it when Celeste gave her a credit card and asked her to pick up an order she'd placed at a James Avery jewelry store. One of the items, she said, was a ring that she was buying for Jim Madigan to give his wife Dawn. At the store, amid the display cases of gold and silver, Kristina walked around, choosing gifts for friends and writing the item numbers on a slip of white paper. She jotted down the number of the ring and went to look at it. When she found it, it was the Simplicity Wedding Band, a simple gold and silver ring, identical to one Christopher had given Jennifer in October for their one year anniversary.

Dawn has a wedding ring, Kristina thought. *Why would Jim give her that?*

By December 7, Steve had had seven operations in two months, from the original surgery, through installing and removing the tracheotomy and laying in the skin grafts. His wounds slowly healed, until seventy percent were covered by new skin. With so much progress, Dr. Coscia discharged him to HealthSouth, a rehab facility next door to Brackenridge. Its proximity gave the doctor the opportunity to look in on Steve and monitor his recovery.

That month, Dr. Coscia rarely saw Celeste when he visited Steve's room. Celeste hated to go, complaining it interrupted her day. Perhaps Steve complained, again pushing her to tell him what she wanted, to be with him or to be apart. Days before Christmas, they battled in his room, Celeste screaming and shouting, taking a key and pressing it against her skin, threatening to cut her wrists.

That night at home, she screamed at Kristina. Grabbing a framed photo, she threw it against the wall, and pulled out a shard of glass. "You know what your father looked like when he blew his brains out," she taunted, pressing the glass against her wrist. "His face, his whole head, was gone. I read the autopsy. His whole face was nothing but a big hole."

"Stop it," Kristina shouted, crying.

"What do you care? You're Kristina Beard now," Celeste screamed sarcastically.

Shaking, Kristina ran outside and dialed 911 on her cell phone. She watched her mother through the window as Celeste paced manically through the house. Within minutes two deputies arrived to handcuff Celeste and transport her to St. David's. All the way to the car, Celeste cursed at Kristina and called her names. That night, at Justin's parents' house, Steve called Kristina on her cell phone.

"Don't listen to what your mother says when she's like this. She doesn't know what she's doing. She's sick," he said. "She doesn't mean those things."

The following morning Celeste's therapist, Dr. Hauser, signed her release papers. When Celeste saw Kristina at home, she acted like nothing had happened.

In the park, days after Christmas, Celeste handed Tracey a small box wrapped in silky white paper with a silver James Avery gift tag. Tracey opened it, and inside was the Simplicity Wedding Band that Celeste had asked Kristina to pick up, gold with silver edges.

"This ring means that I love you and that we're supposed to be together," Celeste told her, slipping it on her finger. "Remember, you belong to me."

For once, Tracey didn't worry who might see, and they kissed openly in the park. Afterward, Celeste glanced about nervously. "Do you think anyone saw us?" she asked.

Hurt that at such a time she'd be worried, Tracey said, "I don't think so."

"That Justin is such a snake. I wouldn't put it past him to be following me," she said. "I don't know what he knows about all this, but he knows something."

The check Jimmy Martinez expected from Bank of America for the security work he'd done at the house arrived just after the first of the year. Instead of being for the amount of the invoice, $8,000, it was made out for $74,499.38. Jimmy called Celeste and said there'd been a mistake. She had a simple solution. "Sign the check over to me and I'll give you one to replace it," she said.

Jimmy did, and Celeste wrote him a check for his work plus a $1,000 tip.

Another check came in that month. Stacy Sadler, the travel agent, received the refund on the trip to Europe. Looking at it in her hand, Stacy thought about Steve and all the rumors that Celeste was involved in the shooting. She decided she couldn't just hand the money over to her. It didn't seem right. So she walked a few doors down from the travel agency to the PakMail store where she knew Steve had a personal mailbox. She handed the envelope to the owner and asked, "Would you put this in Mr. Beard's box for me?"

"Sure," he said, looking at the envelope. "It's all taken care of."

She didn't know that Celeste had Steve's key. Just after the first of the year, on January 11, Celeste deposited that $50,124 check, along with the $74,499.38 check made out to Jimmy, into her bank account.

At HealthSouth the social workers discussed Steve's discharge needs. His skin grafts were healing slowly and needed special care, to be kept clean and checked for infection. His ileostomy needed to be changed daily. The risk of infection was high, and in his weakened state, any infection could prove fatal. "You really need to hire a nursing service," they told Celeste. "You're not equipped to handle this type of care."

Celeste, who didn't even like to brush her own hair, refused. "I want to do this myself," she told them.

Justin brought brochures on home nursing services, but she wouldn't read them.

"No," she said. "I want to take care of Steve myself."

At the park, Tracey begged her not to do anything to hurt him, fearing his death would raise the stakes and the charge against her to murder.

"It'll be easy," Celeste said. "I just won't wash my hands."

The morning of January 18, Celeste called Donna Goodson, the receptionist at Studio 29. A statuesque redhead with a wild side to match Celeste's, Donna had listened in for months to her diatribes against Steve as she dished with Joseph, her stylist. "I can't believe he didn't die," Donna heard Celeste say one day. Others at the salon talked well of Steve, but listening to Celeste, Donna thought he sounded like the vilest of men.

This day, Celeste called with a request: "Steve will be getting out this afternoon. I want to bring him in for a haircut, pedicure, and manicure."

"Sure, I'll juggle things and make room," Donna said. When she worked things out, it required Celeste giving up her nail appointment and rescheduling it for two days later. Celeste sounded miffed, but she agreed.

That afternoon, Celeste signed Steve out of HealthSouth and, with the physical therapist, helped him from his wheelchair into her Cadillac. At Davenport Village, Justin and Christopher helped him back into his wheelchair. Moments later, although she'd pledged to be his nurse, Celeste left. Instead, Kristina and the two boys pushed Steve around the shopping center. It was the first time he'd seen the completed Davenport II, and he grinned proudly at the sprawling two-story shopping center.

"Look at that," he said. "Look what I built."

He stopped in at PakMail and said hello to the owner. Then they made their way to Studio 29 for his haircut. At the salon, every task proved painful for Steve. Getting in and out of the stylist's chair, bending his head back for a shampoo, even putting his feet on a stool for the pedicure, brought pain. The stylist hurried him through, and Kristina and the boys helped Steve into her car. For the first time in nearly four months he drove into the long, tree-shaded driveway at Toro Canyon. He was home. But he couldn't get inside.

The carpenter had been there for months working on projects for Celeste, including new bookshelves, but she hadn't gotten around to ramps for the stairs until the day Steve came home. When he arrived, the ramps weren't done.

Justin and Christopher couldn't wheel him into the front of the house with the three flights of stairs, so they rolled him around to the back. There, too, there were stairs without ramps. Finally Justin, Christopher, and the carpenter all hoisted him up to the landing and wheeled him into the living room. Inside the house, the railings had been installed, but again they encountered an obstacle, this time the stairs to the master bedroom wing. Steve stood up and, with Justin helping, tried to walk up the stairs. His abdomen covered with scar tissue, with each step he grimaced in pain.

It took half an hour from the time he pulled into the driveway until Justin wheeled Steve into the master bedroom, and he and Christopher helped him into the four-poster bed. The last time he'd laid there was the night he was shot, but that didn't appear to dull the excitement for Steve. He looked elated to be home.

Kristina kissed him good-bye, and she and Justin ran off to a photography class. Soon, Christopher left. By then Jennifer had arrived from work, and she climbed on the bed beside him. With Meagan on the floor at his feet and his new puppy, Kaci, on the bed between them, they watched *20/20* and talked. Steve looked exhausted but happy. When he fell asleep, Jennifer put on his oxygen machine, covered him with a blanket, kissed him on the forehead, and tiptoed off to bed.

Celeste still hadn't come home.

"I can't keep my nail appointment. Steve's dying," Celeste told Donna Goodson at Studio 29 on the phone the next morning. "I don't want him to die in the house, so I'm taking him back to the hospital."

"Don't worry," Donna said, amazed that she'd bothered to call with Steve so ill.

That morning Celeste had taken Steve to HealthSouth for a physical therapy session. She complained the entire time, saying they'd discharged him too soon.

"I don't want to come back here," Steve told her. "I want to stay at home."

"He can't even go to the bathroom. It took two of us to help him last night."

"I did things here," he said. "I did things in rehab. I can do it."

Ignoring what Steve wanted, Celeste called Dr. Coscia. "I want him readmitted," she said. "He's complaining of chest pains and he's not talking right. He's confused."

At Brackenridge Hospital just after 8:00 A.M., the physician on duty examined Steve, who complained of chest pains. Noting no indication of a heart problem, he examined a rash on Steve's groin. Diagnosing it as a yeast infection, he saw no reason to admit him. Hospitals can be dangerous places, with infection a high possibility. Steve, he said, would be better off at home. But when Dr. Coscia examined Steve, he overruled him.

"Let's keep him here a couple of days," he ordered. "See if we can treat the rash."

When she heard Steve was back in the hospital, Jennifer called Kristina on her cell phone to tell her what had happened.

"Did he look sick?" Kris asked.

"No," Jen said.

"That's so mean. She just doesn't want him home."

When Celeste called Tracey to tell her that Steve was back in the hospital, Tracey at first didn't believe her. "Why?" she said.

"He's really sick," she said. "I think he has some kind of infection."

"That HealthSouth is a disgusting pigpen," Celeste complained to the case worker at Brackenridge. "He had a rash, and they didn't do anything about it. They told me to put vinegar on it. He never should have been released. They said he could take care of himself, but he can't. They sent him home too soon."

Checked into another room, his fourth at the hospital, Steve was treated for the rash with antifungal creams and showers. He seemed well, ate, and talked to the twins. "I'm fine," he said. "I'll be home again in a couple of days."

That afternoon, Steve looked so good that another debate ensued between Coscia and a physician who saw no reason he should be in the hospital. A social worker was called in to explain to Celeste that with no clear reason why he should be there, Medicare might refuse to pay the bill.

"I don't care," she said. "We have money. We'll pay."

The following day, Steve fared well. His rash had improved and the doctors argued again about whether he needed to be hospitalized. The twins and their boyfriends stayed with Steve as Celeste came and went, saying she had errands to run. While disappointed at being back in the hospital, he was in a good mood, watching television and joking.

"This is just a setback," he told a friend who called. "I'm fine. I'll be out in no time."

The first real indication that more troubled Steve than he knew was the next day, when a cardiologist ran an EKG and did an ultrasound of Steve's heart. "*I don't believe this is ischemic chest pain*"—coming from any problem with the heart—the doctor wrote on his chart. "*I am concerned about infection given his warm, tender lower region.*"

Later that day blood work noted an elevated white blood cell count, another sign something was brewing.

In pain, Steve was given Vicodin, but his temperature had crept up overnight, another possible sign of infection. At just after three that afternoon it reached 102.5 degrees. More blood work was drawn, and this time it came back positive for infection.

Worried, Kristina called Dr. Handley, Steve's physician, and told him that he was back in the hospital.

"Lots of people get infections in hospitals. If they caught it early, he'll be all right," he said. "Try not to worry."

Meanwhile, Celeste seemed more preoccupied with her nail appointment. "I can't make it today. I think Steve's gonna die," she said to Donna when she called. "Just don't make an appointment for me."

"Celeste, forget about the salon," she replied. "Take care of yourself and Steve."

"Okay," Celeste said, and hung up.

By eight-thirty that evening drugs had brought Steve's temperature back down to 100.2 and he was resting comfortably. Yet he slept little that night, with nurses waking him every hour to take his temperature. By three-thirty the next morning, his temperature was up again, this time to 102.3. And something else was wrong; his pulse had climbed to 120 beats per minute. He was delirious, talking but making little sense.

"You owe me money," he told Kristina, who held his hand. "Twenty dollars."

"Okay, I'll pay you later," she said, humoring him.

Soon after, Celeste's mind, too, had turned to the issue of money.

Just after nine that morning she called Chuck Fuqua at home. "Steve's really sick, and I need to get on his bank account," she said.

"I can't do that," Chuck said. "Not without a new signature card."

"What if Steve signs a signature card?" she asked. "He wants me on there so I can take care of the bills."

Remembering all the times she'd forged Steve's name, Fuqua said, "If we can independently verify that it's his signature, yes, we can do it."

When he hung up the phone he thought, *Well, she found some way to finish him off.*

At 11:30 A.M., Steve's blood pressure dropped to 80 over 60. He wheezed and tossed uncomfortably in bed. He was disoriented, his breathing was shallow, and his heart raced at 140 beats per minute.

"You need to come home," Justin said when he called Jennifer in Houston, where she was with Christopher attending his great aunt's funeral. "Steve's taken a turn for the worse."

She and Christopher left the funeral and immediately drove west to Austin.

While his doctors treated Steve, Celeste fumed about HealthSouth, blaming the infection on poor care she said he'd received there. She even called the social worker at the facility. "There may be a lawsuit if he dies," she threatened.

As bad as Steve looked, and as concerned as the doctors appeared, Kristina didn't believe he would die. She kept remembering what Dr. Handley had said and about how many times Steve had been sick before and recovered. She'd already lost one father, and she couldn't grasp the possibility that she could lose another.

"Hello, Elise," Kristina heard Steve whisper. It gave her the chills. *He's just confused,* she thought.

Dr. Coscia wasn't at the hospital that day. With Steve in increasing respiratory distress, the doctor on duty ordered an infectious disease consult. The infectious disease doctor feared Steve suffered from septic shock, a rampaging and often fatal infection. "We're going to move your husband to the ICU," a nurse told Celeste at one-forty that afternoon. "Why don't you all go get some lunch and then go there to see him?"

After a night at his bedside, they were tired, and Kristina, Justin, and Celeste did as the nurse suggested. They drove to a nearby restaurant called the Brick Oven. In the car, Celeste called someone she told them was Dawn and talked to her throughout lunch. Later, Tracey would say that she was on the telephone with Celeste, her own pulse racing when she realized that if Steve died, she could soon be charged with murder.

Meanwhile at the hospital, at 2:31 that afternoon, a nurse and an aide wheeled Steve into the ICU on a gurney. By then his heart fluttered at a dangerous 162 beats per minute, his breathing was shallow, and his oxygen levels were low.

Four minutes later his pulse dropped to 60. And moments afterward his exhausted heart simply stopped.

In the minutes that followed, the ICU staff converged on Steve's bed. They intubated him, putting a tube down into his throat and pumping oxygen into his lungs. They gave him shots of epinephrine to stimulate his heart, then gave him CPR and jolted him with paddles to electrify his heart to beat.

It didn't work.

At 3:15 P.M., Steven Beard Jr. was officially declared dead.

The cause noted on his chart: septic shock, overwhelming infection.

"Are you the Beard family?" a nurse asked when they returned to the hospital.

"Yes," Celeste said.

She pulled them to the side, into a private room. "I'm sorry, we did all we could," she said. "But we couldn't save him."

Celeste let out a shriek that echoed off the walls and down the hospital corridors. Inconsolable, she screamed and cried until a doctor ordered her taken to an empty room and given Haldol to calm her. In the darkness, they laid her on a gurney.

"Steve's dead," Justin said when he called Jennifer on her

cell phone. He caught her and Christopher rushing back from Houston. At that point Jennifer cried and Christopher pulled over to comfort her. They no longer had a reason to hurry.

With Steve's body being escorted to the medical examiner's wagon to be taken for autopsy, Celeste called Donna at Studio 29, a woman she barely knew.

"Steve's dead. He's dead," she shouted.

"Celeste, calm down," Donna said. "You're going to be all right."

"No, he's dead, Donna. He's really dead."

When she hung up, Donna told the others who worked at the salon. Many had known Steve and liked him. Except from Celeste, Donna had never heard a bad word about him.

"God, he gave her everything," Petra Mueller, the owner, said.

Celeste left the hospital that afternoon and drove home in Steve's Cadillac with the twins and their boyfriends. As they got out of the car, she went inside. Justin opened the center console to retrieve a parking ticket they'd gotten at the hospital. Inside, he discovered something odd, an unfamiliar cell phone. As much time as he'd spent with Kristina and Celeste, he thought he knew all their phones. This was one he'd never seen.

"What's that?" Christopher asked as he walked over beside him.

"Have you ever seen this cell phone before?" Justin said.

Christopher took it from him and held it. He flipped the buttons and pulled up the opening screen with the phone number. "No," he said. He then flipped through the numbers recently dialed. Tracey's home and cell phones popped up.

Justin and Christopher looked at each other with a sinking feeling.

"She's still talking to Tracey," Justin said. Christopher nodded. He was thinking about all the times Celeste just disappeared. Usually, she told everyone where she was going, but since the shooting, she'd left the house or the hospital and was gone for hours, never mentioning where she'd been when she returned.

Just then Celeste ran from the house toward the car. They stepped to the side, Justin holding the cell phone behind him.

"I'm missing something," she said, throwing open the car door and searching. She opened the center console, then the glove compartment, then checked under the seats. While she was distracted, Justin dropped the cell phone and kicked it under the car.

Celeste jerked up and stood inches from him, pulling her body straight. Staring Justin in the eye, she held out her hand. "You have it. Give it to me."

"What?" Justin said.

"You have it. I want it now," she insisted as she frisked him down, like a cop searching a suspect. Seeing what was happening through the window, Kristina and Jennifer ran outside.

"What's wrong?" Kristina asked.

Celeste didn't answer, but again searched the car. Finding nothing, she ran inside.

"This is what she wanted," Justin said, bending down to retrieve the telephone. He handed it to Kristina.

Kristina grabbed the phone and looked at it. She, too, had never seen it before. But instead of investigating any further, she walked inside and gave it to her mother. "Is this what you wanted?" she said.

Celeste snatched it and disappeared into the guest bedroom, locking the door. Then Kristina heard her talking to someone on the telephone.

Later that night Celeste asked Kristina if she'd heard Steve's dying wish.

"No, what was it?"

"Steve said he forgave the person who shot him, and he didn't want to pursue the case. He didn't want any of us to have to go through the pain of a trial," she said. "He wouldn't want any of you to cooperate with the police."

Sad and confused, Kristina said nothing.

Chapter
15

Within hours of Steve's death Celeste left a message on the home voice mail of C.W. Beard, his cousin and banker in Dallas. "Steve's dead," she said. "I want to be put on his bank accounts right away. I have bills to pay."

When C.W. got the message, he called Becky. By then the bad news was filtering through the family. "We didn't even know our dad was back in the hospital," says Paul. "Celeste never told us."

The loss hit all of them hard as they looked back at the final years of their father's life. They'd had so little time with him since their mother's death. With Celeste pushing them away, they'd felt like outsiders. When they tried to visit, she always had reasons why it wouldn't work. "I knew she was behind the shooting," says Paul. "She wanted him dead, and she found someone to kill him."

That Saturday, after Steve was gone, Jennifer called Anita and told her the bad news. Anita did what she'd grown up doing when a friend had a death in the family; she bought two pies and went directly to the Toro Canyon house to console the family. She thought the house would be filled with friends and family; instead she found the twins and their boyfriends making phone calls to tell people about Steve's death while Celeste, in her chenille robe, smoked on the patio. After the incident with the telephone, she was in a foul mood.

"Those kids better do what I tell them," she snapped. "The money's all mine now. If they don't do what I want them to, I'll leave it all to the dogs."

"Celeste, you don't mean that."

"Sure, I do. And I'm going to spend every penny I can."

When Anita asked about the plans for the funeral services, Celeste frowned. "I'm not going to do anything but a small funeral," she said. "I don't want Steve's damn kids in my house."

"You have to do something. People will be expecting it," Anita argued. She suggested a small luncheon at the club following the funeral service, for family and close friends. "I'll even take care of setting it up for you."

Reluctantly, Celeste agreed.

That afternoon, Christopher put in a call for Brett Spicer, a deputy with the Sheriff's Department who'd sometimes worked security for the Beards. The twins were worried, afraid that with Steve gone, Tracey might show up at the house. When Spicer talked to Celeste, she was unconcerned. "I've talked to my therapist about it," she said. "Tracey's more likely to kill herself than to come after us."

Still, she told Spicer to bring in security, "so the girls feel safe."

At the house that night, with their adoptive father dead only hours, Celeste put the twins to work. Along with Justin and Christopher, they cleaned Steve's closet, taking everything he owned to a Goodwill bin except what she was burying him in and a few things she wanted to send to Steve III. The following night, when Spicer arrived, he found piles of boxes spread throughout the formal dining room with the names of family and friends on the outside. Inside were Steve's personal possessions, the things he loved. When they had it all organized, Celeste chose who received what. Then Jennifer and Christopher hauled the boxes to the PakMail store to be shipped. Within forty-eight hours of Steve's death, Celeste had removed nearly every trace of him from the house he'd so lovingly built.

"You need to figure out what part Celeste played in this," Paul Beard urged Detective Wines on the phone the Monday morning following his father's death.

"I can't tell you about the investigation," Wines said. "All I can say is we're working the case."

What he didn't want to and couldn't tell Paul was that the case was deeply in trouble. Early that morning he'd gone to the District Attorney's Office to talk to Bill Mange, the prosecutor. With nearly four months between the shooting and Steve's death, Mange explained that he'd wait for an autopsy to decide if Steve's death was related to the homicide. If so, the charges against Tracey could be upgraded to murder. Then Mange, a thin man with sloping shoulders and a big-toothed grin, got very serious. "You did talk to Steve Beard, didn't you? You interviewed him before he died?"

Bristling under Mange's steady gaze, Wines admitted that he'd never gone back to the hospital to talk to him. He'd been waiting for Steve to be released. Wines had planned to attempt to talk to him when he was healthy.

"You never interviewed the victim?" Mange blustered. "You let that woman bully you into not doing what you had every right to do?"

"I guess I did," Wines admitted, knowing immediately that he'd made a mistake he would never have the opportunity to repair. Mange simply shook his head in disgust. Later Wines would say that when it came to the Beard investigation, the cooperation between the D.A.'s Office and the Sheriff's Department ended that day.

Hours later Mange was even angrier. After going through the materials Wines had left with him, he was appalled by the lack of care the investigation had been given. At first he thought there might be other crime scene photos, which weren't included in the packet. He went so far as to call the crime scene officer on duty that day. "You must have a roll of film you didn't develop," he said. "Where are the photos of the crime scene?"

"You have everything," the deputy said. "That's all they told me to take."

Mange was furious. Wines hadn't made a diagram of the house and the crime scene. While he had access to the house, he hadn't conducted a test to see if the sound of the gunshot carried to the guest wing, where Kristina awoke to find her mother standing at the door. Instead of photos of the bloody sheets and the blood spray against the wall—in an investigation like this he usually had dozens—he had one photo of blood on the bed and a stack of photos of Hummel figurines and the homes' opulent furnishings. Mange blamed Wines. Although he'd worked with the detective on other cases and found him to be thorough, he judged that in this case he'd allowed himself to be distracted by the Beards' wealth, losing his focus on the crime. Perhaps when Steve Beard seemed to be recovering he'd given the case a lower priority. And then there was Burton, the formidable criminal defense attorney. "He'd allowed his presence to intimidate the investigation. It never should have happened," says Mange. "Rick was usually a good cop, and he was a good guy. I liked him. He just did a bad job on this case."

The mistake couldn't be undone. Steve was dead. Celeste had withdrawn the consent to search and disposed of the mattress, repainted the walls, and replaced the carpeting. Everything was gone. Mange didn't think it could get much worse, but he was wrong. That afternoon an e-mail circulated from Ronnie Earle, Travis County's district attorney, saying he wanted to meet with the prosecutor working the Beard case. Now Mange knew he not only had a botched investigation, but a high-profile one.

"Rich Oppel, the editor of the *Statesman*, called me about this case," Earle said. "He knew Beard. How do we stand on this?"

Mange swallowed hard and then told him the truth. "We've got a mess," he said, talking about the crime scene photos and Celeste's bullying tactics. "We don't even know what the victim had to say. We never asked him."

Earle looked angry. "Work the case," he told Mange. "And keep me informed."

A snowstorm in Virginia kept Paul and his wife from flying out on Monday, and Celeste agreed to push the funeral back until that Wednesday, January 26. She was busy anyway. Early in the morning, she sent Kristina to the bank along with a signature card with Steve's name on it to give Chuck Fuqua. When the teenager walked in and handed it to him, Fuqua was embarrassed for her. Later, a stack of checks would also pour into the bank dated January 22, the day Steve died, bearing his signature. It would seem that despite having spent much of the day unconscious, he'd somehow been able to sign the card and checks. Fuqua wasn't buying it, but in truth it didn't matter. With Steve dead, the trust kicked into effect, and he was no longer involved.

"I'll accept the card but I can't change anything," he said. "Now that your father's dead, it's up to the trust department to administer the estate."

When Kristina told Celeste, she was livid.

"That's my money, not theirs," she said. "We'll see who controls it."

When she called Fuqua to complain, he said only, "There's nothing I can do."

She was better off with Steve alive than with him dead, Fuqua thought after he hung up the telephone. *Steve made decisions with his heart. The bank makes them by the book.*

The business of death is a sad and often confusing one, with families rushing to make arrangements. Always a careful man, Steve had ensured that when he died that wouldn't be the case. Years earlier, when he buried Elise, he planned his own funeral as well. Still, one unforeseen glitch appeared. Steve had chosen a beautiful mahogany casket, but in the years since, the policy at the funeral home had changed to only allow metal caskets in the mausoleum where he'd be interred in a crypt with his first wife. Bonita Thompson, a saleswoman from Cook Walden Funeral Home, asked Celeste to come in to pick out a new one. Monday afternoon Celeste drove to the funeral home with the twins.

At Cook Walden, Thompson led them into a showroom, where she pointed out the choices. Celeste walked through and chose a casket for Steve. Then she turned to the twins. "While we're here, why don't you pick out your coffins?" she said.

Jennifer looked at Kristina in alarm. "No, we don't want to do that," she said.

Startled as well, Kristina protested, and both the girls

turned to walk away. As teenagers, they didn't want to ponder their own deaths. What they didn't know was that their mother had been contemplating their deaths since their births. While at Timberlawn, she told a therapist that from the twins' first years she kept special outfits in their closets, ones she considered their burial clothes.

"Come on," Celeste said. "Pick them out."

They refused.

"Then I'll do it for you," she said. With that, Celeste walked through until she stopped in front of a white casket with a lilac interior that shone pink.

"Pink's my color," she said to Thompson. "I'll take one of these for myself and two for the girls."

Steve's obituary ran in the *Statesman* on Tuesday, January 25. After recounting the highlights of his life, from his military service to founding KBVO, it continued with a tribute from Celeste: "*You were a truly gifted, generous, and strong man. You were my darling husband and you brought nothing but joy to my life, and I will love you and miss you forever.*" Visitation began at two that afternoon and continued until nine that evening. Celeste didn't attend.

"Don't tell anyone, even Kristina, that I wasn't there," she told Jennifer. "They'll just all think I left, that they missed me."

Jennifer did as she was told, even taking Steve's yellow rose boutonniere to the funeral home for Celeste. Jennifer rarely questioned her mother, and now she didn't ask what was so important that she couldn't go to her own husband's wake.

At the funeral home, Jennifer looked down at Steve's kind face in the casket. He looked so alive that she thought he must have been breathing. For a moment she waited, hoping he'd sit up and talk to her, or just open his eyes. Jen held the boutonniere in her hands but couldn't bring herself to pin it on the sweater Celeste had chosen for him to wear, a gift they'd brought back from Australia. Instead, one of the funeral home attendants pinned it on while Jennifer sat by herself and cried over the second father she'd lost in three years.

As guests arrived, Kristina acted as hostess. The twins had rarely seen Amy since the shooting, but she came, as did Justin's family. Many of Steve's friends were there, including his employees from KBVO. Kristina handled the day like she'd handled much of her life with her mother: She tried not to think too carefully about any of it. Stunned, she talked to people and circulated through the crowd.

Making matters even more uncomfortable was the worry about what the people walking in were thinking. Along with the obituary, an article on Steve's death had run in the *Statesman* that morning. In it, Travis County Medical Examiner Roberto Bayardo announced the autopsy results: pulmonary embolism, a blood clot to the lungs, caused by months of inactivity. Bayardo ruled the blood clot a complication of the gunshot and listed the cause of death as homicide.

On the day of the funeral, Celeste went to Tramps to have her hair styled into a chic French twist. She brought Dawn Madigan with her. In the salon, her hairdresser, Denise, watched as Celeste pawed through the accessories and knickknacks. She carried them up to the counter by the handful. When they'd all been rung up, she signed a charge slip for $1,000 and handed the overflowing bag to Dawn as a gift. "I don't know if Dawn wanted them or if Celeste just thought she should have them," Denise said later.

On the way to the services, the limo was filled with Celeste, Dawn, the twins and their boyfriends. Celeste was animated and full of life, throwing her head back and laughing.

"Pull over in Davenport Village," she ordered the driver. "I want to stop at the pharmacy."

At Northwest Hills Pharmacy, Celeste and the others left the car and ran inside. The twins assumed she had a last minute item to pick up. Instead she made her way to the pharmacist. "Now I own this place. It's time for you people to kiss my ass like you kissed Steve's," she taunted. Then she turned and left.

In the limo again, she chuckled as if she'd just pulled off a great coup. "Did you see her face?" she said, laughing even harder.

They drove around Austin, then north to the funeral home. As if someone had turned a switch, when the limo pulled into the parking lot, Celeste stopped laughing. As she emerged from the limo for the 11:00 A.M. service, she had tears in her eyes. Two hundred people, most Steve's friends, attended. Paul, still snowed in, couldn't be there, but Steven III held up his cell phone so he could listen to the eulogy. During the sermon the minister—the same one who'd performed their wedding five years earlier—talked about Steve and his many talents as a businessman and a father. Then he turned the subject to his marriage to Celeste. "Yes, they had the differences all couples do, but they loved each other dearly. After he lost Elise, I saw Celeste bring Steve out of his depression," he said. As he spoke those words, Celeste dabbed at tears while one of Steve's closest friends walked out.

It was when the minister said, "Ashes to ashes and dust to dust," that Kristina finally cried. The last week had been a hell for her, losing Steve and worrying about her safety and that of her mother and sister. She couldn't take any more. Justin wrapped his arm around her to comfort her.

After the service the twins and Celeste were alone with Steve's body before they closed the casket. Jennifer and

Kristina walked up to say their last good-byes. Then they tucked two small gifts into the casket, a small photo album of all of them together during happy times and a teddy bear they'd given him in the hospital. When it was Celeste's turn, she, too, had brought something for Steve to carry into eternity. From her bag she pulled a small bottle of Wolfschmidt vodka.

"For the trip," she said, slipping it in beside him and smiling.

In the limo as they followed the hearse to the mausoleum, Celeste laughed again. "Did you see what I put in his coffin?" she said. Then she bragged about buying the trip insurance. "I knew we'd never go."

Steve's adult children kept their distance at the funeral, hanging back and watching their stepmother. That night they were on Celeste's mind. "The attorneys are such chickens they haven't told Steve's kids they aren't getting anything," she snickered to Brett Spicer, when he was on security duty at the house. "Under Steve's will, I get every penny."

Later Spicer would return to his office and tell Wines about the evening. "She didn't appear at all sad," he said.

Boxes from Celeste began arriving the day after the funeral at the homes of many of Steve's friends. When Gus Voelzel unpacked his, he found Steve's stuffed and mounted jackalope, a jackrabbit head with antlers attached. He and Steve had laughed about it together when they'd first met. McEachern's box held Steve's beloved KBVO license plates. Others received crystal snifters and martini glasses. It was a grand gesture many found thoughtful. Yet, they wondered why Celeste was doing it. Did she simply want them to have something to remember him by? Or did she want them to think well of her, to discount all the rumors about her involvement in Steve's murder?

* * *

Days after the funeral, Celeste arrived at Studio 29 early, before the shop opened, in her bathrobe and lamb's wool slippers, to have her hair done. She hoisted her black-and-white cocker spaniel, Nikki, onto the counter while she talked to Donna. The dog urinated, and Celeste laughed. "Oh, well," she giggled.

As Joseph cut Celeste's hair, Donna listened in. "People are being so mean. They all think I was involved," she said.

"No," he said. "I'm sure they don't."

"Yes they do," she whined, saying she'd just gotten back from a meeting with her bankers in Dallas. "They're trying to put me on a budget. They think I don't need five telephone lines and that I ought to be able to live on ten thousand dollars a month. I told them next time I go to Dallas I want them to put all my money in a room, every bit of it, so I can sit there and look at it."

Donna smiled, envisioning Celeste doing just that in her Chanel suit with her Gucci sunglasses and dripping in diamonds.

At Charles Burton's office, Celeste called often, worried that she was a suspect. She called so often, she told friends Burton had threatened to drop her as a client.

"I don't know why the police department would think I was involved," she told Brett Spicer, the deputy she had working off-duty as security at the house. "I hate Tracey for what she did. I hate her so much I have dreams where I'm running over her with my car."

What she didn't mention was that she was still meeting Tracey at the park two to three days a week. Somehow, despite changing the phone numbers three times, Tracey always seemed able to get the new unlisted numbers.

"Put your mother on the telephone," Tracey told Jennifer one day.

Jennifer hung up. When she asked her mother about it, Celeste just shrugged.

"I know she's still talking to Tracey," Jen told Christopher. "I see her number on the caller ID."

In Dallas, the bankers questioned Celeste's household expenses and refused to pay the way they had before Steve died. Once, she called one of the bank officers and claimed to have breast cancer. "I need money," she said. When the woman refused, she screamed. "I'm going to cut off my fucking breast and mail it to you."

Trying to mediate, David Kuperman came out to the Toro Canyon house to explain to Celeste the way the trust worked. She was entitled to disbursements from the trust's income. With the stock market down and Davenport Village not yet fully leased, that would be between $10,000 and $15,000 a month. Under the terms of the estate, the bank, he said, would pay off the mortgages on both the house and the lake house, so her monthly stipend would only need to cover her living expenses.

Celeste was incensed. She wasn't to be calmed, even when Kuperman explained she could easily sell the lake house and have hundreds of thousands of dollars in the bank to cover extra expenses.

"That's my money!" she screamed. "My money! Not the bank's!"

A second Dallas meeting with Bank of America didn't leave her in any better a mood. "The bank has the sole discretion on the distribution of the funds," Janet Hudnall, the officer in charge of the trust, informed her. "With the house paid off, you can expect about fifteen thousand dollars a month."

While she had Celeste there, Hudnall questioned her about the expenses incurred while Steve was in the hospital, including the $74,000 check to Jimmy. Confronted, Celeste admitted it had been inflated. On a sheet of paper, Hudnall then added up the expenses that were out of line, including an $80,000 eight-carat diamond Celeste bought for herself, claiming the stone had been ordered by Steve before the shooting. Hudnall didn't know that the Christmas before, Celeste had asked for such a diamond and Steve had refused to buy it, but the banker had her suspicions. By the time she was done, the banker had a chart that showed that in four months Celeste had spent $717,610 of Steve's estate. At that rate she'd work her way through his fortune in five years.

Days later Hudnall called with more bad news for Celeste. After reviewing the checks she'd written over the previous months, the bank was charging many of the items—including the check she'd written to Jimmy Martinez—against the $500,000 onetime payment she was entitled to under Steve's will. Celeste had unwittingly used up her security cushion, thrown it away on needless house repairs.

With the bank coming down hard on her, money was all Celeste talked about. To raise funds, she sent Jennifer to return racks of her clothes hanging in the master closet, things she'd bought that still had the tags affixed, to Talbots, Dillard's, and Foley's. In all, Jen returned so many of Celeste's unworn clothes that they totaled $20,000. Yet the clothes had been bought so long ago, she was given only store credits.

She also began talking about suing HealthSouth for malpractice, claiming unsanitary conditions there caused Steve's death. When her hands broke out in a nasty infection just days after his death, Celeste had Justin photograph the ugly sores, saying the photo proved Steve died of an infection, because she'd contracted it from him. Justin had no way of knowing that the photo could one day be used as evidence of something vastly different: not that Steve infected Celeste, but that she might have done as she threatened, purposely infecting him.

* * *

Little about Celeste's behavior seemed to make sense that February. While she threw away money with abandon, she schemed to find ways not to have to pay bills. In early February she went up to Studio 29 and called the police. "I don't want the cops in my house," she told Donna. "Last time they were there they tore the place up."

When they arrived, she told them that the maid had stolen from her, that her white gold Baume & Mercier watch with the diamonds was missing. The officer took the report and said he'd talk to the woman. After he left, Celeste turned to Donna and laughed. "Now I won't have to pay the lazy bitch unemployment."

With the girls' nineteenth birthday approaching, at first Celeste said she'd take them to New Orleans, then backed out. "The bank won't give me money," she said. That year, Celeste failed to even give the girls birthday cards.

Perhaps Celeste was beginning to realize what Chuck Fuqua had known all along—that she had been better off with Steve alive than with him dead. Without him, she was at the mercy of a faceless bank, one that didn't succumb to ravings or sad stories. That, coupled with the constant stares from those who believed she was responsible for Steve's death, must have seemed overwhelming. She talked often about the newspaper article that questioned her involvement, and her name came up often on the radio talk shows, usually followed by the word murder.

On February 9, little more than two weeks after Steve's death, Celeste called the twins from the lobby of Studio 29, ordering them to meet her there. When they arrived, she sat on a bench, glassy-eyed. Worried, Kristina and Justin sat beside her, while Jennifer and Christopher knelt at her feet.

"Tracey and I made a pact that when things got too tough,

we'd kill ourselves together," she told them. "I don't want to die alone. Will all of you die with me?"

None of the kids answered. Weeks earlier she'd bought the girls and herself coffins. Now she wanted them to agree to kill themselves. While Jennifer fought back the terror building inside her, Christopher simply changed the subject. They left the salon that day acting as if nothing had just happened.

A week later Celeste wasn't talking about suicide anymore. By then she had a new plan, and a new friend she'd enlisted to erase all her problems.

Chapter
16

"I used to be a guy. My name was Don Goodson," Donna told people, in her deep, whiskey voice. At nearly six feet tall, with angular features and a prominent Adam's apple, she looked as if she might be telling the truth. But she simply enjoyed the quizzical stares she got from such a remark. Donna Rose Goodson was just a big girl, the kind who in high school wears flats not to tower over every guy in her class. That wasn't Donna's style, however. Instead, she had a personality to match her height, bold and brash. In a crowd, she never went unnoticed, not just because of her size or her thick mane of long red hair, but her attitude. "Donna's aggressive," says an old friend. "She's the type of person who moves into a situation and uses it to her advantage."

Throughout that fall and winter, Donna, who had just turned thirty-nine to Celeste's thirty-seven, had been a sympathetic voice. When the girls came into Studio 29, she'd told them to give her best wishes to their mom and to watch over her so Celeste didn't become depressed. The girls passed her kind words on. In February, Jennifer came into Studio 29 and said, "Donna, we're going to the Houston rodeo for our mom's birthday. My mom wants to know if you want to come along."

"Sure," Donna said.

That Friday, February 11, Celeste arrived at Studio 29 ready to go, and they were off, leaving Donna's 1998 Buick Regal in the salon parking lot.

The drive from Austin to Houston in Celeste's bronze mist Cadillac was anything but leisurely. The kids drove behind in one of the Cateras, and they talked back and forth between the cars on walkie-talkies. At times Donna held on to the dashboard to keep from sliding out of her seat as Celeste, smoking a cigarette and talking on the telephone, wove in and out of traffic, setting such a frantic pace that they covered the 160 miles in less than two hours. On the way, Celeste talked about her marriage, bragging about the money Steve spent on her. When it came to the shooting, Donna was surprised when Celeste admitted she'd told the teens not to mention Tracey to the police.

"Why'd you do that?" Donna asked.

"I couldn't imagine Tracey did it," Celeste said.

In Houston, they pulled into the circular drive of the Doubletree Galleria Hotel, a curved edifice that overlooks Post Oak Drive, one of the most exclusive shopping districts in the country. On their way up in the elevator Celeste turned and grinned at Donna. With pride, she said, "You're with a woman who fucked her way to the top."

When a guy named Bubba called the suite, Donna realized Celeste had plans for that night. Someone Celeste had met at the lake, Bubba was supposed to bring a date for Donna, but his friend had backed out. Celeste appeared annoyed but said little when Bubba picked them up that night and drove them to Sullivan's, an art deco chophouse. There, they met Bubba's friend George and his girlfriend. Donna, not interested in a blind date, was relieved.

George's girlfriend said she was sorry about Steve's death and she asked Celeste, "How are you doing?"

"You don't look like you're letting it slow you down," George observed.

"Don't make me shoot you," Celeste snapped back with a wide grin, forming a pistol with her fingers and pretending to pull back the trigger.

The others groaned. "That's pretty cold," Bubba said.

"You need not to say things like that," Donna said.

But Celeste just laughed.

Next, they drove to a hole-in-the-wall bar in Bubba's Jaguar. Celeste whispered to Donna, "Bubba's got more money than Steve. You're looking at my next husband."

On the dance floor, Bubba and Celeste held each other and kissed.

Near closing time, Donna left. At the hotel, Kristina and Justin slept in the pull-out couch, and Donna bedded down in one of the two double beds with Jennifer, leaving the other open for Celeste. Before long she was asleep.

Sometime later Jennifer awoke—to the sound of Celeste undressing Bubba.

"No," he whispered. But Celeste pulled at his clothes, unzipping his pants, and then her face disappeared between his legs.

Angry, Jennifer elbowed Donna.

Startled, Donna bellowed, "What's going on?" She opened her eyes just in time to see Bubba grab his clothes and run to the bathroom. Jennifer switched the lights on.

Drunk, Celeste giggled. Minutes later Bubba emerged and quickly left.

The next morning, Jennifer and Kristina were angry. "I can't believe you did that," Kristina said.

"So what?" Celeste shouted, going on the offensive. "It's none of your business."

That afternoon, Donna and Celeste headed to Saks Fifth Avenue, to have their hair brushed into curls. Twice they missed their appointments, but the hairdresser didn't complain when Celeste handed her a hundred dollar tip. In the store, Celeste bought a fringed cowgirl outfit she wore that night when Bubba, dressed in jeans and cowboy boots, picked them up for the rodeo. After the show—a mixture of bull riding, calf roping, and music—they ate sushi, then ended up at a country western bar.

After midnight, Donna, still stinging from the previous night's episode, announced, "Bubba's not coming to the room tonight."

The man Celeste pegged as her next husband flushed with embarrassment. When she said she'd go home with him, he refused. He wouldn't even drive by his house to show it to her, no matter how much she pleaded. After he dropped them at the hotel, the two women made their way to the Doubletree bar.

"He's loaded," Celeste told Donna. "He's spent eight hundred dollars on us in the past two days."

The following morning Celeste awoke to the kids holding a cake they'd baked for her before leaving on the trip. Candles lit, they sang "Happy Birthday." A little while later the girls and Justin left for Austin. Once they were gone, Celeste called her bank.

"My money hit my account," she said. "Let's smoke a joint and go gamble."

Celeste pulled a pot cigarette from her suitcase. She took a Coke can and used a pen to poke holes, then lit it and dropped it inside, breathing in the smoke as it wafted from the openings. Stoned, they lay around the hotel room, missing their checkout time, then their late checkout. After consuming a bag of the hotel's chocolate chip cookies from room service, they finally called the bellman to bring down their suitcases. In the Cadillac, Celeste called OnStar and rattled off Bubba's address. "I want to see his house before we leave," she said.

"There aren't any houses there, just apartments," the operator said.

"No," Celeste insisted. "He has a house."

They drove until they were at a block of apartments. "We must be in the wrong place," Celeste said. But just then the gates opened and Bubba drove out in his Jaguar.

"He's poor," Celeste said. "Guess he's out of the picture."

Driving east, they stopped at an ATM machine and Celeste pulled out money, then they headed to Lake Charles, Louisiana, to gamble. On the two and a half hour drive, Donna prodded Celeste, curious about her relationship with Steve. Three weeks after his death, Celeste talked about him like he'd been the love of her life. Perhaps she didn't realize that Donna had eavesdropped on conversations in which she'd called Steve a fat old bastard and said she hated the thought of going to Europe with him.

Then Donna talked about her own life. Two years earlier she'd been living with her fiancé, a cop. "I was crazy in love with him," she said. The relationship ended badly, so badly that she narrowly escaped jail. As Donna explained it, her fiancé brought home sensitive police documents that ended up in the hands of those he was investigating. Donna was charged with misuse of public information, a third-degree felony. In a plea bargain, she got a thousand dollar fine and five year's probation. Six months later, they fought, and the court ordered her to attend domestic violence counseling.

After telling Donna about her Arizona charges for insurance fraud, Celeste commented, "I wonder why Tracey's not in jail by now."

"Maybe she's working with the District Attorney's Office," Donna said. "Has she got information to bargain with?"

Celeste said nothing at first, then mused, "My attorney says they need two pieces of information to make a murder charge stick. One is the gun. The other one is Tracey. If I could get rid of Tracey, I could justify Steve's death."

"You've got a good lawyer?" asked Donna.

"I hired Charles Burton," Celeste bragged. "He's only lost one murder case. That was some guy who left his bloody clothes in a Dumpster and they found them. They're not going to find my clothes in a Dumpster. I'm no dumb blonde like Anna Nicole Smith."

Later, Donna discovered Celeste had a thing about the busty actress, even listing her OnStar password as Nicole. Then Celeste took the conversation where Donna had suspected it was headed. "How much would it cost to get rid of Tracey?" she asked.

Donna smiled and said, "For the right price you could get rid of anybody."

"Do you know anyone who could do it?"

"There's this guy, Modesto, he's part of the Mexican mafia," Donna said.

"How much do you think Modesto would charge?" she asked.

"About five hundred," Donna answered, taking a long drag from her cigarette.

"When can he do it?" Celeste asked.

Donna smiled, "He'll need the money first."

Later, Donna insisted that she never intended to hire anyone to kill Tracey and that from the beginning she was playing along to squeeze money out of Celeste. "It was a you-don't-con-a-con situation," she says with a smirk.

In Lake Charles, Celeste handed Donna $500 to play the

slots, which the tall redhead pocketed. At the craps table, Celeste dropped another thousand, then hooked up with a guy at the bar. A big loser that night, he took them for a comp dinner, and Celeste bankrolled him for $400, which he quickly lost.

"Let's go," Celeste said at about eleven.

This time, not wanting a replay of the trip to Houston, Donna drove.

"Pull into that ATM," Celeste ordered as they passed a bank. When she did, Celeste withdrew $500 and handed it to her. "For Modesto," she said.

The rest of the five hour drive, Celeste slept. As they pulled into Austin, at four that morning, a heavy fog clung to the road. "I want to drive you by Tracey's," Celeste said. "So Modesto can find it."

Celeste then directed Donna to the corner house on Wilson. In the early morning hours of February 14, Tracey's maroon Nissan Pathfinder was parked in the driveway.

"When can he do it?" Celeste asked again.

"I just need to talk to him," Donna said.

Celeste dropped Donna at the salon to get her car. After driving home and changing, Donna headed to work. It was Valentine's Day, and the salon was booked solid. But when she arrived, her check wasn't what she thought it should be. Angry, she left and went to the Toro Canyon house.

"You don't have to work there, you can work for me," Celeste told her. "I can pay you four hundred dollars a week, and you don't have to pay for anything. I'll pick up all the tabs."

From that point on, Donna worked for Celeste.

That day, Donna called Bruce Reynolds, a friend who owned a small plumbing company, to see if he wanted to go out. He agreed, met Donna at her house, and they drove to Toro Canyon at seven that evening. "She lives here?" said

Reynolds, who was tall with an aquiline nose and a runner's body. On the porch, Donna rang the doorbell, then ran and hid behind a tree, like an adolescent playing a prank.

"Donna, are you fooling with me?" he said as Celeste opened the door.

"Nah, this is the place," Donna said, laughing and walking toward him. Then she pointed at the door. "This is Celeste."

Donna immediately sensed a connection between them. At dinner at Louie's 106, a small, posh downtown eatery, they talked and drank, Bruce seated beside Celeste in the booth. On her way back from the rest room, Donna saw them kiss. That night, Bruce slept with Celeste, and Donna bunked in Kristina's room alone. By then the twins were rarely home. Kristina spent most nights at Anita's or at Justin's parents' home, while Jennifer overnighted with friends or Christopher. Since the shooting, the house had become a frightening place for them. And once Donna entered Celeste's life, they stayed away even more, wary of her brashness and what they'd heard about her past, including that she was on probation. At times they stared at her, wondering if what else they'd heard was true—that she'd once been a man.

"When will Modesto do it?" Celeste asked off and on during the ensuing days.

"Pretty soon," Donna said.

For a week Bruce hung so close he seemed physically attached to Celeste. During the day, they slept in the master bedroom. At night, they circulated from bar to bar, with Donna as driver. Later, who brought up marriage would be a point of dispute. Donna and the teens would say it was Bruce, who seemed entranced with Celeste and her wealth. But he maintained that Celeste asked him to elope with her to Las Vegas. At times Donna thought that Bruce wanted to keep her separated from Celeste. She grew tired of it, worried he'd get in the way of what she wanted: more of Celeste's money.

One day she told Celeste, "Modesto needs another thousand." Celeste sent Kristina to an ATM machine and handed the envelope full of cash to Donna, who had noticed that Celeste seemed increasingly on edge. She didn't like the rumors circulating through Austin, gossip that speculated Tracey hadn't acted alone.

On the morning of February 16, Bruce had to work. Donna drove him home and then went to her mother's house, where Donna lived with her teenage son, Henry. Celeste called, frantic. "I heard they're talking about me at Studio 29," she squealed, a manic edge to her voice. "Kim's telling people I put Tracey up to killing Steve, and that the twins' father died mysteriously. I want you to go there with me."

Donna drove to the house to pick her up. She didn't notice Celeste slip a butcher knife into her purse as they walked through the kitchen to the car, to head for the salon.

As Celeste had ordered when she called her, Kristina and Justin were waiting when Donna pulled into the parking lot. They immediately spotted Kim, a blond nail technician, smoking a cigarette outside the back door. Before the Cadillac even stopped, Celeste jumped out, charging at her with the knife. Kim turned and ran, her ankles tottering in her high heels. The following minutes could only be described as bedlam. Kristina and Donna grabbed Celeste and pleaded with her to throw down the knife. Appearing to acquiesce, Celeste tucked the knife inside her shirt, then stormed inside the salon.

"I want an apology," she demanded, pulling out the knife. "And I want it now."

Kristina again struggled with her mother, but couldn't wrestle the knife away.

"I want an apology!" Celeste shouted even louder.

By then Jennifer had arrived, after seeing Celeste's and Kristina's cars in the parking lot. She grabbed Celeste's arm and tried to wrench the knife from her. They struggled and Celeste pulled away. In the confusion, the knife grazed Kristina's knee, cutting her, and plunged into Celeste's forearm once and her left thigh twice.

By the time police arrived, Kim had fled, and no one pressed charges. Donna wrapped Celeste's leg and arm in bandages, and they left for North Austin Medical Center. Celeste looked up at Justin as he helped her into the car. "Did you see how frightened they were of me?" she asked with excitement.

At the hospital Celeste said, "This was an accident. I wasn't trying to kill myself."

The doctor sutured her leg wounds and dressed the cut in her arm. The six-inch knife blade had come close to a large artery in her inner thigh, so he ordered that she be kept overnight for observation.

The next morning, Celeste was released, and that afternoon she and Donna dressed and primped to go out. When Donna was ready, she searched the house for Celeste and found her in what had been Steve's office. "Oh, I shouldn't have called you," Celeste said, hanging up the phone as Donna walked into the room. Donna assumed Celeste had been talking to Tracey when she said, "It hasn't been taken care of."

"Modesto needs more money," Donna said. "Another thousand."

Celeste didn't argue. She picked up the telephone and called Kristina. "I need you to get some cash for me," she said. When Kristina and Justin showed up with the money and handed it to Celeste, she gave it to Donna. They both watched, eyes wide, wondering what was happening.

Bruce saw it as well. He'd been suspicious of Donna's relationship with Celeste, assuming that Donna had an angle.

The following afternoon he locked himself and Celeste in the master bedroom and called out to Donna, demanding she leave. "Celeste and I are getting married," he said "We don't want you here."

"I need my things," Donna replied. "Then I'll be gone."

He opened the door, and Donna ran inside and jumped on the bed. Celeste laughed when she crossed her arms and refused to move. When Justin overheard what was going on, he convinced Bruce to talk to him in the hallway and minutes later Bruce was gone.

"I told him to leave," Justin said. "He won't be back."

That night, when they were partying at a club, Celeste said to Donna, "I hope no one ever says it's him or you again, because you're my best friend."

Donna smiled, but she had no doubts about why Celeste wanted her as a friend: Celeste thought she could get rid of Tracey.

At the Toro Canyon house the days fell into a pattern. The cleaning lady circulated in and out, and the dry cleaner picked up the laundry, all of it, including the sheets and Celeste's panties and bras. Most days, Celeste and Donna slept until three in the afternoon, then rose and dressed to go out for the night. Celeste always had a man around. The night after Bruce departed, she met Joey Fina, a tall, dark Italian with a melodic accent. He told her he'd solve all of her problems by taking her to Italy, where they'd live on a hillside vineyard. At the same time, she dated Cole Johnson, a good-looking, sandy-haired construction worker who tended bar at the 311 Club. Ironically, Johnson had the same name as Celeste's older brother. Soft-spoken and polite, he was an old friend of Donna's. On his nights off, the three of them bar-hopped together.

Celeste's erratic behavior hadn't gone unnoticed. Charles Burton cautioned Kristina to rein in her mother, lest there be talk about the young widow who wasn't grieving. And not long after the Studio 29 incident, Petra Mueller, the owner, filed a lawsuit, charging that Celeste had destroyed her business by frightening away her clientele. Livid, Celeste told Donna she was going to hire someone to hack into the salon computer and delete all the customer files. For weeks after she learned of the suit, Celeste made a game of avoiding the process server who sat outside the gates on Toro Canyon. Evenings, Donna drove and Celeste ducked down in the backseat as they pulled out of the driveway. A block away, she sat up and laughed. Finally, Charles Burton called Donna, asking her to convince Celeste to take the papers. To get her to agree, Donna turned it into a game.

"She'll be home in an hour," she told the process server. "Come then."

When he arrived, Celeste waited on the patio. Despite temperatures in the seventies, she wore a full-length mink with a matching hat and sunglasses. Covered in diamonds, she had on Chanel shoes and held a bag with diamond clasps. She had a martini in one hand and a see-through plastic bag filled with prescription drugs at her side. As the man stared at her, Celeste popped pills, then washed them down with a swig of vodka.

The man laughed, but Celeste never broke a smile.

When he tore the papers apart to give her the receipt, a staple fell to the floor.

"You can't leave that. Somebody else will die around here," Donna deadpanned. "Get on your knees and find it."

With that, the man dropped onto all fours, searching around the patio, chuckling.

With his client acting so oddly, that spring Charles Burton told Kristina he wanted her to have power of attorney over her mother's affairs. He said he worried about Celeste's behavior, throwing away money and frequenting bars. It bred suspicion. Burton said he wanted Celeste back at Timberlawn. Perhaps he thought she belonged there. Or maybe it was as Donna and Kristina later maintained, that he said the police wouldn't be able to arrest Celeste for Steve's murder while she was hospitalized.

There was also the matter of the girls' statements to the District Attorney's Office. Mange wanted to talk to them, but every time it came up, Celeste became hysterical. Once, she had an anxiety attack on the steps to Burton's office, and an ambulance had to be called. "He told us once Celeste was in the hospital we could talk to the D.A.," Kristina said. "I was scared, but I wanted to help them."

In truth, Burton didn't need to be so concerned, since the investigation had stalled. Wines's admission to Mange that he hadn't interviewed Steve had caused a rift between the men. The detective thought about the case often but felt cut out of the investigation. Mange, on the other hand, couldn't build a case on beauty shop gossip; he needed solid evidence, which he didn't have. The prosecutor had no doubt Celeste was involved, but unless Tracey talked, he feared Celeste would go unpunished. The only way he had a case against her was to cut a deal with Tracey, and Tracey wasn't interested. Loyal, she rebuffed every suggestion her attorney made that she work with the D.A.'s Office to get a lesser sentence. Even if it meant life in prison, Tracey was determined to protect Celeste.

Still, the investigation haunted Celeste. Donna thought her guilt ate at her. She rarely talked bad about Steve. Instead she portrayed him as her fallen hero, her one true love. And she mused often about what the police might be doing. One day, she complained that Burton refused to get her a copy of the police report, which was available to the public. "Call that detective and get the case number. I'll get it for you," Donna offered.

Celeste dialed Wines's phone number, and when she asked, he quickly read it off.

"It must be right on his desk," she said to Donna after she hung up.

"I think that cop's mad at you," Donna said. "He's not going to let this drop."

Celeste frowned.

Donna was fascinated watching Celeste. Like a chameleon, she acted one way with some people and like a different person around others. With Anita and her friends from the lake—Dawn, Marilou, and Dana—Celeste played the vulnerable widow, grieving for her husband. "With me, she was the promiscuous drunk," says Donna. "Every night in the bars, and nothing she wouldn't do."

Always, she asked when Modesto would murder Tracey. "Maybe tomorrow," Donna said. Or, "Later today." Celeste called Tracey often, which Tracey interpreted as Celeste missing her. But when Celeste hung up, she frowned because Modesto hadn't done the job yet. When she asked why, Donna made up excuses. Modesto was busy, had another job first, or planned to wait a few more days. Celeste took it well, never pushing.

If Celeste knew how to handle men, Donna knew how to handle Celeste; Donna led her on, and Celeste refused her nothing. When Donna mentioned liking something, Celeste gave it to her. One day it was a diamond cocktail ring, another, a jeweled pendant of the Dallas skyline. "She wanted Tracey dead so bad, I could have asked for her car and she would have signed over the registration," says Donna.

Out every night and sleeping much of the day, Donna performed a job that evolved into shuffling Celeste to therapy sessions, brushing her hair, arranging for hairdressers and manicurists to come to the house, and running her errands. She never had time to do paperwork and pay bills.

Soon the unopened mail piled up until it mounded over a corner of Steve's desk. "You could hire my mom to do it," Donna suggested.

The following day Donna's mother, Frances Tate, came to the Toro Canyon house and spent the day sorting bills. There were credit card statements with hundreds of thousands of dollars waiting to be paid. After two hours of organizing, Celeste handed her a check for $800 for her services.

More and more, Kristina and Justin took over the work of running the house, so much so that Celeste made up lists for them, telling them what needed to be done, everything from buying new garbage cans to typing her letters. Celeste even sent Justin a thank-you card: *"You've been really wonderful with everything you do for us . . . I couldn't have survived the last two months without you."*

On the porch one afternoon, Celeste and Justin sat in rocking chairs looking out at the bluebonnets. As usual, she was on the telephone, this time with her psychiatrist, Michele Hauser. For weeks she'd told the doctor that she felt guilty over Steve's murder. "If I hadn't brought Tracey into our lives, he'd still be alive," she said.

Justin listened as Celeste told Hauser she couldn't sleep, blaming it on depression. When she hung up, she laughed. "Well, I told the partial truth," she said. "I'm not sleeping, but it's because I'm having so much fun at the bars."

Busy with Donna, Celeste rarely saw Tracey. "Celeste. Call me—important," Tracey wrote on a sheet of paper, faxing it from an Office Depot in late February. Later she wouldn't remember what had been so urgent. "I think I was worried about her," says Tracey. "When we talked on the telephone, she sounded like she was unraveling."

Days later Celeste called Tracey in the middle of the night. "I'm out on Toro Canyon. Come get me."

When Tracey got there, she found Celeste walking on the

road. Tracey opened the door for her and they drove through the quiet neighborhood while Celeste talked. On the side of the road, Celeste cried over what the police might do. Tracey, the one already facing a life sentence, comforted her. "By then, I wasn't in love with her," Tracey said. "But I loved her."

And still, every day, Celeste asked Donna if that would be the day Modesto would fulfill the contract and kill Tracey.

In early March, Donna told Celeste, "Modesto needs $2,500 to finish the contract. He has expenses."

Again, Celeste told Kristina to go to the bank.

"Why?" Kristina asked.

"Because I said so," she answered.

When Kristina returned, she found Celeste and Donna in the master bathroom. She handed Celeste the $2,500 in an envelope and watched as her mother gave it to Donna.

"What's going on?" Kristina asked. "What's between you and Donna?"

"Never mind," Celeste said. "It's none of your business. And I don't want you asking Donna any questions. Stay away from her."

With the hit imminent, or so she believed, Celeste had an idea. She and Donna left the next day for New Orleans. It was Mardi Gras. What better place to set up an alibi than with thousands of people to testify she wasn't even in Austin?

That week, Anita had plans to help Celeste write thank-you notes for the flowers and remembrances that had poured in for Steve's funeral. Instead her fax churned out a letter from Celeste: *"I'm just too distraught. I can't handle Steve's death. I feel like I want to kill myself and be with him. I'm going back to Timberlawn."*

Days later Anita mentioned it to Christopher, who worked part-time in her office. "I'm worried about Celeste," she said. "She's really taking Steve's death hard."

"She's partying in New Orleans," he said. "I think she's fine."

Meanwhile, Celeste and Donna jumped from hotel to hotel in New Orleans, and what was to have been a three-day trip turned into ten. During the day they shopped, buying wild costumes and long, shiny metallic green, purple, and silver wigs. At night they walked Bourbon Street in leopard leotards, their hair concealed beneath the wigs. In platform shoes, they towered over the other revelers, attracting attention. One night they dressed like members of the rock group KISS, their faces painted white with black stripes. Nearly every night, Celeste slept with a different man. On the street during the parades, she tore open her blouse, flashing her breasts for the bright plastic beads thrown off the floats. A few nights, Celeste's current boyfriend, Cole Johnson, flew in. When he left, she partied again, picking up a new guy in the bars or on the streets. While Celeste brought her latest man upstairs, Donna slept in the lobby.

When Celeste once again urged Donna to find out when the hit would take place, Donna pretended to call Modesto; no one answered. "Maybe he's taking care of it right now," she'd say.

With that, Celeste called Tracey. When she answered, Celeste hung up.

Finally, on the tenth day after they'd arrived, Donna said, "I need a phone card to call Modesto. We don't want it traced." They walked over to an Eckerd and Celeste bought one. While Celeste waited, Donna dialed her mother's house on a pay phone. Donna's teenage son answered, and they talked for half an hour or so while Celeste waited.

"When are you coming home?" he asked.

"Soon," she said, feeling guilty about being gone so long.

"We have to leave now," she told Celeste when she hung up. "Modesto has pulled out. I have a new guy who says he'll do it, but he wants more money."

"I need the car loaded in five minutes," Celeste barked at the bellman. "I've got an emergency at home."

This time, Donna called her fictional assassin Sam. "Sam's going to do it, but we need to get the cash to him," she said. Celeste pulled $500 out of the ATM. So far she'd paid Donna $5,500, without any results.

Back in Austin, Donna told Celeste she had to meet Sam at the Waterloo Brewery, a restaurant brew house. Once there, the two of them waited for a man who didn't exist. When Cole showed up, he knew nothing about why they'd come. While Celeste had been watching Donna carefully, he distracted her, kissing her and nuzzling her neck. Donna got up and left for the bathroom.

"Did you see him yet?" she whispered to Donna when she returned.

"Yeah," she said. "He's come and gone."

"Damn, I missed him," she said.

"You have to be patient. He's going to Mexico to take care of business. He'll do it when he gets back."

Celeste nodded.

Two days later Celeste had a limo take her to Donna's mother's house to pick her up for a night of clubbing. That night, they argued. Cole had a friend with him, and Celeste pushed Donna to sleep with him. When Donna threatened to leave, Celeste told her that if she did, she'd report her for driving while intoxicated.

As usual, Donna slept in Kristina's room alone.

Still angry, early the next morning Donna packed her things. After she threw her bags in the car, she popped her head into the master bedroom. "I'm going now," she said. "You two need to lock up the house. I've got my stuff. I'm not coming back."

Outside, Donna pulled away in her Buick, and in her rearview mirror saw Celeste in her robe running toward the Cadillac. On the highway, Celeste chased Donna, blowing her horn and pulling in front of her and slamming down the brakes. Donna pulled onto the left shoulder and stopped. She walked back and found Celeste crying in her car.

"Don't leave," Celeste said. "Please come back."

"No, this is over," Donna said. "I'm leaving."

With the car keys, Celeste stabbed at her wrist. "I'm going to kill myself if you leave!" she screamed.

"Here," Donna said, pulling Celeste's diamond ring off her finger and tossing it at her. "Take this and leave me alone."

"I don't care about the ring. I want you to come back," she said.

Donna got in her Buick and left. Again Celeste followed, pulling beside her and trying to veer her off the road. At the next exit, Donna pulled off the highway and into a Container Store parking lot. A man walked by. "Call the police!" Donna shouted.

By then Celeste had screeched into the lot and pulled up directly behind her, preventing her from leaving. "Please come back to the house. I need you."

"No, I'm not having anything to do with you," Donna shouted. "Leave me be."

They were still arguing when police arrived. One officer pulled Donna off to the side. "I used to work for this woman, and I'm quitting," she said. "She doesn't want me to go."

In the end, the officers ordered Celeste to move her car. Then they called Kristina and asked her to pick up her mother.

"Please come back," Jennifer told Donna on the phone the next day. "My mom won't hurt you."

Later, Donna and Celeste talked. When they hung up, Donna agreed to one more night together, to see if things would be different.

The limo arrived at Donna's house about seven to drive them to the Dog and Duck, an Austin pub, for St. Patty's day. Celeste had on a long, shiny green wig, and she'd brought another for Donna.

At the house, before they left, Donna handed Celeste an envelope in front of Cole and her mother, Frances. "That's the money I owe you, the twenty-five hundred," she said. "Count it. It's all there."

Frowning, Celeste took the envelope and threw it in her purse. Perhaps she decided money alone wouldn't compensate Donna, that she wanted something else. Later, at the bar, the room swirled and Donna thought people were staring at her. Celeste leaned over and kissed her on the lips; Donna didn't kiss her back. A short time later, Cole and Celeste left, leaving the limo behind. Donna had the driver take her home, and she woke up the next morning certain Celeste had slipped something into her drink.

That day, Donna left a message on Celeste's answering machine. "I know what you did, and it wasn't cool," she said. "If I don't hear from you in the next fifteen minutes, I'm taking the photos of you from New Orleans and selling them to the newspaper."

Minutes later the phone rang. Celeste acted as if nothing had happened. "I'm out with Jennifer," she said. "What do you need?"

"We have some unfinished business," Donna told her. "Meet me at Baby Acapulco tomorrow."

Celeste agreed.

The colorful Mexican restaurant off I-35 was busy the following day when Donna waited for Celeste. As soon as she arrived and sat down, Donna told her, "If you really want this done, I need the twenty-five hundred back."

Celeste pulled the envelope from her purse and gave it to her. "I'm going back to Timberlawn on the twenty-first. My lawyer thinks I should," she said. "Do it while I'm there."

On March 21, Donna drove out to the Toro Canyon house and helped Celeste pack for Timberlawn. When they finished, Celeste handed Donna a check for $2,400 to keep her on her payroll for an additional six weeks. She also gave her a Texaco gas card, "So you can drive to Dallas to visit me." Finally, she handed her a cell phone. "Remember, I want it done while I'm gone. Use this to call me."

The code for the voice mail, she told Donna, was 10-02, the day Steve was shot. "That was the day he really died for me," she said with a smirk.

Later, Tracey would say Celeste called her daily from the hospital. "I'm just feeling really guilty about Steve," she told her. But perhaps, as she had from New Orleans, Celeste was calling to see if Sam had killed her yet.

With everything going on around her, not knowing when the District Attorney's Office would change the charge to murder or when she'd be arrested, Tracey still didn't blame Celeste. "I could have said no when she asked me to do it," she says. "I didn't."

A week later Donna drove to Timberlawn with Joey Fina, who wanted to see Celeste. While she was there, Donna decided to line her pockets further.

"I want to get out of here," Celeste told Donna. "Is it done?"

"No. If you want it done, that's what it will take," she said, handing her a scrap of paper on which she'd written $10,000. Celeste looked up at her, searching her face. Then she pulled out her checkbook and wrote a check for $7,650 to add to the $2,500 she'd already given her.

"It'll be done when you get home," Donna said, tucking it away.

When Joey asked what the check was for, Donna dismissed it by saying she was spending money for Celeste when she returned to Austin. Days later, Donna cashed the two checks, pocketing the $2,400 for her payroll check in cash and asking for a cashier's check for the bill money. She then left for Lake Charles to meet a girlfriend and gamble.

On April 1, Kristina took the day off from Concordia College where she and Jen took classes and drove to Timberlawn for a joint session with Celeste and her therapist. Much of the talk was about money. Where in the past Steve had attempted to restrain Celeste, with him dead that job fell to Kristina. She had Celeste's power of attorney, paid her bills, and saw the money flowing out faster than it came in. Much of it went to Donna Goodson.

First Dr. Gotway met with Celeste alone. Throughout the session, Celeste raged, calling Kristina disloyal. Gotway tried to calm her, to tell her Kristina was trying to protect her from her own destructive spending. When Kristina joined them, Celeste cursed at her and called her names, threatening to disinherit her. "There has been a role reversal," Gotway noted in Celeste's chart. "The daughter . . . finds herself in a difficult situation."

"You hate me!" Celeste screamed at Kristina.

"That's not it," Kristina pleaded. "I'm just trying to take care of you."

Three days later, back in Austin, Kristina called Donna Goodson. "Why's my mom paying you all this money?" she asked.

For weeks, Kristina had been wondering about Donna, trying to figure out what part she played in her mother's life.

They partied together, but it seemed more than that. Celeste had told her not to ask Donna questions, to stay away from her. But when Kristina saw the $7,650 check on the bank statement, she couldn't keep quiet any longer.

While Celeste had been occupied with Donna, Kristina had also started to consider the way her mother treated *her,* acting like she was an employee or a servant, someone to be ordered about. From Timberlawn, Celeste had continued calling and ordering her to do things, yelling and screaming. Both the girls considered the family sessions they had with Dr. Gotway a joke since Celeste coached them on what to say and what not to say. They weren't allowed to mention Donna, for instance, or the parade of men coming and going from Celeste's bedroom.

Not only had the time and distance allowed Kristina to take a good look at her life with her mother, but Justin pushed her to consider it as well. "She shouldn't treat you like that," he said. "She has no right."

For the first time, Kristina began to believe that he was right. She deserved more.

"I don't work for your mother anymore," Donna told Kristina that evening on the telephone. "If you have any questions, you need to talk to her."

Then Donna thought about Celeste and what she was capable of. "Listen," she said to the teenager. "You and Jennifer do whatever you need to do to stay safe."

After she hung up, Donna called Celeste. She'd been looking for a way to get out of the mess she was in with her, and this appeared to be the answer.

"We need to call this off," she said. "Kristina is asking too many questions. She wants to know what's happening with the money. Sam got nervous and took off with your money. We both got played."

"God damn it!" Celeste screamed. "I'm getting out of here now!"

"You're a liar," the nurses heard Celeste blare at Kristina over the telephone. "You fucking little bitch, I told you not to talk to Donna. Now, come get me. I'm checking out of this hellhole tonight."

Kristina was silent.

"Kristina, you and Justin drive up here to get me now. I told you I'm getting out."

"No," Kristina said.

"No? I told you to come get me now!" she screamed. "I want you and Justin to drive up here tonight and get me. I'm coming home."

"No," Kristina said again. "I won't."

"If you don't pick me up, you'll regret it," Celeste threatened.

"I won't," Kristina said.

When she hung up the telephone, Kristina was both frightened and exhilarated. It was the first time she'd flatly refused to do as her mother ordered; it felt at the same time liberating and terrifying.

Minutes later Jennifer's cell phone rang while she and Christopher were eating dinner in a restaurant. "Jennifer, I don't know what's wrong with your sister," Celeste told her. "I need you to come up here right away and get me. I'm checking out."

"We were just—"

"I don't care!" Celeste screamed. "Get in your car and come get me!"

When Christopher and Jennifer arrived at Timberlawn three hours later, Celeste had her suitcases packed and was ready to go. "Take these," she ordered Christopher, thrusting them into his hands. Then she ran for the elevator, not even bothering to sign herself out. In the car, Christopher drove with Celeste in the seat beside him. In the backseat, Jennifer stared at the back of her mother's head, panic eating away inside her. She'd feared an event like this for weeks. Too much hung over all of them. Bill Mange, the prosecutor, had contacted Christopher and had a meeting scheduled with him later that same week. Jen knew her boyfriend wouldn't lie for Celeste. He'd tell Mange everything. She wanted to talk to the prosecutor, too, but she was frightened. Every time the police came up, Celeste shrieked at her, "You don't talk to them, ever."

Like Christopher, Jennifer knew she wouldn't lie for her mother. She had to tell the truth. When that happened, she knew Celeste would take revenge. But now the situation had become even more complicated; Celeste was furious at Kristina, and when her mother got this angry, bad things happened.

"I don't know what's gotten into Kristina. That little bitch," Celeste stormed, dialing the telephone.

"Yes," Kristina said when she answered.

"I want you home when I get there, young lady."

"You shouldn't treat me like this," Kristina said. "You shouldn't talk to me like this."

"When I get there, I expect you to be home."

The shouting escalated, Jennifer and Christopher jarred by the hard edge to Celeste's voice. Finally, Kristina hung up.

Celeste seethed. "I am so angry I could physically kill Kristina," she said.

In the backseat, Jennifer's chest tightened. To her, Celeste's words weren't an idle threat. She believed her mother had manipulated Tracey into killing Steve. She'd spent her life watching her hurt and take advantage of people. She'd grown up fearing her, and believed that Celeste was capable of murdering both her and Kristina.

Christopher looked in the rearview mirror and his eyes met Jennifer's. Without speaking a word, they both knew Celeste had crossed a line that night, and that the situation had just become even more terrifying.

The hours in the car on the way back to Austin were agony. Jennifer knew she could never go home again. It was simply too dangerous. And if she left, she had to find a way to hide, for Celeste never let go of anyone without a battle, and for her daughters she would mount an all-out war.

When they pulled into Austin, Christopher came to the rescue. "Celeste, drop us at my apartment, so we can get my car," he said. "We'll meet you at the house."

Celeste did as they asked, screeching out of the parking lot.

"You can't go home," Christopher said as soon as she pulled away.

"I know," Jen replied.

They also couldn't stay at Christopher's; that would be the first place Celeste would look. Instead, they went to Anita's office. It was closed, but Christopher, who worked there part-time, had a key. They sat in the office in the darkness, afraid Celeste would find them. When she was angry, Jennifer knew her mother was capable of anything.

Kristina didn't follow her mother's orders that night either. She stayed at the Grimms' house with Justin. "We can't go home, Kris," Jen said to her on the telephone the next day. "I've never seen Mom so angry. She said she could actually kill you."

"I know," Kristina said. Yet she wasn't ready to sever the ties permanently. "We have to let her cool down."

It wasn't what Jennifer wanted to hear, but she wasn't pushing Kristina. She knew how important Celeste was to her sister and how hard it would be for her to break away. Ever since Steve died, Kristina had worked hard to try to restore order to their lives. All to no avail, for with Celeste chaos always won.

The phone calls started that first night. At times Celeste pleaded; at other times she shrieked. The message was clear: She wanted the girls home.

When Kristina heard the voice mails, she felt ill. She'd never denied her mother anything, never blatantly disobeyed. But she knew she couldn't go home, not yet, not until her mother changed how she treated her. When she pondered how to convince her mother that her screaming was abuse, Kristina came up with a plan. She and Justin would tape record the phone calls and messages; then Kristina could play them back for Celeste, letting her hear what Kristina heard on the telephone—emotional battery. From that point on, when Celeste called, Kristina and Justin turned on their tape recorders.

"Kristina, just because you're nineteen doesn't mean that you don't have to do what I tell you to do. You want to move out, is that what you're telling me?" Celeste screamed.

"I don't know," Kristina replied.

"That's what you're saying by deliberately disobeying me?"

"No."

"If you want to continue going to college, if you want to continue to have your expenses paid without working, then you better get your ass home tonight, do you understand that?"

"Yeah."

"Because I'm going to come over there tonight and get your car keys . . . I will change all the locks . . . I'm not playing games with you . . . are you willing to just say fuck it?"

"I don't know."

"What don't you know? Because I'm—I'm a worse person than my father, who molested me? Is that what you don't know?"

Over the days following Jennifer's and Kristina's refusal to return home, the calls became increasingly desperate. Celeste ranted and raved. She called Justin, Justin's parents, Christopher, Christopher's family, the twins' friends, Anita, and everyone she could for help, but no one would tell her where the girls had gone. One afternoon Celeste pounded on the Grimms' front door, pleading with Justin's father to let her in. He told Celeste to leave. Inside the house, Kristina cried. The ties that bound her to her mother were strong.

"I'm not going to have my life run by a nineteen-year-old who thinks she knows everything in the goddamned fucking world," Celeste raged during her next call. "I am your mother. You are not going to tell me what to do . . . I'm telling you this. If you choose to stay at the Grimms', you'll be sorry. I will get a restraining order first thing in the morning. You will not be allowed at my house, ever."

Celeste tried to elicit Kristina's sympathy, talking about her abuse, ranting about the horrors of her life. When that didn't work, she argued that Kristina wasn't acting as an adult. "If you had a problem, you should've said, 'Mom, I don't want to do this,' instead of holding all this resentment and hatred inside of you . . . That's the adult way . . . All you want to do is hurt me," Celeste cried.

"That's not true," Kristina said, her voice heavy with sadness.

Hour after hour Jennifer's and Kristina's cell phones rang. When they didn't answer, Celeste left long messages on their voice mails, or Justin's, his parents', or Christopher's.

"I like how everybody's avoiding my phone calls, Kristina. You're just making it worse on yourself."

On Justin's cell phone, Celeste left a message saying,

"Kristina stole Kaci, which is valued over five hundred dollars, so it's a felony . . . I do not want to do this to my children, because I love them and Mother's Day is coming up, but they're leaving me no choice . . . The other thing to tell the girls is if—if, um, they don't come here at five tonight, I'm not psycho or anything, I'm as calm as can be, but I will report them for stealing the keys to the house and everything else, since they don't live here anymore. I will hire a private detective and track them down, because they were stupid enough to charge on the gas card. And I know, I know the area of town that they're in, and I know where they go to school . . . If they don't do it tonight at five, they will be sorry.

"I've disconnected both girls' phones, and neither one have car insurance . . . please make sure you tell the girls that I love them, but I will have them arrested at school, because they've hurt me, and I think it's only fair that they get humiliated."

The days were torment for the twins. They were afraid, of both staying away and going home. Celeste accused them of stealing money and jewelry. At times they talked with their mother and agreed to meet her, but they never showed up at the Toro Canyon house. And always, Celeste called again.

It was the last conversation she had with her mother that finally convinced Kristina that Celeste wasn't just abusive, she was evil.

"Why are you doing this to me?" Celeste said.

"Why are you doing this to me?" Kristina answered.

"You don't care about me at all?"

"Yes, I do care about you."

"Then, why don't you come home? Why? Why don't you come down and talk to me?"

" 'Cause I don't want you to throw a scene."

"I wasn't going to hurt myself, Kris. What the hell do you

think I went to the hospital for? I'm not gonna hurt myself anymore. I'm not gonna throw a scene anymore . . . Do you think that I'm worse than my father?"

"When you call me names, like 'you little bitch,' and you always say that I'm worthless and selfish. When all I ever do is do everything for you," Kristina said.

"I just want you to know that I do not appreciate you butting into my business when I asked you not to," Celeste warned. "And I was gonna when you gonna home, I was gonna tell you exactly why, exactly what Donna has on me."

"What does she have?" Kristina asked.

"I'm not telling you over the phone. 'Cause you'll just go and tell Justin and everybody else, right?"

"No," Kristina said.

"What?"

"No."

After a momentary pause, Celeste said, "I hired somebody to kill Tracey."

Chapter
17

I hired someone to kill Tracey. The words echoed in Kristina's mind. Suddenly, so many things became clear. She'd spent a lifetime yearning for a storybook mother, loving and kind. Instead she'd been born to Celeste, who'd told Jennifer and Christopher, "I could physically kill Kristina." She'd even bought them both caskets. It wasn't hard to imagine what Celeste might have planned for them. For the first time, Kristina believed her mother was capable of anything, even murder. And if that were true, it wasn't hard to conclude she was behind Steve's death. Tracey Tarlton squeezed the trigger, but Kristina realized her mother must have put her up to it.

When Kris told Christopher about the tape and her mother's words, he said, "You need to talk to Jen."

"I think Mom murdered Steve," she told her twin when they met.

Finally, Jennifer thought. *Finally you understand.*

"I do, too," Jen said. "Kristina, we have to tell the police, and we can't go home. We can never talk to Celeste, never see her again."

Kristina nodded. "I know," she said.

The two sisters held each other and cried, over their lost childhoods and a mother who'd never known how to love them.

The following day the twins told Anita what they now believed, that Celeste was behind Steve's murder. At first Anita seemed doubtful. Her faith had been shaken in Celeste when she learned that rather than going to Timberlawn, as she'd told her, she had gone to New Orleans to party with Donna Goodson. Still, lying about where she went was a long way from murder. Yet, as the girls talked, things started to make sense. She'd noticed how Steve always got drunk when they visited him at home, and he didn't when they were at a restaurant. When the girls told her about the Everclear and sleeping pills, she saw the explanation. Then they asked her what had happened to the $30,000 in Social Security money Celeste had invested with her for them.

"Mom said you lost all our money in the stock market," Kristina said. "Did you?"

"No," Anita said, pulling out the file from a drawer. There, they saw recorded the withdrawal their mother had made; at a time when she was spending hundreds of thousands of dollars on clothes and jewels for herself, Celeste had emptied their accounts.

If the money had been there, it might have served as a cushion, to help them hide. But it was gone. The girls were frightened. Where would they go? How would they live? Being on the run would take money, and they had none. It was then that Kristina decided to do something she'd later regret. Months earlier, Celeste had told them they could have the money from the sale of Steve's Cadillac, to invest and use to pay tuition. Earlier that month, Kristina had sold the car for $21,000. Over the coming days, Kristina would write checks against a joint checking account she had with Celeste for that sum, money she and Jennifer could use to hide.

- Just days later, at four-fifteen, on the afternoon of Friday, April 7, Bill Mange walked into the lobby at the D.A.'s Office to greet Christopher for the interview he had scheduled. Instead, he found not only Christopher and his attorney, but Justin with his attorney, and both Kristina and Jennifer with their attorney.

"We all want to tell you what we know," Christopher said. "And I'd like to go first."

"Let's get started," Mange said.

That day and the days that followed, the prosecutor let the teens tell their stories. Then he slowly questioned each about specific points. With Christopher, the interview took little over an hour. For the first time, Mange heard about Celeste's bizarre behavior the night of the shooting, from sending them to the lake house, to dropping off Meagan and ordering them not to mention Tracey's name. "I thought Celeste was involved from the beginning," Christopher said. "Lots of things made her look guilty."

When Justin began his statement, Mange listened carefully. While Christopher had been animated and forceful, Kristina's boyfriend gave a deliberate recounting, point for point, of all that had happened since he'd first met Celeste, including her affair with Jimmy Martinez. Mange judged that Justin had been thinking long and hard about Celeste's involvement and that the teenager felt like the dams were opening, all his suspicions finally free to spill out. Justin, it appeared, didn't want to leave out anything potentially important. Before he left that afternoon, Mange had in his hands the evidence the boys had brought with them: Celeste's journals, cards from Tracey, and even her secret personal calendar. After they left, Mange paged through the cards, including the one in which Tracey remarked on Celeste's "long, slender body."

Taking it all in, Mange felt sure Celeste was involved. Still, he wondered, was there enough evidence to seek an indictment? *No,* he thought. *Not yet.*

"We believe our mother was in on it," Jennifer told him two days later, when she and Kristina returned for their interviews, "She put Tracey up to murdering our dad."

As Mange listened, Jennifer described her mother's ruthlessness and the callous way she'd treated Steve. To Celeste, Mange was learning, nothing was more important than money. "I saw her signing Steve's name to checks," Jennifer said. "We were all afraid to tell Steve anything, afraid she'd come after us if we did."

When it was finally her turn, Kristina added other facts to the mix. Justin, Christopher, and Jennifer had all already told him about the Everclear and sleeping pills, but they didn't understand the extent of Celeste's actions. "She called the drinks the 'Graveyard,'" Kristina said, frowning. "She laughed about it."

Finally, Kristina handed over to Mange her stash of audio tapes of Celeste's phone calls. The first she played—the conversation about Donna—sent chills through him. "I hired someone to kill Tracey," Celeste said on the tape.

"Play that again," Mange said.

Just like the first time, he heard Celeste say, "I hired someone to kill Tracey."

It was there, recorded, Celeste's admission that she'd solicited Tracey's murder. Why did Celeste want Tracey dead? To shut her up, Mange thought.

"I didn't want to believe our mom was involved," Kristina told him, crying. "All my life she's done bad things, but this was just too horrible. Are you going to arrest her?"

Mange wasn't sure exactly what he had yet. Was there enough evidence for a murder charge, for solicitation of murder? It was something he'd have to take a close look at. "I'm not going to do anything until I'm sure I can take her into a courtroom and make the charges stick," he said. "Let me look into this, and we'll talk again."

One thing had come through loud and clear during his interviews with all the teenagers: They were terrified of Celeste. Both girls cried when they talked about the caskets and Celeste's admission: "I could physically kill Kristina." Since that night, they'd been in hiding. Mange didn't ask how he could reach them. He didn't want to know. "I'll call your attorneys to get messages to you," he said. "I'll be in touch."

Then Kristina said something that brought home to him just how helpless she felt. "I'm afraid to see my mom on the street. If I do and she tells me to, I'll get in the car and drive away with her," she said, crying. "I do what she tells me to do. I always have."

"Would you get in the car, too?" Mange asked Jennifer.

"No," Jen said. "Not me."

The prosecutor realized that although the twins were identical in appearance, they were very different people, especially when it came to their mother.

The possibility that Celeste would find them was a real one. For days she'd been searching, showing up at Jennifer's orthodontist's office and trying to get their schedules at Concordia, where they were both taking classes. The phone rang repeatedly at Anita's house, and Kristina heard their mother screaming into the answering machine. She'd called Jimmy, asking him to help look for the girls, and she'd hired a private investigator. Justin, Christopher, and Amy had all noticed him shadowing them.

"I'm not strong enough to say no to her," Kristina told

Mange. "She'd tell me her side and I'd believe her. I can't risk that."

"Then hide," he said. Writing down his home phone number on the back of his business card, he handed it to her. "And call me if you need help."

After they left, Mange considered what he'd just learned: Celeste had a contract on Tracey's life. He walked to the office of Rosemary Lehmberg, the first assistant district attorney. "You have to let Tracey know," she said. "She has to be protected."

Mange put in a call for Wines. After they talked, the phone rang in the office of Keith Hampton, Tracey's attorney. "We have reason to believe your client's life is in danger, that there may be a hit out on Ms. Tarlton," Wines said. "We'll have police drive by to check on her house, but you need to warn her to watch her back."

When Tracey heard, she called Celeste.

"It's the twins," Celeste told her. "They're mad at you for killing their father. But don't worry. I'll take care of it."

The next day, Celeste and Tracey met at their bench in the park. Celeste was distraught and crying. "The girls have turned me in," she said. Tracey had just learned someone wanted to kill her, yet she found herself comforting Celeste, who rambled on about the girls and the atrocities that were taking over her life. On top of everything, she claimed she had breast cancer. "I'm going to go to California to live with my sister, Caresse," she said. "I don't know when I'll come back."

The months since the shooting had been a hell for Tracey. She was plagued by guilt and feared each time the phone rang that it would be more bad news. She missed Celeste and she worried about her. To Tracey, it appeared her lover was slowly crumbling under the weight of what they had done. And now cancer.

"I understand," Tracey said.

* * *

"I should hire a hitman to kill Tracey Tarlton," Celeste said to her therapist a few days later. "She's ruined my life."

"Celeste, don't go there," Hauser told her. "That's not good judgment."

Throughout the session, Celeste raged against what she described as the treachery of the twins. They'd stolen money and jewelry, she claimed. "I'm embarrassed that they're lying and committing crimes. It reflects on me, as a mother."

"I think you ought to go back to Timberlawn," Hauser said. Celeste agreed, and left a few days later.

At Timberlawn, Gotway tried to disarm the hatred overflowing from Celeste toward the twins. At times she cried, saying she feared that they had fled from her life forever as she'd fled from her own mother. Other times, she succumbed to verbal rampages, blaming them, especially Kristina, for all of her problems.

She wrote the twins a letter: "*I'm typing this letter to you because I can no longer write. I am falling a lot, too . . . I understand that you are growing up and want to be on your own. I can accept that. I can't accept your hiding from me. You both are tearing me up inside . . . I verbally abused you and I am deeply sorry. I was hoping you would be an adult, accept my apology and realize that I was sick. It will never happen again . . . If I do not hear from you by Friday, I will know that the path you chose is to be out of my life. You will leave me no choice but to cancel your insurance, gas cards, phones, and OnStar . . . I love you more than anything and would do absolutely anything for you . . . I love you both,*"

The signature was barely a scratch, "*Mom.*"

Twelve days after she checked back into Timberlawn, Celeste returned to Austin. By then nothing in her world was the same. While she was gone, Donna Goodson had packed her possessions into her Buick Regal and taken off for Florida. "I figured I was next," she says. "I was scared shitless Celeste would hire someone to kill me."

Her fears were no less real than the twins'.

"Your mother says she has the gun loaded and she's going to kill herself tonight if you don't go home," Peggy Farley, Kristina's former therapist, told her one day.

When Kristina explained to Farley that they couldn't go home, that they were afraid of their mother, Farley offered to let them stay with her family on their ranch. Kristina agreed, and when the twins arrived, Justin and Christopher came with them.

It was easy for Farley to see how frightened the teens were. On their first day there, Justin and Christopher disconnected the OnStar systems in the Cateras, afraid Celeste would use the signals to track them. But they still didn't feel safe. With the money she'd brought, Kristina bought an old Jeep, one their mother wouldn't recognize.

When Celeste left a message for Justin, they knew they'd done the right thing. "OnStar can't find the girls, but I left a message with them for the girls," she said. "Tell Kristina to push the OnStar button so they can get the message."

Justin knew the minute the button was pushed, OnStar would have a fix on their location. "It would be like, gotcha," he said.

As Farley talked to them about what happened, she sensed they'd all been through a terrible trauma. "The kids seemed overwhelmed," she said later. "They talked about it all the time. They couldn't seem to think of anything else."

"Our mom was planning our deaths," Kristina told her.

At night the twins were plagued by nightmares of their mother finding them and taking revenge. During the day, they were afraid to leave the ranch. While they were there, Christopher and Jennifer broke up. Jennifer would later say that she believed all the pressure was just too much for them.

Although Celeste had written in her letter from Timberlawn that she'd never again attempt to contact them, she enlisted the aid of the police in her search. In early May she left messages on Justin's voice mail, threatening to turn the girls in to the police for taking Kaci and for stealing money. "Tell Kristina to call me today or I'm calling the police," Celeste threatened. "This is the last warning."

On May 5 she carried through on her threats, filing a report with the Travis County Sheriff's Department that alleged Kristina and Jennifer had stolen from her—not only money, but jewelry worth tens of thousands of dollars. A deputy went out to the Toro Canyon house and took the complaint. When he got there, Celeste said she couldn't open the safe but that she knew the jewelry was gone.

"They changed the combination," she argued. "In effect, they robbed me of being able to get to it." The deputy told her to contact a locksmith. When the safe was opened, three of the seven missing pieces were inside, and the deputy wrote up a complaint on the remaining four items.

"I can't believe you're falling for this," Mange told the deputy when he heard. "She's using you to get to the kids, to control them."

"Maybe they took the stuff," the deputy insisted.

"This woman is a suspect in a murder," Mange told him. "Don't help her find the kids. They're terrified of her."

Reluctantly, the deputy agreed.

Celeste wasn't to be quieted. Days later the phone rang at Donna's house. She'd just returned from Florida a week earlier, and wondered how Celeste knew.

"Come out to the house. I have a job for you," Celeste said.

"Tell you what," Donna countered. "Meet me at Baby

Acapulco's. You can buy lunch and we'll talk." Donna took one precaution; before she left the house, she told her mother who she was meeting and where, just in case she never came home.

In the busy, loud lunchtime crowd, Donna ate quesadillas and chips and listened to Celeste's proposal. She was still afraid of her, but she was intrigued. Maybe there was a way to make more money. "I want you to find the girls," Celeste said. "They've taken off with their cars, the dog, and some of my stuff."

To find them, Celeste suggested Donna search through wedding announcements and make phone calls to their friends. The girls were standing up in a wedding that month, she wasn't sure where. "Once you find them, call me and I'll take over," she said.

Donna wondered what Celeste had planned for the girls. To her, it didn't sound good.

Celeste explained that she was willing to put Donna up in a hotel for a week, to let her use the telephone there to search. That way, she said, the calls wouldn't be traceable to either of their homes. Donna, always looking for a little fun, agreed.

That day, Celeste checked Donna into the Red Lion Inn and left. As soon as she was out the door, Donna called a friend to join her. They watched pay-per-view movies, ordering champagne and dinner from room service.

She partied for a week, then called Celeste.

"I didn't find them," she said. "I'm going home."

At the Farleys' ranch, Jennifer and Justin watched Kristina, worried she might break down and call Celeste. When Justin played his voice mails with their mother ranting about missing them and wanting them home, Kristina cried. Sometimes Jennifer wondered how much more her sister could take before she picked up the telephone, dialed Celeste, and said, "Come get me." They were so frightened that Justin took Kristina's cell phone away from her.

"Kristina, this is it," Jen said. "This is reality. Our mother is a murderer."

The good days were the ones they spent working at the ranch. While there, they helped Peggy and her husband repair fences, lay down a floor, and remodel a bathroom. They'd never done such tasks before, but the work kept their minds off their mother and helped distract them from the very real possibility that at any moment Celeste could pull in the driveway and demand that they come home. Although legally adults, they were afraid she'd find a way to make them.

They called Bill Mange almost every day, hoping to hear that she'd been arrested. The news, however, was never good. After looking at the evidence, Mange feared that, despite everything the twins and their boyfriends had pulled together, the case he had against Celeste wouldn't convince a jury. It was all circumstantial. What he needed was for Tracey Tarlton to implicate her. Then, he judged, he might have a case.

Tracey's lawyer, Keith Hampton, hinted they had information to deal with. At one point he even asked for complete immunity for his client.

"What is this, Commit a Murder Free Week?" Mange scoffed. "Keith, that's not on the table, and it never will be."

After that, Hampton's allusions to a deal stopped.

Despite everything, Tracey hadn't had any second thoughts about standing by Celeste and taking the entire wrap for the killing. The innuendos about the possibility of a deal were her attorney's idea, not hers. "I was determined to go down for this and not take Celeste with me," she says. "I told him that wasn't on the table."

Still, although Celeste had never gone to California, Tracey rarely saw her. One day when they met outside BookPeople, Celeste railed at her, telling her that she'd lost the twins over the murder and that her life was in shambles. A few days later Celeste called, shrieking, "You're just like everyone else! You don't love me!"

Fearing Celeste was suicidal, Tracey drove to Toro Canyon and arrived just as Celeste pulled in. When she saw Tracey, Celeste slammed on the brakes. "Oh, my God, that's the woman who murdered my husband," she shouted to Dr. Dennison, who was supervising two yardmen nearby.

"Drive up to the house," he said. "Nothing will happen with me here."

Celeste pulled forward and Tracey followed. In front of the house, both cars stopped and the two women argued. "Get out of here. They'll see you," Celeste said. "And don't come back. I don't want to see you anymore."

"Fine!" Tracey shouted.

"You can tell people whatever you want," Celeste cried. "I can't do this anymore."

By then Bob Dennison was walking toward them. Angry and hurt, Tracey got back in her car and screeched out of the driveway. Without even thanking her neighbor, Celeste ran in the house.

After that day, it seemed to Tracey that the horror of what they had done was consuming them both. Yet, even with Celeste telling her she never wanted to see her again, Tracey didn't question if what she'd done was right or why she'd done it. What happened next would change that.

The article in the *Austin American Statesman* ran on June 23, eight days after Tracey and Celeste argued in the driveway. Worried that Bill Mange wouldn't be able to arrest Celeste, the girls had filed a request for a restraining order to keep her away from them. According to their affidavit, Celeste had contact with Tracey after the shooting, and Celeste had become increasingly unstable. They believed she was behind their father's murder. But it was the final line in the second paragraph that Tracey read and reread that morning: *"Kristina said she taped her mother saying that she had hired a hit-man to kill Tarlton. The tape has been turned over to investigators."*

At her house on Wilson that night, Tracey downed pills and drank the bottle of vodka Celeste had left behind. Later that night an ambulance pulled in front of the house on Wilson and Tracey was rushed to the hospital for yet another suicide attempt.

The twins' secret tape recording was the talk of Austin. For months the city had speculated on Celeste's involvement in her husband's murder. Now Celeste, with her millions, was being accused by her own daughters of hiring a hit man. The twins were frantic with worry, knowing how vindictive their mother could be. They'd not only left her, but were working with the prosecutors.

The hearing for the restraining order was coming up, and they didn't know if Celeste would be seated across from them as they testified, with the cold, hateful stare they both knew well. As Jennifer and Kristina took the stand that day, they were flanked by four uniformed, armed deputies. The twins scanned the courtroom. Their mother wasn't there.

The twins' testimony was riveting. Reporters jotted pages of notes as they recounted how Celeste had bought them caskets and been involved in the murder of their father. "We're afraid of our mother," Jennifer said. "Celeste drugged our father. She gave Steve sleeping pills and spiked his vodka."

"When we were babies we had seizures," Kristina testified. "I believe our mother not only used to poison our father but us."

"Celeste loves her daughters," her attorney argued. Yet, she did not contest the order.

That day was a victory for the girls. Judge John Hathaway granted the restraining order and ordered Celeste to pay $13,500 toward the twins' legal fees. "You're strong and courageous," he told them. "Not only can she not come within two hundred yards of you, she can't throw a spitball at you. She can't use a gun or a knife; she can't come anywhere near you or touch you in any way.

Despite their victory in the courtroom and the judge's assurances, the girls felt anything but safe.

Not even generating a headline was what happened at Donna Goodson's house. One morning the police arrived with a search warrant. They took her computer, her zip drive, and pawn tickets. Although the audiotape had been played in open court, it wasn't about involvement in a murder-for-hire. It was about four pieces of jewelry.

Months earlier, Celeste had reported the jewelry stolen, blaming the twins. Although the investigation had been dropped, an alert went out to pawnshops describing the pieces. A call came in regarding one of the pieces, a stunning diamond cocktail ring worth thousands. When deputies investigated, they found Donna had pawned it for a few hundred dollars. Pawn tickets found in the search turned up the remaining three pieces, including a pendant with the Dallas skyline encrusted with jewels, all in pawnshops on her way to Florida. Later, Donna argued that the jewelry was a gift, not stolen. "Celeste wanted me to take care of Tracey so bad, all I had to do was say I liked something and she gave it to me," she says. "I didn't have to steal anything."

The day of the search, Donna was arrested and booked in the Travis County Jail on a probation violation. Since she'd pawned the items in Louisiana, they knew that she'd left

Texas without permission. To her, the arrest was a relief. Ever since news of the audiotape had broken, she'd been looking over her back, watching faces, waiting for Celeste to strike. At times she thought it was imminent, like the week the windows on not only her car but her mother's and her stepfather's were smashed in their driveway. Another night she awoke to the crack of shotgun fire in front of her house. After that she moved her bed away from the window. "In jail I was safe," she says. "For the first time in weeks, I knew she couldn't get me." Donna hated to leave jail ten days later, when a judge reinstated her probation. "From that point on, I watched my back," she says.

Spurred by the twins' testifying against their mother, that summer the older Beard children asked Kristina and Jennifer to join them in a wrongful death suit against Celeste, to keep her from squandering Steve's fortune. They agreed. In August, seven months after Steve's death, the girls came out of hiding long enough to take the witness stand in a hearing on the case. This time Celeste was in the courtroom. "We didn't want to see her," says Kristina. "We were scared."

Newspaper, radio, and television reporters were all in the courtroom when Kristina took the stand. The testimony was grueling. As attorneys questioned them, the girls answered carefully, keeping their eyes averted from Celeste as they recounted the months leading up to and the night of the shooting. The following morning the lead sentence in the paper would recount the hamburger night at the Beard household, when Tracey slipped her arm over Celeste's shoulder, then kissed her hard on her lips.

"Was it your impression that your mother and Tracey Tarlton were having an affair?"

"Yes," Kristina said.

Unlike the protection hearing, this time Kristina also described the way Celeste threw away Steve's money, testifying that she paid large sums to friends and to her ex-husband Jimmy Martinez for little work. In some cases the money came back to her, through refunds on overpayments. As it would every time she took the stand, on cross examination Kristina was questioned vigorously about the checks she'd cashed in the weeks following her decision to go into hiding.

"You violated your mother's trust, didn't you?" Celeste's attorney challenged

"I was doing what she said I should," Kristina said. "And I had her power of attorney. She opened up a joint bank account and put me on it."

Despite their fears, both the girls held up well, answering questions and not backing down. When they'd finished, however, it was evident how big a toll the testimony had taken on them. In a room behind the courtroom, they sat together, crying. Neither had looked her mother in the eye. That was something they weren't yet ready to do. But they could feel her in the courtroom and knew how much she now hated them.

Over the next two days, the Beard children's attorneys pulled in witnesses to show how Celeste was squandering Steve's money.

"How much money did Mrs. Beard spend in the past seven months?" an attorney asked.

"Half a million dollars," Janet Hudnall, a vice president of Bank of America, replied.

Celeste had gone through so much money, in fact, that she'd eaten up the $500,000 gift in Steve's will.

"It's gone?" asked the attorney.

"All of it," said Hudnall.

Yet, Steve's own actions served to undercut his children's case. On the stand, David Kuperman testified not only that Steve approved many of the bills, but that he increased Celeste's portion of the estate in the trust after the shooting, by adding Davenport Village II to the estate's holdings. Still, the evidence was compelling, especially when Petra Mueller, the owner of Studio 29, took the stand and recounted how days before the shooting she overheard Celeste say that she wished Steve were dead.

Throughout the hearing, Celeste, carefully dressed and manicured, watched the proceedings from the chair beside her attorney. She showed little emotion, her eyes narrowing as so many spoke against her. Yet she never took the stand. Instead the twins' attorney read part of a deposition Celeste had given earlier that summer. In it, one attorney questioned her about her meetings with Tracey. Celeste admitted that she'd met with Tracey once behind BookPeople, after Steve's death. "I was distraught," she said. "And I just wanted her to know I was losing my whole family."

There she was, admitting she'd talked to the woman accused of murdering her husband. Astonishingly, Celeste insisted she didn't ask Tracey the one question it seemed would be on her mind more than any other: Did you kill Steve?

On August 31 the judge came down with his ruling. Citing insufficient evidence, he ruled against the Beard children and refused to stop Celeste from spending the money in the estate while they pursued other action against her.

In the newspaper article on the hearing, Steven III was quoted as saying that the criminal investigation into his father's murder continued. But it was something else, something near the end of the article, that caught Tracey's interest: The reason Celeste hadn't been at the twins' protective hearing in July was that she'd gone to Aspen, *on her honeymoon.*

Tracey had never heard of Celeste's fifth husband, Spencer Cole Johnson. A thirty-eight-year-old bartender and carpenter, he'd been introduced to Celeste by Donna that spring while they bar-hopped Sixth Street. Friends say he had little more than his clothes—mostly jeans—and a motorcycle and a run-down truck when he started dating Celeste. "He's a nice guy, sweet, worked hard," says a friend. "He's a little on the wild side, loved to party. And he was head over heels in love with Celeste."

Tracey was devastated by the news. "She was married just weeks after she told me she didn't want to see me anymore," she says. "Even I could figure out that they were together before we split."

If Celeste had lied when she'd told her she wasn't seeing anyone else, Tracey wondered, what else had her former lover misled her about? Her mind grazed over the past year, since they'd met in St. David's. Was it all a lie? One thing had never stopped bothering her: On the night of the shooting, Tracey had wondered about Celeste's story about why she'd removed Meagan—that she was protective of Steve—when all along she'd said Steve beat the dog. If the dog was faithful to him, didn't that say something about who he was?

Maybe he wasn't the way she portrayed him, Tracey thought. *Maybe it was all a lie.*

Soon Tracey came to the conclusion that she had never really known Celeste as she thought she did. "I wondered if Celeste broke me in gradually or just found a way to make me more malleable. She wanted Steve dead, and she knew I would do it for her," she says. "I wondered if she just planted a seed within me and let it grow."

What Tracey had been dreading happened the following February, when Mange took the evidence against her to a grand jury for a murder indictment. For more than a year, she'd been out on $25,000 bail, awaiting trial on a charge of injury to the elderly. Since Steve Beard's death, Keith Hampton, Tracey's attorney, had fought hard to keep the shotgun out of evidence, arguing that Wines and Knight had intimidated her into turning it over. Consistently, the judges had ruled against him.

As the grand jury met, Hampton called Tracey and told her that once the indictment came down, she could expect to be arrested. After a year of working only off and on, she didn't have the money for bail. That week, Tracey stayed home and boxed up her possessions. She had no illusions about her future. From the beginning, she believed she'd one day enter jail and never emerge. Her dog, Wren, seemed to sense something was wrong. All weekend he stayed beside her, following her from room to room, nestling against her when she sat on the floor and cried.

On Friday, February 16, the grand jury added capital murder to the charges against her. Immediately her bail jumped to $500,000.

"We are still investigating the matter and still looking at Celeste Beard's involvement," Mange's boss was quoted as saying in the *Statesman* the following day. "This is one of the most complicated cases I've ever seen."

Days later officers showed up at the house on Wilson. One handcuffed Tracey and led her to a squad car. By then she'd taken Wren and her cats to a friend's house, and made arrangements for her things to be stored and her home sold. Still, as she entered the Travis County Jail, it all seemed surreal. "It was like it was happening to someone else," she says. "It felt like everything was over and Celeste had gotten away with it."

Meanwhile, Celeste cashed in, and Steve Beard's children were helpless to stop her. The week after Tracey entered jail, Celeste and Cole signed a contract to buy a brand new home, a stately edifice on Yeargin Court in the town of Southlake, Texas. An exclusive enclave where the average house cost more than $400,000, Southlake lay halfway between Fort Worth and Dallas, a suburban refuge with a charming town square and a Fourth of July celebration that included fireworks sprayed across the sky.

By April she'd sold the Austin homes—the lake house for $280,000, of which $120,000 went toward paying her attorneys on the civil matter; and Steve's dream house on Toro Canyon, for $1,890,000. The mortgages paid up by the trust, after expenses she pocketed more than $2 million.

The day of the Toro Canyon closing, Celeste gave the title company a list of cashier's checks she wanted drawn from the proceeds: more than $50,000 to American Express, $10,000 to Louis Shanks Furniture stores, and a string of checks for banks, from $15,000 to Bank of America to $250,000 to Wells Fargo. Just under half a million went into her trust fund, and $516,892 went to First Fidelity Title Company to pay cash for their grand new home. She asked for the rest, $227,000, in a check made out to her.

Steven Beard's death had made Celeste, the former waitress, a very wealthy woman.

By then Jennifer was living with Anita's aged mother in Midland, but Kristina and Justin moved back to Austin and in with his parents, where they hired on at a Best Buy store. Always, they were on alert, watching for Celeste, knowing that at any moment she or someone she'd sent to look for them could walk through the door.

One day Jimmy did just that. Kristina had been out on a lunch break. When she returned, Justin played the security tape for her, showing Jimmy walking the aisles, looking about but buying nothing. He finally stood in the computer department, staring at Justin, watching. Finally he turned and left. Kristina thought he was there for her.

Even separated from them, Celeste continued to haunt their lives. The twins were reminded of her every time they tried to get a cell phone or a credit card. Over the years, they discovered, she'd used their Social Security numbers, beginning when they were just twelve. The bills were paid late or not at all. When Kristina tried to get a Sprint cell phone, the company turned her down, saying that someone named Celeste had been in there with her Social Security number and that she'd screamed at the clerks. When they contacted the credit reporting agencies and tried to clear up their credit reports, they were told there was nothing they could do. Although the twins were just children when the charges were made, they were unable to prove they hadn't been the ones who made them.

When Paul Beard called Mange that summer, the prosecutor was blunt. He'd been over the evidence again and again and found no way to convict Celeste on what he had. "The only way we get Celeste is if Tracey testifies against her," Mange said.

"We all want Celeste," Paul said.

"Well, then the best thing we can do is put pressure on Tracey. Let her sit in jail and stew, knowing Celeste is out enjoying the good life."

Throughout 2001, Bill Mange continued to build his case against Tracey, always keeping in mind that he also wanted Celeste. His office was filled with boxes of subpoenaed phone, medical, and financial records. Tracey's bank records were carefully searched, and Mange found no indication that money had passed between the two women. That didn't surprise him. He'd never thought the murder was about money, not on Tracey's part. He'd had no doubt that was precisely what it was about for Celeste.

In October another motion came before the court. Stuart Kinard and Mike Maguire, two white-haired, well-respected criminal attorneys, had taken over Tracey's case. Like Hampton before them, they argued to keep the gun out. Like

Hampton, they failed. Tracey had not been intimidated, the judge ruled. Her .20 gauge shotgun would be evidence against her at her trial, scheduled for March of the coming year.

After the hearing, Kinard and Maguire approached Mange about the possibility of a deal. If Tracey could build the case against Celeste, was there a chance for a deal? Mange balked. First, they were asking for transactional immunity, meaning that Tracey would walk out the jail door and serve no more time for murder. Second, neither Kinard nor Maguire would say exactly what Tracey had. Instead of one hypothetical outline of the evidence they had to bargain with, as defense attorneys often do, they floated four possible scenarios. When they wouldn't be more specific, Mange refused to bargain. "I wasn't letting her walk, and I wasn't buying a pig in a poke," he says. "I wanted to know exactly what they had to offer."

Off and on when their paths crossed at the courthouse, the defense attorneys tested the waters. Mange stood firm.

"I thought you wanted Celeste Beard," Maguire said.

"I want the person I've got enough evidence to put away," Mange replied. "Right now, that's your client. That's the case I'm taking to trial."

In Del Valle, the sprawling Travis County Jail annex southeast of the city, Tracey was silent. She said little to anyone, quietly staying in her cell thinking about the past. "I realized Celeste had played me. All along for her it was a game," she says. "But I still agreed to do it, and I wasn't going to pull her into the mess I was in."

Then she met someone. On the courtyard one day, during exercise period, Jeannie Jenkins, who'd been in and out of jails and prisons all her life on charges from prostitution to burglary, saw Tracey walking quietly in circles and crying. She thought she'd never seen anyone who looked so totally alone. Jeannie went up to her and began to draw her into a conversation. Before long Tracey spilled out her story, telling her everything that had led to Steve's murder.

"Did that woman just leave you here to rot?" Jeannie asked.

"I guess you could say she did," Tracey admitted, thinking back on all the promises Celeste had made and not kept, everything from paying for her attorney to putting money into her commissary fund. She hadn't even taken care of her animals.

"That's not right," Jeannie said. "You shouldn't be doing all the time. That woman's as guilty or guiltier than you are."

After that day, Tracey thought often of Jeannie's words.

In March 2002, a year after Tracey entered jail, Mange had his case against her lined up. He had traveled to Timberlawn and interviewed Susan Milholland. He knew about Tracey's obsession with Celeste and her threat aimed at Steve: "All my problems would be solved if someone met an untimely death."

On top of that, he had the shotgun shell tying her to the murder, and he had Terry, the Tramps manicurist who'd heard Tracey say that if Steve ever hurt Celeste, she'd kill him. Still, the case was a difficult one. Early on, Tracey had told the detectives that Celeste had a key to her house. At trial, Mange figured Maguire and Kinard would argue Celeste had the opportunity to get Tracey's shotgun and kill Steve herself. It wasn't as open-and-shut a case as he would have liked. Still, he wasn't too worried. Everyone at the D.A.'s Office knew the investigation was flawed. If he lost, he lost. They'd pat him on the back and say he'd put up a good fight. The upside was that if he won, he'd be a hero.

"You're really going to go ahead against Tracey and leave Celeste hanging out there?" Kinard said to him one day at the courthouse.

"You bet I am," Mange said. "And I'm going to win."

In his office, Mange had a list of facts he'd pulled together on the Beard case, indicators that pointed to Celeste's involvement, everything from dropping Meagan at the lake house to the birthday card she'd sent Tracey, which read, "To the one I love." Still, he didn't have the thing he needed most: Tracey's testimony. He wanted Celeste, and he was willing to deal to get her; but he couldn't give Kinard and Maguire what they asked for: immunity that would free Tracey. Mange wasn't buying it now any more than he had when Hampton brought it up nearly two years earlier. "No way I'll let someone who shot a helpless old man in the middle of the night walk," he said. "Forget it."

In February, as Tracey's trial approached, Maguire and Kinard met with Mange again. This time they were ready to deal. In Del Valle, Tracey had told them she was willing to talk. In fact, she said whether or not they worked out a deal, she wanted to tell Mange everything, including Celeste's role in the murder. With an eager client, they didn't dance around the issue. This time they floated only one hypothetical scenario for Tracey's testimony. Mange was interested. From what he heard, it fit the evidence. With something concrete, the bargaining began. Still, they were worlds apart. Mange wanted Tracey to serve forty years, while Maguire pushed for probation. Gradually, they came to a compromise: Tracey would plead guilty to Steve Beard's murder and serve twenty years. But before it was set in stone, Mange needed to hear from her what she had to say.

"We'll talk to our client and get back with you," Maguire told him.

That afternoon Mange called Paul Beard in Virginia. "Are you willing to plea out Tracey Tarlton on a reduced sentence to get Celeste?" he asked.

"Yes," Paul said. "Tracey was a pawn. We want Celeste."

"Okay," Mange said.

The following day Kinard called Mange. "You've got a deal," he said.

In late March, a week before her trial date, Mange, Kinard, and Maguire all traveled to Del Valle for the debriefing. There, in one of the rooms reserved for attorneys and their clients, over a period of four hours, Tracey talked. She started with the first day she met Celeste at St. David's and went through to the night of the shooting and their confrontation in Celeste's driveway the June after Steve died, when Celeste had told her she wanted nothing more to do with her. Then Mange brought out photos of the crime scene and an architect's diagram of the house he'd gotten from Gus Voelzel.

"Show me how you entered and left the house," he asked.

Using her finger to trace her path, she talked him through that night, telling how Celeste had done a walk-through with her, then changed it, having her drive up to the back of the house and enter through a door off the pool. While she talked, Mange assessed her. Her intelligence surprised him. It was rare that he'd run across a defendant so bright and articulate. On the witness stand, she'd be powerful. More important, everything she told him matched the physical evidence. It all rang true.

When they parted that day, Mange told the defense attorneys he believed they had a deal. "Now we just need to make sure your client isn't lying."

Mange hadn't talked to Wines about the case in more than a year, but that afternoon he called the detective. As angry as he was about the way Wines had investigated the case, he was the lead detective and Mange felt stuck with him. "We're taking Tracey to DPS for a polygraph tomorrow," he told him. "I'd like you to be there."

On March 28, four days before her trial date, Tracey was transported to the Texas Department of Public Safety office for a polygraph. Mange and Wines, with Maguire and Kinard, watched from behind smoked glass. She stared up at the window often. *She knows we're here*, Mange thought.

For three hours the examiner shot her questions, at first those with verifiable answers—like what's your name, your birthdate, what month is this? Then he honed in on Celeste and on Steve's murder. Before he finished and tabulated the results, the examiner stuck his head into the room where Mange and Wines waited.

"This looks really good," he said. "I think she's telling the truth."

Mange smiled at Wines. "Go get your warrant," he said. "And find Celeste Beard."

"I already know where she is," Wines told him. "I've been keeping tabs on her."

An hour later Mange called Wines at his office. By then Wines had checked in with the Southlake police and alerted them to the impending arrest. "Forget about the warrant," Mange said. "I'm taking this to a grand jury. I want the indictment sealed until we round her up."

With all Celeste's money, Wines understood Mange considered her a flight risk.

That afternoon Tracey told her story again, this time in front of a grand jury. The session lasted thirty minutes, and she was the only witness. Mange listened, looking for inconsistencies, anything that would indicate that despite the lie detector test, which she'd passed without a glitch, she was lying. As she had throughout the debriefing, Tracey stayed true to her story. When he walked out later that afternoon, he had an indictment charging Celeste with injury to an elderly individual, murder, and capital murder.

The following morning, March 29, Good Friday, Mange

called Paul, who'd already packed to fly to Houston for Tracey's trial. "We've struck a deal with Tracey," Mange said. "We're going to arrest Celeste."

"Finally," Paul said.

Mange reached Kristina and Justin in the car on their way to Port Aransas, on the Texas coast, for the Easter weekend. "We're arresting your mother this afternoon," he said. "I'll notify you as soon as we have her in custody."

When Kristina hung up, she began sobbing. "She cried for the rest of the trip," Justin says.

"We've got her," Wines said when he called Mange later that day. "Southlake police have picked up Celeste."

At the jail, Tracey heard the news on television. "I knew she'd be coming," she says. "Once they had her, she was on her way." Inside, she felt no happiness, only resolve.

"It has taken two years to unravel the mystery surrounding the death of Steve Beard," Travis County District Attorney Ronnie Earle told the press that day. "This indictment is the result of dogged persistence by Bill Mange and the Sheriff's Office. They never gave up."

The first time Mange saw the woman he'd pursued for more than two years was at the bond hearing. There, Celeste Beard Johnson, thin, blond, her designer suits replaced by an orange and green jailhouse uniform, looked subdued. She didn't resemble the monster he'd heard so much about. At her side were six lawyers, including Charles Burton, the criminal defense attorney she'd hired the day of the shooting.

"She has ample funds to flee," Mange argued. "She's not involved with her family and has nothing to keep her from running."

To bolster his claims, Mange brought Bank of America records that showed that in the year after Steve's death, Celeste had collected $3.5 million from the estate.

"She doesn't have that now," Burton argued. "The money is gone, and Mrs. Johnson doesn't have the resources to pay a high bail."

With that, State District Judge Julie Kocurek set bail at $8 million, the highest in the history of Travis County, Texas.

Not long after Celeste arrived at the jail, Tracey saw her for the first time, across the exercise yard. Soon, messages began arriving, relayed through other inmates. "Celeste says it's not too late," one inmate told Tracey. "She still loves you. You can still be together."

The messages continued until Tracey told the messenger, "Tell Celeste to put it in writing."

Then something unexpected happened. The previous December, Mange had been transferred out of his position as chief of a court to head the motor fuels division, investigating white collar crimes. He hated the paper-heavy workload. A month after the judge set Celeste's record bail, Mange announced he was leaving the prosecutor's office, and the Beard murder case became the bastard stepchild no one wanted.

Chapter
18

The Travis County D.A.'s staff had murmured for months about the Beard case. How could they not? A multimillionaire shot by his trophy wife's lesbian lover. "It had all the makings of a soap opera," says one prosecutor. It wasn't just the sensational aspects that begged their attention. When Bill Mange said he was leaving, more than one prosecutor eyed the file boxes of Beard documents climbing his office walls. The case was set for trial in December, and he had months of work to get trial ready. And then there was the investigation. They all knew it was flawed. As strong as the circumstantial evidence was, the case rested on the testimony of one person: Tracey Tarlton. Few prosecutors want a case where the star witness is a confessed murderer.

Making matters worse, Celeste was angry at Charles Burton for not getting her bail lowered and replaced him with Houston's Dick DeGuerin, one of Texas's best known and most accomplished defense attorneys. Over the years, DeGuerin's talents had taken on nearly mythical proportions in the state. Wealthy Texans in trouble flocked to him when trouble knocked, including Senator Kay Bailey Hutchison. His phone rang again when four New York Mets were arrested in a spat in a Houston nightclub. The well-heeled paid into the high six-figure fees for his tenacious brand of defense, where he maximized every seed of evidence in his client's interest. DeGuerin made no apologies for charging those who could afford to pay, yet he also took on cases where the only remuneration was a sense of self-satisfaction. In 1987 he championed the cause of a mentally ill and desperately poor Houston woman who tried to drown six of her seven children, killing two of them, and saved her from the death penalty.

Six years later DeGuerin was in the Branch Davidian compound in Waco, Texas. Outside, the FBI and ATF camped out in a standoff with David Koresh and his band of followers. As Koresh's attorney, DeGuerin tried to negotiate a peaceful solution, one that would bring his client and his followers out alive. It wasn't to be, and on the fifty-first day of the siege the compound exploded in a hail of bullets and tear gas into a furnace, incinerating all eighty-four men, women, and children.

"High profile, bad investigation, mountains of work, Dick DeGuerin, and the very real possibility that you'd lose, you'd have to be crazy to want the Beard case," says Assistant District Attorney Allison Wetzel. So when an e-mail from her boss popped up on her computer in August, she opened it with trepidation. *"We'd like you to take the Beard case,"* it read.

Damn, she thought. *Just what I need.*

As the chief prosecutor in child abuse cases, Wetzel already had an overwhelming workload. But this wasn't an instance where she got to pick and choose. "When you're handed a case, you run with it," she says. "It's part of the job."

In the District Attorney's Office, Wetzel had a strong reputation and a colorful one. She'd grown up in Houston, the daughter of an Exxon engineer and a secretary, in a home where she was expected to achieve. She graduated from high school at sixteen, college at twenty, and only took the law school entrance exam, the LSAT, because she couldn't think of anything else to do. At the University of Houston, she made law review, then clerked for two of that city's most prominent, high-dollar criminal attorneys, Racehorse Haynes and Jack Zimmerman. She found criminal law fascinating, learning the stories behind the headlines of their high-profile cases. Then, in the late eighties, any thought that she had about becoming a defense attorney faded.

At the time, she worked in the Dallas District Attorney's Office, gathering experience before moving into private practice. One night an undercover officer she knew was gunned down during a drug bust. That changed things for her. "I saw the impact the murder had on people, including the family," she says. "After that, I didn't want to defend criminals anymore. I liked being one of the good guys, even if most of the prosecutors I knew were middle-age white guys in bad suits."

In Austin she found a good match; Wetzel was a natural for a job where she prosecuted the murders and sexual assaults of children. With two young sons of her own, she identified with the victims and their families and fought hard to do her best for them. Nearly six feet tall with a tussle of chin-length, dark auburn hair, in a courtroom she bristled with nervous energy. She knew her evidence the way she'd once studied for law school exams, front to back, and always had it ready to pounce on a defense attorney's misstep. Wetzel may have had a Sunday school bearing, but everyone who knew her well realized that was only one side. Scratch the surface and she became a feisty opponent with a vocabulary that could strike a cowboy pale.

Wetzel had been glad the Beard case was Bill Mange's problem. "No fun to get your butt kicked with the world watching," she says. But now it was hers.

That same afternoon, she met with her boss, who looked at her schedule and decided there'd be no time for the other cases crowding it, even a capital murder trial of a woman who'd killed her own child. Those were handed out to others on the staff. Moving the case files from Bill Mange's office to hers—enough to have filled two pickup trucks—convinced her that had been a good decision.

Still, until she sat down with Jennifer and Kristina, the case felt foreign to Wetzel. In them, she saw the small victims she'd come to know so well, bowed by years of parental abuse. The girls didn't want to testify against their mother. They were frightened. That was something Wetzel understood. She'd had young victims crawl under a witness stand to get away from an abusive parent's gaze. "We're going to take this one step at a time," she told them. "There's one big thing to remember here: You're not trying to put your mother in jail. The state is doing that. You're just telling the truth."

Over the following days, Wetzel interviewed other witnesses, from Amy Cozart, the twins' friend who'd been with Jennifer at the lake house the night of the shooting, to David Kuperman, Steve's attorney. The interview that most concerned her was the one she had with Tracey Tarlton at the Del Valle jail. Wetzel had already read her statement. Much of it seemed hard to believe; yet the evidence suggested she was telling the truth. As Tracey talked, Wetzel sized her up. Cases based on accomplice testimony are difficult. Most often the accomplices are poorly educated and have records that undermine their credibility. Tracey didn't fit that mold. Instead, Wetzel was impressed by her intelligence, and, despite her psychiatric history, Tracey didn't appear the least bit crazy.

"Why are you testifying against Celeste?" Wetzel asked.

"I understand that I shot Steve and I deserve prison," Tracey said. "But I'm not the only one who does. I want to explain why I did what I did."

Wetzel left the jail that day relieved, and more hopeful than when she'd arrived. *Maybe I can do this*, she thought. *It just might work.*

At night, she cooked her family dinner, then curled up with Timberlawn records instead of a good novel. In the end, they were as fascinating, offering insight into what went on behind the institution's locked doors. In the office, during the day, she combed through financial records. A pattern emerged. Celeste's flagrant spending, she reasoned, showed motive. By the time Wetzel perused the phone records, she felt even more confident. It was easy to see that Celeste hadn't cut off contact with Tracey after the shooting; the women had talked often even after Steve's death.

"Why don't we put those in a more usable format," Sergeant Debra Smith, who with Sergeant Dawn McLean, transported Tracey to and from the jail for conferences, mentioned one day. "We can put the financials and phone records on spread sheets and draw up summaries."

Wetzel had an undergraduate degree in business, but the thought had never occurred to her. Smith, a no-nonsense woman with short dark hair and glasses, however, was a former auditor who worked as an investigator in the D.A.'s White Collar Crime Unit. With a master's degree in criminal justice management, she was an expert at honing complicated records into a form a jury would understand.

"Go for it," Wetzel said, glad to have Smith take over the

task. She had more pressing problems: DeGuerin had filed a motion asking an appellate court to lower Celeste's bail. If he succeeded, Wetzel had no doubt Celeste would flee.

With the trial rescheduled for late January, just weeks away, DeGuerin and his staff took over the second floor of a gracious, old, brown brick house a block from the Travis County Criminal Justice Center. The owner, a lawyer with offices on the first floor, had offered the apartment as DeGuerin's base through the trial. A porch overlooked the street, shaded by an ancient live oak, its thick trunk camouflaged by heavy broad-leafed vines.

Inside, it was a stark contrast to Wetzel's modern beige office. The wood floors creaked, and the furniture mixed Salvation Army and vintage antiques. A sign over the kitchen door read, ABSOLUTELY NO CREDIT, and the dining room had the look of a war room. A battered table groaned under stacks of files, documents, and transcripts of prior testimony—from the protection hearings and the wrongful death suit—while on the walls, beside battered tin ads for Grapette soda, Cobb's Creek Whisky, and Southern Select Beer, hung sheets of yellow legal paper suspended on strips of clear tape. Each bore a list of names under a heading: Need Subpoenas, Interview, and Find.

DeGuerin had family in Houston, including his first grandchild, a boy named Eli, after his father, Elias McDowell DeGuerin. Better known as Mack, the elder DeGuerin was an Austin civil lawyer, an LBJ Democrat who served on Johnson's congressional staff and several times as assistant attorney general in the days before Texas turned conservative and Republican. Dick and his younger brother, Mike, followed their father into law but took the other side of the practice, representing criminal defendants. Although he'd grown up in Austin, DeGuerin had made his mark in Houston courtrooms. Fresh out of law school in the early sixties, he worked at the Harris County District Attorney's Office, where he quickly became a courthouse presence. A few years later the brothers became protégés of the legendary Percy Foreman, one of the most powerful defense attorneys to ever argue before a jury. Years later, in the tough cases, Dick DeGuerin still asked himself, "What would Percy do?"

Although slight and spare, DeGuerin cut an imposing figure in a courtroom, perched hawklike on the edge of his chair beside his client, his eyes intent. In his early sixties, he ran three miles a day and looked a decade younger. He always carried the same worn, golden brown leather briefcase made by a client who couldn't pay any other way. That wasn't the case with Celeste where his bill was $450,000. While DeGuerin was busy with her, his next defendant awaited trial in a Galveston jail: Robert Durst, the heir to a New York real estate fortune, accused of murdering and dismembering his next door neighbor.

On October 2, 2002, the third anniversary of Steve's shooting, in one of his first tasks as Celeste's attorney, DeGuerin went before a three-judge panel of the appeals court to argue for a reduction of her $8 million bond on the charge of capital murder. It was then that Wetzel pulled Donna Goodson out of her hat. Armed with a signed immunity agreement she'd crafted with Goodson and her attorney, Wetzel took the solicitation case before a grand jury. When the indictment came down, Celeste was charged with soliciting the murder of Tracey Tarlton with an additional $5 million bond.

In a November hearing, DeGuerin argued again that Celeste didn't have the funds to post such high bail. An accountant's report he produced suggested she had little left of the $3.5 million she'd gotten after Steve's death. In Southlake, Cole had sold the house, but much of that money had gone to pay bills. In 2001, according to the records, Celeste paid $223,000 to American Express and $197,453 in improvements on a brand new house. Many of her jewels, furniture, and antiques, the treasures she'd paid so dearly for with Steve's money, had been sold at a distress sale.

The decision went against DeGuerin, and the battle was over. Celeste wouldn't leave jail unless acquitted in the trial. Now both sides prepared for the war.

With the Beard trial date set in stone for January 27, Wetzel had a problem. She needed a prosecutor to second-chair—act as cocounsel on the case. Considering the attorneys within the D.A.'s Office, she quickly settled on Gary Cobb.

Wetzel reasoned she and Cobb would be a good match. They had something in common: Before she'd arrived, he had held her slot as chief of the child abuse unit. Cobb had a reputation for having an unusual ability to connect with juries. In front of a courtroom, he appeared smooth and effortless, never anxious, worried, or rattled. Going up against DeGuerin, self-confidence was an important asset. And there was little Cobb liked better than trying a tough case.

"You should just see the evidence in this Beard case," Wetzel said to him at the office. A little at a time, she talked about the challenges of the upcoming trial: the mental health issues, the accomplice testimony, the testimony of the daughters. None of it would be an easy sell to a jury, but she hoped the case's complexity would lure Cobb.

"It all sounded unbelievable," he'd say later. "I found it fascinating."

That DeGuerin was involved didn't frighten him. In fact, he relished a good fight. In his thirteen years as a prosecutor, Cobb, who grew up one of nine siblings in a small Mississippi town where black men weren't expected to go to col-

lege, much less law school, had won more than his share of
bizarre cases. One involved a husband who claimed his wife
committed suicide during sex. Cobb tore down his version
of the woman's death by demonstrating a history of domestic violence. Another case yielded a life sentence without a
body. The verdict relied on a single spec of DNA.

"So, what do you think about trying this case with me?"
Wetzel finally asked.

"I think it could be fun," Cobb answered.

While the prosecution would rest with Wetzel and Cobb,
DeGuerin had amassed a team for the trial. His partner, Matt
Hennessy, thin, with a mop of dark hair, would play a small
role, but Hennessy's wife, Catherine Baen, would function
as DeGuerin's point person and second chair. Tall and lithe,
Baen had been raised the daughter of a country doctor and
had the ramrod straight bearing of a horsewoman. At Texas
Tech University she'd participated in a Texas tradition—ba-
ton twirling.

Her credentials as an attorney spoke for themselves.
She'd clerked at one of Houston's biggest firms, Bracewell
and Patterson, and had worked on such high-profile cases as
the Oklahoma City bombing and the David Graham case,
better known as the cadet murder, where Graham, an Air
Force cadet, and his fiancée, Diane Zamora, a navy cadet attending Annapolis, were convicted of murdering a girl he'd
had a fling with, Adrianne Jones. More recently, Baen had
gone international, working on the Bosnian war crimes tri-
bunal in The Hague, Netherlands.

From her first meeting with Celeste, Baen found her client
funny, bright, and personable, with the vulnerability of a
child; hardly the characteristics of a killer, she'd insist.

While DeGuerin concentrated on his other clients, Baen
did the groundwork, readying the Beard case for the courtroom with the help of three law students from a criminal law

class DeGuerin taught at the University of Texas. They conducted interviews and combed through the formidable load of exhibits prosecutors had collected, including medical, telephone, and financial records. As she talked to Celeste, she formed a theory on what had happened. Celeste told Baen that Tracey and Kristina were close. Perhaps, Baen theorized, Kristina, not Celeste, conspired with Tracey. She also latched onto possible financial motives for the twins wanting their mother out of the way. "It was only after Kristina cashed those checks and took her mother's money that she went to the District Attorney's Office and said, 'I think my mother killed Steve,'" says Baen. "These were greedy kids out to get rid of their mother to get the money for themselves."

When it came to Tracey, Baen didn't mince words. "This is a very defensible case," she says. "The bottom line is that Tracey Tarlton is bat crazy. She's insane. She was obsessed with Celeste, and she killed Steve because she wanted him out of the picture."

The first major hearing on the Beard case in the 390th District Court, where Celeste was scheduled to be tried, took place that November 2002. The 390th was presided over by Judge Julie Kocurek, who could have been the prototype for TV's *Judging Amy*. Trim, with large hazel eyes and straight, dark blond hair, Kocurek looked more like a soccer mom than a criminal court judge. Looks can be deceiving, however. As a prosecutor, Kocurek had tried rapists, child abusers, and murderers, including an eleven-year-old boy who stabbed a man ninety-nine times, then fed his ears to a dog.

Appointed by then-Governor George W. Bush, Kocurek came to the bench in 1999 as the first woman to head a Travis County felony court. At the time, she was pregnant with twins, a boy and a girl. In the 2000 election she became the first Republican judge elected in Austin, a city so liberal that a Green Party candidate once totaled twenty-five percent of the vote. One reason: She bore a familiar name. Her grandfather-in-law, Willie Kocurek, was an appliance dealer turned civic leader, known for his humor, who'd worked to improve public schools. Beyond that, the courthouse scuttlebutt was that Judge Kocurek belonged on the bench; she knew the law and ran a fair courtroom.

That day in Kocurek's courtroom, the issue was the admissibility of evidence—the journals, cards, and calendars the twins and their friends had collected from Celeste's storage bins. Even the way DeGuerin titled the motion elicited strong emotions: "Motion to Suppress Evidence Stolen from the Defendant's Home."

That first day of pretrial testimony would be the hardest for the twins. The thought of seeing Celeste again, this time in her jail uniform, of having to testify in front of her, sent chills through both of them. Yet one thing had markedly changed for them both: They no longer felt alone. Months earlier, Ellen Halbert, director of the district attorney's Victim Witness Division, called Mange, offering to help with the case by acting as an intermediary with the Beard children. Exhausted by calls from the twins and Justin, Mange eagerly turned that portion of the case over to her.

With short, highlighted brown hair and a maternal manner, Halbert understood the emotions the girls battled. She, too, had been through a horrific ordeal. Years earlier an eighteen-year-old drifter hid in her home and raped and stabbed her. She barely survived. Helping others victimized by violent crime brought her to the attention of then-Governor Ann Richards, who appointed her to the board that oversees prisons, probations, and paroles. Two years after Richards left office, District Attorney Ronnie Earle asked her to join his office, supervising eight counselors and four staffers who work with more than four thousand victims and their families each year.

Halbert had heard people talking about the Beard case around the office for months before she met the girls for the first time. At that first meeting, she knew they were frightened. She thought they looked like scared children, and her heart went out to them. Yet, before long the girls opened up, glad to have her to confide in. On the day of the pretrial, Halbert accompanied them to the courtroom and sat in a front row seat, where they could look at her instead of their mother while they testified.

"You stole those things from your mother's storage, didn't you?" DeGuerin accused.

"Some of it looked like it didn't need to be thrown away," Jennifer countered. "It looked interesting, so we kept it."

Calling the twins "spoiled brats," DeGuerin railed against them.

At one point, when Celeste looked away, Jennifer shot her a quick glance. There sat her mother, laughing with the attorneys clustered about her. *She must think the whole thing's a joke,* Jennifer thought.

In the back hallway, after Jennifer finished testifying, Wetzel put her arm around her as she sobbed, her shoulders heaving at the emotional turmoil of testifying against her own mother. Later, Jennifer would remember being grateful Kristina had taped their mother saying she'd hired someone to kill Tracey Tarlton. *If she hadn't,* Jennifer thought, *no one would have believed us.*

The hearing went on with DeGuerin insisting that the twins and their boyfriends had stolen their mother's possessions. As garbage, it was fair game, admissible in court. If stolen, the evidence would be tainted and inadmissible.

Seven days later, as the hearing drew to a close, Celeste

hobbled up to the stand. In jail, she'd broken her leg. How it happened remained a mystery. The official story was that she'd fallen after fainting. The story circulating through the jail was very different—that she'd broken it herself by battering it against a bench, perhaps to illicit sympathy from the jury, perhaps to get out of the general population and into the hospital ward.

On the stand, Celeste denied ever asking the girls and their friends to clean the storage areas. Those were her things, things she never intended to throw away, she said.

Cobb had something else he wanted an answer to: "Why did you have your husband murdered?"

The question caught the courtroom off guard.

"I did not murder my husband. I'm not guilty," she snapped.

DeGuerin jumped up and objected. Celeste, he said, was there to talk about the journals and cards, not to testify about the murder. The judge sustained the objection.

In his closing, DeGuerin claimed Mange had put the girls up to "stealing" from their mother. "He apparently played the part of the three monkeys: Hear no evil, see no evil, speak no evil," DeGuerin charged. "The authority to enter the house does not equate to the authority to take things without permission."

"It may hurt Celeste Beard's feelings to know that someone went through her trash, but it's not against the law to do so," Wetzel countered.

When Kocurek's ruling came on Thanksgiving week, the prosecutors won. The evidence would be admissible. Yet Kocurek gave DeGuerin an olive branch by reducing Celeste's bail to $2 million. By then an appeals court had lowered the $8 million bond on the capital murder case to $500,000. None of it did any good, DeGuerin argued, insisting Celeste had little more than a few thousand dollars in the bank and owed $750,000 for attorneys' fees and the fees of experts he'd enlisted to testify on her behalf at the trial.

Yet Wetzel thought she'd gained much more than the use of the evidence from the pretrial hearing. She'd been able to see Jennifer, Kristina, Justin, and Christopher on the stand. No longer teenagers, they'd put out strong testimony, refusing to let DeGuerin rattle them. Justin had come off as a bit stiff, something she'd work on with him. She didn't want him to hesitate, analyzing each question. The jury could interpret that as being evasive. But that was a minor issue. For the most part, Wetzel was pleased.

As the trial approached, both sides carefully groomed their cases. Wetzel got a court order to use the Toro Canyon house for a demonstration. She wanted Tracey to show them how she'd picked her way through the house the night of the shooting. Wetzel also ordered a sound test, to see if Celeste should have heard the shot. As Tracey walked through the house that day, a shotgun fired a blank in the master bedroom. Standing in the girls' wing, she heard it clearly. Like everything else, she now believed Celeste had lied when she told her she'd slept through the gunshot. "It was complete bullshit," she says. "The sound of that gun shook the house."

As her case came together, Wetzel saw only one issue as truly worrisome: the cause of death. With four months between the shooting and Steve's death, she knew DeGuerin would bring in medical experts to testify that he'd died of causes unrelated to the shooting. When she brought it up to Cobb, he did exactly what she counted on him to do—he told her not to worry. "This isn't any different than any other trial we've done in the past," he assured her. "We'll take this step by step and prove our case."

At the same time, DeGuerin had no trouble summing up how he saw his case. Celeste—or "Les," as he called her—was innocent. Tracey Tarlton was "a sick, mentally ill woman, who was obsessed with her," and Donna Goodson "a hanger-on who only wanted money." Celeste's sin, he would argue, was nothing more than being "overly generous and trusting." As for the twins, DeGuerin called them "devil children" and felt sure the jury would see them as he did—"spoiled brats."

As the trial neared, the defense settled on their trial haiku, the three points they would drill into jurors' minds:

1. Celeste's lifestyle was not evidence of guilt.
2. She was better off with Steve alive.
3. Celeste didn't kill Steve.

Yet, DeGuerin admitted he had obstacles ahead. First, the jury had to see Celeste as a woman who loved her husband, not as a gold digger. And they had to be able to "see through" the prosecution's case. "I don't think Allison Wetzel is all that convinced her case is solid," said DeGuerin, his face hard, and thoughtful. "I think she's worried."

Through the courthouse grapevine, Wetzel heard that DeGuerin thought he was getting to her. She was determined not to let that happen. Still, she'd griped enough about him at home that one night when he called her house, one of her sons answered. "It's your archenemy," he said, handing her the phone.

Deciding to make a joke of a potentially embarrassing situation, Wetzel picked up the phone and said, "Well, hello, archenemy."

DeGuerin didn't laugh.

* * *

On the morning of Wednesday, January 29, a panel of ninety-four potential jurors gathered in numbered seats in Kocurek's courtroom. Behind the bench, the judge sat flanked by the Stars and Stripes and the Texas Lone Star flag. By the end of the day she was determined to whittle the panel down to twelve jurors and two alternates willing to devote the coming two months to the trial of Celeste Beard Johnson.

Celeste sat between DeGuerin and Baen. Gone was her jail-house attire, replaced by a charcoal gray sweater set and a long gray skirt, both shades darker than the gray cloth paneling on the courtroom's walls. The cast still cocooned her leg, and her crutches were stowed under the table. Her blond hair had grown out, leaving it long and brown at the roots. She had it pulled sternly back and, although the twins never remembered her wearing glasses, she wore oval wire-rimmed ones that made her look like an injured schoolteacher, far from the sultry femme fatale who had married five times.

Yet it wasn't the defendant, but a figure at the far end of the defense table, who caught Wetzel's attention: Robert Hirschhorn, a well-known jury consultant who worked many of the state's highest profile cases. While DeGuerin asked questions, attempting to bond with the jurors, Hirschhorn would analyze the answers and look for clues in body language and facial expressions. Behind them sat the rest of the team: Matt Hennessy and DeGuerin's law students who'd volunteered to help with the case.

It was Hirschhorn's job to predict how each juror would react to testimony and vote once deliberations began. He needed to have twelve impaneled who could be persuaded to view Celeste as a victim, not a murderer. A bonus would be a juror who would have difficulty, under any circumstances, judging another human guilty, to hang the jury if they were leaning toward a conviction.

As voir dire—the process of truth telling—began, Wetzel introduced herself and the other attorneys to the panel, standing before an easel with a poster-size blowup of the indictment: *State of Texas v. Celeste Beard*. "I thank you all for coming," she began. "This may be the most important part of the trial. We need to make sure we have a jury that will be fair to both Mrs. Beard and the state of Texas."

Even before the questioning started, much was already known. The week before, the potential jurors had met in the courtroom and been given questionnaires. The lawyers had plumbed the most important issues of the case: How did the jurors feel about young women who married older men? Would they find it difficult to convict a young, attractive woman? Did they have experiences with law enforcement or mental illness that would color their verdict? Both sides had carefully considered and tabulated their answers.

With Steve Beard's millions and the twisted details of the alleged plot involving the young wife and her lesbian lover, the Beard case hadn't needed any more of a draw to bring in publicity, but DeGuerin tended to help make any trial an event. In this case, drawn by the sensationalism and what promised to be a hard fought trial, *PrimeTime Live*, Court TV, and *48 Hours* had cameras throughout the courtroom.

Wetzel began her presentation, explaining the process. Texas has a bifurcated trial system. First, the jury would judge guilt or innocence. Before trials began, defendants were given the option of who would decide their sentence if convicted. "Mrs. Beard has decided her punishment will be handled by the jury, not the judge," she said.

DeGuerin jumped to his feet. "Your Honor, that doesn't need to be talked about with the jury yet," he said. "That gives the impression my client expects to be convicted."

Wetzel agreed; of course that would depend on the jury's

decision, but then she launched a second volley: "It isn't until the punishment phase that the jury learns if the accused has committed other bad acts." She wanted to implant in jurors' minds that Celeste may have committed crimes they'd only learn later.

As Wetzel worked her way around the room, she asked questions to weed out jurors who had a grudge against the state and those who would not be able to make a decision. She also had the task of determining who would not be able to get past Celeste's wholesome looks. "Juror number twenty-three," she said. "You said on your questionnaire that you would not be able to find someone who looks like Mrs. Beard guilty of murder."

"I couldn't," answered the man. "She just doesn't look like a murderer to me."

Cobb noted in his records that juror 23 was unacceptable. At the end of the process, jurors would be stricken for cause—those who admitted they were prejudiced either for or against the defendant, those who maintained they couldn't make a decision. Then, each side would be given ten preemptory strikes, enabling them to weed out jurors they judged were not in their side's best interests.

Wetzel went on, "We all know that people aren't as they appear. How do we judge whether people are telling us the truth?"

From that, the jurors launched into a discussion that included the characteristics by which they judged others as liars: a lack of eye contact, body language, a tone of voice, whether their words were logical and credible based on other facts, whether or not they had personal gain at stake. Wetzel agreed those were all indications.

She then detailed the counts against Celeste. First: capital murder. For that charge the jurors would have to find Celeste caused her husband's death for the promise of remuneration;

namely, his money. In liberal Travis County—unlike much of Texas—prosecutors rarely asked for the death penalty. In a case where the defendant hadn't pulled the trigger, it would be especially difficult to get. So the prosecutor had taken the ultimate punishment off the table. A conviction on capital murder meant an automatic life sentence.

Second, Celeste was charged with murder. Unlike capital murder, here the jury didn't need a financial motive. The punishment, too, differed. A murder conviction offered options from probation to life.

Last, Celeste was charged with injury of an elderly person, another third-class felony, with punishment ranging from probation to life.

All the charges required that to find her guilty, the jury had to decide Celeste acted knowingly and with intent to grievously harm Steve. That brought Wetzel to the role she charged Celeste had played—that of the planner and conspirator.

"Can someone be guilty of murder without pulling the trigger on the gun?" she asked.

Hands went up around the room. Before long nearly all the panel agreed that the planner was as guilty as the shooter in a murder—a simplification of what's called the Law of Parties in criminal statutes.

The prosecutor didn't fare as well when it came to her next concept: the proposition that some evidence would come from a coconspirator, a self-avowed murderer. Many in the jury pool found Wetzel's suggestion that they give such testimony as much credibility as that of a police officer preposterous. DeGuerin agreed, jumping from his chair. "That's ridiculous," he said. "Judge, how can she ask the jury to overlook where the information comes from? The law doesn't ask them to do that."

Tracey Tarlton's testimony, Wetzel said, could be judged

based on whether it was corroborated by other evidence. With that, many jurors agreed, but some staunchly insisted that they could never, under any circumstances, judge someone guilty based on the testimony of an admitted murderer. "That would be like looking at a guy in a dress and asking me to ignore the dress," said one man, a tall, heavy-set business type in a starched white shirt, khakis, and a tie. "That's not gonna happen."

That afternoon it was DeGuerin's turn. Where Wetzel had come off as strident, he approached the jurors softly, introducing himself and his fellow attorneys. He stood behind Celeste, placing his hands on her shoulders. "This is my client, the most important person in the courtroom," he said. "As jurors, you'll be deciding her fate."

When he introduced his three law students in the courtroom, he said, "They're here because they want to help." DeGuerin talked of his teaching at the University of Texas, an institution that permeates Austin. And he talked of David Koresh, saying he was proud of what he'd done in Waco, "trying to bring a peaceful solution. I'm proud of what I do, proud of being a defense attorney.

"Now I'm going to do what one of you suggested earlier," he said with a warm smile. "I'm going to get on with it."

To begin, DeGuerin went row by row, allowing those who'd already formed opinions on Celeste's guilt to disqualify themselves. A dozen jurors said they'd already judged Celeste, even before the first word of testimony.

From there he talked of the law that allowed a defendant to decide whether she would take the stand. Many people, he said, felt they had to hear from the accused. If a defendant didn't testify, they judged, it was an admission of guilt. Again hands rose from a sampling of jurors who said they could not ignore the failure of a person accused of a crime to take the witness stand. These jurors, too, were disqualified.

DeGuerin then tried to defuse a hot button issue: the Beards' May-December marriage. "I'm seventeen years older than my wife," said one juror. "I know she didn't marry me for my money."

DeGuerin chuckled. "How many of you do have a problem with it?"

Four women and three men raised their hands. " 'Money hungry gold digger' comes to mind," said one of the men.

Hirschhorn noted strikes against more potential jurors.

In the end the jury that would judge Celeste Beard consisted of eight men and four women, with two male alternates. Nine were white, one Asian American, one black, and one Hispanic. One was a software engineer who'd gotten a laugh when he said that if his team waited to release software until it was a hundred percent, "we'd never get anything out."

Another was a woman in her fifties, whose twenty-year-old daughter had been kidnapped and murdered thirteen years earlier. "I have serious issues with the Austin P.D.," she'd admitted. "But they wouldn't impact my decision in this case."

Also on the final jury was a white-haired, bearded man, the one who'd laughed about being married to a woman seventeen years his junior. Would that influence his decision? No one could truly know, for despite the eight hours they'd spent choosing the jury, despite Hirschhorn's analysis, no one could predict how any of the fourteen people seated in the jury box would react to the testimony they would hear. Would they believe that the woman seated so demurely before them could orchestrate murder?

As she scanned their faces, Wetzel felt good about the jurors who'd decide Celeste Beard's fate. They were bright, well-educated, and looked interested. Yet, she was worried. That DeGuerin and Hirschhorn also seemed pleased bothered her. What did they see in these same fourteen people that led them to believe the opposite, that this jury would find their client not guilty?

Chapter
19

The flags flew at half-mast at the Texas State Capitol the following Monday, February 3, 2003, on the first day of testimony in the Celeste Beard case. Over the weekend, the U.S. had suffered a tragedy; the space shuttle *Columbia* had exploded in the Texas skies as it descended toward earth. Austin and the country mourned.

Two hundred fifty miles northeast in Nacogdoches, searchers retrieved shuttle debris, while at Woolridge Park, a green, public square with a gracious white-pillared gazebo across from the Travis County courthouse, the gnarled branches of graceful oaks reached out across the sloping grounds like arms offering shelter. Under them, the city's homeless rearranged shopping cart estates. The winter had been a difficult one, at times bitterly cold, but this day was a balmy respite, 60 degrees by the nine o'clock start time. It was expected to be near 80 by afternoon.

Even on quiet days courthouses are unsettling places. Those who work there try to make them homey, bringing family photos, their children's grade school art, and doughnuts to share. Opening day of a big case, the anxiety is so powerful it seems nearly palpable. It bristles in the faces in the hallways, sparks from the fluorescent lights overhead, and sends a static tension through those who file into the courtroom. The Blackwell-Thurman Criminal Justice Center was no exception that morning, as it buzzed with anticipation. Half a block away, on Tenth Street, TV-news satellite trucks waited for sound bites. Inside, lines formed at the first-floor metal detectors and elevators filled with the curious.

Just after nine, Judge Kocurek announced the beginning of the case styled *State of Texas v. Celeste Beard Johnson*. The 390th District Court was standing room only as Celeste, looking reserved in a pink sweater set and beige skirt, stood with her crutches beside her attorneys as Assistant D.A. Gary Cobb read the indictment: one charge each of capital murder, murder, and injury to the elderly.

"How do you plead?" Kocurek asked.

"I am not guilty," Celeste said firmly.

"Is the state ready?" asked the judge.

"The state is ready," replied Allison Wetzel.

"Is the defense ready?"

"The defense is ready," said Dick DeGuerin.

"Ms. Wetzel, you may begin your opening statement," said the judge.

With that, Allison Wetzel stood before the jury. "On October 9, 1999, just before 3:00 A.M., Steven Beard woke up suddenly, in excruciating pain," she said. "His intestines were spilling out of the front of his body. He didn't know what had happened to him. Police found a spent shotgun shell at the foot of his bed. He was rushed to Brackenridge Hospital. The doctors didn't know if he'd make it . . ."

Nervous, perhaps intimidated by the cameras stationed throughout the courtroom or the reputation of the attorney who glowered at her from the defense table, Wetzel began tentatively, reading her statement. But soon she gathered momentum, her voice growing secure and her eyes flashing as she commenced where Steven Beard's troubles had begun, the day he met an "opportunistic country club waitress."

As the story developed, Wetzel told of Beard's vulnerability, after nursing his beloved Elise through cancer. She recounted his first months with Celeste, when she entered his life as a housekeeper, then divorced Jimmy Martinez and set her sights on Steve and his millions. They married, yet Celeste quickly showed her true nature, emptying his safety deposit box. Steve initiated divorce proceedings, which would have left Celeste with nothing. "That divorce filing taught Celeste Beard a lesson," Wetzel said, explaining that if Steve divorced Celeste, she got nothing. If he died, she got it all.

Celeste sat between DeGuerin and Catherine Baen, shoulders rounded, arms wrapped about her, with her head draped to the side, her chin pinned to her left shoulder. She looked pitiful, like a beaten dog or a cowering child. At times she teared up. Over the coming weeks, the reporters would dub her frequent tears as the "daily cry." Often, she glared at witnesses and prosecutors, her blue eyes flashing pure hate.

The portrait Wetzel painted of Celeste was a damning one, a woman who married for money, then abhorred her husband, ridiculed him, and drugged him. She recounted Tracey Tarlton's version of her romance with Celeste, asserting Celeste "worked on Tracey to convince her Steven Beard was a terrible man."

To the world, she said, Tracey and Celeste held themselves out to be a couple. They attended a wedding together, sent each other cards, talked on the telephone "all the time." Then Tracey came to hamburger night and kissed Celeste in front of Kristina. It was Tracey who went to the girls' graduation party at Jimmy Martinez's house, not Steve. He wasn't invited. That August, Steve told his wife to rid herself of

Tarlton, and Celeste, Wetzel said, "stepped up her campaign to do harm to Steven Beard . . .

"A few days before they were to depart for Europe, Celeste asked Tracey Tarlton to shoot Steven Beard. She promised if Tracey got caught she'd take care of her pets, pay for her lawyer, and support her."

Wetzel recounted that night in October, detailing the plans Celeste made, claiming she'd told Tracey to shoot Steve in the stomach, not the head or chest, because that would make a mess. Afterward, Celeste attempted to wipe all remnants of Tracey from the house, anything that could tie her to the killing. When Steve died the following January 22, "Celeste's mourning was short."

With her final words, Wetzel delivered a punch: "This is a simple case of a greedy, manipulative defendant who took advantage of a mentally ill woman who loved her."

For a few moments the courtroom remained silent. Then Dick DeGuerin stood. It was his opportunity to address the jury, to convince them to see the case his way. Unlike Wetzel, he showed little nervousness. For the first moments, however, he did seem overwhelmed. He knew jurors would find many of his client's actions reprehensible. "This is a case of fatal attraction," he said. "This is a case of a fatal obsession."

While Celeste had barely looked up from her chin-to-shoulder pose during Wetzel's opening, as DeGuerin spoke she sat up, listening intently. DeGuerin agreed with Wetzel that Tarlton was mentally ill. In fact, he went even further, labeling her psychotic and saying she heard voices and experienced auditory and visual hallucinations. "She is a lesbian," he said, spitting out the words, "predatory and aggressive."

A self-satisfied smile flashed across Celeste's face as he spoke. Branding Tarlton that way was risky in liberal Austin, yet DeGuerin had reasoned it through. While the jurors might not condemn Tracey's sexuality, he intended to draw her as a sexual predator, obsessed with Celeste. DeGuerin felt certain the jury wouldn't condone that.

Tarlton killed Steve to get him out of Celeste's life, DeGuerin charged, because she wanted her for herself. She then turned on Celeste, fingering her as the planner, to escape the death penalty or a life sentence. To defuse later testimony, he admitted parts of what Wetzel had charged. Yes, he said, Celeste married Steven Beard for his money, for security, for his promise that he would support her. Steve knew that. He was a kind, generous, outgoing and friendly man. He was bighearted with Celeste and gave her everything she wanted. "He was generous," said DeGuerin, "to a fault."

The twins were "spoiled brats," he said, who turned against their own mother to get their adoptive father's money.

Yes, Celeste was unfaithful, had a relationship with her ex-husband. But, he implied, Steve knew and didn't object. He was sexually impotent, DeGuerin said, requiring a shot in his penis to get an erection. He drank too much, had heart problems, breathing problems. He knew Celeste married him for his support and money and didn't care. And Steve was happy with her, happier than he'd ever been.

On the overhead projector, he displayed photos of Steve and Celeste at their wedding, on rafting trips to Colorado, in Hong Kong and San Francisco, and at the lake on their matching wave runners. Then Celeste had a breakdown, caused by post-traumatic stress from years of sexual abuse when she was a child. She tried to kill herself, and met Tracey Tarlton in the psychiatric unit at St. David's.

There, he said, they became friends. He showed pictures of the two women at the wedding in Atlanta and at the lake house party Celeste threw for Tracey. He described it not as a lover's gift but a favor for a friend, because "Tracey's house wasn't big enough." On the screen he projected a snapshot of Celeste and Tracey dancing.

Yet, in the world DeGuerin portrayed, the relationship on Celeste's part was never more than platonic. The two women had never been lovers.

Perhaps DeGuerin didn't know how openly the women had courted. Or he may have felt hamstrung by his client, who insisted to him as she had to Steve, "I don't eat at the Y." Of course, proving Tracey had lied about the nature of the relationship offered an intriguing upside for DeGuerin. The question before the jury wasn't if Celeste and Tracey were lovers or friends, only if they conspired to kill Steve. Yet disproving Tracey's story of the love affair would brand her a liar. It then wouldn't be difficult for him to persuade the jurors to view her entire testimony as a lie.

DeGuerin then brought out the written evidence, bits he'd pulled from the journals and cards to bolster his version. First: a note from Timberlawn, where Celeste wrote to Tracey, "I just want to be your friend. Nothing more." Second: a snatch of Tracey's voluminous psychiatric reports, the day she'd said all her problems would be solved "if a certain person met with an untimely death."

Where Wetzel's conclusion had been that Celeste loaded Tracey with anger toward Steve and then pointed her, as one might a gun, at her husband, DeGuerin took the opposite stance. The relationship, everything Tracey said about Celeste's involvement, was all a fabrication of Tarlton's sickness.

"It's just in Tracey's mind," he said.

He admitted Celeste's actions in the months following her husband's death would raise eyebrows. "She drank, partied, spent money, she mutilated herself," he said. "She threatened Tracey." Yet, no matter what, it was all unimportant, because Steve, he insisted, hadn't died of a complication from the gunshot wound but an unrelated infection. It was the argument that worried Wetzel the most, that he'd be able to rewrite the autopsy and change Steve Beard's cause of death.

"The state's evidence will make Celeste look bad," he admitted. "It will make her look like a gold digger."

But he wanted the jurors to remember: To believe a confessed killer like Tracey Tarlton, the state had to have corroborative evidence. DeGuerin said the evidence they would present was tainted. The sources, particularly the twins, were clouded with suspicion. They were after Steve's money, he said. And the only way they could get their hands on it was to get rid of their mother. "Corroborative evidence must show Celeste was involved in the commission of the crime," DeGuerin concluded. "It is not enough to just make her look bad."

Before he sat down, DeGuerin looked at the jurors and made one last statement: "Celeste Beard is not guilty."

In the front two rows behind the prosecutors sat the elder Beard children, Becky, Paul and his wife Kim, and Steve III. They'd waited three years for this day in court. Paul glanced at Celeste, remembering the one time he'd seen her before, with his father on their visit in Virginia. That day, she'd catered to Steve and acted as if she loved him. Now, Paul judged, like so much else in Celeste's life, it had all been a sham.

Next to the Beard children sat Ellen Halbert, the prosecutor's head of victim assistance. Steve's friends filed in, including the Baumans, eager to see justice done. The rest of the seats filled with the media and those who were drawn by the sensational headlines. Noticeably absent was anyone supporting Celeste. Neither her mother nor her sister attended. Even her husband, Cole, wasn't there. Catherine

Baen dismissed questions about his absence by saying simply, "He has to work."

Celeste's only constant supporter in the courthouse was Marilou Gibbs, the elderly woman she'd befriended at the lake. Gibbs wasn't allowed in the courtroom because she would later testify, so she sat in the hallway reading novels. "Celeste asked me to come," she said. "It makes her feel better to know I'm here."

Meanwhile, Wetzel brought Steve into the courtroom. As her first piece of evidence, she presented the 911 tape from the shooting. The jurors listened intently to the frightened, gravelly voice of a dead man:

"My—My—My guts are coming out."

"Do you need an ambulance?"

"I need an ambulance, hurry."

The prosecutor wanted Steve to become a presence for the jurors, and the tape accomplished that. As his voice filled the courtroom, it was easy to hear his pain and picture his bloody hands holding in his internal organs.

"My guts just jumped out of my stomach . . . my wife in the house . . . call her."

One after the other, Cobb called to the stand those first on the scene: Deputy Alan Howard, Stephen Alexander, and Sergeant Greg Truitt. At three A.M., three years before, they responded to a call from an elderly man at a mansion in an exclusive residential neighborhood in the hills over Austin. Lights flashing behind him, Howard rang the bell. No response. With the others trailing, he picked his way around the side of the house and onto a patio. Through a window, he saw Steve, critically injured.

Howard broke the glass.

"Did you make a lot of noise?" Cobb asked Truitt.

"When Howard broke the door, we did," he replied.

"No one came?"

"No."

Truitt later encountered Celeste and Kristina in the living room.

"Don't let my husband die," she cried.

STAR Flight had already been called to the Beard residence when Deputy Russell Thompson noticed something yellow visible under the corner of an EMS bag: a spent shotgun shell. "This is a crime scene," he announced. "Secure the area."

The officers agreed on nearly every point, except one: Celeste Beard's demeanor. One described her as very upset; others disagreed, saying she seemed intermittently concerned and calm. One said, "She cried, but there weren't any tears."

This was the prosecutors' case, and they offered DeGuerin little to work with. Still, on cross examination, he pulled together what he could. He repeated every entry from every incident log that described Celeste as distraught. He drew the image of her as a hysterical wife, worried about her husband. "Kristina didn't seem worried?" he asked.

No, they said. In fact, Kristina comforted her mother.

Again and again he asked about the handles to the bedroom door, the ones through which the officers and medics entered. Brass, they appeared to pull open, but instead slid. Why were the doors important? Later it would seem he wanted to establish that the doors were locked from the inside. If so, Tracey couldn't have left as she said she did and locked the door behind her. If that was his hope, it never materialized.

With that night carefully drawn, Cobb led the jury into the investigation, and Knight, by then a lieutenant, and Detective Wines each took turns on the stand. They described the disarray of the master bedroom—drawers pulled out—saying it looked like a staged robbery. Knight implied Celeste offered an alibi too quickly and that her suggestion of a robbery seemed suspicious. Knight and Wines recounted their trip to Tracey's house and how they followed Tracey into a back room, where she retrieved the shotgun.

In the courtroom, Cobb brought Wines the shotgun. He checked the serial number, the case number, and Tracey's name etched in the metal. "This is it," he said, displaying the weapon with its polished wood handle and long black metal barrel for the jury. Cobb also used Knight and Wines to introduce Celeste's lack of cooperation with police. Even after Knight heard Tracey Tarlton's name from the teens and asked Celeste pointedly if she had any relationship that could put Steve in jeopardy, Celeste said no. She refused to let them interview her husband and removed her consent to search her home.

"Was she a help or a hindrance?" asked Cobb.

"A hindrance," said Wines.

When he took over, DeGuerin disputed the image of his client as uncooperative. Celeste, he pointed out, signed the consent to search and initially allowed them into her home. Then he questioned the integrity of the investigation, asking what had happened to items, including the cell phone Knight found that displayed Tarlton's phone numbers.

"They went into evidence at the Sheriff's Department," Truitt said.

But the phone had disappeared, something for which no explanation was offered.

"Patients in ICU can only have visitors for so many minutes a day?" DeGuerin said, suggesting the officers' visits ate into Celeste's time with Steve. "Isn't that true?"

Knight at first balked, then agreed, "That's probably true."

Through it all, the two attorneys went toe-to-toe, Cobb revealing suspicious details and DeGuerin offering alternative scenarios to lessen the implication of guilt. He also did what he tells law students to do during his criminal defense law classes at UT: He "embraced the ugly baby," the element in the trial that would stun the jury. While questioning Wines, he flashed photos on the overhead projector of Celeste and Tracey, arms around each other, dancing and sitting on each other's laps. By doing so, he lessened the shock value of the photos, taking from prosecutors the opportunity to introduce them at a more dramatic moment. Yet again, he insisted the women were no more than friends.

With the gray-haired and goateed Wines on the witness stand, Cobb explained the long delay in the case. Steve Beard was shot in October 1999 and died the following January. Tracey at first denied the charges, fighting the admission of the evidence against her. Then, nearly two years later, she confessed and implicated Celeste.

On cross exam DeGuerin made the most of Tracey's early statements. "She denied shooting Steven Beard?" he said.

"Yes, sir," said Wines.

"It was a lie, wasn't it?"

"It turned out to be. Yes, sir."

When Wines searched Tracey's house, he found her journal, including passages about her love of Celeste. "Did it seem to you that Tracey Tarlton had an obsession with Celeste Beard?" asked DeGuerin.

"Yes, sir," said Wines.

One passage DeGuerin read from her journal said that with Celeste gone so much on family trips, it was "hard to pretend I have a girlfriend."

"That means she's making it up?" DeGuerin said.

"It could," said Wines.

One photo from the party Celeste threw for Tracey, the "Fashion Victims" soiree, seemed to especially interest DeGuerin. Perhaps it offered an explanation for photos that showed Celeste and Tracey looking very much like a couple. In it, Celeste munched a brownie. "Is that a marijuana brownie Celeste is eating?" he asked.

"It could be," Wines said.

DeGuerin's final words to Wines hung in the air. They were about the twins and their friends. "Did they seem to you to be spoiled little brats?"

Wetzel objected, and DeGuerin said, "No further questions, Your Honor."

"She would say, 'Oh, God, I wish he would just die already,'" Amy Cozart testified. "Celeste made it clear she married Steve for his money."

By then a University of Texas student, Cozart was the first of the teens to take the stand. She'd changed over the three years since Steve's death. Heavier, she looked world-weary and reluctant to be there. Yet she answered questions calmly. With Cozart, Wetzel gave jurors their first glimpse of Celeste's world, filled with greed and sex. Celeste hated her husband, Cozart testified, and she hid things from him. "If Steve found out she had sex with Jimmy Martinez it would nullify their marital agreement. She wouldn't get any money," Cozart said. "She said when Steve died, she'd act like she was mourning. Based on her reaction, no one would know she never loved him."

Wetzel and Cobb had carefully laid out their trial plan. Since the trial would be a long one, they wanted to keep the jury from losing interest. Interspersed among the financial and medical testimony, which could become tiresome, they planted the more interesting witnesses, including the teens. Every day, they wanted the jury to have something to spark their attention. They'd also made a decision not to begin with any of the Beard children. With their court battle over Steve's estate, DeGuerin could suggest their interest was money not justice. Cozart and Jennifer's old boyfriend, Christopher Doose, had no such exposure and no reason to lie.

At the same time, DeGuerin tried hard to bend each of the prosecution witnesses' testimony to his view of the case. "You're only recalling the bad times, aren't you?" he asked Cozart, after which she admitted there were times when Celeste was affectionate toward Steve. From Tracey's journals, he read her ramblings about her love for Celeste. That Celeste planned extended trips left Tracey feeling "short of breath and anxious," adding details to back up his theory of a fatal attraction.

The trial continued with the prosecutors shoring up their case, laying the groundwork for the twins and Tracey to take the stand. Without a thick layer of corroboration to bolster the coming testimony, they worried that what their star witnesses had to say would be judged as just too strange to be true.

For days, they put those on the stand who'd crossed paths with Tracey and Celeste the summer before the shooting. Eight who'd attended the lake house party testified. Yes, they'd seen the women openly acting like a couple. More than one had walked in on them kissing. Some had seen them wander off to bed together. Yes, they believed the women were lovers. Cindy Light told how Celeste called her days after the shooting, wanting the photos from the party, including one in which she and Tracey kissed.

When it came to his cross exam, DeGuerin's tactics began to suggest someone caught in the era of *Leave It to Beaver* when the rest of the world had moved on to *Will & Grace*. Though one of the jurors had answered on the pretrial questionnaire that he was gay, DeGuerin still talked of "predatory lesbians." At times his questions seemed archaic, as when he suggested that in lesbian relationships one of the women played a masculine role. "That went out in the fifties," scoffed a witness.

Rather than a romance, DeGuerin suggested the physical touching seen by witnesses and in the photographs of the Fashion Victim party was a product of impaired reasoning. On the overhead, he again displayed the photo of Celeste seated on Tracey's lap with a brownie poised near her lips. DeGuerin insisted Tracey had used the marijuana it contained to break down Celeste's defenses, despite the fact that Celeste, not Tracey, held the brownie and that the women were kissing before the drugged desserts arrived.

From the Studio 29 employees, the jurors heard about Celeste's bizarre behavior, how she bragged about her disdain for Steve. As DeGuerin fought to make Celeste appear a victim, the prosecutors refined their portrait of the woman on trial. They wanted jurors to see her as cold and ruthless, a woman who cared for nothing more than money. The testimony of Kuperman and Steve's other advisers backed them up as they detailed how she grabbed every cent she could—even taking Elise's jewelry from Steve's safety deposit box—and how quickly she spent it. The message came through clear: If Steve divorced Celeste, she got nothing beyond her half-interest in the houses and her personal possessions. If he died, she got millions more.

As it had been at the hearings on the civil case, Steve's own actions raised doubt. "Didn't Steve increase the amount of money Celeste was entitled to under the trust while he was in the hospital?" DeGuerin asked.

"Yes," Kuperman answered.

"Did Steve want to divorce Celeste?"

"No. Steve didn't want a divorce."

Still, the image of Celeste as a gold digger never faded. C. W. Beard and Chuck Fuqua testified that with her husband gravely ill, she called them, demanding access to

Steve's bank accounts. While Steve loved Celeste, any doubt about the way she felt about him was answered by Amy MacLeod, the nurse who testified about his September hospitalization. The day he was discharged, Celeste refused to pick him up for five hours.

With MacLeod and the medical professionals who'd treated Steve, DeGuerin picked away at the gentlemanly image of Steve the prosecutors were building. While he might have been kind and generous when he was sober, he maintained, Steve was an alcoholic. "He denied dependence on alcohol, didn't he?" the defense attorney railed.

"Yes," MacLeod said.

Of course, another explanation was offered by the prosecutors' witnesses: Steve had never known how much alcohol he was ingesting, unaware he drank Everclear instead of vodka. Christopher Doose backed up Amy Cozart's testimony, but further exposed Celeste's bizarre actions. On the trip West, he testified, he and Justin had to help Steve to the car, because Celeste fed him ground-up sleeping pills in his cottage cheese.

Then Wetzel turned her attention to the night of the shooting.

"Had she ever brought Meagan to the lake house late at night before?" she asked.

"No," Christopher said, looking directly at the jury. "It was definitely out of the ordinary."

"How did she look that night?"

"Frantic," he said.

"Did you bring up a name of who you thought might have shot Steve?"

"Yes, Tracey," Christopher said. "Celeste had been crying. She stopped. She got really serious and said, 'No, it wasn't and don't say that. That's not true.'"

"Her demeanor changed?"

"One hundred and eighty degrees," he said.

During cross exam DeGuerin went on the attack. "You never told Steve that Celeste called him names behind his back?"

"No," Christopher admitted.

"You never told him about the Everclear or the sleeping pills?"

"No."

"I thought you liked Steve."

"I did," Christopher said.

DeGuerin came down hard on the somber-looking young man on the stand, dressed in a suit, his sandy brown hair closely cropped. As hard as he pushed, Christopher didn't back off, even when the defense attorney accused him and the other teens of stealing the evidence they'd given prosecutors. The only time he resembled DeGuerin's spoiled-brat theme was when he decribed ten million dollars as "a modest amount."

For a moment the entire courtroom gasped.

"Didn't Celeste fall apart after Steve's death, have to go to Timberlawn?" DeGuerin asked, implying she had loved her husband.

"She went to appease the bank," Christopher answered.

"I didn't ask you that," DeGuerin said, furious.

At the end, Wetzel had Christopher on redirect. "Why didn't you tell Steve Beard the bad things his wife was doing?" she asked.

His face flushed and his eyes filled with tears. "I was young, but that's no excuse," he said. "I didn't understand what was really going on, the implications."

"Knowing what you know now, if you could go back and tell Steve Beard these things, would you?" Wetzel asked.

"Absolutely," he said, crying harder. "Every day, I wish I could change what happened."

In the gallery, Steve Beard's grown children wept softly, and in the jury box some of those who would decide Celeste's fate wiped their eyes.

"Did Celeste talk about her husband?" Cobb asked Justin when he took the stand.

"She called him, old, evil, fat, mean, and controlling . . . Prior to meeting him I believed he was an evil person."

"Did your opinion change?"

"Yes. He would joke with me, tell stories, and talk to me about how I was doing in school . . . I liked him."

"Was there a point where it was assumed without asking [that you would stay over in Kristina's bedroom]?" Cobb asked.

"Yes."

"Was there a night you were told you couldn't stay there?"

Justin stared straight ahead, never looking toward the defense table. "Yes. The night Mr. Beard was shot."

"Who told you that you couldn't stay that night?"

"Celeste."

On the stand, Justin hesitated at times, yet his answers came more quickly than at the pretrial, where he'd paused, analyzing each question before answering. With Justin, Cobb laid out the night of the shooting, including the orders not to mention Tracey's name, and the days after, when Celeste barred the police from Steve's hospital room. He then wove back to that summer, to the times Justin saw Tracey and Celeste together, including the time at the lake house, where they shared the same bed.

Years of worrying Celeste might find the twins had all led Justin to that day on the stand. As he testified in a somber dark suit, he looked old beyond his years, filling in for the jury more of Celeste's bizarre world, where she jumped from man to man and treated the teens like they were her servants and her entourage, confiding in them about her sex life, including the "Sunday suck." Earlier, Dr. Handley had contradicted DeGuerin's opening statement. No, Steve had never needed penile shots for erections, he testified. Rather, he, like millions of men, took Viagra. Justin testified that Celeste hated the encounters, complaining loudly and often.

"I need to go make some money," she'd say, on her way into the master bedroom.

Celeste had a secret life, with secret parties and P.O. boxes she hid from her husband, Justin said. Then he told of the chaos at Toro Canyon: While Steve lay in the hospital fighting for his life, Celeste remodeled. She bought new furniture, three new televisions, the Cadillacs, shrubs; had the garage floor, crown moldings, and rain gutters all painted. She regrouted the pool, something that had been done a year earlier, sending the bills to the trust to pay. When Steve came home, she refused to hire help. "Did you ever talk to Celeste about bringing in an aide to take care of Mr. Beard?" Cobb asked.

"Yes," Justin said. "She didn't want that."

Celeste told him and the twins that she cut off all communication with Tracey after the shooting, but when he found the secret cell phone, they suspected that wasn't so. "She told us Tracey got fired from BookPeople," Justin said. "I wondered how she knew."

From Celeste laughing in the funeral limousine to her wild partying with Donna Goodson, Justin had seen it all. Then he told how Celeste had given Donna money, lots of money.

On cross exam, again DeGuerin attacked. "It's true that Steve Beard didn't like you at all," he charged.

"No," Justin said.

"He called you a loser."

"No."

After talking about the sleeping pills and the Everclear, the parties that Steve wasn't to be told about, DeGuerin said, "In all the bad things you said Celeste was doing to Steve Beard, you participated, didn't you?"

Grimacing, Justin admitted, "Yes."

DeGuerin kept at him, suggesting he and the other teens had been the ones who bad-mouthed Steve, not Celeste, and that Kristina—even more than Celeste—had been close to Tracy. He slammed Justin for having been party to tape-recording Celeste's calls and implied they'd been edited and changed. Justin, as DeGuerin described him, was a computer nerd easily capable of altering the phone calls. About Celeste's juvenile behavior, like pilfering For Sale signs and sticking them in the lot at the lake, DeGuerin mocked, "Now that's something that really shows Celeste to be a killer, doesn't it?"

"I object, Your Honor," Cobb said.

"No more sidebars or comments," Judge Kocurek warned DeGuerin.

Over and over again DeGuerin suggested that Justin lied. He insisted that he couldn't have seen the women in bed together at the lake house, maintaining that the line of sight from the doorway to the bed wouldn't have allowed it. It was Tracey who acted like a couple with Celeste, not the other way around, he said. Although at times he appeared shaken, Justin held his own.

An avid photographer, Justin had photos of so much, from Celeste's infected hands to marijuana brownie crumbs after the lake house party, that DeGuerin asserted, "If you'd actually seen Tracey and Celeste in bed you could have taken a picture, couldn't you?"

"No," said Justin.

At the end of the cross examination, DeGuerin charged, "You and Kristina are still together. You have a financial stake in this case."

"You could say that my stake would be for justice," Justin shot back.

"For justice or for Justin?" the defense attorney countered.

Jennifer felt her mother's eyes on her when she took the stand. At twenty-three years old, she'd grown into a woman. Still, a chill ran through her. She, more than anyone, understood her mother's wrath. The trial promised the end of their ordeal; yet Jennifer felt only dread. She and Kristina had discussed what they would do if their mother were acquitted—they'd run. Celeste, they felt certain, would hunt them down. And if she found them? "She'd kill us," Jennifer says.

So that day on the stand, Jennifer concentrated on Ellen Halbert's face in the gallery and on the attorneys' questions. The one person she couldn't bear to look at was Celeste. Throughout her testimony, as Jennifer talked about the horrors of her childhood, her mother took her stricken pose, tucking her chin against her shoulder, as if to shrink behind the defense table. Every so often, however, she looked up. When she did, Celeste's eyes flashed rage.

"Who took you to the foster home in Arizona and left you there?" asked Wetzel.

"Celeste," Jennifer replied. While the jury had already heard much about Celeste's life with Steve, what Jennifer filled in was who her mother had been before she'd married him, the woman who flitted from marriage to marriage, dragging along two small daughters, unless they became inconvenient, at which times she shuttled them off to be cared for by whichever state she was currently in.

"What was the Sunday suck?"

"Celeste giving Steve a blow job," Jennifer replied.

Through her testimony, the entire tawdry picture of Celeste's life came into focus. Nothing, it seemed, was beyond this woman, not shocking her teenagers with talk of sex nor bedding her ex-husband after drugging her current one. As Jennifer added to the texture of the prior testimony about events on the night of the shooting, one thing came through clearly. While they disagreed about small things, including who said Tracey's name first, the teens were consistent about what had happened that night, including that Celeste had not been at Toro Canyon at midnight.

Another thing became clear as Jennifer talked: When Celeste told her to do something, she didn't ask why.

"Did you ask Celeste why you weren't to mention Tracey's name?" Wetzel asked.

"No. I was afraid to. She would be upset."

"And that would scare you?"

"Yes."

"Why didn't you meet your mother alone?"

"I was afraid to. Little things kept adding up." Before long Wetzel had artfully led Jennifer through what frightened her, including the pink-lined caskets.

During cross exam, DeGuerin grilled Jennifer. "When did you start calling your mother Celeste?" he charged. "Was it when you were suing her over Steve's money?"

"No."

"You refuse today to call your mother your mother?" he said, flushed with fury.

Wetzel jumped up and objected. Judge Kocurek sustained her objection, and DeGuerin fumed. After a pause, he said, "You didn't like Steve, did you?"

"That's not true."

But then he said some things that struck home for Jennifer. "You laughed at him getting drunk, didn't you?"

"Yes," she said sadly.

"Not to his face but behind his back."

"Yes," she said again. Now, with Steve dead, she regretted

those actions. At the time, she had been a teenager making fun of an adult.

The prosecutors had laid it all before the jury. In fits and starts, they'd heard about hamburger night and the way Tracey kissed Celeste; the graduation party at Jimmy's house and finding Tracey on top of Celeste. DeGuerin did what he could, objecting, flustering, accusing. Jennifer and Kristina were kept by the bank, he suggested. Earlier he'd accused the bankers of depriving Celeste of her own money, by not funding the trust. Now he asked how Jennifer and Kristina managed to not only live but buy cars and an Austin triplex.

"We work, and we got a loan," Jennifer said.

Still, at times, she seemed shaken. On redirect, Wetzel returned to the main issues. "Was it all right with your mother if you told authorities what you knew?" she asked.

"No," said Jennifer. "It wasn't all right."

"Celeste told me to tell the others not to mention Tracey's name," Kristina said when she took the stand. With her, Wetzel filled in more of Celeste's past life, including the period when she moved into Steve's house and his bedroom. She showed how Celeste began slowly, adding sleeping pills to Steve's food. "I didn't realize it could hurt him," Kristina said. "I thought he was a nice man. Celeste was never married to anyone else for very long. I didn't think he would last, either." Instead, Steve had stuck with Celeste, and with Kristina and Jennifer. "He became our dad."

Much of Kristina's testimony mirrored that of her sister and friends. On the stand, neither she nor Jennifer bore any resemblance to the spoiled brats DeGuerin described. She talked about Steve and Celeste's arguments, mostly over money, and her mother's suicide attempts, usually when one husband or another threatened to leave. When she saw Tracey at St. David's, Kristina said, "She looked sad, and I felt bad for her."

The jurors didn't hear about Kristina's sleepless nights as the trial approached. Even in a room full of deputies and a judge, she couldn't look at her mother. If she met her mother's gaze, she feared she wouldn't be able to testify against her. She felt certain that somehow Celeste would get to her. To the twins, Celeste remained supremely powerful.

Wetzel had been looking forward to putting one item in particular before the jury. Approaching the witness stand, she handed Kristina a receipt from James Avery. When she'd discovered it in Celeste's records, Wetzel had been delighted.

"What is this for?" Wetzel asked.

"My mother sent me to pick up an order she'd placed."

"Is there a ring on there?"

"Yes, a wedding ring."

"Is this the ring?" she asked, bringing to the stand a plastic bag that held the wedding ring Celeste had given Tracey, which had been placed in evidence.

"That looks like it," Kristina said.

As Wetzel turned on the recorder to play the phone calls Kristina had taped after Celeste left Timberlawn, all present heard what the twins had heard throughout their lives: their mother emotionally manipulating and verbally abusing them. "Do you know what it feels like, do you?" Celeste screamed. "Do you know what it feels like when you're four years old, you aren't even in kindergarten, and some guy has a big dick sticking in you? Do you know what that does to you? . . . I don't think I can ever forgive what you said to me tonight. Because as soon as I get home I feel like just fucking sticking a knife down my throat, you bitch."

One sentence to the next Celeste's mood changed. From talking calmly, she launched into terrible attacks, calling

Kristina names and threatening to cut her off and leave her with nothing. On the witness stand, Kristina stared down at her lap, crying softly. Even years later it hurt her to listen to the tapes. It was, after all, her mother's voice.

Next to her attorneys, Celeste cried, too. Her face red, she sobbed, with her head on the table. Looking back, it would seem Celeste's tears nearly always came when someone said something nice about her or when her alleged abuse came up in testimony. Now, Celeste cried listening to her own voice on the tape, harder than she had at any other time during the trial.

Wetzel let the tape run out to the final sentence.

"I hired someone to kill Tracey," Celeste said.

"Okay," Kristina answered.

Then the tape went silent.

The courtroom became utterly quiet. As the judge ordered a break, Wetzel looked at the stunned jurors.

At 11:35 A.M. on the Tuesday of the third week of the trial, Tracey Tarlton walked into the courtroom wearing an orange V-neck jailhouse uniform over a yellow T-shirt. Heavier than in the photos the jury had seen, two years after entering jail, she was pale and somber. After being sworn in, the prosecutors' star witness took the stand, clasped her hands in her lap, and braced for what she knew would come. At times she looked over at Celeste. Unlike the twins, she showed no fear. More than once, she smiled. When she did, Celeste averted her gaze. No one on either side doubted how important the coming testimony would be. "Tracey was crucial," says Cobb. "For the defense to win, they had to destroy her."

Slowly Wetzel led her star witness through her life, from her childhood in Fort Worth, through her jobs at the U.S. Fish & Wildlife Service, to BookPeople, where she managed a staff of 150. Then she talked about the nights Tracey drank and played Russian roulette, and how friends brought her to St. David's.

"Did you meet someone named Celeste Beard there?"

"Yes, I did."

Wetzel developed the relationship carefully with Tracey, showing how she and Celeste began spending more and more time together, Tracey talking about the first times they were sexual. "Your hands on her?" Wetzel asked.

"Our hands on each other," she replied.

Soon the jurors had before them testimony about a relationship that built quickly, one in which Tracey cared for Celeste, worrying about her and taking care of her. Through it all she saw Steve as the enemy. "I only knew him through what Celeste told me," she said. Tears in her eyes, Tracey talked of the night of the shooting, steeling her resolve to walk into the house, stand at the foot of the bed, and pull the trigger.

With Steve wheelchair bound and in terrible pain, Celeste met Tracey in the park and gave her the wedding band.

"This ring?" Wetzel asked, handing her the bag.

"Yes," Tracey said. After she'd identified it, Wetzel handed it to the first juror to look at and pass to the others. She wanted them to satisfy their curiosity firsthand, that it was, in fact, a wedding ring.

For two days Tracey remained on the stand, and the prosecutors and defense attorneys warred, with her as the battleground. Wetzel wanted jurors to see an intelligent yet troubled woman drawn into Celeste's web of lies. DeGuerin needed to drill his vision of Tarlton into their minds: that of an obsessed mentally ill woman. During cross exam, on a large tablet of paper beside her he wrote words he wanted jurors to identify her with: suicidal, homicidal, delusional, and psychotic. Soon it became a war of medical charts, journals, and cards. Wetzel read snatches out of the materials before her. In the journal, she asked, who'd written that they needed to go to the day program, quick?

"Celeste," Tracey said.

As Wetzel drew out the testimony, the affair between the women developed, erratic but consensual. To the facts already before the jury, Tracey added Celeste's attempts to poison Steve with botulism. "She laughed that he was so fat it didn't even make him sick," Tracey said.

Then Tracey recounted the night Celeste called her to Toro Canyon after Steve passed out. "She gave me the plastic bag and I held it around his neck," she said. "But he moved and I couldn't do it. I dropped it."

If not for Steve's children watching from the front rows, the tale of an old man whose young wife flittered from inept scheme to inept scheme in her quest to murder him might have seemed funny, as if it could have been the script for a Coen brothers' movie. But this was real, and Steven Beard had suffered the consequences. In the gallery, Paul squirmed in his seat, furious at all his father had suffered.

When DeGuerin took over, he found no shortage of snatches of writings from Tracey's cards, letters, and medical chart to suggest that the obsession had been one-sided and that Celeste had never wanted to be more than friends with her.

"It's a fair statement that your notes to her were very expressive of sexual themes, and her notes to you were not expressive of sexual themes. Is that a fair statement?" he asked.

"That's a fair statement," she agreed.

From the pile of papers on the defense table, DeGuerin pulled out a journal that none of the prosecutors had ever seen before. "Is this yours?"

"Yes," Tracey admitted.

"Didn't know we had this, did you?"

"No," she said.

For all Wetzel knew, her case had just blown wide open. She had no idea what was in the journal as DeGuerin placed it into evidence. She wondered, as he talked, if she should have objected. But instead she sat tight, not wanting the jurors to see how shaken she felt as DeGuerin read a quote from the journal in which Tracey mused, wondering why she wanted a relationship with a married woman she couldn't always see.

"Wanting means you're not having one," he said.

"It means, I'm wanting this. I'm wanting myself to put on the brakes, but I'm not."

At times DeGuerin shuffled through his legal pads, looking for his next quote. When he settled on one from Tracey's Timberlawn chart he read from Milholland's notes: "*Patient's dream is to have an affair with peer.*' You had suicidal and romantic patterns. You had a history of convincing heterosexual women to try lesbianism. Haven't you?"

"No sir," Tracey said. "I've never recruited anybody."

"Wasn't Zan Ray a heterosexual woman before your relationship?"

Wetzel had warned Tracey that DeGuerin would do all he could to anger her. She was determined not to be rattled. "These women both came voluntarily to the relationships," Tracey answered calmly. "They weren't coerced."

At times the defense attorney tried to draw a picture of Kristina as having been close to Tracey, perhaps even closer than Celeste. Kristina, he pointed out, went to her house the night she'd threatened suicide, to take the guns away from her. She'd had a key to Tracey's house. Somehow, it never came off. Perhaps because he couldn't show they spent time together other than at Celeste's behest. When it came to the relationship counseling the two women attended with Barbara Grant, something Wetzel had put in earlier when Grant was on the stand, he said, "Wasn't that the reason you went to see Barbara Grant, because you were recruiting Celeste?"

"No," Tracey said. "I didn't bring her to recruit her. That's not the reason."

"You were hoping Barbara Grant would counsel Celeste to be more comfortable."

This time Tracey agreed. She had wanted Celeste to become more comfortable with their sex life. "Yes, sir," she said.

Pointing out that nowhere in Tracey's journals did she ever recount a sexual experience with Celeste, he asked, "Is there a single journal entry in which you wrote Celeste stayed all night?"

"That wasn't an issue for me."

"Is there a single journal entry in which you say it finally happened, we finally had sex?"

"No," Tracey admitted.

"It was all in your mind, wasn't it?" he charged.

"No," she replied.

Through it all, DeGuerin hammered at his themes. One was that Tracey had misrepresented the house and the way she'd walked through it on the night of the shooting. He contended that she couldn't have parked where she said she did without jumping down a wall. All of this, he suggested, meant she was lying when she said that Celeste had walked through the house with her, laying out the route.

Behind the prosecutors' table, Cobb and Wetzel objected when they could and watched as DeGuerin attacked the woman who formed the centerpiece of their case. Even at pretrial, Wetzel and the defense attorney had clashed. Yet she had to admit he was using everything he possibly could against the witnesses she called to the stand. He rarely left an opportunity unexplored.

Finally, the defense attorney pulled an old prosecutor's

trick out of his portfolio; he got Tracey's shotgun. Calling her out of the witness box, he put it in her hands. It was empty, but still threatening. "Show us how you shot Steven Beard," he ordered.

Tracey looked toward the prosecutors and the judge, but neither interceded. Instead, looking tired and deflated, she aimed at a wall. "I aimed at him and squeezed the trigger," she said, poising the shotgun on her shoulder, like a hunter in the field. Quickly, she put the gun down.

"Show us again," DeGuerin ordered. Again she complied, and again she immediately lowered the gun and put it on a counter. As she walked back to the stand, instead of danger-ous, Tracey Tarlton appeared beaten and regretful. She'd shot and killed Steve Beard. She admitted that. But the demonstration made her look more victim than killer.

"Aren't you testifying here today because the prosecutors gave you a sweetheart deal?" DeGuerin charged. "Isn't that the truth?"

"No," Tracey said, but the implication hung in the air.

At the end, before Tracey left the stand, Wetzel asked, "Why are you testifying?

"I owe it to Steve Beard," she said. "We were both fooled by the same woman."

As Tracey left the courtroom, Wetzel felt confident she'd done well. Despite DeGuerin's attacks, Tracey had never lost her temper or appeared "a crazy woman," as he at-tempted to paint her.

It wouldn't be the end of the bad news for the defense, as Wetzel introduced summaries of financial and phone rec-ords. By the time the expert witnesses left the stand, the state's case had two more linchpins: Celeste had cashed in after Steve's death, spending wildly and using every tactic she could to pull money from his estate, and she hadn't cut off the relationship with Tracey. Rather, they talked often and for long periods on the secret cell phone, well after the shooting. More often than not, Celeste had initiated the calls. If she felt she was being stalked by Tracey, as DeGuerin implied, why would she do that?

After the emotional roller coaster of Tracey's testimony, Donna Goodson's afternoon on the stand seemed a needed break. The day of Steve's death came into even sharper focus as Goodson quoted Celeste as saying she "took him to the hospital because she didn't want him to die in the house." After the funeral, Celeste recovered quickly, Donna said, describing their wild forays to Houston, Lake Charles, and New Orleans. Back in Austin, Celeste bedded one man after another, talking about marriage with all of them. One day Donna found two of Steve's robes in a closet.

"I thought I got rid of all his shit," Celeste said, throwing them in the garbage.

While Kristina was on the stand, the jurors had heard the tape in which Celeste admitted hiring a hit man. At times it was comical, as Goodson described how she'd reeled in more and more money from Celeste.

"Did you try to find anyone to kill Tracey Tarlton?" Cobb asked.

"No. I never did."

"Did you steal any items from Celeste Beard?" Cobb asked.

"No," Goodson replied.

"You had pawn tickets for the jewelry you pawned, didn't you?" DeGuerin countered. On the overhead projector he put up slides of the jewelry Celeste had reported stolen, the same items Goodson pawned. She insisted they were gifts.

"For two years you had information that Celeste had asked you to find someone to kill Tracey, and you didn't tell anyone?" DeGuerin said.

"That's right," Goodson answered.

"Fourteen days in jail, and you weren't worried at all," DeGuerin said, referring to the time she'd spent there after the police had raided her house.

It would prove to have been one question too many, as Goodson answered, "I was safe in jail. I feared for my life. I thought Celeste had found someone to do away with me because I knew too much."

The last witness before the state rested was Becky Beard. On the stand, she cried, describing her father as a good man. Her tears reminded everyone in the courtroom that someone very real had been brutally murdered. Steve had suffered for months and then died a horrible death. After weeks of sensational testimony, the prosecutors wanted to bring the jurors back to basics.

A full month after the trial began, Allison Wetzel rose in the courtroom and said, "The state of Texas rests."

As she gathered her files, she thought about the forty-six witnesses she'd put on the stand. All had done well, she thought; yet she worried. More than any other issue, the cause of death gnawed at her. During the course of the case, she'd put Steve's surgeon, Dr. Coscia, on the stand, who'd testified that the damage from the gunshot had been extensive and that he'd never been able to fully repair Steve's colon. The physician said such a wound bred infection. Yet Dr. Coscia maintained infection hadn't killed his patient. He agreed with Dr. Roberto Bayardo, the Travis County medical examiner, who'd conducted the autopsy: The cause of death was pulmonary embolism, blood clots to the lungs caused by the months of inactivity, a direct result of the shooting.

On the stand, Bayardo had detailed how he'd made his diagnosis, showing slides taken of Steve's lungs. Reading from hospital charts, Cobb listed Steve's symptoms.

"Is that consistent with infection?" he asked.

"No, it's consistent with a blood clot in the lungs," Bayardo said.

Yet, DeGuerin had come back hard, suggesting that his experts would disagree and testify that Steve died of an overwhelming infection not linked to the shooting. If so, Steve had died of natural causes, not homicide.

"Do you know a Dr. Charles Petty?" DeGuerin asked Bayardo,

"Yes, I admire him," he said.

"It's not unusual for physicians to disagree, is it?"

"If he disagrees with me, I'll be very angry," Bayardo said in his Latin accent, his tone highly skeptical. "Not in this case when the evidence is so clear-cut."

The jury chuckled at the Latin doctor, who became huffy with insult. Yet, Wetzel couldn't find it humorous. In the wings waited Dr. Petty and a second physician, both hired to blow a fatal hole through her well-crafted case.

Chapter

20

On the morning of Monday, March, 3, 2003, Dick DeGuerin began Celeste's defense with four Dallas mental health professionals from Timberlawn: her psychologist, Dr. Bernard Gotway; her psychiatrist, Dr. Howard Miller; the art therapist, Melissa Caldwell; and Tracey's therapist, Susan Milholland. Under Texas law, no privilege exists that exempts physicians from testifying in criminal cases, and all raised their hands before Judge Kocurek and promised to tell the truth, the whole truth.

Wearing a tweedy sport coat fit for a college professor, his gray hair curly, Gotway, the first on the stand, estimated he'd treated, if not thousands, at least hundreds of patients. Licensed for eighteen years at the time he first saw Celeste, he specialized in patients who'd suffered severe trauma. Concerning his client on trial for murder, he described her as a needy woman who had flashbacks, overwhelming anxieties, and the need to spend lavishly on others to buy their friendships. "This is the kind of thing we treat every day," Gotway said, adjusting his glasses. "She was ripe for treatment when she got to Timberlawn."

Much of the turmoil in her marriage to Steve, the therapist said, involved her spending. Yet, here, he suggested, Celeste was merely a pawn of her history. "Whenever she got to feeling bad, she'd buy something," he said. "She'd hide her anxiety by trying to make things perfect, especially in the house."

While Celeste was his primary focus, he worked on the marriage as well through couple's therapy. "Steve told me he wanted Celeste to be happy. I thought these were people who wanted to be together," Gotway said. "Celeste is complex. She's had a lot of trauma in her life, and she tends to be histrionic. She seeks attention." Then he went on to say something that caught Wetzel's undivided attention. "Celeste isn't capable of making long-term plans. She's too impulsive, jumping from one thing to the next. She's not a strategic thinker able to plan over a long period of time."

"Could she have planned for months to influence Tracey Tarlton to kill her husband? Could she do that?" DeGuerin asked.

Wetzel jumped up. "I object your honor. That's a question the jury has to answer."

"Sustained," Judge Kocurek ruled. Yet DeGuerin had made his point: Celeste's psychologist judged her incapable of the murder.

"Are there some people who say things to their therapists that aren't true?" Wetzel asked during cross examination.

"Yes," Gotway said.

"Would the failure of a patient to disclose make a therapist's opinion less valid?"

"Yes."

"Did she tell you she was having an affair with her ex-husband?"

"No," Gotway said.

"Did the defendant tell you this was the first time she'd ever told anyone about her sexual abuse?"

"That's what I wrote in my notes," he said.

"Would it surprise you that she told a therapist in 1995 about the abuse?"

"No," he said.

Yes, he agreed, the nurses described Celeste as demanding and manipulative.

"Did she manipulate you?" Wetzel asked.

"In little ways, yes," he said.

As Wetzel asked questions, a very different image of the sessions with Gotway emerged than his answers to the defense attorney revealed. Yes, she'd called Steve names and said that she hated him. While Gotway suggested under direct testimony that the relationship with Tracey had been one-sided, he admitted not knowing many things, including that the women slept in the same bed and that Celeste had given Tracey a wedding ring. Before long there seemed to be much about his patient that Gotway didn't know.

Then Wetzel got a surprise. "Did she mention to you that she'd hired someone to kill Tracey Tarlton?" she asked.

"She said she'd discussed that with someone," Gotway said.

Wetzel looked startled, then pointed out, "That's not in your notes."

"I didn't write it down."

"Why?" Wetzel asked, staring at Gotway. "Were you trying to protect her?"

"Probably," Gotway answered. "Yes."

When Susan Milholland took the stand, it was clear that she had reacted very differently when Tracey told her, "All my problems would be over if a certain person met an untimely death." Though a less blatant threat than the one Gotway had testified to hearing, it was enough for Milholland to call a meeting and for Tracey to be transferred out of Celeste's unit.

Next, Dr. Howard Miller, Celeste's psychiatrist, a thick-necked man with a quiet voice, wearing a quiet suit, took the stand. "Tracey may have been delusional about her relationship with Celeste," he said, well into his testimony. "She was certainly delusional about other things. She has a strong need to believe that the relationship was what she wanted it to be."

Wetzel and Cobb assumed that Celeste's therapist would testify only about his patient. Instead, DeGuerin had asked about Tracey. Although Miller never treated her, he voiced his opinions.

"We'd like to take Dr. Miller on a sidebar," Wetzel said, wanting to stop the testimony and argue outside the jury's presence that he shouldn't be allowed to comment on the mental state of a woman who wasn't his patient.

"Not timely," the judge ruled, saying the objection came too late.

With that, DeGuerin dug out the chart he'd branded Tracey with, the one that read: suicidal, homicidal, delusional, and psychotic. The defense attorney placed it beside Miller, asking him if those words fit Tracey Tarlton. Yes, Miller said, they did, "Tracey's illness makes her likely to give in to her feelings and act on them in violence."

When it came to the relationship between the two women, Miller said that he urged his patient to distance herself from Tracey. "I believe Tracey sustains a delusional belief system," he said. "She believes the relationship with Celeste was more than it was."

On the stand, Miller came across as sincere and believable. The first day of his case and five weeks into the trial, DeGuerin was making headway. Then he turned the witness over to Wetzel for cross examination.

"Isn't it true that in August, September, and October of 1999, Tracey Tarlton reported no auditory hallucinations of any kind?" Wetzel asked.

"In July of 1999 the notes indicate some auditory hallucinations," Miller answered.

"My question was later in 1999, say in October?" Wetzel replied pointedly.

"The notes I have don't indicate any," he said.

"When Tracey hears these voices, does she know they're not real?"

"Yes," he said. "I believe she does."

With Wetzel prompting him, Miller discussed the rules at Timberlawn, including those that barred sexual contact. Yes, if Tracey had admitted a sexual affair with Celeste, they would have been separated, so there were reasons for her not to flaunt a relationship with Celeste or write about it in a journal that could be read by others.

"If Tracey had told you about a sexual relationship, you'd shut it down?" she asked.

"We'd try to interrupt it," he said.

"You were Celeste's therapist, not Tracey's," Wetzel pointed out.

"Yes," Miller agreed. At the defense table, DeGuerin frowned. Wetzel then began what would become a routine tactic throughout the trial: to prove Miller knew little about the real Celeste. She showed photos of Tracey and Celeste together on the overhead projector and listed many of the things the women had done together, from parties to kissing on the lips at social events, ending with the wedding ring. "If ten people saw them together [acting as a couple], would they be delusional?" she said.

"Tracey was delusional at the time she was at Timberlawn," Miller said.

"Is it possible that their relationship changed after Timberlawn?"

"It may have," Miller conceded.

"Dr. Miller, do people in relationships, whether mentally ill or not, want to believe the person they love?" asked Wetzel.

"Yes," he said.

"Is it possible that the defendant encouraged Tracey to believe their relationship was closer than it was?"

"Yes."

Over the weeks of the defense, DeGuerin had fought to tear apart the evidence the prosecutors had put before the jury, but made little progress. The prosecutors, meanwhile, insinuated doubt into the testimony of one defense witness after another. An attendant from St. David's who insisted the women couldn't have kissed while there found himself staring at photos taken on the hospital grounds, a place where cameras were forbidden. If the women broke one rule, what kept them from flouting others? When Dr. Michele Hauser, Celeste's Austin psychiatrist, took the stand, DeGuerin worked on the twins' remarks that Celeste went to St. David's to prevent Steve from divorcing her, not because she was truly ill.

"Was she depressed?" he asked.

"Yes," she said.

In some ways, Hauser's testimony helped Celeste. She painted her patient not as a leader, but a follower, someone easily manipulated. Still, other points in her testimony hurt DeGuerin's case. Yes, Steve was angry late that September, aware that Celeste was not including him in her plans. He discovered she'd used aliases to get credit cards. As she had with the others, on cross exam, Wetzel turned Hauser's testimony to her advantage. Again, Celeste had hid much from Hauser. One thing came through loud and clear—an indication of Celeste's personality. When Tracey overdosed before Celeste's trip to Australia, Celeste told the therapist she was worried. "Celeste had concerns that Tracey would try to kill herself and that this would interrupt her vacation," Hauser said.

More than one juror stared at Celeste, who glared at the therapist on the stand.

To Hauser, like Gotway, Celeste had said she "should hire a hit man to kill Tracey."

"What did you tell her?" Wetzel asked.

"I told her that wasn't good judgment, not a good way to handle things."

On the stand, Jimmy Martinez smiled at the spectators and swiveled nervously from side to side in the chair. For two days he'd waited in the hall to be called. Now it appeared he'd rather be anywhere but testifying at his former wife's capital murder trial. Seated next to DeGuerin, Celeste beamed. Later, one spectator would say she "lit up like a Roman candle with Martinez on the stand." Another thought he actually detected flirting between the defendant and the witness.

Yes, Martinez testified, the alarm system in the Toro Canyon home was faulty, and he'd fixed it. He testified that Celeste loved the twins and would have done anything for them, and that his sexual liaison with her was more of a close friendship than an affair. Yes, he agreed with DeGuerin, Tracey "bird-dogged" Celeste at the graduation party. "Celeste told me to tell Tracey that she wasn't a lesbian," Martinez testified.

When Cobb took over, he concentrated on the money, mainly the check Celeste had written for Martinez's work, inflated by tens of thousands of dollars, money Celeste pocketed.

"She gave you a lot, didn't she?" Cobb asked.

"Yes," said Martinez.

"You'd do anything for her?"

"Yes," he said again.

Those first days of the defense, with DeGuerin and the prosecutors squaring off in front of the judge with opposing objections, tempers flared. DeGuerin called Cobb and Wetzel unprofessional for talking while he asked questions, and Cobb countered that DeGuerin objected simply to interrupt his cross exams. At the bench, Baen and Wetzel towered over their male counterparts. When witnesses like the executives from Bank of America brought in their own attorneys, the judge was swarmed by business suits. At one point nine lawyers clustered about her, each listening to every word, waiting to argue for his or her client's best interest.

The animosity between the two sides was exemplified by one of the final witnesses in the fifth week. DeGuerin brought a Houston accountant named Jeff Compton to the stand to testify about Celeste's finances. With colorful charts, Compton argued that Celeste hadn't profited from Steve's death, as the prosecutors maintained.

"Did expenditures increase after Steve's death?" DeGuerin asked.

"It was stable to declining, as far as expenditures from those accounts," Compton said.

"Was Celeste better off financially with Steve dead or alive?"

"She had access to more property with him alive," Compton said.

On cross, Wetzel pointed out that the figures Compton quoted as spending from before Steve's death included major onetime expenses, like the cost of building and decorating the two houses. Those skewed the figures, she argued.

On the stand, Compton bristled, angrily insisting she was wrong, that the Beards had continued to spend. With that, Wetzel pulled out a chart she'd pulled together with Kuperman, when he was on the stand. In two vertical columns, she compared what Celeste got under the trust to what she would receive in a divorce. Under the divorce column, she was entitled to nothing other than the half interests in the two houses and her personal property. If he died, she received a hundred percent of the value of the houses plus the income from the trust for the rest of her life, a difference of millions of dollars.

Compton shot back, insisting the prenup might not hold up in a divorce. But then he conceded that, at least at face value, Celeste had more money of her own if Steve died.

"Would you agree with me that having access to something is not the same as owning it and being able to sell it for cash if you wish to?" Wetzel asked.

"Yes," Compton agreed.

Throughout the trial, DeGuerin fought no issue as ferociously as his contention that the relationship with Celeste existed only in Tracey's mind. If he could convince the jury that the affair was a figment of a diseased mind, he might persuade them that Celeste's involvement in the murder was untrue as well. To do that, he'd put on a parade of mental health professionals.

With his furrowed brow and graying mustache, Dr. Randy Frazier, Tracey's psychologist, made an affable witness. That fall, after the shooting, he said, Tracey was consumed by a lack of access to Celeste. It was all she talked about. "What did Celeste and Tracey do together?" DeGuerin asked.

"She alluded to sexual contact and social contact," Frazier said.

While DeGuerin appeared to gain nothing of importance from Frazier, Wetzel scored when she asked him to point out in his patient's charts when and where he'd noted evidence that Tracey suffered from psychotic episodes. From June 1999 through the time frame of the shooting, Frazier had seen no sign of either hallucinations or delusions.

"If Tracey believed Steve was standing in the way of her relationship with Celeste, would that get in the way of reality?" DeGuerin asked on redirect.

"If there was no reality basis to that, I would consider that delusional," Frazier said.

"Assume there was a friendship, nothing more, is that delusional?"

"If she's getting clear information from Celeste," Frazier said.

"Suppose there was actual sexual contact?" DeGuerin asked, and Wetzel looked up from her notes to listen carefully, as DeGuerin seemed to abandon his entire strategy mid-witness.

"Then Tracey would be getting mixed messages," Frazier said. "The word that comes to mind is confusion."

DeGuerin handed him Celeste's birthday card to Tracey, reading, "To the One I Love," and asked, "Would that be a mixed message?"

"It would fuel a hope Tracey had," Frazier said. "It doesn't sound like such a distortion in that context to think this person cares."

"Could there then have been a delusional hope that with Steve out of the way she'd have what she wanted?"

"It certainly could," Frazier said.

Clearly, in the sixth week of the trial the defense attorney had backed off his declaration that the affair had all been a figment of Tracey's mind. With so much evidence against him, perhaps he'd simply decided it was time to move on.

From that point on, the defense witnesses taking the stand fell into groups: the lawyers, from Charles Burton to Philip Presse, whom Celeste had hired after the shooting; and the friends, from Ana Presse and Dawn Madigan to Terry Meyer, her manicurist. As Mange had planned if he'd taken Tracey Tarlton to trial, DeGuerin used Meyer to introduce Tracey's words at Tramps: "If that old man hurts Celeste, I'll kill him." One of Celeste's hairdresser friends, Denise, never made it from the hallway to the witness stand. Although she was prepared to testify, she'd later say the defense decided not to call her. She suspected it was because of what she might say that would bolster the prosecution, including that Celeste had told called Steve names and told her about putting the sleeping pills in his food.

On the stand, Celeste's friend from the lake, Marilou Gibbs, a heavyset woman with a thick helmet of gray hair, at first charmed the courtroom. She laughed about Celeste and Steve, describing them as very much in love. Rather than add Everclear to his vodka, Gibbs said Celeste watered it down, to keep him sober. It was true that Celeste argued with him, "even flipping him the bird," she said, but she did it to his face, and Steve loved her more for it. Rather than Celeste and Steve arguing, Gibbs suggested it was Kristina who clashed with her adoptive father. "She called him names behind his back," Gibbs said. "She complained about having to sit down to dinner with him."

The jurors warmed to Gibbs, laughing along with her. Perhaps they thought that if Celeste had such a good friend, she couldn't be all bad. But during her second day on the stand, the mood in the courtroom turned dark when Gibbs insisted that Steve was the one who convinced Celeste to go to relationship counseling with Tracey. The picture before the courtroom of the old-fashioned businessman contrasted sharply with the new-age notion of a husband sending his wife to relationship counseling with her gay lover. Gibbs even maintained that she'd found a bottle of sleeping pills at the lake house when she cleaned it up, and had taken the time to count them. None were missing. DeGuerin suggested this implied the teens were lying and that Celeste hadn't put any in Steve's food.

On the stand, Gibbs systematically addressed nearly every issue in the trial. Yes, she said, Tracey "bird-dogged" Celeste at the graduation party, stalking her, obsessed with her, giving her long, glaring looks when she talked to or danced with others. Celeste, on the other hand, was merely friendly. Before long the jury, which had been sitting up and smiling at the old woman, sat back in their chairs, frowning.

Listening to Gibbs, it seemed that she'd been friends to all in the family, especially Steve, who she said confided in her about personal matters, including his concerns about Tracey. Then DeGuerin used Gibbs to introduce Defendant's Exhibit 15. the "Hey Dyke" letter, which read: *"No one believes anything you tell them. You are never going to ever have another friend ever again. No one will ever like you again. You need to prove to everyone that you really do love Steve and join him. It is the only way that anyone will like you. I promise."*

Unsigned, Celeste maintained she'd received it in the mail after Kristina and Jennifer went into hiding. Gibbs said she'd been the one to notice an indentation of a signature in the note. "It was Kristina's," she said. "I advised Celeste to take it to her attorney."

On cross exam, Gary Cobb pointed out that Gibbs had been right outside the courtroom door for most of the trial, often with her daughter, Dana, the realtor who had sold

Steve the lake house lot, circulating in and out. "Every issue in this case, you've come up here and given testimony on," he said. He then asked if Celeste had done things for Gibbs, from allowing her to live rent free in the lake house to loaning her $4,000 when her car broke down.

Gibbs said she'd repaid the loan and denied that the other instances were true: "I did not live at the lake house rent free."

"You've said Celeste wasn't a person who kept secrets. Did she ever tell you she had a sexual relationship with Jimmy Martinez?"

"No," Gibbs said.

"Nothing would make you believe she had a sexual relationship with Tracey?"

"Not unless I saw it with my own eyes," Gibbs said.

"Were you given some bedroom furniture by the defendant?"

"No," Gibbs insisted, leading Cobb to ask again.

"She gave me a mattress and a box spring," Gibbs said.

"Your answer is that I was not specific enough to name individual bed parts?" he said, raising one eyebrow. "You put yourself out to be a good friend of Steve Beard's. How often did you visit him in the hospital?"

"I didn't," she admitted.

"Did you visit him in rehab?"

"No," she said.

Throughout the defense, threads emerged that went nowhere. DeGuerin convinced Judge Kocurek to have Kristina—who denied writing the letter—fingerprinted, but her prints failed to match the one on the "Hey Dyke" letter. The indentation, an expert said, matched her signature, but on cross she admitted it could have been traced. A defense audio expert suggested the tape on which Celeste was heard saying she'd hired a hit man to kill Tracey might have been edited, but under cross examination he described editing as including turning the tape recorder on and off.

Yet, no testimony was as bizarre as that of Katina Lofton.

The issue with Lofton—a repeat felon serving a six-year sentence for theft and forgery—had cropped up late in 2002, as Wetzel and DeGuerin readied for trial, when Celeste wrote to DeGuerin telling him that Lofton had information about the case. On the stand, Lofton described having bunked in the same cell with Tracey for a period of a month, from March to April 2002.

"Did Tracey ever say if Celeste knew she was going to kill Steve?" DeGuerin asked.

"She didn't," Lofton said. "Tracey said she shot him. She never said that Celeste knew she was going to shoot her husband."

"Did Tracey Tarlton say what she was going to say on the stand?"

"She was going to say Celeste did it to get out of jail quicker," Lofton said. "She said she wasn't going to rot in jail while Celeste lived the good life."

"Did Tracey say they were lovers?" DeGuerin asked.

"She said they were friends, that Celeste helped her out."

"Do you have anything to gain by testifying before this jury?"

"No," she said. Yet she did admit that Celeste had once given her $200, stationery, and envelopes.

DeGuerin then led Lofton through a series of questions about a meeting she'd had with Wetzel and Sergeant Debra Smith, her investigator. Lofton claimed that Wetzel told her not to testify, that she'd get torn up on the stand.

A short, heavyset black woman, Lofton wore her green jail uniform. DeGuerin described her as taking the stand reluctantly, fearful for her own life for testifying. Wetzel countered that by calling her a liar, willing to say anything for money.

It wasn't the first time the prosecutor's path had crossed with the witness. Lofton was the mother in the "spiked baby case," a horrific case of child abuse that had stunned Austin just a year earlier, when her husband, Jermaine Lofton Sr., dangled their infant son out of the window of a moving car, then carried him on a long foot chase with police. While officers begged him not to, he laughed and spiked the baby against the ground like a football. The child was left brain damaged. Wetzel had been the prosecutor, and she'd wanted Katina Lofton to testify against her husband. Even to help punish the man who'd nearly killed her baby, Lofton refused to take the stand. Without her help, Wetzel got a guilty verdict and a seventy-five-year sentence for Jermaine. She wouldn't testify for her own child, but now Lofton was on the stand defending Celeste.

"Is it hard for you to remember all the different things you have told different people?" Wetzel asked when she took over.

"No," Lofton said. But when Wetzel gave her the opportunity to amend her testimony, Lofton admitted she'd also gotten fifty dollars from one of Celeste's friends, in her commissary fund.

With that, Wetzel pulled out Lofton's jailhouse correspondence. After Celeste's arrest, Mange had the jail copy everything coming in and out for her. "I'm here to support you," Lofton wrote to Celeste in one letter. "You know, I'll be looking out for you."

In the letters, Lofton called Celeste "Dimples," and asked her for many things, from school tuition, to full-body contouring, to support letters from Celeste's friends for her parole. In a letter from July of the previous year, Wetzel asked, "Do you tell the defendant, 'There's no limit to what I would do for you?'"

"Yes," Lofton said.

Lofton wrote Celeste fractured poems, extolling her platonic love, describing her as a good woman, then said, "I got some shit your attorney need to know."

"Did you tell the defendant not to write you back until she's had time to do these things and to remind her friend to do the support letters?"

"Yes."

From one of Lofton's letters, in which she told Celeste she wasn't gay, Wetzel read, "I like Dick too much."

"You're not talking about Mr. DeGuerin here, are you?" Wetzel asked, straight-faced.

Above his suit collar, the defense attorney's neck turned scarlet as Lofton said, "No."

In the end, it would seem that Lofton would sum up her own testimony, saying, "Ain't nobody here ever going to fess up to what's really going on."

The two witnesses DeGuerin fought the hardest to get on the stand would never be allowed to testify before the jury. The first was Tracey's old girlfriend, Zan Ray. Tracey had been with Ray when she found her husband's body, after he committed suicide. It would have been an enticing morsel to place before the jury to show Tracey had another girlfriend whose husband turned up dead, even if he had left a note and died of an overdose. The second: Reginald Breaux, the man Tracey had shared beers with then brushed against with her car. She'd been jailed overnight, but never charged with anything from the incident. DeGuerin argued the incident showed Tracey had attempted to kill someone before Steve Beard. Judge Kocurek ruled that neither witness was relevant.

As the defense rested, Wetzel worried the most about the impact of two of DeGuerin's expert witnesses: Drs. Terry Satterwhite and Charles Petty.

A UT professor in infectious diseases, Satterwhite was an

elderly, pale man with trembling hands, who seemed fascinated by the courtroom. DeGuerin had asked him to review the Brackenridge Hospital records for Steve's final stay there, in the days leading up to and including his death.

"Did you review them?" he asked.

"Yes," Satterwhite said.

"What did you conclude was the cause of death?"

"Group A strep, a blood infection, the same strain that causes a sore throat and acute rheumatic fever," he said. Satterwhite went on to say Steve's age, heart condition, asthma, alcohol abuse, and diabetes made him more vulnerable.

"What relation did his death have to the gunshot wound?" DeGuerin asked.

"I don't think it had any relationship," Satterwhite said. As evidence of the infection, DeGuerin led the physician through Steve's chart, citing the notations as his temperature climbed. The groin rash, he said, may have been the point of entry.

"Could this Group A strep have been caused by changing his ileostomy bag with dirty hands?"

"No."

"Did this infection have anything to do with the gunshot wound or the recovery from the gunshot wound?" DeGuerin asked again.

"No, in my opinion, it did not," Satterwhite said.

On cross exam, Gary Cobb asked Satterwhite, "Did you look at the autopsy?"

"Yes," he said. "Just a few days ago."

"Did you look at the photos?"

"I'm not qualified to interpret the photos," Satterwhite said. "I'm not trained in it."

"Pulmonary embolisms are common with trauma surgery when a patient has not been ambulatory?"

"Yes," Satterwhite said. "I haven't seen the slides. There

weren't any microscopic findings in the autopsy report."

"Wasn't the rash a complication of the gunshot wound?"

"Not in my opinion," Satterwhite said.

"But if he got it in HealthSouth, the reason he was there is because of the gunshot?"

"Yes," Satterwhite said.

After Satterwhite, Dr. Charles Petty took the stand. An elderly, balding, 1950 Harvard Medical School graduate, Petty had established the Medical Examiner's Office in Dallas and resembled a favorite uncle. In his career, he'd done more than 13,000 autopsies and testified in court 1,300 times. Unlike Dr. Satterwhite, Dr. Petty had reviewed not only the records, but the autopsy and slides.

"Mr. Beard died of overwhelming infection," he said in a still strong voice. "His blood cultures showed GAS or Group A strep."

Both on where the infection started and its relationship to the gunshot wound, Petty agreed with Satterwhite: It began in the rash on Steve's groin and had no relationship to the gunshot. If the two doctors were right, Steve Beard had died not of homicide, but of natural causes. Perhaps it could even have been malpractice, DeGuerin suggested, since Steve went for a full day after lab tests found the infection before receiving an antibiotic. For this testimony, the jurors sat up straight, and some leaned forward.

As to the blood clots Dr. Bayardo had noted in Steve's lungs, Dr. Petty saw them in the slides but disagreed about their significance. They were of different ages, some old, he said. They may have been associated with Steve's chronic lung condition.

"Just because you have a pulmonary embolism, does that mean you're going to die?" DeGuerin asked.

"No," Dr. Petty said. "An area of this patient's lungs was infarcted, dead, the blood supply from the artery cut off. It had been that way for some time. It indicates that these clots had gone on over a period of time."

"Can a person survive such clots?"

"If they're not big enough to cut off the blood to the lungs."

"Could it cause death?"

"If it is predeath, yes," he said. "I can't tell if these were."

Under cross exam, Dr. Petty said that the last time he'd conducted an autopsy had been seven years earlier and that he knew Dr. Bayardo well and considered him a good medical examiner. Since retiring, Petty had testified at other trials, sometimes for the prosecutors and other times for the defense.

"You lectured at a class with Mr. DeGuerin entitled, 'You Sure It Was the Bullet and Not the Chili?—Cross Examining the Pathologist,' didn't you?' On getting alternative causes of death in front of a jury?" Cobb asked.

Petty agreed he'd participated, but said he didn't remember the seminar's title. Then, while he said he'd discussed Dr. Satterwhite's findings with him, Petty insisted he'd made up his mind about the cause of death in the Beard case on his own.

"The pulmonary embolism you mentioned, was that sufficient to cause death?" Cobb asked.

"He had an old pulmonary embolism that didn't cause his death," Petty said. "I'm just giving my opinion. He died of infection."

"Could it be that Dr. Bayardo's opinion is correct and yours was incorrect?"

"Could be," he said.

"Are you familiar with the case of David Gunby?" Cobb asked, and DeGuerin objected. Shot in 1966 when Charles Whitman fired a high-powered rifle off the UT tower, Gunby lived until 2001, when he died after a failed kidney transplant. The medical examiner ruled his death a homicide, caused by longstanding complications of his wounds. Kocurek ruled in DeGuerin's favor, disallowing the line of questioning.

"Can complications of a gunshot wound ultimately cause death even years later?" Cobb asked.

"Yes," Petty said.

Although she believed Cobb had done well with both physicians, Wetzel worried. If jurors believed the testimony that Steve had died of an unrelated infection, they'd have to vote to acquit.

After the defense rested, both sides brought rebuttal witnesses to the stand, including battling psychologists. Yet, none opened up new territory. DeGuerin didn't put Celeste on the stand. Instead, the final thing the jury heard was her videotaped deposition from the civil case. On the television screen, she dressed casually, in an orange sweater and jeans, her dyed blond hair pulled back in a ponytail. Wetzel wanted to play only a portion, but DeGuerin insisted the jury hear the entire three-hour deposition.

"Did you ever have any romantic involvement with Tracey Tarlton?" she was asked.

"No, I did not."

"Why did you leave Meagan at the lake house that night?"

"Because Amy begged me to leave her."

"How did it come about that Jennifer was at the lake house that night?"

"She had asked to stay there."

"Did you talk to Tracey on October second?" The day of the shooting.

"She called me on my cell phone."

"What did she say?"

"That the police had talked to her."

"Did you ever ask Tracey Tarlton if she shot Steve?"

"I don't believe so," she said.

On the screen, Celeste contradicted points that DeGuerin had laboriously pushed during the seven weeks of testimony, including that Steve had ill feelings for Tracey. About one thing she held firm: "Tracey and I didn't have a relationship. We had a friendship."

Then, after more than one hundred witnesses, both sides finally rested. Judge Kocurek dismissed the two alternates and sent the jury home for the night. The following morning, closing arguments would begin.

Chapter
21

"It's been a strange and weird trip, hasn't it?" Gary Cobb began the following day, March 17, as he opened closing arguments. Agreement murmured through the overflowing room, spectators standing in the aisles for lack of seats.

The front rows behind the prosecution were filled with Steve Beard's grown children and their families. They'd sat through painful testimony about their father's last years. At the same time they abhorred what Tracey had done, they pulled for her. "We believed she'd been manipulated, like our dad was," Paul says. "She was used by Celeste."

Among them sat many of the witnesses, including the twins and their friends, who held hands in solidarity. Their protectors, Anita and Ellen Halbert, were with them. Both the twins were on edge. For weeks Jennifer had been having nightmares in which Celeste called out to her from the street in front of her house. If she went to meet her, she felt certain her mother would kill her.

More than anyone in the courtroom except their mother, the twins' futures rested on the twelve jurors seated in the box. If Celeste were found not guilty, they were prepared to leave Austin and run, they believed for their very lives. Kristina feared they'd never be able to stop running, for she knew Celeste had a long and vengeful memory.

As they laid out their closing arguments, Cobb and Wetzel had split up tasks. Cobb would explain the law and how it pertained to this case. Then the defense had the floor for their closing, arguing the defense haiku: Celeste was better off with Steve alive; lifestyle was not proof of guilt; and Celeste did not kill her husband. Finally, Wetzel, the lead prosecutor, would close, summing up evidence she said proved Celeste Beard Johnson had committed murder.

"To judge the defendant is guilty of capital murder," Cobb began. "You must find that she had her husband killed for remuneration. That's easy, for the only motive for this murder was Steven Beard's money." Effortlessly, he moved from topic to topic, explaining the criteria for judging Celeste guilty of murder and injury to the elderly. Sizing up their star witness, he said: "Tracey Tarlton was a credible person on the stand, the same credible person people saw in September and October of 1999 . . . She's not the first person to do something crazy for love."

The defense said Steve didn't die of the gunshot wound or anything related to it, but Cobb argued, "Dr. Bayardo was in the best position to determine cause of death. He conducted the autopsy . . .

"The love of money is the root of all evil. People loved Celeste Beard, but all she loved was money," Cobb said, picking up the white placard that held the defense's exhibit of Celeste's money with and without Steve. On the front, their expert had listed houses, jewelry, cash and investments, arguing Celeste was better off with Steve alive than dead. The trip to Europe was a test, to see if the marriage could be saved. If it couldn't, "he would have divorced her skinny butt," Cobb said, flipping the chart over to a blank, empty white. "And this is what she would have gotten, a big pocketful of nothing.

"Listen to the witnesses who do not have Celeste Beard's money in their pockets," he urged, "and come to a verdict: Celeste Beard Johnson is guilty of capital murder."

Beginning the defense's closing argument, Catherine Baen took over the courtroom floor. She set up a computer for a PowerPoint demonstration, and then her voice filled the courtroom for the first time since the trial began.

"Celeste Beard Johnson is not guilty," she began. In the four weeks of evidence the prosecution presented, she maintained, they'd been unable to make their case. To make her point, she brought up the secret cell phone and the phone records. "The only person who put that cell phone in Celeste's hands was Tracey Tarlton," she said. And Tracey, she went on, was not to be believed.

Even if the jury believed Celeste was involved in the shooting, she said, it couldn't be proven that she'd done it for money. Even Kuperman had testified that Steve didn't want a divorce. If they did divorce, she argued, the state gave a wrong impression as to what Celeste would get—half the houses, and closets full of clothes and expensive jewelry. "That doesn't sound like nothing to me, folks," she said.

The jurors had to find Celeste was guilty beyond a reasonable doubt. "The prosecutors say this is the type of evidence on which you'd base a serious decision, like buying a home," she went on. "You're not deciding whether or not to buy a home. You're deciding whether or not to put this woman in a cage for the rest of her life."

Nearly all the evidence against Celeste, she said, came from questionable sources: Tracey, the twins, and Donna Goodson. "Everyone would agree this family is dysfunctional with a capital D," she asserted. "The twins have two million reasons to lie against Celeste," the money they'd inherit with Celeste out of the way.

"Tracey Tarlton killed Steve Beard on her own, for her own selfish reasons," DeGuerin said, addressing the jury. "Her own sick reasons."

Quickly, his passion built. Where Baen was analytical, DeGuerin packed a strong emotional punch. "You need to believe that Steve died without a reasonable doubt from the gunshot wound," he said, saying that they couldn't do that.

When it came to the two women, DeGuerin said it was "insulting to say that Celeste was the aggressor." Holding up Tracey's journal, Defense Exhibit 98, he said, "If you do nothing else, please read this journal. Please look at the medical records."

Reading snatches in which Tracey pined for Celeste, DeGuerin, his face flushed with fervor, said, "Delusions, lies, or fantasies, but it's not the truth . . . The truth is that Tracey Tarlton is an aggressive lesbian who pursued heterosexual women who were married."

On the screen, Baen flipped up the chart with the terms DeGuerin had used to paint Tracey: suicidal, homicidal, delusional, psychotic. He lowered his voice from what had become a roar and read from Tracey's Timberlawn chart. "That's not normal. That's a crazy woman . . . She had nothing to lose and everything to gain," he said, as Baen flashed on the screen a photo of Tracey aiming the murder weapon.

Walking back toward the defense table, he said: "Tracey told you Celeste ordered her to shoot him in the stomach so it wouldn't make a mess."

With that, DeGuerin lay down on the defense table, a pillow across his midsection. He pulled a white sheet over him, as if he were an obese man in bed. "Steve Beard's stomach is the only thing Tracey could see!" he shouted. "She shot him in the stomach because it was the biggest target she had."

Back on his feet, DeGuerin stared at the jurors and demanded: "You must return a not guilty verdict if you believe she was absolutely innocent, if she was definitely not guilty, if she was probably not guilty, and if she might not be guilty . . . The state did not prove guilt beyond a reasonable doubt because they don't have the evidence. All this other trash, this soap opera, does not prove Celeste is guilty."

At 6:45 that evening the rest of the courthouse was dark and the crowds had thinned as Allison Wetzel rose to give the final closing argument. She began by thanking the jurors on behalf of the state of Texas, Steve's family and his children.

"Gary Cobb ran out of time earlier," she said. "He'd like you to look at the two date books and compare what Steve writes on the family one versus what is in Celeste's own book. You'll note there's no mention of the trip to Europe in hers. That's because she never planned to go."

After DeGuerin's highly emotional pleas, Wetzel wanted to be calm. The jury, she judged, had had enough. This was a different prosecutor from the one who'd given an opening statement, one more self-assured. If DeGuerin had once gotten under her skin, he was there no longer. "I wish we'd known in the beginning of the trial that Mr. DeGuerin was going to admit the relationship between the women was sexual," she said. "It would have saved us a lot of time."

Tracey had told Barbara Grant that Celeste insisted she be monogamous. "Monogamy isn't just I want to play house," Wetzel said. "It's you-and-me-babe."

Then she talked of the twins' testimony: "Ninety percent of what Kristina and Jennifer told you is the same as what Christopher and Amy told you. The defendant looked forward to Steve's death. She hated having sex with that old man."

For the jury, Wetzel organized the evidence, drawing together the elements that pointed to Celeste's involvement, everything from banning the teens from revealing Tracey's name to the cell phone bills. Scoffing at the notion that the killing wasn't about money, she held up the state's financial chart, showing a sharp rise in Celeste's spending, and then pointed out that the day Steve died, Celeste's overriding concern was getting on his bank account. "That tells you something," she said.

When it came to the cause of death, she quoted from Bayardo and Dr. Coscia, Steve's surgeon, who'd said the symptoms matched pulmonary embolism. But for any juror not convinced, she held up a photo Justin had taken of Celeste's hands after Steve died, with pockets of infection across her fingers. Wetzel's implication was that if Steve died of an infection, it had come from Celeste.

"Celeste Beard gave Donna Goodson ten thousand dollars. That wasn't just for brushing her hair, folks," she said. "Even Dr. Gotway admits Celeste talked about hiring a hit man to get rid of Tracey. Who was their star witness? Katina Lofton, a ten-time felon who asks Celeste for money."

Lofton, Wetzel said, thought Celeste was going to be her Santa Claus.

"When you're rich like Celeste Beard, you can buy lawyers and witnesses. Maybe in some places special people get special treatment. But when it comes to the courtroom, that stops," she said. "If you find Celeste Beard not guilty, you're basically telling her money can buy anything. The defendant is guilty of capital murder. This defendant is guilty of injury to the elderly. I believe in this jury."

Forty-eight days after it began, the trial of Celeste Beard Johnson ended. With that, the jury was led from the courtroom.

Deliberations were agony for both sides. Steve's children spent much of their time in Halbert's office, thinking back over all that had happened. At times they were seen outside the front doors, smoking quietly, looking tired and sad. They were all furious at DeGuerin for his final tactic—lying on the table with the pillow over his middle. To them, he'd ridiculed their father, a dead man not there to defend himself. Paul was especially angry, remembering the way Celeste giggled as DeGuerin lay on the table.

The twins rarely left the courthouse, worried about being pounced on by reporters and television cameras. They were taken in hidden elevators and out private doors. At the jail, Tracey Tarlton watched for snatches on the television news, and at home, Donna Goodson found she couldn't turn off the TV, afraid the jury would come in without her hearing.

As the first evening of deliberations turned into the second day, the defense lawyers grew more confident. An old adage said that a quick verdict was usually a verdict of guilt. The longer a jury stayed out, it was thought, the better it was for the defense. DeGuerin, however, was still gnawing on his closing remarks. He'd had plans that in the tight time constraints he hadn't gotten to, including drawing a timeline he said would have proved Celeste couldn't have done all Tracey said she did the night of the shooting. And he was angry, spitting angry, about the judge, who'd ruled that he wasn't allowed to present the testimony from Zan Ray and

Reginald Breaux. "If we'd been allowed to put on the case we wanted to, I'd feel better," he said. "She didn't let us do that."

For her part, Catherine Baen prowled nervously through the tight quarters of the small defense room and the courthouse corridors, the hours wearing her down. She'd received a call inviting her back to The Hague to work on another war crimes trial. She'd agreed to go, but any excitement was squashed under the weight of what this jury would decide.

Rumors floated through the courthouse that this was an organized jury. Many were managers at their companies. When lunches were brought in, it was noticed that charts and lists were taped to the walls. They were dissecting the case, moving from issue to issue.

Meanwhile, Wetzel and Cobb weren't worried about the passing hours. The jurors had asked the bailiff for evidence to be brought to them: the two calendars and the phone record summary. All were items they'd suggested the jury consider in their closings. Still, they had asked for other things that didn't bode as well for the prosecutors, including Tracey's journal, which DeGuerin had urged them to read.

On the third day, Wednesday, March 19, at 10:00 A.M., the jurors sent out a request for more evidence, including the photos from the lake house party, the cards the women had sent to each other, and Justin's photos of Celeste's infected hands. But it was something else that caught all the attorneys' attention: The jurors wanted the photos from the autopsy—the autopsy itself—and Steve Beard's death certificate.

To Wetzel this held good news and bad news. The good news: It appeared the jury had decided Celeste was involved, otherwise they wouldn't be considering cause of death. The bad news: They were discussing the cause of death.

Nearly seven hours later, at 4:40 P.M., the attorneys were called. The jury had reached a verdict.

The interested flooded the courtroom, even more than for closing arguments. Again Steve's family, including the twins and their friends, packed the front pews. Justin, Kristina, Jennifer, their friend Amanda, and Ellen Halbert sat together, holding hands. Moments earlier Justin had led them all in prayer. "Help the jury see what we know in our hearts," he said. "Give us justice for Steve."

Behind Celeste and her attorneys sat her friends, Marilou and her daughters, and Celeste's husband Cole, who'd told the media he stood behind his wife's innocence. The only one missing from the courtroom was Gary Cobb, who'd gone to pick up his youngest son at school. The jury walked in without smiling. The bailiff handed the decision to the judge, who read it and returned it to him. He then took it to the jury foreperson, Shelly Rosales, a blond, matter-of-fact woman, who looked directly at Celeste.

"We the jury find the defendant, Celeste Johnson, guilty on the charge of capital murder," she read.

Tears flooded Celeste's eyes. DeGuerin and Baen put their arms behind her, as if to hold her up. Steve's children, including the twins, sobbed. Later, Jennifer and Kristina would say they felt a tremendous sadness, to think that their mother would be spending the rest of her life in jail. Justin smiled down at Kristina and kissed her.

As the judge calmed the chaos, Rosales continued.

"We the jury find the defendant guilty of injury to the elderly," she read.

Amy and Christopher hugged and cried. In the excited courtroom, the judge ordered that the jury be taken to their room. She didn't want them to witness the highly emotional display. With the guilty ruling on capital murder, Celeste would automatically be given a life sentence and wouldn't be eligible for parole for forty years. The jury, however, had another duty before them for the following day: to decide her punishment on the second charge.

As soon as they'd disappeared behind the back courtroom door, DeGuerin jumped up, arguing that the injury to the elderly charge was double jeopardy. If an appeals court overturned the capital murder charge, he didn't want to have to fight the injury to the elderly charge as well. Judge Kocurek overruled him, saying it was too late to bring up that argument. That decided, DeGuerin asked that the Arizona fraud case not be put before the jury during sentencing. With that, Wetzel and all the defense attorneys converged on the judge's bench. About that time, Cobb, who'd heard the verdict on his car radio, arrived and hurried to the bench to join the fray.

Finally, DeGuerin returned to the defense table, where he sat, arms crossed, face flushed, glaring at the judge and the prosecutors, beside his client, who sobbed.

The following morning the principals in the case all collected in the courtroom for what would be the final day of the trial. Beginning business, Kocurek ruled that the Arizona conviction would be put before the jurors. The jury was then led in and seated to hear testimony and arguments before sentencing. The options for the injury to the elderly sentence covered a wide span, from probation to life in prison. As the first item put before them, Judge Kocurek read the Arizona fraud conviction, letting the jurors know this wasn't the first time Celeste had committed a crime.

Then prosecutors called their first witness, Kelly Beard Brand, Steve III's daughter. "Steven Beard was my grandfather," she said. On the stand, she tearfully recounted how he'd loved his family, especially her daughter, Allison, his great-grandchild. He was already dead when her second child, Claire, was born. She would never know her great-grandfather.

On the stand next, Paul Beard, the career navy man, stared at Celeste with hatred as he described how she'd segregated them from their father during the final years of Steve's life. He sobbed, explaining how his father's death had devastated the family. The hole his father's murder had wrenched into his life was so great, he said, that it could never be repaired. When he retired from the service later that summer, he didn't plan to attend the ceremonies. Without his father, who'd urged him to join the navy, everything had lost importance.

A lion throughout the trial, DeGuerin didn't question the children or object. Instead he sat behind the defense table visibly angry. "We offer all the evidence in the trial for the jurors' consideration in sentencing," he said when it was his turn to put on a rebuttal. Perhaps it would have been too risky to put on witnesses. Anyone who testified on Celeste's behalf could have been cross-examined by the prosecutors. Throughout the trial, those called to defend Celeste had ended up hurting her by adding to the sordid details of her life.

Testimony was concluded, and once again the attorneys began closing arguments. Cobb thanked the jurors, then argued for a life sentence. "A poet once wrote about people who die before their time," he said. "What they expect from us is that we gently remove the stain of injustice from their death." The jurors, he said, could do that for Steven Beard, give him justice and allow his soul to rest.

Next, DeGuerin stood before the jury, seething. "I'm not going to stand here asking for mercy," he said. Instead he argued that their decision had been wrong. He charged that the deliberations had taken three days because some on the panel didn't agree with the verdict and the cause of death. "By God, I disagree with your verdict. I disagree strongly . . . The evidence before you shows that Celeste is innocent."

Then he went down what he described as a timeline that proved she was innocent, something he'd forgotten during the trial closing, and he asked those on the jury who he suspected were uncomfortable with the verdict to stand up to the others, to hang the jury on the punishment phase. It was a desperate twist in a strange case, a tactic few in the courtroom had ever seen before, the equivalent of a Hail Mary pass, a risky football play used by losing teams in the final moments of a game. "Those of you who have reasonable doubt . . . you can stand up and say, 'I was wrong,'" he argued. "'I shouldn't have compromised. I shouldn't have surrendered' . . . Don't give in."

"Your verdict was the right decision," Wetzel told the jury, as the last one to address them. "Beginning many years ago, this woman has hurt people fraudulently . . . She's not the victim . . . Steve Beard is the victim . . . he has a great-grandchild he'll never see."

As angry as DeGuerin had been, Wetzel was calm. It was by far the best argument she'd put on during the case, eloquent and measured. "It strikes me how vulnerable Steve Beard was, asleep in his own bed . . . asking the operator to call his wife . . . don't you know he was reaching out to her for help. How ironic that he didn't know she was the one behind it . . . We trust that you will reach a verdict. What Celeste Beard did to her husband has earned her a life sentence. We trust you'll give her what she deserves."

At 11:25 that morning the jury again began deliberations. One hour and twenty minutes later they had a decision.

As Celeste stood before them, she stared at the jurors as if she hated all of them, looking every bit the monster her own children had labeled her. The jurors would later say DeGuerin had read them wrong and that there'd been no dissent in their ranks. "We wanted to make sure everyone felt comfortable with it," says the foreman, Rosales. "We just took our time."

As before, they dealt out the maximum penalty, a second life sentence, and, to send a message that they had no doubt about their verdict, a $10,000 fine.

"I'd like the jury polled," DeGuerin challenged. Later that year, in Galveston, he'd mount a masterful defense and win an acquittal for Robert Durst, the New York heir who admitted killing his neighbor, then dismembering and disposing of his body. That victory would make worldwide headlines. But this day, in an Austin courtroom, the man who was arguably Texas's most famous living defense attorney had lost to two talented prosecutors and it tasted bitter.

The judge did as he asked and polled the twelve jurors, but to no avail. They all agreed that, for what she'd done to Steve, Celeste should spend the rest of her life in jail.

As a final matter of business, Kristina walked to the witness stand one more time, wearing a skirt and a serious blue blazer. In her hand, she held a white spiral notebook. For weeks she and Ellen Halbert had talked about whether she would deliver an allocution, a victim's statement, in which she would finally address her mother. Ellen had told her of the one she'd done at the trial of her own assailant and said it had given her a feeling of strength and a sense of peace.

"I have a lot of things I want to say to you," Kristina began, looking straight into her mother's eyes. "What did I ever do to you? What did Jen ever do to you but love you? . . . You don't deserve us. You never deserved us. You said we turned on you, but you turned on us. Steve gave you his love. He took you into his family, and you violated him. You murdered him, and you are guilty."

As Kristina left the witness stand, she walked past her mother. Celeste's hands shook, but no tears filled her eyes. Instead of sadness, her eyes were fixated on the face of her favorite daughter with utter rage.

Author's Footnote

On a dreary day in early 2004, nearly a year after the trial's end, I drove to Gatesville, Texas, to the prison where Celeste and Tracey were housed in separate units. I pulled into the parking lot of the Mountain View Unit as a thin rain misted from a cold, tented gray sky. By that summer, Donna Goodson would also be behind bars, serving a six-month sentence in a jail outside Austin for falsifying a Texas driver's license. Celeste, on the other hand, wouldn't be eligible for parole for forty years. Barring the success of an appeal Dick DeGuerin had filed, this complex of small red brick buildings would probably be her home for the rest of her life. All that recalled her previous world was the razor wire curled atop the cyclone fence that surrounded the unit's perimeter, like that she'd installed at Toro Canyon after the shooting.

The inmates in Mountain View were the most serious female offenders in the Texas prison system, on death row or, like Celeste, serving long sentences. Darlie Routier, the Dallas mother prosecutors said killed her two beautiful young sons, was there, along with Clara Harris, the Houston dentist who ran over her philandering husband with the family Mercedes Benz. In prison, Harris and Celeste, both assigned to work typing books into Braille, had become friends. When Celeste emerged, she was markedly changed from her appearance at the trial. Her leg, which had required surgery, remained in a walking cast, and she shuffled into the visitors' area on crutches. Her hair, pulled back into a too-tight ponytail, looked dirty, her skin had a prison pallor, and her eyes peered unblinking out of dark, tormented circles. Gone were the trial sweater sets, replaced by wrinkled, off-white scrubs, her official prison garb. In the visitors' area we talked through a black wire mesh and cloudy Plexiglas cage.

"Did you have anything to do with Steve's murder?" I asked.

"No," she snapped. "Of course I didn't. I said I didn't."

"Actually, you never took the stand, Celeste. You never really said anything."

"Biggest mistake of my life," she mused angrily. "I never should have listened when Dick DeGuerin told me not to."

"Did you have a sexual relationship with Tracey?" I continued.

"No. My only mistake was not telling Tracey myself that I didn't want anything to do with her. That's why she killed Steve, because she was jealous."

"That was your only mistake?"

"That and raising my daughters as I did, as a friend instead of a mother, teaching them to lie and to love money more than people," she said. She then launched into a verbal assault of the twins. She said she loved them more than anything or anyone, that she'd tried to be a good mother, and for that she'd paid a price. Her eyes grew black and her hands shook as she accused them of manufacturing evidence against her and working with the District Attorney's Office. Then she concentrated her venom at Kristina, the daughter who had catered to her every whim, who'd yearned for her love. "Kristina was in cahoots with Tracey," she said. "I think of her and Jennifer like the Menendez brothers, who killed their parents. I want them to spend time in prison. They belong here, not me."

"Tell me something that points to your innocence," I challenged. "Anything."

In response, she told me about a letter her attorneys received while the jury was sequestered, from a man she identified only as Robert. This stranger, she said, had written stating that he'd seen Tracey, Kristina, and Justin in a Sear's store the month before the shooting. "Tracey shouted, 'If you don't help me, I'll get someone who will.'"

When I pressed Celeste for his last name, she suddenly changed her story, saying Robert wasn't sure the couple Tracey talked to was Kristina and Justin. "He said it was someone who *looked* like them."

That morning, Celeste made statements I knew weren't true. She misquoted trial testimony and personally attacked those who testified against her. When I called her on the lies, she shouted that I was in the pocket of the "evil twins."

In contrast, at the Gatesville Unit, Tracey sauntered calmly into the visitor's area to meet me. Her hair cropped close to her ears, and her uniform clean and neatly pressed, she smiled. Although she hadn't been on medication for many months, she appeared bright-eyed and well. Looking back, she said, she thought it was the alcohol more than anything else that had led her to thoughts of suicide five years earlier, when she'd met Celeste in St. David's. "It's easy to say I was mentally ill. I was in a psychiatric hospital," she said. "But that's a label, and it was more than that. I've come to realize that there were lots of loopholes in my thought processes. I was willing to believe that there were situations when it was permissible to take another person's life. I now know that's not true."

Although only seven years remained before she'd be eligible for parole, she insisted she thought little of that. Instead of planning a future, she said prison had taught her to live in the moment. In the laundry where she worked five days a week, just the folding of a shirt gave her a sense of satisfaction. She'd learned to enjoy the small moments in life and to cherish the few family and friends who'd stood by her.

When she talked of Celeste, her voice rang with sadness. "I think she's numb. No one can make her feel. She sees only her own needs," she said. "She kept throwing men, women, money, and things into herself to try to fill up, but she couldn't feel any of it. No matter how much she had, she was still empty inside." Often, she said, she thought of Steve Beard and the night she pulled the trigger of her shotgun while he slept. When the sadness came, she envisioned a cloud and let the pain float away.

"I can't change this," she said, her eyes filling with tears. "I did a horrible thing. I'm not angry about being in prison. I understand why I'm here. I walked into Steve Beard's bedroom and shot him in his sleep."

The twins, too, remembered Steve.

In many ways, they'd picked up the pieces of their lives, working and returning to school. Kristina, still with Justin, moved out of Austin to Houston, for college and the anonymity of a big city. Jen kept her job selling insurance and shared the twins' triplex with a friend. Their mother wanted only pain and suffering for them, but they had to fight the urge to feel sad for her. "We talk sometimes about what it must be like for her in prison," said Jennifer. "She can't go out and enjoy the sun on a beautiful day, or take car trips and eat junk food, just the dumb stuff she used to love to do."

"But then she'll say something to someone and it will get back to us. Something hateful," said Kristina. "And we remember that she never loved us or Steve. We're forced to think about how wicked she really is."

"I wish our mom was different, but she isn't," said Jen. "We were never really people to her. She was never really our mother, because she didn't love us the way a mother loves her children. She's incapable of loving anyone."

Still, they struggled with all that happened. Although they both understood their mother was behind bars, for them, Celeste was all-powerful, and they continued to fear her. Kristina was afraid to venture out alone at night, afraid Celeste lurked in the shadows. "I check my rearview mirror," she says. "I'm afraid I'm being followed."

Jennifer still grieved over losing two fathers, one to suicide, the other to murder. Their mother continued to stalk her in nightmares where Celeste waited unseen for an opportunity to take vengeance. "I'd like to go on with my life," she says. "But so far, I just can't."

Neither planned to ever see or speak to their mother again. "She doesn't deserve us," says Kristina.

In yet another twist, in the fall of 2004 Kristina and Jennifer were reunited with their long-lost sister, the baby girl Celeste had put up for adoption. A college freshman, she'd looked for her biological family and found her father dead and her mother in prison. Only Kristina and Jennifer were there to tell her all that had happened. "She looks just like us," says Kristina. "We recognized her the moment we saw her."

At Christmas, the twins have a ritual. In Austin, Jennifer and Kristina gather at a church with other victims of violent crimes and their families to decorate a tree of remembrance. In honor of Steve, they hang an ornament, an ethereal gold angel. The ceremony, surrounded by so many others who have lost loved ones, gives them a sense of community and a moment of peace.

"We don't have much family left," says Jennifer sadly. "And we want to make sure Steve's not forgotten."